MS

The
Causes
and
Consequences
of
Antitrust

The Causes

and

Consequences

of

Antitrust

The Public-Choice Perspective

Edited by

Fred S. McChesney
and William F. Shughart II

E ran F J
9/19/96 bt

The University of
Chicago Press
Chicago and London

FRED S. McCHESNEY is the Robert T. Thompson Professor of Law and Business and professor of economics at Emory University.
WILLIAM F. SHUGHART II is the P. M. B. Self, William King Self, and Henry C. Self Free Enterprise Chairholder and professor of economics at the University of Mississippi.

The University of Chicago Press, Chicago 60637
The University of Chicago Press, Ltd., London
© 1995 by The University of Chicago
All rights reserved. Published 1995
Printed in the United States of America

04 03 02 01 00 99 98 97 96 95   1 2 3 4 5

ISBN: 0-226-55634-4 (cloth)
　　　0-226-55635-2 (paper)

Library of Congress Cataloging-in-Publication Data

The causes and consequences of antitrust : the public-choice
　perspective / edited by Fred S. McChesney and William F. Shughart
　II.
　　　　p.　　cm.
　　Includes bibliographical references and index.
　　1. Trusts, Industrial—Government policy—United States.
　　2. Public interest—United States.　3. Monopolies—United States.
　　4. Antitrust law—Economic aspects—United States.　I. McChesney,
　　Fred S., 1948–　　　II. Shughart, William F.
　　HD2795.C27　　　1995
　　338.8'0973—dc20　　　　　　　　　　　　　　　　　　94-27435
　　　　　　　　　　　　　　　　　　　　　　　　　　　　　CIP

⊗ The paper used in this publication meets the
minimum requirements of the American National Standard
for Information Sciences—Permanence of Paper for
Printed Library Materials, ANSI Z39.48-1984.

To the memory of my mother and
to my father, who together taught
me so much

FSMcC

To Hilary, Willie, and Frank

WFS

Contents

	Preface	ix
1	Introduction and Overview FRED S. McCHESNEY AND WILLIAM F. SHUGHART II	1
2	Public-Choice Theory and Antitrust Policy WILLIAM F. SHUGHART II	7
Part One	**In Search of the Public-Interest Model of Antitrust** FRED S. McCHESNEY	**25**
3	What Do Economists Think about Antitrust?: A Random Walk down Pennsylvania Avenue PAUL H. RUBIN	33
4	The Economic Effects of the Antitrust Laws (1966) GEORGE J. STIGLER	63 ——
5	A Statistical Study of Antitrust Enforcement (1970) RICHARD A. POSNER	73 ——
6	The Economic Determinants of Antitrust Activity (1973) WILLIAM F. LONG, RICHARD SCHRAMM, AND ROBERT D. TOLLISON	95 ——
7	Is Collusion Profitable? (1976) PETER ASCH AND JOSEPH J. SENECA	105— /O7
Part Two	**The Positive Economics of Antitrust Enforcement** BRUCE YANDLE	**119**
8	Did Antitrust Policy Cause the Great Merger Wave? (1985) GEORGE BITTLINGMAYER	127 ——
9	Antimerger Policy under the Hart-Scott-Rodino Act: A Reexamination of the Market-Power Hypothesis (1985) B. ESPEN ECKBO AND PEGGY WIER	147 ——
10	The Employment Consequences of the Sherman and Clayton Acts (1991) WILLIAM F. SHUGHART II AND ROBERT D. TOLLISON	165 ——

11   Antitrust Enforcement and Foreign Competition   179
            WILLIAM F. SHUGHART II, JON SILVERMAN, AND
            ROBERT D. TOLLISON

Part Three The Public-Choice Model of Antitrust   189
            LOUIS DE ALESSI
12   Antitrust Pork Barrel (1982)   201
            ROGER L. FAITH, DONALD R. LEAVENS, AND
            ROBERT D. TOLLISON
13   Bureaucracy and Politics in FTC Merger Challenges
            (1990)   213
            MALCOLM B. COATE, RICHARD S. HIGGINS, AND
            FRED S. McCHESNEY
14   Monopolies and Mergers Commission, Merger
            Reports, and the Public Interest: A Probit Analysis
            (1992)   231
            CHARLIE WEIR

Part Four   Public Choice and the Origins of Antitrust   243
            WILLIAM E. KOVACIC
15   Antitrust before the Sherman Act   255
            DONALD J. BOUDREAUX,
            THOMAS J. DiLORENZO, AND STEPHEN PARKER
16   Business Restraints and the Clayton Act of 1914:
            Public- or Private-Interest Legislation?   271
            ROBERT B. EKELUND, JR., MICHAEL J.
            McDONALD, AND ROBERT D. TOLLISON
17   Output and Stock Prices When Antitrust Is Suspended:
            The Effects of the NIRA   287
            GEORGE BITTLINGMAYER

Part Five   Retrospect and Prospect   319
            WILLIAM F. SHUGHART II
18   Be True to Your School: Chicago's Contradictory
            Views of Antitrust and Regulation (1991)   323
            FRED S. McCHESNEY
19   The Unjoined Debate   341
            FRED S. McCHESNEY AND
            WILLIAM F. SHUGHART II

            Selected Bibliography   351
            List of Contributors   365
            Author Index   367
            Subject Index   372

PREFACE

This book aims at nothing less than a paradigm shift. For some four decades, antitrust analysis has pitted devotees of the "Chicago school" against old-guard structuralists and their game-theory successors, a group sometimes known as the "Harvard school." Debates between the two camps have focused on what antitrust law ought to do, what kinds of cases it ought to bring. Harvard wants the antitrust laws applied vigorously, even creatively, to a wide range of industries and business practices. Chicago suggests that the scope of antitrust enforcement should be more limited and its application more cautious. The two sides have no disagreement, however, about whether antitrust has a useful role to play in the first place. Antitrust's importance in maintaining freely functioning competitive markets is taken as self-evident.

The Causes and Consequences of Antitrust seeks to move the debate away from the familiar question, What should antitrust do? It asks instead, What has antitrust done, and why? It addresses these questions in methodologically familiar ways, using standard economic models and statistical tests. The empirical answers are revealing. The evidence suggests that the well-worn debates dividing Harvard and Chicago, while important, have overlooked more fundamental issues. If successful, the book will return the attention of antitrust scholars to first principles, forcing them to consider seriously whether antitrust has any legitimate place in a market-based economy.

Answers to questions about the purposes and effects of antitrust are as important nowadays as they were in 1890 when Senator John Sherman's bill was before Congress. Following the collapse of Russian communism and the Soviet bloc, Harvard school economists have fanned out across eastern Europe to urge the enactment of antitrust laws in the emerging republics. Antitrust's domain has expanded considerably in Western Europe during the past two decades. Taiwan recently adopted an antitrust policy for the first time. One of this volume's contributors has advised the Mongolian government on a proposed antitrust statute; one of its co-editors has taught antitrust in Russia. Closer to home, more stringent antitrust enforcement, including repeal of the McCarran-Ferguson Act's antitrust exemption protecting the insurance industry and closer scrutiny of hospital mergers, is a key policy of the Clinton administration.

Thus, antitrust's political future has been reaffirmed. Curiously, however, politicians' faith in antitrust's ideals persists despite economists' inability to find any systematic benefits from its application. In fact, there is widespread acknowledgment that antitrust has repeatedly failed to protect the interests of consumers. Individual case studies and more systematic evidence demonstrate that the laws have actually been used not to enhance competition but to reduce it.

By applying the fundamental assumptions and empirical methods of public choice to the analysis of antitrust, we seek to dispel the naive view that antitrust is the bulwark of free markets. Our goal is to place antitrust within the same behavioral system that has been successfully brought to bear in explaining other public policies toward business. Closing the behavioral system requires recognizing that, like government regulation of price and entry in general, antitrust enforcement is shaped largely by private interests and not by the public interest. We do not claim that the public-choice model explains everything about antitrust, only that it illuminates a good many more of the causes and consequences of antitrust than alternative models do.

The use of standard economic theory and methods to analyze government is a hallmark of what has increasingly come to be called the "Virginia school" of political economy, a term coined to identify the work of James Buchanan, Gordon Tullock, and their students. It is fitting in that respect that we acknowledge our great professional debt to Robert Tollison. As readers of this volume will discover, Bob Tollison was a pioneer in the positive analysis of antitrust, and he remains one of the central contributors to ongoing research in this area. His intellectual influence on the two of us has been great.

Indirectly, this book owes its existence to Bob Tollison. Each of us, unbeknownst to the other, had talked to Bob about putting together a volume of this sort. He then informed us of our common interests, suggesting co-authorship and -editorship. The idea was a felicitous one, and we here acknowledge Bob's role as intellectual middleman.

Others have helped as well in the book's production. Foremost, of course, are our many contributors. We also thank our referees at the University of Chicago Press, notably Richard Posner, for useful suggestions. David Galenson, of the University of Chicago, was also instrumental in the review process. Karen Peterson handled all technical details and questions promptly and courteously. Shirley Kessel made indexing fun. Mike Belongia, Steve Graham, and Paul Pecorino of the University of Mississippi read and commented on various portions of the manuscript, offering friendly criticisms that, while not always adopted, were invariably helpful. Cathy Phillips of Emory University handled many administrative duties most capably and always cheerfully.

Finally, both of us are grateful to our academic benefactors. Fred McChesney thanks the members of the Robert T. Thompson, Sr., family for their generous support of the Robert T. Thompson Chair in Law and Business, which has made possible the opportunities for research that led to this book. William Shughart thanks Peyton Self and the other members of his family for their commitment to the University of Mississippi and the financial generosity that sustains the P. M. B. Self, William King Self, and Henry C. Self Free Enterprise Chair.

FRED S. MCCHESNEY
WILLIAM F. SHUGHART II

Of course I know, and every other sensible man knows, that the Sherman law is damned nonsense, but if my country wants to go to hell, I am here to help it.

—Justice Oliver Wendell Holmes, Jr.

CHAPTER ONE

Introduction and Overview   L 40

FRED S. McCHESNEY AND WILLIAM F. SHUGHART II

Antitrust policy commands widespread scholarly support. Its intellectual champions reside not only in Cambridge, but in Chicago as well. For example, Frederic Scherer (1980, 491), the author of a popular industrial organization textbook, characterizes antitrust as "one of the more important weapons wielded by government in its effort to harmonize the profit-seeking behavior of private enterprises with the public interest." Similarly, the late George Stigler, one of the leading lights of the Chicago school, has called antitrust a "public interest law in the same sense in which . . . having private property, enforcement of contracts, and suppression of crime are public-interest phenomena" (Hazlett 1984, 46). And Richard Posner (1976, 4) suggests that the importance of economic efficiency as a social value "establishes a *prima facie* case for having an antitrust policy." Superficially, at least, antitrust seems to be "one of those rare issues that cuts across even the most formidable of ideological barriers" (Elzinga and Breit 1976, ix).

But while the ideals of antitrust are widely accepted, scholars have long been critical of its specific applications. An extensive literature suggests that enforcement of the antitrust laws often works against the interests of consumers by interfering with the efficient allocation of society's scarce resources (Shughart and Tollison 1985; Shughart 1990a). As Paul Rubin discusses in chapter 3 of this volume, many of the leading precedents in the antitrust case law have been studied in depth both by economists and by legal commentators and, it is fair to say, the verdict is that many more "bad" than "good" cases have been brought. A typical antitrust case study finds that the evidence presented in behalf of the plaintiff was "weak and at times bordered on fiction" and that "neither the government nor the Courts seemed able to distinguish between competition and monopolizing" (Peterman 1975a, 143). Even when the law conceivably has struck against anticompetitive acts and practices, the effectiveness of the relief granted to the plaintiff has likewise been called into question (Elzinga 1969; Rogowsky 1986, 1987).[1]

Despite these numerous and telling criticisms, the commentators ordinarily treat each example of failed antitrust enforcement as an aberration. According

---

1. In summing up his detailed study of the Federal Trade Commission's lengthy prosecution of the Brown Shoe Company, John Peterman (1975b, 393) concludes that at best "nothing was accomplished by bringing this case."

to the conventional wisdom, antitrust's many failures are due not to defects in its principles but to errors in its application. So the critics of antitrust policy preach reform, calling on the public law enforcement agencies to do a better job; or calling on lawyers, judges, and enforcement personnel to apply more correctly the relevant economic theories; or calling for the replacement of incumbent policy makers with others better able to enforce the antitrust laws in ways that promote the public's interest.

In short, antitrust is one of the few remaining examples of a public-policy process in which it is still widely assumed that government is motivated by the goal of serving the public interest. The purposes of antitrust seem to be beyond debate; the enforcement agencies and the courts, despite their tendency to err, are basically regarded as benevolent maximizers of the public welfare. As a consequence of this fundamental assumption, the standard approach to the analysis of antitrust policy consists primarily of efforts to identify good and bad laws and good and bad cases, ending with recommendations for better laws, better cases, and better bureaucrats.

The study of antitrust would thus seem to be at an intellectual dead end. Supporters and critics alike are locked into a normative debate that neither side can win, because both *assume* that the antitrust laws were enacted in a public spirited attempt to promote competition and that the officials charged with enforcement responsibility have no motivation beyond achieving that goal. It is our purpose in putting together this volume to challenge that fundamental presumption.

In doing so, we contribute to the development of a growing body of research that applies the insights of public-choice theory to the analysis of antitrust policy. The public-choice model questions whether public policy toward business is in fact driven by the goal of promoting competition so as to enhance some vague conception of the "public interest." It suggests instead that public policy emerges from political bargains in which special-interest groups purchase protection from the forces of unfettered competition, benefiting both themselves and politician-suppliers of protectionism at the expense of other groups.

The papers collected in this volume elaborate the public-choice approach to antitrust by making previously published contributions to the literature more accessible, and by presenting new analyses of antitrust policy that extend the insights of public choice in a number of important new directions. Moreover, previously unpublished background material for each of the volume's major sections has been contributed by leading public-choice scholars. This background material provides the reader with an overview of the relevant antitrust issues, including extensive citations to important studies not included in the present volume, and supplies an intellectual roadmap that situates the selected readings in the context of the pertinent issues.

The previously published papers included in the volume have all been edited and, in some cases, shortened to streamline the exposition. Appendices, data descriptions, and similar supporting material comprise the bulk of the deletions. Internal citations to references not essential to the main flow of ideas have also been omitted.

We make no claim that the papers collected here resolve all the interesting or important questions concerning antitrust. To paraphrase Winston Churchill, this volume does not represent the end, or even the beginning of the end, of the task of explaining the origins, purposes, and effects of antitrust policy. But, if successful, the book will be the end of the beginning—the end of decades of hand-wringing over antitrust's failures coupled with credulous expressions of faith in policy makers' ability to avoid repeating their regrettable but understandable mistakes. Much of antitrust admittedly remains unexamined. But additional light will be cast into its dark corners only with more widespread appreciation of the fact that underlying antitrust there is a rational, self-interest-seeking process at work.

The distinction between the public-interest and public-choice views of antitrust is developed further in the next chapter. William Shughart provides an overview of the public-choice model that underscores its insistence that self-seeking motives be attributed to all individuals, in or out of government. The principal implication of this analysis is that antitrust is no different from economic regulation in general. While in theory antitrust can be employed to promote the public's interest, it can also be used politically to further the private interests of some groups at the expense of others.

The remainder of the book is divided into five major parts, each presenting one aspect of the new thinking about antitrust. Part One sets the stage for the revisionist analysis in succeeding sections by questioning the public-interest basis of antitrust. It opens with a background piece by Fred McChesney that examines the process by which economists, during the century following the Sherman Act's passage, came generally to agree on the desirability of having an antitrust policy. As McChesney points out, the Sherman Act was greeted with little enthusiasm by economists of the day, yet by the middle of the century the profession had been won over. But this transformation was not based on any systematic empirical evidence that antitrust enforcement had enhanced consumers' welfare. Indeed, as Paul Rubin describes in chapter 3, an extensive economic literature raising doubts about the wisdom of many individual cases brought by federal antitrust enforcers had already begun to develop.

The numerous government cases seemingly at odds with antitrust's intended purpose of promoting competition sparked several attempts to inquire more methodically into the actual effects of antitrust enforcement; several of these are reprinted in Part One. The chapter by George Stigler is an early attempt along these lines, based on comparisons of very rough and highly aggregated industrial concentration data for the United States and the United Kingdom. Stigler and others who might have inquired more thoroughly into the impact of antitrust enforcement on economic performance were hampered in part by a lack of systematic information on the law enforcement activities of the federal antitrust agencies and of private parties. Richard Posner began to fill the gap with "A Statistical Study of Antitrust Enforcement," a portion of which is reprinted in chapter 5 of this volume.

Relying on Posner's data, the chapter by William Long, Richard Schramm, and Robert Tollison provides empirical evidence that the prevention of welfare losses to consumers, the supposed goal of antitrust policy, does little to explain how the antitrust enforcement agencies actually select cases to bring. The following chapter by Peter Asch and Joseph Seneca investigates a sample of government cases alleging unlawful price fixing, a major target of the antitrust laws to stop firms from increasing prices and profits at the expense of consumers. Asch and Seneca find, however, that the defendants in the price-fixing cases sampled were not extraordinarily profitable.

Part Two of the volume is devoted to positive analyses of the actual effects of antitrust enforcement. Bruce Yandle's background article heeds George Stigler's (1975, 140) instructions, explaining how the intended purposes of antitrust are properly deduced not from its stated purposes but from the record of its impact on competitive conditions in the economy. In chapter 8, George Bittlingmayer shows how one episode that has long puzzled scholars, the "Great Merger Wave" that dramatically increased industrial concentration at the turn of the century, was in fact *caused* by antitrust enforcement. He argues that the early efforts of the federal trust-busters prompted the leading firms in a number of industries to substitute mergers for the price-fixing agreements that the Sherman Act made illegal in 1890.

Espen Eckbo and Peggy Wier look at federal efforts to block mergers thought to have anticompetitive purposes and effects. They present evidence that the mergers targeted by the antitrust authorities are in fact procompetitive. Taking a more macroeconomic view, William Shughart and Robert Tollison measure the effects of antitrust enforcement on aggregate employment. Their findings suggest that antitrust has tended to affect employment negatively; the evidence shows that by restricting output and raising prices, antitrust is itself anticompetitive. The final chapter in Part Two, by Shughart, Jon Silverman, and Tollison, finds that the federal antitrust authorities step up their enforcement activities during periods when domestic firms face increased competitive pressures from foreign producers, a result that lends additional support to the view that antitrust is protectionist.

If antitrust enforcement does not achieve its stated objective of promoting competition and, in fact, has had such negative economic consequences overall, how can its survival be explained? As Louis De Alessi discusses as background to Part Three, one must begin looking for answers by examining the ways that antitrust can be used for the private benefit of certain firms, politicians, and bureaucrats. The chapter by Roger Faith, Donald Leavens, and Robert Tollison provides empirical evidence that the antitrust policy process is valuable to politicians, who are afforded the opportunity to sell protection from antitrust intervention when their constituents are targeted by the enforcement authorities. Along these same lines, Malcolm Coate, Richard Higgins, and Fred McChesney analyze the process by which the Federal Trade Commission selects mergers to challenge, and show how this selection process is influenced by congressional political pressure. The chapter by Charlie Weir presents similar empirical evidence from the enforcement activities of Great Britain's Mergers and Monopolies Commission.

Part Four explores the origins of the antitrust laws. As William Kovacic explains in his background piece, there is a longstanding debate among lawyers and legal scholars about whether the antitrust laws were enacted to strike, on behalf of consumers, at anticompetitive business practices, or whether the legislation was politically motivated by a desire, on behalf of inefficient firms, to place their rivals at a competitive disadvantage. Questions concerning the origins of antitrust, however, did not attract the attention of economists until much later, when the lack of economic evidence to support the public-interest model could no longer be ignored. Moreover, questions about the extent to which special interests inspired the enactment of antitrust became increasingly of interest to economists as evidence of political influences on the enforcement process accumulated. If protectionist forces explain much of antitrust policy nowadays, they ask, were these same forces at work in the beginning?

The chapter by Donald Boudreaux, Thomas DiLorenzo, and Stephen Parker finds that anticompetitive purposes in fact underlay the passage of the state antitrust statutes, which preceded federal antitrust legislation by several years. Chapter 16, by Robert Ekelund, Michael McDonald, and Robert Tollison, reports evidence of political forces at work in the Senate's roll-call vote on the Clayton Act of 1914. Part Four closes with George Bittlingmayer's analysis of antitrust policy during the Hoover and early New Deal years. He focuses on the suspension of antitrust enforcement under the National Industrial Recovery Act (NIRA) and its administrative creation, the National Recovery Administration (NRA). Contrary to what antitrust's proponents would expect, its suspension was apparently beneficial economically.

Part Five concludes by setting the stage for future debate. Fred McChesney's chapter argues that the normative economic analysis of the "Chicago school," which is now so dominant in antitrust thinking, rests on a number of fundamental inconsistencies that Chicagoans have yet to address. The volume's final chapter, by McChesney and Shughart, points to a number of other unresolved questions raised by the public-choice perspective on antitrust. The authors challenge the proponents of the public-interest model either to supply evidence that supports its predictions or to abandon their naive faith in its promises.

CHAPTER TWO

Public-Choice Theory and Antitrust Policy

WILLIAM F. SHUGHART II

Private markets, the norm in the United States and most of the developed world, represent a proprietary setting in which individual economic agents bear the full costs and reap the full benefits of their own resource allocation decisions. The suppliers of private goods and services sink or swim according to how well they satisfy the demands of their customers. The satisfaction buyers derive from consumption, in turn, depends largely on the prudence of their own purchase decisions. The profit motive that animates the privately owned firm and the utility-maximizing objective of the consumer provide powerful incentives for the parties interacting in private markets to use resources efficiently and to honor their commitments.

Government, by contrast, operates in a nonproprietary setting in which the costs of resource allocation decisions are less fully borne by individual decision makers.[1] Incentives to use resources efficiently are weakened because, on the one hand, property rights are ill-defined and the "owners" of government agencies—the taxpayers—consequently cannot credibly threaten to withdraw their capital when their interests are not well-served. On the other hand, because the salaries and other pecuniary rewards of public office are subject to statutory ceilings, government decision makers are less able to personally benefit from holding costs down or from remaining attuned to taxpayers' wants.

In one setting, then, resource allocation decisions are made self-interestedly in the pursuit of personal gain. In the other setting, decision makers operate under constraints that limit their ability to benefit personally from the choices they make. But the conventional analysis of government ignores the wide divergence in incentives created by these two different property-rights regimes. Rather than specifying a general model that helps explain the behavior of individuals in both settings, this analysis simply *assumes* the motivations of the relevant decision makers to be different. In contrast to decision makers in private markets, who are supposed to be selfish, government decision makers are conceived of as selfless. Hence, the out-

---

1. Armen A. Alchian, Some Economics of Property Rights, 30 Il Politico 816 (1965). Reprinted in Economic Forces at Work (1977).

comes produced in the public sector are seen to differ from those produced in the private sector, not because the constraints on behavior are different, but rather because the motivations of the decision makers are. Government decision makers are assumed to be guided not by their own self-interests but by the interests of others.[2]

Hence, when private markets fail to produce some socially desirable outcome, the failure is attributed to the unrestrained pursuit of self-interest. Government is then called upon to intervene and to correct this failure in ways that promote the public's interest. But when government fails, the failure is blamed on error, on ignorance, or on the human fallibility of otherwise well-meaning public officials.

The theory of public choice to which this chapter is devoted insists, however, that the same behavioral model be applied to all decision makers in the economy. The conventional analysis of antitrust, for example, is content to assume that government policy toward business is formulated and implemented solely with the objective of promoting freely functioning markets that enhance the well-being of consumers. This chapter argues instead that legislative and policy decisions in the realm of antitrust are shaped not by some ideal conception of the public interest, but rather by the interactions between well-organized private interest groups seeking protection from the forces of competition and politicians and other government officials seeking to maximize their own personal welfare.

The Fundamental Assumptions of Public Choice

Most discussions of governmental processes assume that public policies toward business are formulated and executed by somewhat imperfect but basically well-intentioned public servants. Government intervention to correct perceived sources of market failure in the private economy is still widely believed to operate in the "public interest."

From this point of view, the purposes of most public policies toward business are beyond dispute: Were it not for environmental regulation, profit-seeking firms would plunder the nation's natural resources, denuding the

---

2. This assumption has led some observers to conclude erroneously that *competition* is a more important determinant of efficiency in the supply of public goods and services than is *ownership*. An extreme version of this argument holds that, when entities are forced to compete for service-provision rights, there are no significant differences in the cost efficiencies of private for-profit firms, private not-for-profit organizations, and public enterprises. For a collection of anecdotes supporting this point of view, see David Osborne and Ted Gaebler, Reinventing Government: How the Entrepreneurial Spirit is Transforming the Public Sector (1992). Systematic empirical evidence that public enterprises—even when these face competition from rival suppliers—are less efficient by market standards than are comparable privately owned firms is reported by Aidan R. Vining and Anthony E. Boardman, Ownership versus Competition: Efficiency in Public Enterprise, 73 Pub. Choice 205 (1992).

forests and fouling the air and water. Were it not for consumer product safety standards, firms would sell shoddy and dangerous goods that maim or kill their purchasers. Were it not for advertising regulation, firms would mislead consumers into buying products they do not want at prices they cannot afford. Were it not for occupational health and safety regulation, firms would expose their employees to unacceptable workplace hazards. Were it not for the antitrust laws, unchecked monopoly power would foreclose markets, raise prices, and stifle innovation.

Because of these preconceptions, whenever public policies toward business fail to achieve their stated goals (as they do quite often, by many accounts), the failures are attributed to one or more of a number of correctable errors. The critics accordingly prescribe reforms that urge the enforcement agencies to do a better job, recommend that legislators and government officials learn economic principles, call for the replacement of incumbent policy makers with people better able to serve the public interest, or endorse higher levels of funding for the relevant bureau.

The standard approach to the analysis of public policies toward business thus treats market failure and market power as arising from the activities of individuals and firms seeking only their own private gains, on the one hand, and government intervention into the economy as necessary corrective actions taken by public servants seeking only to promote the general welfare, on the other. In one setting, individuals are assumed to be self-interested; in another, they are assumed to be public-interested. The analyst cannot have it both ways. A decision must be made about how individuals in general behave.[3]

The model of public choice insists that the same rational, self-interest-seeking motives that animate human action in ordinary markets be applied to decision making in the public sector as well. The assumption that *all* individuals, in or out of government, pursue their own self-interests is the fundamental tenet of public choice. Just as consumers want to maximize their utility and firms want to maximize their profits, public policy makers want to maximize their own welfare.

The objective attributed to policy makers and other government officials is the maximization of political support. Depending on the particular policy process being analyzed, the goal of self-interest may be more specifically thought of in terms of the maximization of the probability of election or of reelection to political office, the maximization of the probability of appointment or of reappointment to a position of public responsibility, or the maximization of personal wealth, which includes the salary and perquisites of public office as well as the income expected from post-government employment.

In short, *homo politicus* and *homo economicus* are the same. The critical

---

3. James M. Buchanan, Toward Analysis of Closed Behavioral Systems, in James M. Buchanan and Robert D. Tollison, eds., Theory of Public Choice (1972).

implication of this assumption of universal self-interest is that the observed differences between public choices and private choices emerge not because individuals adopt different behavioral objectives in the two settings, but rather because the constraints on behavior are different. Different outcomes emerge not because public choices are guided by motives different from those guiding private choices, but rather because in private markets self-interested producers and consumers make choices that mainly affect themselves, while in political markets self-interested voters and politicians make choices that mainly affect others.

Public-choice theory focuses on modeling and deriving testable implications about behavior in the nonproprietary institutional setting that characterizes public decision making. In doing so, public-choice theory stresses that the proper unit of analysis is the individual, not "society" or some other vague collective entity. "Society" does not make choices, individuals do. Traditional economic theory studies how the interactions of large numbers of self-interest-seeking producers and consumers in ordinary private markets determine outcomes such as prices, quantities, incomes, and profits; modern public-choice theory studies how the interactions of large numbers of self-interest-seeking demanders, suppliers, and brokers of wealth transfers in political markets determine outcomes such as tax rates, income subsidies, and regulatory intervention.

The deceptively simple insights of public choice move the discussion of public policy away from nonscientific debates about "good" and "bad" law or "good" and "bad" enforcement toward a more hard-nosed analysis of how public institutions actually function. One implication of the public-choice approach is that, in order to uncover the actual objectives of a particular public policy or program, it is necessary to look behind the stated intentions of the policy's supporters. When we seek to explain why a policy was adopted or why it persists, "the theory tells us to look, as precisely and carefully as we can, at who gains and who loses, and how much" (Stigler 1975, 140).

If we find evidence, for example, that until the enactment of deregulation in 1978, public regulation of commercial airline fares and routes provided large benefits to the established air carriers while imposing substantial costs on passengers, then rhetoric about protecting the flying public notwithstanding, the conclusion that regulation was intended to benefit the airlines themselves is warranted.[4] Similarly, if we observe that the public antitrust law enforcement agencies frequently attack mergers that promise to enhance economic efficiency (and, consequently, lower costs and prices) rather than deter

4. See, for example, Theodore E. Keeler, Airline Regulation and Market Performance, 3 Bell J. Econ. 399 (1972); and George W. Douglas and James C. Miller III, Quality Competition, Industry Equilibrium, and Efficiency in the Price-Constrained Airline Market, 64 Amer. Econ. Rev. 657 (1974).

anticompetitive mergers that might lead to increased market power, then despite the concern for consumer welfare expressed by antitrust's proponents, the conclusion seems justified that the law on mergers was intended to protect inefficient rival producers from increased competition (Eckbo 1983; Stillman 1983; chapter 9 of this volume).

Errors can of course be made out of ignorance or failure to foresee all of a policy's "unintended" consequences. "But errors are not what men live by or on. . . . [A]n explanation of a policy in terms of error or confusion is no explanation at all—anything and everything is compatible with that 'explanation.'" Hence, if "the announced goals of a policy are . . . unrelated or perversely related to its actual effects," and this divergence persists through time, then as a first approximation it seems reasonable to conclude that the actual effects are not only known, but desired. The *"truly intended effects* [of a policy] *should be deduced from the actual effects"* (Stigler 1975, 140; emphasis in original).

In short, public-choice theory suggests that what the conventional wisdom treats as policy "failures" are in fact the predictable consequences of self-interest-seeking behavior on the part of rational individuals operating under a particular set of institutional constraints. To public-choice scholars, economic markets and political markets are one and the same in the sense that the individuals who interact in these markets are motivated by similar goals and their behavior can be analyzed with the same set of tools.

The Market for Wealth Transfers

If "majority rules" were in fact a meaningful way of characterizing political outcomes in a representative democracy, there would be no minimum-wage law, no agricultural price supports, no import tariffs and quotas—in short, none of the many and varied government programs and policies that benefit the few at the expense of the many. Yet such special-interest measures exist—indeed flourish—in the United States and elsewhere. This simple observation about politics raises two important questions. If a large number of public policies generate few discernible benefits for the majority, why are such policies adopted? Given the very real costs, both direct and indirect, borne by the taxpaying majority in financing the machinery of wealth redistribution, why do such policies persist?

The answer to both of these questions is that there is a market for wealth transfers just as there are markets for automobiles, shoes, and thousands of other ordinary goods. The existence of this market for wealth transfers derives from the fact that government's powers to tax and spend and to compel or prohibit put it in position to selectively help or hurt a large number of individuals and firms. The political machinery of the state can be used to secure direct cash payments, relief from tax obligations, control over prices charged and wages paid, restrictions on entry and conditions of employment, and many other similar favors. And because public authority is so enormously valuable, it represents "a blank check on which everyone wants to write."[5] But only certain groups will be successful in using the political process for their own gain, while other groups will bear the costs. The problem is to determine which special interests will tend to receive wealth transfers and which will tend to supply them.

The proposition that private interests—and not the "public interest"— drive policy outcomes was articulated in its modern form by George Stigler (1971). In its simplest construction, what has since become known as the interest-group or "capture" theory of government is usually stated in terms of traditional economic regulation of price and entry, because the theory was first applied in explaining the wide divergence observed between the actual and the purported effects of this type of government intervention into the private economy. By asking why it is that the application of regulatory controls to industries like trucking and commercial airlines, and the imposition of licensing requirements on occupations like doctoring, lawyering, and barbering, rarely seem to benefit consumers, Stigler formalized the notion that coalitions of producers will often find it profitable to use the apparatus of public regulation for their own gain (see also Posner 1974; Peltzman 1976).

This conclusion follows, on the one hand, because producer groups are usually small enough in number and their financial interests are usually sufficiently concentrated that the potential benefits from organizing and lobbying for governmental favors will exceed the associated costs. On the other hand, the more diffuse nature of consumer interests coupled with the fact that each will bear only a small share of the cost of financing producers' benefits means that the relatively high cost of organizing to oppose expropriation of their wealth will exceed the expected gains from doing so. As a result of the higher rate of return to them of acting collectively, producer groups will often be successful in using the political process to obtain regulatory benefits for themselves at consumers' expense.

The interest-group model is much more general, however. It does not consistently pit producers against consumers or "capital" against labor. The model can be applied to any situation in which political authority can be mobilized to selectively help or hurt various interest groups. Indeed, public policies toward business are often tailored to redistribute wealth between groups of producers.

Generally speaking, the political coalitions with a comparative advantage in lobbying activities will be the demanders of wealth transfers in the interest-group model. This conclusion follows because certain information and trans-

5. John E. Chubb and Terry M. Moe, Politics, Markets, and America's Schools (1990), at 29.

actions costs must be borne in order for individuals or firms to act collectively.[6] Smaller coalitions with a strong community of interests will tend to
have stronger political voices because each group member has a larger financial stake in the outcome, given that the potential gains (or losses) will be
divided among fewer hands. These greater financial interests raise the expected rate of return to investments in information about the wealth effects
of transfer activity.

At the same time, smaller coalitions face lower costs of reaching agreement
on a common course of action and of monitoring and controlling free-riding
behavior by individual members. Taken together, these observations help
explain why small, cohesive interest groups are often successful in obtaining
wealth transfers at the expense of the general "public," whose interests are
more diffuse and whose costs of organizing to avoid supplying transfers are
relatively high. (Saying that a coalition faces high costs for organizing to
demand transfers is the same thing as saying that the group will find it costly
to organize to avoid having a portion of its wealth expropriated for transfer
to some other group.)

In addition, however, it is worth noting that a significant portion of the
costs of engaging in transfer-seeking activity are start-up costs. Once they
have been borne, the cost of supplying additional collective effort is relatively
low. Groups that have already organized for some other purpose, therefore,
have an important advantage in the market for wealth transfers: To the extent
that political lobbying is a byproduct of performing some other function,
these groups can avoid a large part of the initial costs of transfer seeking.
Labor unions, industry trade associations, professional societies, agricultural
cooperatives, and so on are well situated to act on political issues that affect
their wealth precisely because the costs of identifying and organizing a community of interests have already been incurred.

The role of political representatives in this setting is to match demanders
and suppliers of wealth transfers. In order to perform this brokerage function,
politicians have incentives to seek out issues on which the prospective winners are well-organized and well-informed, while the losers remain rationally
ignorant about the wealth effects of transfer activity. Policies and programs
whose benefits are narrowly focused on small, well-organized interest groups
but whose costs are spread more diffusely across the polity as a whole are
politically popular precisely because the expected political payoff to the broker is larger. When the prospective gains will be shared by relatively few
individuals, the winners have a strong incentive to provide the broker with
political support (votes, campaign contributions, and the like) in exchange
for the benefits conferred on them. On the other hand, when the bulk of the

6. Mancur Olson, The Logic of Collective Action: Public Goods and the Theory of Groups
(1965).

cost of financing these narrow benefits will be borne by taxpayers in general, the losers will not find it worth their while to become informed about and to withdraw their political support in an effort to block the broker's expropriation of their wealth.

This asymmetry in the payoffs facing brokers of wealth transfers is particularly evident in a geographically based representative democracy. A legislator in such a setting can expect a high return from taking positions that provide benefits narrowly tailored to the local (district or state) interests he or she has been elected to represent in the national legislature—and little or no return from taking vague positions in support of the "public interest." Because nonresidents cannot vote in the legislator's political jurisdiction, benefits provided to groups located outside the district or state go unrewarded and any costs imposed on these outsiders go unpenalized.

A political-support-maximizing legislator will accordingly search for programs and policies that transfer wealth to local interest groups at the expense of taxpayers in general. This is just another way of stating the obvious point that the political representatives of rural states and districts will tend to promote agricultural interests in the national legislature, that the representatives of jurisdictions where the local work force is heavily unionized will tend to promote labor's interests, and so forth.

Transactions in this model need not take place in the form of cash. The transfers received by the successful coalitions may be denominated in terms of any of the favors that can be conferred by the selective use of the coercive powers of the state, including forbearance from threatened action.[7] Similarly, the fee paid to the legislators who broker wealth transfers may be denominated in votes, gifts, campaign contributions, travel junkets, or any other convenient form of political barter.

The political equilibrium level of wealth-transfer activity in a geographically based representative democracy is determined through a process known as "logrolling," whereby individual legislators, seeking to further the provincial interests of the citizens they have been elected to represent, search for vote-trading bargains that can be struck with the representatives of other political jurisdictions, each of whom likewise wants to promote the interests of his or her own constituents. In other words, through vote trading and compromise, the legislature attempts to arrive at a level and pattern of wealth redistribution that jointly maximizes the membership's political support. This process of searching for political equilibrium is facilitated by an elaborate system of legislative committees and subcommittees, each of which is charged with the task of becoming informed about and monitoring legislative activity in specific policy areas, and by the adoption of complex legislative

---

7. Fred S. McChesney, Rent Extraction and Interest-Group Organization in a Coasean Model of Regulation, 20 J. Legal Stud. 73 (1991).

rules on such matters as bill introductions, floor action, and voting proce-dures.[8]

The important implication of the foregoing discussion is that political repre-sentatives have much to gain from promoting programs and policies that advance local interests and little or nothing to gain from promoting programs and policies that advance the "public interest." Thus, it is the behavior of rational, self-interest-seeking legislators operating under a particular set of institutional constraints, and not in error or ignorance, that explains the wide divergence often observed between the stated objectives of public policies toward business and the actual effects of those policies. It is not that public policies toward business are well-meaning but deformed in their execution by fallible human beings. Rather, the failure of government intervention to achieve its announced goals is simply due to the fact that "public interest" appears only weakly in the objective function being maximized by public policy makers.

Market Failure and Government Failure

The assertion of market failure is perhaps the most important justification for government intervention into the private economy. *Market failure* refers to circumstances in which private market institutions "fail to sustain 'desirable' activities or to estop 'undesirable' activities."[9] Such situations arise when the benefits or costs of an activity at the level of the individual decision maker diverge from the corresponding benefits or costs of that activity at the level of society, that is, when the relevant economic agents interacting in a market do not bear the full social costs—or cannot capture the full social benefits—of their resource-allocation decisions.

Where "externalities" of this sort exist, less than the socially optimal quantity of some goods, such as education, charity, and inoculation against communicable diseases, may be supplied. More than the socially optimal quantity of some "bads," such as litter, polluted water, smog, and acid rain, may likewise be produced. Indeed, private markets may be completely unable to provide certain "public goods"—national defense, for example—that once produced are freely available to all, including to individuals who have not paid for them.

In an older way of thinking, dealing with market failure was simply a

8. For a theory suggesting that the judicial branch of government promotes wealth-transfer activities by enforcing the bargains struck between special-interest groups and their legislative representatives, see William M. Landes and Richard A. Posner, The Independent Judiciary in an Interest-Group Perspective, 18 J. Law & Econ. 875 (1975). Empirical evidence supporting the Landes-Posner theory of the independent judiciary is reported in Gary M. Anderson, William F. Shughart II, and Robert D. Tollison, On the Incentives of Judges to Enforce Legislative Wealth Transfers, 32 J. Law & Econ. 215 (1989).

9. Francis M. Bator, The Anatomy of Market Failure, 72 Quar. J. Econ. 351 (1958), at 351.

matter of recommending that government levy the appropriate tax or pay the appropriate subsidy necessary to induce private decision makers to take account of the full social costs and benefits of their actions.[10] Modern approaches to the market-failure problem raise doubts about the empirical importance of externalities and public goods,[11] and, moreover, emphasize that even where such phenomena exist, the knowledge limitations of public policy makers and the costs of government intervention must be recognized when corrective action is being considered.

These cautionary notes about the efficacy of government intervention for correcting market failure have been raised because economists have come to appreciate more fully the incentives of private parties to resolve disputes involving property rights in a manner that is mutually beneficial and, hence, improves the efficiency with which society's scarce productive resources are allocated. Just as important, economists have come to appreciate more fully the limitations inherent in public policy solutions to market failure problems.

Government is not perfect and it, like the market, can fail to achieve ideal outcomes. When government intervenes it necessarily acts on the basis of limited information and it must necessarily balance the political demands of the various special-interest groups that will be affected by its policy decisions. Given these factors, along with the costs of the resources used in the execution of public policy and the inevitable time lags involved in the political process, government intervention can be—and often is—ineffective or perverse. Appropriate solutions to market-failure problems in the economy are therefore almost always a choice between imperfect alternatives—between imperfect private solutions and imperfect public policy solutions. Accordingly, the costs and benefits of each must be carefully examined on a case-by-case basis.

The Model of Perfect Competition

In the textbook model of "perfect competition," all rivalry between firms is assumed away. Competition is perfect in the model of perfect competition because the market is assumed to be populated by such a large number of sellers that no one of them can, acting on its own, influence market price. The quantities sold by each firm are so small (relative to the total) that decisions about how much to produce are made under the assumption that the prevailing market price will not be affected by the individual seller's output choices. All firms are *price takers* in the model of perfect competition.

10. A. C. Pigou, The Economics of Welfare (1932).

11. The archetypal public good—the lighthouse—was in fact provided quite successfully by private firms in Great Britain until the early nineteenth century. See Ronald H. Coase, The Lighthouse in Economics, 17 J. Law & Econ. 357 (1974). Also see Harold Demsetz, The Private Production of Public Goods, 13 J. Law & Econ. 293 (1970).

Each seller is required to determine only the level of production that will maximize its profits at the given market price.

The absence of market power in the model of perfect competition is further assured by assuming that the product or service produced and sold by each firm in the industry is identical to that offered by every other seller. This product homogeneity applies not only to the physical characteristics of the good or service itself but to all other dimensions of product supply. No firm has any advantages over its rivals in any aspect of its product that consumers value. Firms consequently need not advertise nor undertake any other promotional activities. Because there is no product differentiation, buyers select among firms solely on the basis of price. They are otherwise indifferent to the identity of the seller from whom they make their purchases.

Resources are assumed to move freely into or out of the industry, and information about prices and costs is assumed to be instantaneously and costlessly available to all market participants. Because any economic profits will immediately attract new sellers into the industry under these assumptions, no firm can charge a price above its marginal production costs in the long run. Price equal to marginal cost is associated with an optimal allocation of society's scarce productive resources.[12] Thus, when output is expanded to the point at which price is equal to marginal cost, the value that consumers place on the last unit produced (the amount they are willing to pay for it) is just equal to the value (opportunity cost) of the resources consumed in producing that last unit of output. Production in the model of perfect competition is therefore said to result in *allocative efficiency*.

In addition, no firm earns positive economic profits (or incurs economic losses) in long-run perfectly competitive equilibrium. Market price is not only equal to marginal cost, it is equal to minimum average cost as well. This observation implies that the good or service in question is produced at the lowest possible unit cost or, to put it another way, that *productive efficiency* is maximized insofar as the industry's output is produced by the socially optimal number of firms each of which employs its own production capacity at the efficient (cost-minimizing) rate.

This combination of allocative efficiency and productive efficiency has been adopted by public policy makers as a benchmark for evaluating the performance of firms operating in the real world. The failure of most firms to achieve the standards set by the textbook model of perfect competition is the principal justification for antitrust and for regulatory intervention into the private economy.

---

12. Marginal cost is measured in terms of opportunities foregone. From society's point of view, it represents the value of the resources consumed in producing an additional unit of a particular good or service rather than in employing those same resources in their next best alternative use.

Monopoly

In contrast to the assumptions of the model of perfect competition, virtually all firms in the real world conduct business in markets characterized by product differentiation. Due to differences in quality, reputation, location, and so on, each seller's product or service has one or more unique attributes that distinguish it in the minds of consumers from the products or services offered by rivals. Tide, All, and dozens of other laundry detergents are available in the market, but buyers typically have a preference for one particular brand. The demand schedule confronting each firm slopes downward under these conditions, indicating that the seller must be prepared to reduce price in order to attract consumers away from the sellers of rival products and to increase its own sales.

Product differentiation leads to a supposed species of market failure that is of great concern to designers of public policies toward business, particularly regulatory policy and antitrust policy. This type of market failure is known as market failure due to "monopoly." In the textbook model of pure monopoly, the industry is assumed to consist of a single firm (or a cartel whose members march in lockstep) that produces and sells a product having no close substitutes. By definition, the demand curve confronting the monopolist is the industry demand curve which, because of the assumption that no other firm produces a closely substitutable product, is downward sloping. This again implies that the firm must reduce price in order to sell more output. But it also means that the firm can raise price without losing all of its sales. The monopolist is therefore said to possess "market power." Rather than taking market price as a given, the firm *searches* for the price that maximizes its profits.

Facing the same demand and cost conditions as the perfectly competitive industry, the monopolist produces a smaller quantity of output and consequently charges a higher price. The monopoly output restriction reduces consumer welfare in two ways. Part of the total welfare loss is measured in income redistributed from consumers to the monopolist in the form of pure economic profit. (This redistribution, by itself, has no impact on *social* welfare because the producer's gains exactly offset consumers' losses.) The remainder is a "deadweight" welfare loss transferred away from consumers but not captured by the producer.

Monopoly thus fails to achieve desirable results in the sense that fewer units of output are produced (and fewer resources are therefore allocated to the production of the monopolized good) than is optimal from the viewpoint of the standard set by the model of perfect competition. The benchmark of allocative efficiency is not met by the monopolist because its price exceeds marginal cost. The value that consumers place on the last unit of output supplied by the monopolist is greater than the value of the resources used in producing that last unit. Moreover, although productive efficiency is achieved by the monopolist under constant-cost conditions, only by coincidence will the monopolist produce at a level at which average costs are minimized with more usual U-shaped cost curves.

Allocative inefficiency and the associated deadweight welfare loss provide a theoretical basis for government intervention against monopoly. The presumption is that appropriate public policies can and will be employed to correct the market failure by moving price and output toward the perfectly competitive ideal. Society will experience a net gain from such intervention if the cost of implementing procompetitive policies is less than the resulting improvement in consumer welfare.

The standard view of antitrust assumes that government will intervene in the economy to restrain the forces of private monopoly with the intention of benefiting that most diverse and unorganized of interest groups, consumers. But the power residing in the antitrust laws to declare illegal certain business practices thought to interfere with the forces of competition is also a power that can be used to subvert the competitive process (Baumol and Ordover 1985). A law that declares mergers to be illegal when they would tend to create a monopoly, for example, is also a law that can be used to block the consummation of an acquisition that promises lower production costs and thereby makes life uncomfortable for the merging firms' rivals.

Selective benefits of this sort are valuable to the firms and industries that secure them. Antitrust's potential for favoring certain interests over others activates the formation of coalitions to seek wealth transfers through antitrust processes and, moreover, triggers the politically self-interested supply response predicted by the public-choice model. In contrast to the naive assumption of the conventional view of antitrust, these favors tend to be supplied not to consumers, but to well-organized pressure groups.

Rent Seeking by Business Enterprise

The term *rent* refers to that part of the compensation received by the owner of a resource over and above the resource's value in its next best alternative use. Economic profit is one example of a rent. Rent seeking and profit seeking therefore have much in common. Both refer to the process by which resource owners strive to put themselves in positions to earn incomes in excess of opportunity costs. But there is also an important distinction to be made between profit seeking and rent seeking.[13] This distinction is made necessary

---

13. This distinction is discussed at length in James M. Buchanan, Rent Seeking and Profit Seeking, in James M. Buchanan, Robert D. Tollison, and Gordon Tullock, eds., Toward a Theory of the Rent Seeking Society (1980). Also see Robert D. Tollison, Rent Seeking: A Survey, 35 Kyklos 575 (1982).

by the fundamental differences in the welfare implications of rent-seeking activities in the private sector as opposed to in the public sector.

In a private market setting, the existence of profits (rents) offers an important motivation to resource owners and to entrepreneurs which induces them to shift scarce productive resources from less highly valued to more highly valued uses. The above-cost payments received by some entrepreneurs or resource owners attract other profit seekers to enter the industry or closely related industries. And as these resource reallocation decisions are made in response to profit signals, output expands, prices decline, and in the limit rents are competed away. Although motivated by entrepreneurs' and resource owners' pursuit of personal gain, profit seeking in the private sector thus tends to improve the efficiency with which society's scarce productive resources are allocated and to increase consumer welfare by redistributing previously lost surplus back to them.

Suppose, however, that the excess returns over costs are due to an artificial output restriction created by government. These above-cost payments might be made available through the granting of an exclusive franchise to supply electricity, cable television, or other public utility services in a specified area; by granting inventors the exclusive right to produce and sell their new products or new production technologies for a specified period of time; by imposing tariffs or quotas on the goods of foreign producers who compete with domestic firms; and so forth.

Resource owners and entrepreneurs will again be motivated to reallocate their resources in pursuit of these returns in excess of costs. But rather than investing their resources to discover ways of producing goods or services that consumers will value more highly than those being supplied by the established firm, these resources will be spent to influence the public officials who have the authority to award the right to receive the above-cost payments. Bribery of government officials aside, resources will be invested in such ways as contributing to the campaigns of politicians willing to advance a particular resource owner's cause, hiring lawyers and lobbyists to fill out the required government forms and to help sway official decisions, and designing advertising campaigns to secure "grass-roots" support for a particular point of view.

Because such resource expenditures do nothing to increase the production of the good or service on which above-cost payments have been made available by government, they do nothing to remove the welfare loss associated with the artificial output restriction. Indeed, the investments made by entrepreneurs or resource owners in the process of competing for the right to receive returns in excess of costs created by the public sector serve to increase the welfare cost of monopoly over and above the simple deadweight loss associated with output restrictions in the private sector.

Consider Richard Posner's (1975) example. Suppose that ten risk-neutral bidders vie for a monopoly right worth $100,000 that only one will win. These returns in excess of cost may represent the present discounted value of a local cable TV franchise, for example. If the bidders cannot collude with one another, if the bids are nonrefundable, and if the selection process for awarding the franchise is unbiased, then each bidder would be willing to invest $10,000 for a ten percent chance of winning the right to capture rents worth $100,000. Although the successful bidder will enjoy a net private return amounting to $90,000, at the level of society the total value of the rents associated with the artificial output restriction is exactly dissipated by the resource expenditures made by the rent seekers—$100,000 is spent to capture $100,000.

To avoid confusion, and to distinguish it from the similarly motivated but fundamentally different profit-seeking activities in the private sector, the term *rent seeking* is used in reference to the resource-wasting expenditures made in pursuit of the above-cost payments associated with artificial scarcities created by government.[14] The important implication of rent-seeking theory is that the welfare cost of monopoly in the public sector may be larger than conventionally thought (Tullock 1967). When artificial output restrictions are created, not only do consumers lose the standard deadweight loss triangle but, depending on the institutional framework within which rent seeking takes place, resources equal to the value of the rent rectangle may be wasted as well.[15]

As the previous example shows, the private gains realized by the recipients of wealth transfers are always more than offset by the cost to society of transfer activity. Moreover, society is made permanently poorer in consequence of these resource-wasting rent-seeking investments. Because the resources spent to secure monopoly rights are by and large sunk (i.e., used to purchase assets with little or no salvage value), little can be gained from a social welfare viewpoint by removing previously created artificial scarcities.[16]

14. The term *rent seeking* was coined by Anne Kreuger in her study of the value of the excess returns associated with trade protections imposed by the governments of Turkey and India. She estimated that in the mid-1960s roughly 15 percent of Turkish and Indian GNP was consumed in competing for import licenses and other valuable monopoly rights. See Anne O. Krueger, The Political Economy of the Rent-Seeking Society, 64 Amer. Econ. Rev. 291 (1974).

15. Tullock, in fact, has provided examples in which rent-seeking expenditures in the aggregate *exceed* the value of the monopoly right. See Gordon Tullock, Efficient Rent Seeking, in Buchanan, Tollison, and Tullock, eds., *supra* note 13. Although the exact-dissipation result was subsequently rehabilitated in Richard S. Higgins, William F. Shughart II, and Robert D. Tollison, Free Entry and Efficient Rent Seeking, 46 Pub. Choice 247 (1985), not all of the theoretical issues have been resolved. See, for example, Gordon Tullock, Back to the Bog, 46 Pub. Choice 259 (1985); J. David Pérez-Castrillo and Thierry Verdier, A General Analysis of Rent-Seeking Games, 73 Pub. Choice 335 (1992); and Gordon Tullock, Still Somewhat Muddy: A Comment, 76 Pub. Choice 365 (1993).

16. Robert E. McCormick, William F. Shughart II, and Robert D. Tollison, The Disinterest in Deregulation, 74 Amer. Econ. Rev. 1075 (1984).

The artificial restrictions on output made available by government thus give rise to what Gordon Tullock has called a "transitional gains trap."[17] The promise of above-cost payments motivates interest groups to seek special privileges from the public sector. These gains are subsequently eroded by competitive forces of one sort or another—the capital value of the rents associated with the artificial scarcity is dissipated up front in pursuit of the monopoly right or, alternatively, is dissipated by competition between the privileged,[18] by newcomers who purchase the right to replace an established producer, and so on. In consequence, incumbent firms in the long run earn only a normal return on their rent-seeking investment.

Yet there is no politically acceptable way to abolish a program or policy that is inefficient both from the standpoint of consumers, who pay artificially high prices, and from the standpoint of the privileged, who no longer make exceptional profits. This is because the current members of the privileged group would suffer a capital loss if the artificial output restriction were abolished. Even though these capital losses would be smaller than the overall social welfare gains from removing the output restriction, it will not generally be possible to devise a compensation scheme for getting out of the trap: "Those persons and groups who have established what they consider to be entitlements in the positive gains that have been artificially created will not agree to change, and those persons and groups who suffer [ongoing] losses will not willingly pay off what they consider to be immoral gainers."[19] This observation implies that the optimal policy is to avoid granting special privileges in the first place.

The owners and managers of private business enterprises are by no means the only seekers of rents in the economy. Wherever the public sector holds a policy monopoly, there will be attempts to influence policy makers to use their authority to compel or prohibit in a way that selectively benefits some individuals or groups at the expense of others. The taxing, spending, and regulatory powers of government represent a valuable resource that can be called upon to help or to hurt a vast array of special interests.

But private business firms are among the most active rent seekers. This is because producer groups are typically small enough in number and their financial interests are sufficiently concentrated that the potential benefits of organizing and lobbying for monopoly rights will exceed the associated costs. Firms are well situated to engage in rent seeking because political favors can often be pursued as byproducts of the activities of industry trade associations

17. Gordon Tullock, The Transitional Gains Trap, 6 Bell J. Econ. 671 (1975).

18. For evidence that the rents made available to the commercial airlines by government regulation of fares and routes were dissipated by nonprice competition between the established carriers, see Douglas and Miller, *supra* note 4.

19. James M. Buchanan, Reform in the Rent-Seeking Society, in Buchanan, Tollison, and Tullock, ed., *supra* note 13, at 365. Also see James M. Buchanan and Gordon Tullock, The "Dead Hand" of Monopoly, 1 Antitrust Law & Econ. Rev. 85 (1968).

and other producer groups that have been organized for other business purposes.

The decision to invest in rent seeking is no different from any other capital-budgeting problem the firm confronts. Faced with a loss of sales to a new or an established rival, for instance, the firm can respond by cutting price, by improving product quality, by increasing its advertising expenditures, or by taking any of a number of other actions, or combinations of actions, that normally characterize the workings of a competitive market economy. Alternatively, the firm can appeal to government for protection. It can lobby for favorable legislation, it can attempt to influence a bureaucratic ruling, or it can instigate an investigation of its rival by supplying information about possible illegal activity—regulatory or antitrust violations, for example—to one of the public law-enforcement agencies. Which of these various options is chosen in any given circumstance will be simply a matter of selecting the strategy offering the highest expected rate of return to the firm.

The moral of this story is that when the opportunity to earn above-cost payments is available, resources will be spent to gain access to them. The motivation to seek private gain is independent of the source of returns in excess of cost. But the welfare implications of such self-interest-seeking activities are fundamentally different in two stylized institutional settings. In the private sector, individuals and firms seek profits by searching out ways of serving consumers better; in the public sector, individuals and firms seek rents by searching out ways of influencing the political process. In one setting, consumer welfare is enhanced as the forces of competition push individuals and firms to keep prices in line with costs; in the other setting, consumer welfare is reduced as a byproduct of a process in which individuals and firms strive for protection from the forces of competition.

An even more basic lesson of the discussion, however, is that political markets and economic markets work in much the same way. Outcomes in both settings are determined by the interaction of large numbers of individuals and firms seeking their own private gain. Outcomes differ in the two settings not because the people interacting in them are motivated differently, but simply because the constraints on behavior are different.

Public Choice and Antitrust

The traditional arguments supporting the idea that government has a role to play in harnessing the self-interest-seeking behavior of private individuals and firms rests on the unstated assumption that the behavior of the public officials who are charged with the responsibility of enacting and enforcing policies and programs aimed at correcting perceived market failures cannot be explained by the economic model. The conventional wisdom on public policies toward business assumes that public policy makers are motivated not by their own self-interest but by the interests of others. It insists that government's power to compel and to prohibit can and will be used with the intention of helping that most diverse and unorganized of interest groups—the "public." Accordingly, whenever and wherever public policies toward business fail to achieve their stated objectives, or achieve their goals at a cost that far outweighs any reasonable estimate of their benefits, "better" policies and "better" policy makers are called for.

The public-choice model, by contrast, recognizes that the same rational, self-interest-seeking behavior that motivates human action in ordinary markets applies to decision making in the public sector as well. Just as consumers seek to maximize their own satisfaction and firms seek to maximize their own profits, public policy makers seek to maximize their own political support. This insight implies that what the conventional wisdom treats as policy failures are in fact the predictable consequences of rational public decision making under a special set of constraints that furnishes higher political payoffs to programs and policies that benefit special interests than they do to programs and policies that serve the "public interest." As such, the public-choice model does not entail value judgments about how public policies toward business *should* work. Instead, it draws testable implications about how public policies *do* work, based on applying sound principles of economic theory to the analysis of political markets.

The public-choice model is rich in empirical content. It has been applied fruitfully in identifying the private-interest basis of a wide variety of public policies. Yet only recently have public-choice scholars entered the debate about the purposes and effects of antitrust.

The remaining chapters apply the insights of public choice to the analysis of this important sphere of government policy toward business. The public-interest and public-choice models of antitrust are evaluated by asking questions such as, Is market failure due to monopoly empirically important? That is, is the existence of an antitrust policy justified by evidence of widespread injury to consumers due to anticompetitive business practices in the private economy? If such market failures occur, does antitrust in fact target those firms and industries in which reductions in market power would provide the largest benefits to consumers? What conclusions can be drawn about the purposes of antitrust by studying the legislative origins of the antitrust statutes? More fundamentally, is there evidence that antitrust has actually been used not to create wealth but to redistribute wealth from unorganized groups to politically well-organized interests?

The answers given to these questions by public-choice scholars are not only interesting in their own right, but also raise the debate about antitrust to a level not addressed by the public-interest model. As the following chapters show, in order to answer the question, "Why has antitrust failed to protect the public's interest?" one must first ask, "Whose public and whose interests does antitrust serve?"

PART ONE

In Search of the Public-Interest
Model of Antitrust

FRED S. MCCHESNEY

Introduction

As economics progresses, it demonstrates an ability to elucidate even seemingly non-economic problems, and in ever-extending realms.[1] Simultaneously, economists have become more introspective. The science increasingly analyzes itself, studying such things as its own methodology,[2] the validity of its empirical evidence,[3] and the production function for economic ideas.[4]

In this era of the new economic introspection, perhaps the liveliest literature explores how economists reach conclusions. The increasing penchant for self-study has yielded the rueful realization that we often fail to practice the science we preach. We profess devotion to scientific method: model, falsifiable implications, empirical tests. Too frequently, though, this process is not the methodology by which economists themselves decide whether fundamental economic propositions should be deemed false or true (technically, refuted or not refuted). Ronald Coase, for example, relates three historical episodes in which economists quickly jettisoned established models in favor of new constructs. Ideally, he notes, "[w]hen a new theory is advanced, economists would compare the accuracy of its predictions, preferably about 'phenomena not yet observed,' with those of the existing theory and would choose that theory which gave the best predictions. Nothing remotely resembling this procedure happened during the three episodes that I discussed."[5]

Suggestions from Robert Tollison are gratefully acknowledged.

1. See, for example, Gerard Radnitsky and Peter Bernholz, eds., Economic Imperialism: The Economic Approach Applied Outside the Field of Economics (1987) and Edmund S. Phelps, ed., Altruism, Morality and Economic Theory (1975).

2. Milton Friedman, The Methodology of Positive Economics, in Essays in Positive Economics (1953). This is not the place to rehash the lengthy debate touched off by Friedman's most influential essay. For a recent discussion, see Thomas Mayer, Friedman's Methodology of Positive Economics: A Soft Reading, 31 Econ. Inq. 213 (1993). See also Donald N. McCloskey, The Rhetoric of Economics, 21 J. Econ. Lit. 481 (1983); Economical Writing, 24 Econ. Inq. 187 (1985).

3. See, for example, Edward Leamer, Let's Take the Con Out of Econometrics, 73 Amer. Econ. Rev. 31 (1986).

4. Robert D. Tollison, Economists as the Subject of Economic Inquiry, 52 So. Econ. J. 909 (1986).

5. Ronald H. Coase, How Should Economists Choose? 13 (1982).

Consider the fundamental paradigm shift of the 1930s, when economists en masse rejected neoclassical principles concerning resource unemployment in favor of the Keynesian alternative. Coase discusses how Keynesianism triumphed in England within just months of the publication of *The General Theory* in 1936.[6] In this country, things were no different. Herbert Stein describes the ambience of economic Washington in 1938, when he first went to work there:

> Washington was a great place for economics and economists then because of the combination of two conditions. The first was that the economic problem had become clear; it was to achieve and maintain 'full employment,' although we did not use that term. The second condition was that we knew the solution to the problem. That was Keynesianism.[7]

Stein does not mention any principled, methodical process by which American economists had come to change their minds because, of course, there had been none.

A similarly unquestioning attitude among economists attended another paradigm shift of the 1930s: acceptance of the basic proposition from Berle and Means's *The Modern Corporation and Private Property* that increasing separation of ownership and control in corporate firms created widespread economic problems (what today would be called "agency costs").[8] The book was a great success, not just popularly, but also among economists. As Stigler and Friedland discuss, economists' swift and generally favorable reception of the Berle-Means message was "astonishingly uncritical."[9] Data were available at the time to subject the principal tenets of the Berle-Means model to testing; other easily derived implications could also have been examined empirically. But none were. "If economists were the professional audience for the economic theses of *The Modern Corporation,* they seldom displayed a deeper understanding of the work than the audience we have labeled 'amateur.' "[10]

More episodes could be cited, but all lead to the same conclusion. When new economic propositions are propounded, economists often make up their minds without demanding the critical tests that would help separate truth from falsity. Principles of science yield to leaps of faith.

6. Ibid., at 9–11.

7. Herbert Stein, When Economics Came to Washington, The American Enterprise (May/June 1993), p. 8.

8. Adolf A. Berle and Gardiner C. Means, The Modern Corporation and Private Property (1932).

9. George J. Stigler and Claire Friedland, The Literature of Economics: The Case of Berle and Means, 26 J. Law & Econ. 237, 258 (1983).

10. Ibid., at 244.

Antitrust

Antitrust law enjoys a positive reputation among most economists. As Paul Rubin notes in the first chapter of Part One, polls of economists by economists consistently show strong majorities in favor of having government intervene in the economy through antitrust law. Indeed, the survey results show that economists agree on the desirability of antitrust more than they concur on almost any other economic proposition.[11]

One might well ask how economists have come to conclude that antitrust is a desirable form of government intervention. If economists generally believe in the price system,[12] on what basis did they come to believe that "market failures" involving lack of competition are both widespread and important enough to justify systematic antitrust law enforcement? The answer appears to be: on no scientific basis at all. Much the same pattern of blind acceptance shown in connection with Keynes and Berle-Means has typified economists' evaluations of antitrust. Antitrust has differed only in the slower speed of its acceptance.

As Stigler reports, economists were not partisans of the Sherman Act. "A careful student of the history of economics would have searched long and hard, on the unseasonably cool day of July 2 of 1890, the day the Sherman Act was signed by President Harrison, for any economist who had ever recommended the policy of actively combating collusion or monopolization in the economy at large" (Stigler 1982b, 41). Stigler also notes that the "lack of enthusiasm, and often the downright hostility, with which economists greeted the Sherman Act" reflected a collective professional view that monopoly was the result either of government favoritism (unreachable by the Sherman Act) or of inevitable "historical force." Today, the profession would refer to the first explanation for monopoly as rent seeking, and to the latter as long-run efficiency. Thus, the terms of the antitrust debate embodied in this volume—politics versus economics—had already been adumbrated in 1890, although economists would not seriously model or test the importance of politics in antitrust for almost a century.

Whatever economists' misgivings about it in 1890, antitrust eventually

---

11. See Bruno S. Frey, Werner W. Pommerehne, Friedrich Schneider and Guy Gilbert, Consensus and Dissension Among Economists: An Empirical Inquiry, 74 Amer. Econ. Rev. 986 (1984). In that survey, economists were asked whether they agreed or disagreed with 27 propositions, including the statement, "antitrust laws should be used vigorously to reduce monopoly power from its current level." Only 12.5 percent of the 936 economists polled disagreed, making the majority in favor of antitrust the third highest percentage in the survey. For an update of these results, indicating that economists still favor antitrust enforcement by a large margin, see Richard M. Alston, J. R. Kearl, and Michael B. Vaughn, Is There a Consensus Among Economists in the 1990's? 82 Amer. Econ. Rev. Papers & Proceedings 203 (1992).

12. Bruno S. Frey, Economists Favor the Price System—Who Else Does? 39 Kyklos 537 (1986).

won the profession over. What better example than Henry Simons, the first
notable "Chicago school" scholar of antitrust? Writing at the nadir of the Depression, Simons in 1934 emphatically blamed collusion and monopoly for a
large part of the economic downturn, and invoked antitrust as the solution:

> [*T*]*he great enemy of democracy is monopoly, in all its forms.* . . .
> There must be outright dismantling of our gigantic corporations and
> persistent prosecution of producers who organize, by whatever meth-
> ods, for price maintenance or output limitation. There must be ex-
> plicit and unqualified repudiation of the so-called "rule of reason."
> Legislation must prohibit, and administration effectively prevent,
> the acquisition by any private firm, or group of firms, of substantial
> monopoly power, regardless of how reasonably that power may ap-
> pear to be exercised. The Federal Trade Commission must become
> perhaps the most powerful of our government agencies. (1948 re-
> print, 43, 58; emphasis in original)

Simons's call to the antitrust barricades is ironic. As George Bittlingmayer
shows in Part Four of this volume, there is empirical evidence that the Depression may actually have been *caused* in part by antitrust enforcement.

But Simons's eulogy to antitrust is particularly remarkable for the fact that
it cites no economic evidence in favor of his claims. Antitrust was in its
forty-fifth year as Simons wrote, yet no analysis of the actual workings of
antitrust, or of the sorts of cases pursued by government, had been done.
Simons is thus typical of the trend among economists, who have, since 1890,
accorded antitrust increasing respect without any scientific reason for doing
so. As Stigler (1982b, 44) remarks, "It would be gratifying to me if I could
report that our profession's changing view was based upon the systematic
study by economists of the effects of the policy, in short, that hard evidence
carried the day. Unfortunately. . . ." The failure to demand evidence in
favor of antitrust is all the more noteworthy, given that Simons was teaching
in a law school. Simons would presumably have been aware of the dubious
economics already perpetrated judicially in the name of promoting competition, such as the per se abolition of such vertical practices as resale price
maintenance.

The papers in this section demonstrate how economists finally began to
use their comparative advantage, applying scientific methods to the study of
antitrust. As Paul Rubin reports, the first steps were taken in the 1950s
with theoretical (e.g., Bork 1954) and especially empirical examinations of
particular antitrust doctrines and cases.[13] The results were remarkably influential; for example, John McGee's (1958) article on the landmark *Standard
Oil* case remains the fundamental analysis of predatory pricing today.

But as Rubin also reports, economists' systematic examination of the cases

---

13. For a brief history of economic theory's advances in the areas of concern to antitrust,
see McChesney (1993).

was not encouraging. In fewer than half the cases from Rubin's sample did the economic merits of the case translate into the appropriate legal result. That is, the courts got it wrong more often than they got it right in the cases sampled. Part of the problem for courts, Rubin points out, is the need, not only to decide correctly on liability, but also to fashion an effective remedy in the event that a violation of the law is found. Several other analyses (Elzinga 1969; Hay and Kelley 1974; Rogowsky 1987) also have found that applying an appropriate remedy consistently bedevils the courts.

Case-by-case analysis of antitrust's economic sense and nonsense continues today (e.g., Kwoka and White 1989). But once it was realized that particular antitrust cases systematically failed to produce the desired results, in terms of either liability or remedy, economists broadened their attention to the overall effects of antitrust. That is the subject of George Stigler's article from 1966 reprinted in this section. The article opens with a strong call for more empirical evaluations of antitrust: "presumption is a poor substitute for evidence."[14] It ends on a more doleful note, concluding that his study's findings are rather "meager." Substantively, Stigler claims that the Sherman Act has somewhat reduced concentration and has diminished the number of horizontal mergers and the extent of collusion. Yet the data at the time were not such, Stigler admits, "that any reasonable man must accept [these] conclusions."

From Stigler's attempt to measure the effects of antitrust, it became obvious that better data on antitrust enforcement were required before strong conclusions could be reached. Richard Posner assumed the onus of amassing that data, and portions of his monumental 1970 study are reprinted in this section. To appreciate Posner's herculean efforts, one must read his full article. He is particularly interested in public (i.e., governmental) enforcement of the antitrust laws, and in the ability of better quantitative information to improve enforcement. His study concludes, "Antitrust enforcement is inefficient, and the first step toward improvement must be, I am convinced, a much greater interest in the dry subject of this paper, antitrust statistics."[15]

One intriguing point emerges from the original Posner article in the portions reprinted in this book. He is apparently the first in recent years to consider (at least in print) whether politics, not just economics, explains government decisions concerning antitrust enforcement. The influence of politics on antitrust is a point he had already included in his study of the Federal Trade Commission published the year before, in which he noted the "politicization of antitrust policy" at the Federal Trade Commission, due to the agency's "dependence on Congress" (Posner 1969a, 54). In the selection

14. The extent to which antitrust economics was unencumbered by data at this time can be seen in Rosemary D. Hale and G. E. Hale, More on Mergers, 5 J. Law & Econ. 119 (1962), the purpose of which was to present the results of a survey asking businessmen the reason for mergers involving their firms.

15. For more recent data of the sort Posner advocates, see James M. Clabault and Michael Block, Sherman Act Indictments 1955–1980 (1981); and Gallo, Craycraft, and Bush (1985).

here, Posner looks at the executive branch to see whether changes in political party at the White House influenced the level of antitrust enforcement at the Justice Department. No difference is evident.

The potential importance of politics in explaining antitrust lay unexplored for years after Posner wrote. Economists chose first to determine to what extent economics, not politics, was a systematic factor in the choice of government cases. The first article to provide an answer to that question—by William Long, Richard Schramm, and Robert Tollison—is reprinted here following the Posner selection. The sequence is fitting, because it was the data collected by Posner that made possible the Long-Schramm-Tollison (L-S-T) analysis.

The three authors develop a cross-industry model of welfare loss potentially caused by anticompetitive acts, then examine whether the Justice Department has brought more cases in industries in which welfare losses from lack of competition would be greater. They find that potential welfare loss apparently exerts little influence on government antitrust activity, and conclude that the explanation for observed patterns of antitrust enforcement must lie outside an economic model. Their analysis is remarkably robust; other authors (Siegfried 1975; Asch 1975) subsequently used different samples and different econometric techniques to check the L-S-T results, but arrived at the same conclusions. Siegfried (1975, 573) concludes, for example, that "economic variables have little influence on the [Department of Justice's] Antitrust Division."

If government was not boldly going where welfare gains were to be had, as the L-S-T and later analyses determined it was not, several disturbing conclusions would follow. It would necessarily be true, for example, that the cases being brought as challenges to particular practices—alleged price fixing or mergers, for example—were not targeting truly important anticompetitive problems. The suspicion was raised, in fact, that the government might be pursuing firms and conduct that did not cause economic harm at all.

This hypothesis was tested by Peter Asch and Joseph Seneca in the final chapter of this section. Asch and Seneca look at a sample of firms charged with price fixing (i.e., firms that had either been found guilty of fixing prices or had chosen not to contest the charges). These firms are compared to a random sample of firms not so accused. If the government was using antitrust correctly, to root out truly injurious collusion, the firms charged with price fixing should have higher prices and profits than the random sample of firms. But Asch and Seneca's results indicate that collusive firms are consistently *less* profitable than non-colluders: they report that "after accounting for other basic influences, the presence of collusive behavior is negatively associated with firm profitability." As the authors conclude, "The finding that collusion and firm profitability are negatively related is, at least superficially, surprising. . . . [T]he findings raise some questions about the effects both of collusive conduct and of public policies to restrict such conduct."

Like the Long-Schramm-Tollison results, the conclusions from the Asch and Seneca investigation of price fixing have proven to be robust over time. Using a different sample of cases and different empirical techniques, Marvel, Netter, and Robinson (1988) also investigated whether the Justice Department can be depended on to identify and prosecute truly injurious price fixing. Apparently it cannot. Marvel and his co-authors found (pp. 572, 575) that "[i]n almost half of the DOJ criminal cases, consumers suffered damages insufficient to justify even the low cost of filing (not litigating) a civil damage claim. . . . [The empirical results indicate] the absence of effective collusion in many of the criminal cases."

Antitrust's partisans point to the fact that some price-fixing cases subsequently produce lower prices (e.g., Block et al. 1981; for some telling criticisms of the Block et al. empirics, see Newmark [1988]). But what does this mean? Penalizing sellers for charging prices that look "too high" to government will cause prices to fall independently of whether the prices were competitive or collusive to begin with. When the revolutionary Marxist government of Ethiopia began executing merchants accused of overpricing, for example, prices reportedly fell by 60 percent. But because there had been no claim that prices were anything other than competitive in the first place, "the drops in price were apparently caused by panicked merchants scrambling to liquidate their stocks and get out of business to avoid 'revolutionary justice' " (Sproul 1993, 742 n. 1).

Lower prices, absent some valid economic reason for issuing an antitrust complaint, are hardly proof of increased consumer welfare. In the long run, expected antitrust penalties just become costs of doing business.[16] Prices will eventually increase to the extent that the conditions of demand and supply allow sellers to pass these higher costs on to consumers. The end result is fewer producers selling at higher prices—just the opposite of antitrust's intended effects.[17]

In other words, even if prices fall in the wake of a price-fixing case, diametrically opposite conclusions about the social welfare consequences of antitrust can still be drawn. On the one hand, producers may have been forced to reduce cartel overcharges, and the case is therefore a "good" case. On the other hand, producers may simply be buying insurance against future antitrust attacks, and the case is therefore a "bad" case.[18] Moreover, because

16. The fact that antitrust law enforcers repeatedly bring cases against the same industries and firms increases the prospect that antitrust will simply become a cost of doing business.

17. In chapter 17 of this volume, George Bittlingmayer discusses further the pernicious economic effects of antitrust attacks on efficient cartels.

18. The same point applies to the claim that successful price-fixing cases will have deterrent effects on other (non-defendant) producers. This may be true, but its normative implications are likewise ambiguous. Indeed, McWilliams, Turk, and Zardkoohi (1993) provide evidence that the adverse wealth effects of government merger policy go far beyond those borne by the owners of the firms involved in the challenged transaction. The values of all mergers—including uncontested mergers—ongoing at the time an unfavorable Supreme Court ruling is announced seem to be affected negatively.

the remedy may be ineffective or the cartel members may simply shift to more costly methods of collusion, it is not at all clear that prices will unambiguously fall in the wake of a "successful" government case.

The issue is largely empirical. And, in fact, while antitrust may cause prices in a particular industry to fall, systematic cross-industry data on price reactions to antitrust enforcement show a disturbing tendency for prices to *increase* when government prevails: "There is little doubt that in the great majority of [price-fixing] cases antitrust prosecution does not lead to lower prices. In general, an indictment for price fixing results in slightly higher prices" (Sproul 1993, 753).

These findings about government's price fixing cases are startling enough by themselves. But they raise wider and more disturbing questions about all of government antitrust enforcement. Price fixing should present the easiest cases for government to locate and to act to stop consumer welfare losses. If antitrust enforcers cannot get it right in those cases, how can they be expected to measure correctly the cost-benefit tradeoffs implicit in more complex horizontal matters, such as mergers? (Indeed, as the chapter by Espen Eckbo and Peggy Wier in Part Two shows, the government generally gets it wrong in merger cases, too.) And if government antitrust enforcers cannot correctly evaluate the competitive merits of relatively straightforward horizontal matters, how much can they be counted on to evaluate accurately more complex matters such as vertical contracting and alleged single-firm monopolization?

Conclusion

In sum, the papers in this section provide a good overview of economists' position on the utility of antitrust as of the mid-1970s. The initial work analyzing individual cases from an economic standpoint was well underway, but the results were disheartening. Courts did not seem to get the cases right as often as flipping a coin would. Moving beyond specific cases, economists had assembled sufficient data to examine more systematically the sorts of cases being pursued under antitrust law. But here, too, the findings were discouraging. Promoting welfare gains appeared to play no role in the government's choice of cases. In fact, firms targeted by the government apparently were not guilty of any economic wrongdoing.

Thus, it was fairly clear by this time what government antitrust was *not* accomplishing. Repeatedly, the null hypothesis that antitrust was a procompetitive force was effectively refuted by the evidence. But no well-formulated alternative hypothesis as to what actually motivated or explained antitrust enforcement had yet emerged.

CHAPTER THREE

What Do Economists Think about Antitrust?: A Random Walk Down Pennsylvania Avenue

PAUL H. RUBIN

Introduction

When asked, a majority of economists generally agree that "antitrust laws should be enforced vigorously to reduce monopoly power from its current level."[1] However, economists themselves are often skeptical of survey results. Another way to measure economists' assessment of antitrust is to examine their writings on particular antitrust cases. That is the purpose of this chapter.

Case-by-case assessments are also a way of determining the efficiency of actual antitrust decisions. An economist can look at the alleged purpose of the antitrust action and then, *ex post,* determine if the action achieved its intended goal. Moreover, as economic theory progresses, it is possible to examine past decisions in the light of current knowledge and determine if the stated justifications for the action would be acceptable given today's increased knowledge. For example, the study of transactions-costs economics has shown that many forms of business behavior previously thought anticompetitive actually have procompetitive justifications (Williamson 1985; Rubin 1990).

Since case interpretations are more subjective than statistical evidence, there are dangers of misinterpretation. Even with respect to current antitrust

The author would like to thank Bruce Allen, George Bittlingmayer, Jinook Jeong, Ron Johnson, Richard Muth, Russell Pittman, Richard Posner, and Oliver Williamson for helpful comments on a previous draft. The usual caveat applies.

1. This question was asked in J. R. Kearl, Clayne L. Pope, Gordon C. Whiting, and Larry T. Wimmer, A Confusion of Economists, 69 Amer. Econ. Rev. 28 (1979); Bruno S. Frey, Werner M. Pommerehne, Friedrich Schneider, and Guy Gilbert, Consensus and Dissension Among Economists: An Empirical Inquiry, 74 Amer. Econ. Rev. 986 (1984); and Richard M. Alston, J. R. Kearl, and Michael B. Vaughn, Is There a Consensus Among Economists in the 1990s? 82 Amer. Econ. Rev. 203 (1992). Kearl et al. find that 85 percent of economists "agree" or "agree with provisions" on this proposition; Frey et al. find 83 percent of American economists and comparable percentages of European economists in these categories. For 1990, Alston et al. find agreement or agreement with provisions among 62 percent of their sample, a statistically significant lower percentage than in the 1979 article based on a 1976 sample.

actions, there are differences in interpretation between different economists.[2] Moreover, there is a possibility of selection bias: an analyst might choose cases that support a particular view of antitrust.

To avoid the second source of bias, I have selected as my sample all of the articles cited in the antitrust chapters of Scherer and Ross (1990) whose titles indicate that they deal with specific cases. This textbook is well-known for being encyclopedic, and it cites many studies. In addition, Scherer is a proponent of an active antitrust policy, so that if there is any selection bias it should be in favor of more successful cases. Therefore, the results may provide an upper-bound of economists' estimate of the efficiency of antitrust. In order to avoid the first type of bias (biased interpretation), I will quote directly from the conclusions as expressed by the authors of the articles in the sample.[3]

In private communications, some have suggested additional sources of bias in my sample. Russell Pittman and George Bittlingmayer have suggested that economists choose a biased sample of cases to write about. Pittman: "How much fun is it to write an article . . . that may be summarized 'case X was investigated correctly, prosecuted correctly, and decided correctly?'" However, anticipating the results, we see below that this is a characterization of a significant number of the articles from the sample. According to the authors' own characterization of the outcomes, in 15 out of 37 articles (40 percent) cases were justified and plaintiff won (see table 3.4). This bias does not seem overwhelming. Bittlingmayer suggests that there is little demand for articles showing that plaintiff lost an unjustified case. There were five such articles among the 37, or 14 percent of the total.

Indeed, as we will see from the sample of cases examined, authors seem to choose cases which provide some innate economic interest, almost independent of the importance of the case itself. We can best see this if we consider those cases analyzed by more than one author. Two authors (McGee 1958; Mariger 1978) wrote about the predation issue in *Standard Oil,* and both came to the same conclusion, that predation was unlikely. Four articles (Allen 1971; Meehan 1972; McBride 1983; Johnson and Parkman 1987) examined the FTC's cases involving vertical integration in cement, and did not fundamentally disagree with one another. These cases were of interest because the motive for the challenged vertical mergers was difficult to understand, but the inefficiency of the cases themselves was not at issue in the articles. There were five articles (Gaskins 1974; Fisher 1974; Swan 1980; Martin 1982; Suslow 1986) examining *Alcoa;* all focused on the issue of the

2. For extreme examples, compare Adams and Brock (1986), who argue that much more antitrust activity would be desirable, with Armentano (1982), who contends that there should be no antitrust at all. While their views are extreme, more moderate economists also differ regarding the net benefits of antitrust both in general and in specific cases.

3. Throughout, all emphasis in quotations is from the original source.

effect of a market for used goods in antitrust analysis, and all concluded that the court got the analysis right. No author considered the overall merits of the case itself. Four authors (Schmalensee 1979; McCarthy 1979; Krouse 1984; Rosenbaum 1987) examined the issue of trademark licensing raised in *ReaLemon,* even though this remedy was not applied. Three articles (Pittman 1984; Levy and Welzer 1985; Petty 1986) examined *IBM,* even though the case was settled. Thus, at least based on cases subject to multiple analyses, the case selection process seems to preclude the hypothesized sorts of bias.

Pittman and Richard Posner both suggest that litigated cases are themselves a biased sample, and that the law may still have a "sound deterrent effect" (Posner) even with "noise" in the litigated cases. However, it is decisions in litigated cases that determine behavior. As Posner (1977) himself shows in his article in the sample, *Schwinn* had a detrimental effect on behavior for ten years until it was overturned by *Sylvania.* It appears that neither source of bias invalidates the results.

Some authors were involved with particular cases as experts on one side or another, and some authors may have worked for agencies (e.g., the Federal Trade Commission or the Department of Justice) which issued complaints. It might appear that this would color the views of an economist. However, I do not believe that this would create a substantial source of bias. First, economists might self-select or be selected by attorneys to advocate positions that the economist would anyway find congenial. Second, and more impor- tant, authors of papers commonly indicate that they have had such an interest in a matter, and referees and editors presumably take such interests into account in reading manuscripts. Nonetheless, I have mentioned all cases in which authors indicate that they have had such an interest.

The rest of this essay is organized as follows. I consider all relevant pub- lished articles cited in chapters 5, 9, 12, 13, 14, and 15 in Scherer and Ross (1990).[4] These chapters deal with particular antitrust doctrines and provide citations to studies of antitrust cases by economists. For each action, articles are discussed in chronological order. Cases are ordered by the date of the first article discussing the case. Thus, the temporal structure of this chapter is in terms of economic analysis of antitrust, not in terms of the antitrust actions themselves.

There are several possible outcomes to antitrust cases, as viewed by an economic analyst. A case may be "justified" (i.e., the behavior challenged may be anticompetitive)[5] or "unjustified" (the behavior is procompetitive).

4. I include only articles published in journals. I omit unpublished articles (including working papers), books, and chapters in books. I also omit articles dealing with a class of cases, such as those included in chapters 7 and 9 below.

5. George Bittlingmayer (personal communication) suggests that "a bad case challenges an efficient *mixture* of competition and cooperation, and not competition per se." I will use "anti- competitive" throughout to mean "inefficient."

Plaintiff (usually the government in the cases cited in Scherer and Ross) may win or lose in each sort of action, justified or unjustified. If the plaintiff wins, still the remedy granted may be effective or ineffective. The only unambiguously desirable outcome is if plaintiff wins a justified case and the remedy is effective; here, anticompetitive behavior is deterred. If the plaintiff loses a justified case, or if the remedy is ineffective, then there are two effects. First, there are costs to being sued, so there is some beneficial deterrent effect even if defendant wins. On the other hand, the victory may entrench the anticompetitive behavior. There are similar effects if the plaintiff loses an unjustified case or if the remedy is ineffective: the defendant firm which is not behaving anticompetitively must nevertheless spend resources on its defense, but the procompetitive behavior is accepted by the courts, or not effectively constrained. Finally, if plaintiff wins an unjustified case and an effective remedy is imposed, there are unambiguous harmful effects.

In what follows, I will classify the outcome as reported by each analyst in terms of the evaluation of the case and the evaluation of the outcome. Some papers deal with a subsidiary issue and do not evaluate the desirability of either the challenged behavior or of the outcome. Nonetheless, I will judge the author's opinion of the case itself based on the interpretation of the issue discussed. (For example, McGee [1958] finds that Standard Oil did not engage in predation, but does not address the monopoly issue. I interpret his analysis as finding that the case was "unjustified" since the aspect of behavior he studied was judged as not anticompetitive.) It should be noted that I use the author's evaluation of a case, even though I may not agree with this evaluation. In all cases, the authors seem to be using the standard economic measures of efficiency in evaluating cases, at least as understood at the time they wrote.

The Sample

The cases and articles constituting my sample, organized as discussed above, are the following.

Cellophane: U.S. v. E.I. du Pont de Nemours and Co., 351 U.S. 377 (1956)

In 1953, the District Court dismissed a charge brought by the Department of Justice against du Pont for monopolizing the manufacture and sale of cellophane. Judge Leahy found that du Pont did not possess monopoly power, so the issue of possibly monopolizing conduct did not arise. Stocking and Mueller (1955) examined this decision and concluded that Judge Leahy was wrong, and that du Pont did possess monopoly power.

They based their conclusion on several factors. After analyzing du Pont's strategic behavior, they concluded that "Du Pont's moves and countermoves to protect its domestic market were the strategy of a producer operating in a monopolistic, not a competitive, market'' (p. 44). They also concluded that du Pont earned monopoly profits on cellophane, in part by comparing return on investment in cellophane with that in rayon, two products that they contended have many similarities. ''From the beginning of the depression in 1929 through the succeeding recovery and the 1938 recession du Pont averaged 29.6 percent before taxes on its cellophane investment. On its rayon investment it averaged only 6.3 percent'' (pp. 62–63).

The final conclusion was:

> Du Pont has used its power with foresight and wisdom. It has apparently recognized that it could increase its earnings by decreasing its costs and prices, by educating its potential customers to the benefits of wrapping their products in cellophane, by improving machinery for packaging, by helping converters and packagers solve their technical problems. It has built a better mousetrap and taught people how to use it.
>
> But du Pont has not surrendered its monopoly power. Its strategy, cellophane's distinctive qualities, and the course of its prices and earnings indicate this. Du Pont's strategy was designed to protect a monopoly in the sale of a product it regarded as unique, and its pricing policies reflected the judgment of its executives on how best to maximize earnings. We think its earnings illustrate Knight's distinction between justifiable profits to the innovator and unjustifiable monopoly gains. They have been ''too large'' and have lasted ''too long.'' (P. 63)

This was viewed as a justified case that the plaintiff lost. However, nowhere in the Stocking and Mueller analysis is there any discussion of the relative size of the efficiency gains from the behaviors listed in the first quoted paragraph and the efficiency losses from the alleged monopoly power. Since du Pont was a monopolist, its specific (but unpatented) investments in packaging technology would have been more profitable; had the firm been competitive, free-rider problems might have eliminated the incentive for such investment. To conclude that du Pont had too much market power would seem to require a balancing of costs and benefits, à la Williamson (1968a).

Standard Oil: U.S. v. Standard Oil of New Jersey et al., 173 Fed. 177 (1909), 221 U.S. 1 (1911)

One of the best known and most influential studies of antitrust enforcement is John S. McGee's (1958) study of Standard Oil. Before McGee wrote, it was an article of faith that Standard Oil achieved its monopoly position through predation: ''According to most accounts, the Standard Oil Co. of New Jersey established an oil refining monopoly in the United States, in large part through the systematic use of predatory price discrimination'' (p. 138). McGee's conclusion is that ''[t]he main trouble with this 'history' is that it is logically deficient, and I can find little or no evidence to support it''

(p. 138). The logical deficiency is that, in general, purchase of a competitor is more profitable than predation. The evidence is based on McGee's reading of the voluminous record in the 1911 case.

McGee reached several specific conclusions. With respect to refining, "I cannot find a single instance in which Standard used predatory price cutting to force a rival refiner to sell out, to reduce asset values for purchase, or to drive a competitor out of business" (p. 157). In marketing, "If Standard's objective was to monopolize marketing—and that would have been irrational to begin with—they failed" (p. 166). And, overall,

> Judging from the Record, Standard Oil did not use predatory price discrimination to drive out competing refiners, nor did its pricing practice have that effect. Whereas there may be a very few cases in which retail kerosene peddlers or dealers went out of business after or during price cutting, there is no real proof that Standard's pricing policies were responsible. I am convinced that Standard did not systematically, if ever, use local price cutting in retailing, or anywhere else, to reduce competition. To do so would have been foolish; and, whatever else has been said about them, the old Standard organization was seldom criticized for making less money when it could readily have made more. (P. 168)

McGee is careful to point out that his conclusion is limited: "It should be quite clear that this is not a verdict of acquittal for the Standard Oil Company; the issue of monopoly remains. . . . The issue of whether the monopoly should have been dissolved is quite separate" (pp. 168–69). McGee does not address this issue. Nonetheless, since he finds that the behavior that he did study was not anticompetitive, I view this as an unjustified case that the government won.

Mariger (1978) extends McGee's results. Mariger allows for some possible effects of predation ignored by McGee. First, predation might be used against one firm as an example to others. Second, Standard might have been unwilling to pay high prices to purchase competitors because this might have induced other firms to blackmail Standard. Finally, Mariger considers the transactions costs involved in negotiating a merger (pp. 344–345). In order to test his hypotheses, Mariger provides empirical evidence on the dominant-firm hypothesis as an alternative to predation.[6] He concludes that "insofar as the dominant-firm model is shown to be a viable alternative to the predatory-pricing hypothesis, our results cast some doubt on the traditional interpretation of Standard Oil's pricing behavior" (p. 361). Thus, Mariger's conclusion is consistent with that of McGee.

Neither Mariger nor McGee address the monopoly issue related to *Standard*

---

6. Because data for a clear empirical test are lacking, Mariger uses a simulation method to determine if the behavior of Standard Oil is consistent with the dominant-firm model.

Oil. The final 1911 antitrust decree split Standard into several companies. Thus, to evaluate the effect of antitrust on the oil industry it is necessary to examine monopolization more explicitly. The closest analysis in the sample is by Burns (1977). Burns uses event-study methodology and examines the effect on stock prices of various events associated with the Standard Oil dissolution. He finds that when the antitrust case was first filed, there was a large reduction in Standard Oil's stock value. However, when the terms of the dissolution were announced, the portfolio of successor companies recovered the entire loss. Thus the dissolution had no net effect on shareholder wealth, and consequently no expected effect on prices or quantities. Burns (1977, 718–19) indicates that "if one accepts the prevailing view that the three defendants [American Tobacco, American Snuff, Standard Oil] were empirical examples of textbook monopolies, the results also imply that there was very little actual or anticipated competition between the [successor] firms . . . and no visible erosion of monopolistic rents." Thus, by this test, *Standard Oil* was a justified case that the government won but which had no effect. (As Burns indicates, this same conclusion applies to his analysis of *American Tobacco,* discussed below.)

Joseph Pratt (1980) analyzes the role of state (particularly Texas) antitrust law on the development of the oil industry. According to Pratt, most historians and many other students of the oil industry have stressed "the primacy of economic forces [as opposed to antitrust] in defining the structure of the modern American petroleum industry" (p. 816). Pratt believes that this view is erroneous and is based on neglect of state antitrust law. The Texas oil field, Spindletop, was crucial: "The discovery of oil at Spindletop in 1901 probably had a greater impact on the petroleum industry's market structure than did the development of any other American oil field in the twentieth century" (p. 817).

The reason was Texas's antitrust law:

> Under the antitrust law in effect in Texas at the time of the Spindletop discovery, Standard could not operate legally in that state. Passed in 1889, one year before the Congress of the United States passed the Sherman Antitrust Act, this strict law prohibited combinations in restraint of trade and blocked one company from owning stock in another. Its passage had been pressed by farmers and ranchers who sought to regulate the companies that controlled the price of cotton bagging, beef, and other similar products, but it applied equally to the oil industry. The general corporation laws of the state reinforced this strong antitrust law by limiting each business chartered in the state to one particular corporate purpose. (P. 819)

The laws were imperfectly enforced, in that Standard did play a major part in the development of Spindletop: "Despite strict antitrust laws and strong political rhetoric, Standard was allowed to operate in all phases of the industry'' (p. 822). Nonetheless, the law had sufficient bite so that the structure of the industry was greatly modified:

> Had Shell agreed to Standard's offer, it is highly unlikely that it would later have merged with the Royal Dutch Company. Also, it would not have grown into a major vertically integrated company capable of competing with Standard. Similarly, the acquisition of Gulf Oil by Standard in 1902 could well have forestalled the emergence of any strong Gulf coast competitors to Standard. Finally, the merger of Gulf Oil and Texaco would have hastened the rise of such competition while limiting it to one, not two, new companies. Each of the above alternatives was considered; each was made impossible by the political environment. (P. 831)

Standard's involvement in the Texas fields had a curious impact, in part because the antitrust authorities could not fully enforce the law:

> Because they lacked sufficient authority, information, or popular support to root out all violations of the law, however, these officials only partially banished Standard, leaving several other vertically integrated companies untouched. So, as much by accident as by design, Texas officials allowed Standard to encourage the growth of its emerging competition but prevented it from absorbing these new companies. (P. 827)

Finally, Pratt concludes that antitrust was responsible for the transition of oil from monopoly to oligopoly:

> Working within public institutions originally designed to deal with a much simpler political economy, officials in both Austin and Washington groped toward ill-defined—if forcefully proclaimed—regulatory goals. Their strained interaction with the young and growing Gulf coast oil companies shaped the transition from monopoly to oligopoly in oil while foreshadowing many of the difficulties that continue to accompany a broader transition at the heart of the subsequent evolution of the petroleum industry, the transition from monopoly control over oil policy by private corporations to shared control between private and public institutions. (P. 837)

Thus, Pratt must be viewed as judging that this outcome was justified: anticompetitive behavior was stopped by antitrust law, albeit state rather than federal law.

Utah Pie: Utah Pie Co. v. Continental Baking Co. et al., 386 U.S. 685 (1967)

Bowman (1967) criticizes this Robinson-Patman case. Utah Pie entered the Salt Lake City frozen pie market in 1957 and built a plant in 1958. It obtained two-thirds of the market in 1958. Its competitors, Pet Milk, Carnation Milk and Continental Baking, responded by lowering their prices. Utah Pie's share then fell to 45 percent in 1960–61, but the company prospered and remained profitable.

Utah Pie sued under the Robinson-Patman Act, which prohibits many forms of price discrimination. It argued that its competitors' prices were lower in Salt Lake City than in some other markets. The jury found for Utah Pie; the Appeals Court reversed; and the Supreme Court again found for Utah Pie. It is this last decision that is criticized unequivocally by Bowman. "The Supreme Court shows a growing determination in its antitrust decisions to convert laws designed to promote competition into laws which regulate or hamper the competitive process" (p. 70). Thus, this is a bad outcome: plaintiffs won a case penalizing procompetitive behavior, lower prices.

Pennington v. United Mine Workers et al., 381 U.S. 657 (1965)

In this factually complex matter, the Supreme Court found that "it is illegal for unions to conspire with any group of employers to limit competition by using wage rates as a barrier to entry" (Williamson 1968b, 89). On this basis, the Supreme Court remanded the issue to the lower court, which found that the behavior had not been anticompetitive. Most of Williamson's analysis sought to determine if the claims of Pennington were theoretically plausible. He found that they were: "wage premiums *can* be used as a barrier to entry . . ." (p. 113). But Williamson was unable to determine whether the net effect of the union agreement under challenge was desirable or not.

Cement

The cement industry was the subject of vigorous antitrust activity beginning about 1962. Through mergers, many cement companies vertically integrated downstream into concrete production and sales. The FTC challenged many of these mergers, alleging that they caused market foreclosure. That is, by integrating downstream, cement producers denied other competitors the possibility of selling to the acquired concrete firm. Foreclosure may have been "offensive" (aimed at gaining additional concrete customers) or "defensive" (aimed at maintaining business with existing customers). As viewed by the FTC, the integration was for the purpose of foreclosure, and there were no offsetting economies.

Allen (1971) was among the first economists to study this series of cases, concluding, "Since no rational firm which knows what it is doing will practice foreclosure *for the sake of foreclosure alone,* concern with foreclosure represents a waste of the scarce enforcement resources" (p. 258). He also finds, consistent with this theoretical position, that "the limited evidence that exists suggests that foreclosure has not been a profitable strategy" (p. 270). Allen finds no evidence for economies of integration, and therefore concludes that much of the vertical integration that did occur (and which was apparently aimed at foreclosure) was due to errors by managers of cement companies who "may or may not know that captive marketing does not pay without trying" (p. 272). Allen concludes (p. 274) that the antitrust policy may have been desirable, but it is by no means a ringing endorsement. "Perhaps a public policy against such vertical mergers protects *both competitors and competition* from firms' mistakes. But it does so by protecting firms from their own mistakes. Whether this is a worthwhile aim of public policy is at least debatable." In sum, we must view this as a bad outcome: behavior that is not anticompetitive is penalized by the antitrust authorities.

Allen's conclusions were debated in a 1972 comment by James Meehan, an FTC economist. While I believe that Allen (1972) successfully refuted Meehan's criticism, nonetheless, the strongest statement Meehan was able to make was that "therefore, we must conclude that public policy with respect to vertical foreclosure was not necessarily 'misplaced' " (p. 465). Meehan does not attempt to demonstrate any inefficiency from the vertical mergers in the cement-concrete industry, or any efficiency gains from antitrust activity against such mergers. His entire analysis is aimed at challenging Allen's arguments regarding foreclosure. Thus, even if there were efficiency gains from the antitrust policy, Meehan would not have been able to find them. His conclusion is neutral with respect to the issue.

A spatial model of pricing and integration in the cement industry was developed by McBride (1983). In McBride's model cement firms have some monopoly power in their local markets because of high transportation costs. However, there are regions of overlap in areas that could be served by more than one firm. During periods of slack demand, the existence of high fixed costs leads to incentives for increasing output for each firm. In this model, there are first-mover advantages for the firm that first integrates vertically. Ultimately, such integration leads to lower concrete prices, but in the short run individual firms can gain by integration. This model has the advantage of providing a rational explanation for such integration, in contrast to Allen's model based on mistake. Ultimately, the model is driven by the *"implicit assumption . . .* that the integrated firm's competitors will react more slowly or less severely to sales lost by vertical integration than to sales lost by cement price cutting" (p. 1017). "[V]ertical integration is a form of nonprice competition that undermines oligopolistic coordination" (p. 1020).

In an empirical section, McBride finds support for his model. More important, he also finds that "although vertical integration in the short run may or may not undermine the rigid cement price, the cumulative effect of vertical integration is to bring the cement price level down. Each additional vertical merger in a region contributed to a $0.10 to $0.26 per barrel drop in realized cement price" (p. 1021). McBride's conclusions with respect to the net results of the FTC action are highly pessimistic. "One cannot, therefore, dismiss the cynical view that the FTC's policy toward vertical integration may provide this very precommitment [to refrain from vertical integration], and thus benefit first and foremost the industry itself. . . . The effect of the FTC actions on consumers appears, therefore, to have been negative" (p. 1021). Moreover, McBride argues that the FTC did not even succeed in achieving its goal. "The FTC stopped vertical integration, but it did not stop vertical control" (p. 1021). Nonetheless, McBride finds that the outcome was bad: procompetitive behavior was stopped by the FTC.

A subsequent comment by Johnson and Parkman (1987) questions the econometric specification of McBride's model; McBride (1987) replies to these questions. This interchange is irrelevant to the policy issues concerned here. As Johnson and Parkman conclude, "What is absent, however, is sufficient evidence that would demonstrate that the vertical mergers in the cement industry have or would create a significant probability of a harmful effect. Apparently, the FTC now concurs as the agency recently rescinded its enforcement policy regarding vertical mergers between cement and ready-mix concrete firms" (p. 753).

In sum, of the articles surveyed, only Meehan's comment argues at all in favor of the FTC's action, and Meehan's argument attempts to show only that one criticism of the FTC was unjustified: he does not claim to show that the policy was justified. As McBride (1983, 1021) points out, the FTC's action was quite costly, and even the FTC has apparently concluded that the policy was misguided. The cement cases are in general viewed as unjustified cases that the government won.

Alcoa: U.S. v. Aluminum Co. of America et al., 148 F. 2d 416 (1945)

In a case begun in 1937 and ultimately decided in 1945, Alcoa was found guilty of monopolization. (Because the Supreme Court could not find a disinterested quorum, the case was decided by a three-judge panel, with Circuit Judge Learned Hand writing the decision.) The ultimate remedy was an order forbidding Alcoa from bidding on aluminum plants built by the government for World War II; these plants were bought instead by Reynolds and Kaiser. An issue in the monopolization case was the proper treatment of reprocessed metal, as opposed to virgin ingot alone. If reprocessed metal were included in the market, Alcoa's share was about 64 percent; if not, it was 90 percent. The court explicitly held that this latter number was sufficient to find monopolization but the former was not. The court ruled that, since Alcoa only controlled the scrap market indirectly, there was monopolization. The literature cited in the sample deals with this issue.

From empirical estimates Gaskins (1974, 270) concludes, "the results of this model support Judge Hand's contention that monopoly control of primary production is nearly equivalent to a pure monopoly in its welfare implication." Fisher (1974), while accepting Gaskins's model (itself based in part on prior empirical work by Fisher) and accepting the conclusion in *Alcoa,* points out that in general it is correct to include reprocessed material in the market. *Alcoa* was nonetheless correctly decided, according to Fisher, because the rate of growth of demand was such that Alcoa's long-run equilibrium market share was between 75 and 78 percent, and thus the use of the actual share of 90 percent was acceptable: "The analytic error of excluding secondary aluminum from the market was of small consequence because the long-run market share (and indeed the short-run share) of such aluminum happened to be small" (p. 359).

Swan (1980, 76) extends the Gaskins model, but does not change the relevant results. "Hand's judgment appears sound." Similarly, Martin (1982, 418) finds that "Judge Hand's decision is correct." Suslow (1986, 400) also concludes that "Alcoa had substantial market power." Thus, while none of these authors evaluates the case-in-chief against Alcoa, all agree that Alcoa did have market power and so that part of the decision was correct.

Brown Shoe: Federal Trade Commission v. Brown Shoe, 384 U.S. 316 (1966)

Peterman (1975b) undertook an unusually detailed study of the FTC's investigation of the Brown Shoe Company's franchising procedures.[7] Under the franchise plan, retailers who "concentrated" their purchases on Brown's shoes received certain minor benefits from Brown (e.g., record keeping and accounting forms and assistance, insurance at perhaps slightly reduced rates, and assistance from Brown's representatives). The agreements did not require exclusive dealing and could be ended by either party at will. But the FTC alleged that the plans foreclosed part of the market to other shoe manufacturers. (Brown produced about 5 percent of shoe output in a very unconcentrated industry, and the franchise dealers represented less than 20 percent of Brown's sales.) Peterman is skeptical of the merits of the case. "This, it seems to me, is 'foreclosure' the FTC should encourage rather than condemn, since it reduces the total cost of shoe production and distribution" (p. 369).

The FTC's original order against Brown Shoe was reversed on appeal, but the Supreme Court upheld the FTC's original finding. However, the remedy was essentially meaningless. Brown was ordered to inform its franchise customers that they could buy shoes elsewhere, but obviously they already had this right and already knew that they had it. Thus, Peterman's final conclu-

---

7. Subsequent to the publication of his article, Peterman joined the staff of the Bureau of Economics at the FTC, and eventually became Bureau Director, the highest position reserved for an economist at the agency.

sion: "But whatever one's point of view it is clear that nothing was accomplished by bringing this case" (p. 393). Nonetheless, since the FTC won (at least nominally) an unjustified case, this must be viewed as a bad outcome.

In an appendix to his study, Peterman discusses a sister case, that against Interco. The consent agreement signed by Interco and then modified after the Supreme Court's decision in *Brown Shoe* was similar in many respects to the one signed by Brown. However, Interco had a division that made loans to new entrants into shoe retailing. The FTC required modification of the terms of these loans; the loan division eventually closed, and Interco concentrated on opening its own stores. Peterman finds that "To the extent that it [the FTC's case against Interco] did [reduce foreclosure], the reduction would be due to the FTC's success in raising Interco's costs of distribution" (p. 402). Again, a bad outcome.

U.S. Steel: U.S. v. United States Steel Co. et al., 223 Fed. 55 (1915), 251 U.S. 417 (1920)

Parsons and Ray (1975) analyzed the 1901 formation (through mergers and other contracts) of U.S. Steel and the 1920 Supreme Court decision not to dissolve the firm. They show that U.S. Steel was able to raise prices and maintain them at supracompetitive levels. The major source of market power was control over iron ore. The effect of the consolidations was to double the value of the firms involved in the mergers, from $700 million to $1,400 million, with J.P. Morgan receiving over $100 million in underwriting fees. U.S. Steel was successful in organizing a cartel (run through the famous Gary dinners) and in continuing to consolidate the small firms that entered the market to benefit from high prices.

Parsons and Ray ask why the Supreme Court did not dissolve the consolidation: "one might well speculate that this was the most socially damaging of all mergers in U.S. history. The failure of the Sherman Act to stop this activity is clearly disquieting" (p. 215). They are unable fully to resolve this issue, but conclude that the court erred by looking for explicit victims of the consolidation. "The search for victims is, in fact, the reason courts have tended to protect competitors and not competition: the 'victims' of competition are vocal and not hard to find" (p. 217). On the other hand, "the 'victims' of the U.S. Steel organization were largely ignorant of the damage they suffered" (p. 218). The case was desirable, but the outcome was incorrect.

The Diesel-Electric Locomotive Case: U.S. v. General Motors, Civil Action No. 63-C-1963, N.D. Illinois

In 1930, General Motors entered the diesel-electric locomotive industry by acquiring the Electro-Motive and Winton Engine companies. Over the next thirty years, GM revolutionized the locomotive business by developing diesel engines for many purposes and greatly improving engine technology. As a result, Marx (1975, 785) shows, from 1936 to 1971 GM had market shares ranging over 50 percent in all but one year and over 80 percent in seven years. In 1961, the Justice Department indicted GM for monopolization in this industry. The civil and criminal cases were dismissed in the late 1960s for lack of evidence. Marx discusses the particular allegations (reciprocity, predation, scale economies and other alleged violations) and argues that this case "demonstrates the need for additional economic input into antitrust proceedings, at both the preliminary and conclusionary stages" (p. 777). To Marx, this was an unjustified case that the government lost.

Sylvania: Continental T.V., Inc., v. GTE Sylvania, Inc., 97 S.Ct. 2549 (1977)

In its *Schwinn* opinion ten years earlier, the Supreme Court had held that nonprice vertical restrictions by manufacturers in sales contracts (such as exclusive territories) were per se illegal. *Sylvania* reversed *Schwinn* and found that such restraints were subject to a rule-of-reason analysis. Posner (1977) analyzes the *Sylvania* decision from a unique point of view. "I briefed and argued the *Schwinn* decision for the government. Subsequently, my views on the proper treatment of restrictions on distribution under the antitrust laws took a 180 degree turn . . ." (p. 2). The purpose of his article was not to defend *Sylvania*: "Obviously I think the decision is good economics . . . and good antitrust law as well" (p. 5). Rather, he examines the implications of this decision for future law.

Most interesting from our perspective is Posner's use of the *Sylvania* decision to attack the entire corpus of antitrust law regarding vertical restrictions. He finds that virtually this entire body of law and the cases implementing it are incorrect. Among the antitrust doctrines potentially affected are resale price maintenance (maximum and minimum); nonprice restraints; franchise restrictions; territorial restrictions; and "tie-ins (not only in franchising), reciprocal buying, exclusive dealing, vertical mergers involving large market shares, boycotts—practices and transactions heretofore regarded as per se illegal or nearly so . . ." (p. 13).

In sum, this article argues that *Sylvania* was a good decision because it reversed an unjustified decision (*Schwinn*) and that the logic of *Sylvania* could be used to reverse many more bad decisions. While the outcome in *Sylvania* was efficient, the article is a rather pessimistic analysis of antitrust law dealing with vertical restrictions generally.

Tobacco: U.S. v. American Tobacco Co., 221 U.S. 106 (1911)

Burns has written several papers (Burns 1977, 1982, 1983, 1986, 1988) analyzing the dissolution of the tobacco trust in 1911, when American Tobacco and American Snuff were divided into fourteen successor companies. In the first article (1977), as indicated in connection with the section on *Standard Oil,* he finds no net effect from the case: the complaint caused a fall in the value of the firm, but this was recovered when the terms of the dissolution order were announced. Burns (1983) finds similar results with respect to bondholders and holders of preferred stock after the *American Tobacco* and *American Snuff* dissolution orders. Burns (1986) does not directly evaluate the antitrust decree. However, he does find that between 1891 and 1906 American Tobacco benefited from successful predation which lowered "acquisition costs directly as well as indirectly through reputation effects on rivals that are subsequently bought out peacefully" (p. 290). Burns (1982, 1989) also finds additional evidence of predatory price cutting. Thus, Burns's analysis indicates that this was a justified case that the government won, but whose remedy meant that the case had no effect.

Cereal: FTC v. Kellogg et al., Docket No. 8863

In the late 1970s, the FTC attempted to order deconcentration in the ready-to-eat (RTE) cereals market. Two witnesses for the FTC, Schmalensee (1978) and Scherer (1979), wrote about the case.[8] Schmalensee believes that the case and the proposed remedy had merit. He analyses a market in which incumbent firms are able to prevent entry through brand proliferation. The results of his theoretical analysis are ambiguous: "In short, we cannot prove rigorously that *all* increases in price competition coupled with free entry would serve to increase W [welfare, the sum of consumers' surplus and producers' excess profits]; we have only shown that *some* range of increase will do this" (p. 320). Also, "the arguments above imply that the basic problem with seller conduct in the market is *not* that too many brands are introduced. It is rather that too little price competition occurs" (p. 320).

The remedy proposed by the FTC was extreme. The three defendants (Kellogg, General Mills, and General Foods) would be required to spin off several brands and trademarks, so that five new firms would be created. There would also be requirements for licensing of existing trademarks and of new brands after five years. Schmalensee believes this remedy useful because it would have caused increased price competition, which is consistent with his analysis of the case. He also believes the remedy beneficial because it would have reduced the "incentive to engage in advertising and brand introduction" (p. 322). It is surprising that Schmalensee views this as a benefit since, as indicated above, his model did not lead to the prediction that too many brands had been introduced.

Scherer's article is not directly related to the antitrust litigation, although much of the data were derived from that litigation. Scherer asks if the brand

---

8. Both articles were written while the case was pending. As discussed in Scherer and Ross (1990, 466), the case was ultimately dismissed by the FTC.

proliferation was on net beneficial or harmful to consumers. His answer is tentative. "In drawing conclusions at the end of such an analysis, one recognizes it is not only the cereal industry's products that can be flaky" (p. 132). However, "it appears probable that product proliferation has, at least at the margin, cost more than it was worth" (p. 133). But this conclusion is not related to the FTC's proposed remedy. Indeed, had the FTC been successful, the structure of the industry would have moved towards monopolistic competition, and there is more product differentiation under this market structure than under monopoly (p. 118). Thus, it is at least arguable that, had the FTC succeeded, there would have been even more brand proliferation and, under Scherer's analysis, more lost surplus.

The government ultimately failed to win this case that the authors believe was justified.

Du Pont: In the matter of E.I. du Pont de Nemours & Co., 96 FTC 683 (1980)

Shepherd served as an expert witness for the FTC in its case against du Pont for monopolization of the titanium dioxide market. His expert testimony was published in the *Antitrust Law and Economics Review* (1979). Shepherd argued that du Pont had a conscious four-part strategy aimed at "capturing all capacity expansion in the industry" (p. 77). Shepherd believed that du Pont's ultimate purpose was to raise prices once it had captured a dominant share of the industry. Ultimately, an administrative law judge dismissed the case. Thus, from Shepherd's perspective, this must be viewed as a justified case with an unfortunate outcome; anticompetitive behavior was not punished by the antitrust authorities.

ReaLemon: In the matter of Borden, Inc., 92 FTC 669 (1978); Borden, Inc., v. FTC, No. 79-3028 CA 6 (1982)

ReaLemon®, Borden's brand of reconstituted lemon juice, accounted for about 90 percent of the reconstituted lemon juice market in the 1960s (Schmalensee 1979, 998). In response to entry by Golden Crown, ReaLemon cut its price in certain markets. Golden Crown complained, and the FTC brought a case against ReaLemon. The initial decision by the administrative law judge in 1976 found that reconstituted lemon juice was a separate product market, so that it was not necessary to include fresh lemons as well; that Borden's pricing policy was illegal (and hence presumably predatory); and that appropriate remedies were an order against selling at "unreasonably" low prices and a requirement that Borden license its trademark for ten years, at license fees aimed only at recovering quality control costs. The full Commission in its opinion in 1977 upheld all of these findings except the requirement for compulsory licensing. The Court of Appeals in 1982 upheld the order of the full Commission.

The key point in Schmalensee's analysis is that the Initial Decision and the Opinion were based on inadequate economic analysis.[9] He finds that "all of these observations [regarding the definition of the market] provide only a starting point from which the analysis of ReaLemon's possible long-run monopoly power can begin" (p. 1016). In connection with predation, Schmalensee concludes, "But without conclusive evidence of intent to do much more than recoup losses and check a rival's expansion, and with no evidence that these goals had been achieved, dismissal of charges seems warranted" (p. 1031). With respect to trademark licensing, Schmalensee concludes that "because a trademark provides a good deal of information quickly to one who has experience with it, one can argue that the trademark licensing relief ordered in the Initial Decision, with the associated quality control provisions, was an efficient way to transmit information to consumers" (pp. 1042–43). Of course, since Schmalensee believes that Borden should not have been found guilty of predation, in his framework no relief would have been granted.

Schmalensee claims also that there is insufficient use of economic analysis in antitrust in general. "If antitrust law is to become a more consistent force for economic efficiency, the selection and analysis of appropriate economic models must be more frequently incorporated into antitrust proceedings" (p. 1045). However, the complex nature of the analysis performed by Schmalensee in this matter indicates that the use of economics will not itself guarantee correct conclusions. (For example, Schmalensee devotes fifteen pages to an inconclusive discussion of economic models of predation.) Nonetheless, with respect to this case, we must conclude that Schmalensee believes that there should have been no finding of liability and hence no remedy because the burden of showing predation had not been met.

McCarthy (1979) discusses compulsory licensing of the trademark.[10] McCarthy believes that the FTC is "very wrong and misinformed as to the competitive impact of trademark ownership per se and as to compulsory trademark licensing as an antitrust remedy" (p. 152). McCarthy goes on to discuss the benefits to consumers of reduced search costs from well-known trademarks.[11]

One aspect of the compulsory licensing scheme was the protection of quality. The allowed license fee would have been set equal to the cost of

9. Schmalensee wrote before the appellate decision, but presumably would also have made the same point about this decision.

10. McCarthy was an attorney and a consultant to the FTC.

11. In the second part of the article, McCarthy argues that the FTC was correct to seek cancellation of the "Formica" trademark and that it is useful for the agency to continue this policy. However, this is not an antitrust issue.

such quality control. Schmalensee does not address this issue, except to say that the Initial Decision "had sensible quality control provisions" (p. 1043). McCarthy does not address this issue either.

The quality-assuring aspects of trademarks are the subject of an article by Krouse (1984). Krouse indicates that "the taste quality of process[ed] lemon juice was shown to be quite sensitive to small variations in the level of the preservative ingredient and thus required strong assurance of quality control" and that "a poor quality processed juice mixed with other ingredients results in a low quality combination" (p. 499). As a result, Krouse indicates that consumers would "be willing to pay a high price premium relative to the processed lemon juice price for quality assurance" (p. 499). Moreover, Krouse indicates that the FTC's licensing provisions would not have led to adequate quality control: "product quality would have uniformly deteriorated as each seller attempted to lower its cost and increase its margin relative to the average market price . . ." (p. 501). In a footnote, Krouse describes the quality-control provisions of the Initial Order, concluding that "these factors pose a number of questions not only about ReaLemon's incentives to assure quality, but its actual ability to do so" (p. 501 note 12).

Rosenbaum (1987) analyzes the pricing issue. He argues that predatory pricing is possible even if price is above average variable cost if the existing firm has an information advantage relative to the potential entrant. (This argument was also considered by Schmalensee.) Rosenbaum further argues that plausible values for unknown parameters in the lemon juice market indicate that this may have been the case here, but that the record is insufficient to be sure. "The lack of information on these parameters in the Borden record suggests that the Courts may want to expand their information search in predation cases" (p. 256). Thus, the strongest conclusion which Rosenbaum can reach is that there may have been effective predation in this matter. He also admits that his proposal is peculiar: "It may seem counter to antitrust intent to require Borden to price, in the short run at least, above average variable cost" (p. 256).

These articles in general view *ReaLemon* as an unjustified case that the government won.

Bread

Block et al. (1981) presented a theoretical model of the deterrent effect of antitrust enforcement on horizontal price fixing. Their theoretical model is based on the assumption that the markup in a cartel depends on the probability of detection. They test this model using the bread industry from 1965–1976, a period in which the Department of Justice brought seventeen price-fixing cases. Block et al. find that the effect of these prosecutions was significant: firms in a region in which there was a case filed in a given year had lower increases in markups than firms in other regions. Moreover, in years when the DOJ's Antitrust Division had a larger budget, markups were also lower. Interestingly, this effect was apparently due to the follow-on class actions that often succeed government price-fixing cases. In the period 1970–1972, such class actions became common following prosecutions in the bread industry. The penalties assessed in the private follow-on cases were approximately ten times the penalties in the initial case. The authors conclude that "deterrence has been a product of both public and private enforcement efforts" (p. 443). Thus, this article shows that in one industry simple prosecution of price-fixing agreements has had a positive effect in reducing markups, both for the firms prosecuted and for others in the same region. The result of these cases was desirable.

Addyston Pipe: U.S. v. Addyston Pipe and Steel Co. et al., 171 U.S. 614 (1899)

Bittlingmayer (1982) indicates that this important price-fixing case was "one of three or four turn-of-the-century cases that established how the Sherman Act was to be applied to cartel agreements" (p. 201). He concludes that the cost structure in the industry was such that "firms could not behave competitively even if they wanted to" (p. 202). There is no long-run competitive equilibrium in an industry with continuously declining average cost curves. In game theoretic terms, the "core" is empty. Moreover, he points out that soon after the case the defendant firms merged, so that even if one did believe that the price-fixing case provided a useful remedy, it would have been short-lived. Thus, this is either a bad outcome (since behavior that was not anticompetitive was penalized) or a neutral outcome, since the merger negated any of the decision's harmful effects.

Chicago Board of Trade: Chicago Board of Trade v. United States, 246 U.S. 231 (1918)

This complex case involved the "call rule," which fixed prices for grain after the Board's daily close. In his discussion of the purpose of the rule, Zerbe (1983) indicates that

> Before 1913, market efficiency, antimonopoly aspects, and aid to commission men in relation to terminal elevator operators appear to have provided the dominant motives. After 1913, however, cartelization of commission rates appears to have provided the primary goal. (P. 29)

Although the case was decided in 1918, "both sides insisted on going forward on the basis of the 1906 rule" (p. 48). Moreover, the case was argued on the basis of fixing of grain prices. Zerbe argues that in fact the issue after 1913 was the fixing of commission rates. Thus, on its own terms, the case was bungled because the truly anticompetitive practices were ignored. Indeed, the case was used later as a justification for carving out an antitrust exemption for commission rates: ''Thus a bungled cartel case involving fixed commissions is invoked to justify antitrust exemptions for just such commissions'' (p. 46). Thus, according to Zerbe, this is a case in which a failure to find antitrust liability for an anticompetitive practice actually served to entrench that practice, and which was therefore positively harmful.

Unlike most of the authors discussed in this essay, Zerbe discusses the political motives for the case, and indicates why it might have been ''bungled'':

> The case was strongly urged by the U.S. Attorney in Chicago, who had been lobbied by some, unfortunately unidentified, members of the Chicago Board of Trade. It was rejected several times by the Attorney General and the Assistant Attorney General for the Antitrust Division because there was no evidence of harm resulting from the restraint and the need for it in terms of making the exchange work seemed convincing. In 1913, the lame-duck attorney general authorized the suit partly because of a recent corner on wheat in Chicago that upset the country. The Democrats who took over were not willing to reconsider the case. (P. 48)

Zerbe indicates that this lack of enthusiasm for the case overall explains why the government's ''heart did not seem in the case it did present.'' It also indicates that the driving force behind the case was not its merits.

AT&T: U.S. v. AT&T Co., 552 F. Supp. 131 (D.D.C. 1982)

This was an unusual case. AT&T was and is intensely regulated by the FCC and also by local regulators. Thus, the Department of Justice's antitrust case, filed in 1974 and settled by a consent decree in 1982, was implicitly an allegation that the regulators were incompetent. A key issue was the disproportionality between local and long distance rates. The regulatory authorities forced AT&T to subsidize local subscribers at the expense of long distance callers. This created a possibility for profitable entry into the long distance market (''cream skimming''). Many of the antitrust allegations dealt with alleged predation by AT&T in an effort to protect these markets from new entrants. However, predation was oddly defined. The government did not allege that AT&T priced below costs, however measured. Rather, it alleged that AT&T priced *''without regard to costs''* and that this was equivalent to predation (MacAvoy and Robinson 1983, p. 27). AT&T did not vigorously contest the government's claim. If it had, MacAvoy and Robinson believe that it might have prevailed on the liability issue, and that even if it had lost, divestiture would have been unlikely (p. 31).

The antitrust settlement severed long lines from local service. MacAvoy and Robinson believe that this outcome was in AT&T's interest and that the firm would not have been allowed by local and federal regulators to unilaterally separate these lines of business. They believe that AT&T will maintain its monopoly position in long distance service, and that local prices will increase. This is because the cessation of cross subsidization of local by long distance callers will lead to local rate increases while allowing AT&T to undercut the prices of long distance competitors. In conclusion, "clearly AT&T has won by losing. . . . As for the public, we seem to have lost by winning" (p. 42). Thus, they view this as an unsuccessful antitrust case.

Noll (1987) does not directly address the antitrust decision. He writes mainly about present and possible future regulation of telecommunications. However, he believes that less regulation and more reliance on competition are desirable. Since this was a major thrust of the antitrust consent decree, Noll must view the outcome of the case as desirable.

U.S. v. IBM Corp., 69 Civ. 200, S.D.N.Y.

Pittman (1984) has examined one aspect of the IBM case, which was filed in 1969 and closed in 1982, the introduction by IBM of the 360/90 "super computer."[12] Pittman believes that the most credible allegation was that "IBM designed, created, and sold this machine as a weapon of predation against the Model 6600 'super computer' of the Control Data Corporation (CDC)" (p. 341). Pittman concludes that IBM did anticipate losing money on the 360/90 computer; that IBM attempted to develop internal analyses that would hide this loss; but that the purpose of the machine was not predatory. Rather, according to Pittman, the machine was developed and sold as a "signal" to customers that IBM was a technologically advanced company. The argument is that "general purpose buyers" would "emulate the purchasing decisions of better-informed purchasers of scientific computers" (p. 363).

Pittman's last paragraph is worth quoting in full because it indicates one hidden cost of antitrust. Firms might be afraid to follow procompetitive strategies that entail losing money on particular sales because of a fear of antitrust liability.

> As a postscript, we may ask why, if the signaling hypothesis presented here is correct, IBM did not simply present the explanation itself, rather than engaging in the extensive and expensive contortions it used in seeking to deny the unprofitability of the 360/90

---

12. Pittman was an economist in the Economic Policy Office, Antitrust Division, U.S. Department of Justice. "His involvement in the IBM case was limited to participation in the internal Justice Department review process which led to the termination of the suit" (p. 341).

system. The answer may lie in the arguably hostile nature of the era as concerned large corporations. This was the period, after all, of the proposal by the Neal Commission of a reorganization-oriented "Concentrated Industries Act" (1968), of Senator Hart's "Industrial Reorganization Act" (1972 and 1973) and "no-fault" monopolization bill (1976), and of a narrow Senate defeat for a bill proposing "vertical dismemberment" of the largest U.S. oil companies. IBM counsel may have believed that an admission of truth to the charge that IBM introduced the System 360/90 knowing that it would lose money would be tantamount to an admission of guilt to the charge of predation. (P. 364)

Pittman thus finds that "the government had the facts right but misunderstood the motivation and likely effect of the conduct" (personal communication); he agrees that the case should be classified as an unjustified case. Levy and Welzer (1985) present a stronger indictment. According to Levy and Welzer, IBM initially anticipated an unfavorable decision, perhaps leading to divestiture. As a result, IBM rationally believed that its future market share would be reduced. In anticipation, it raised prices in order to capitalize on its current market power:

By threatening the firm's right to achieve a future market share, an impending anti-monopolization suit reduces the firm's potential for future profits. The suit thereby encourages the firm to take short-run profits by raising its price towards the monopoly level. (P. 28)

Levy and Welzer show that prices were higher for IBM machines when it looked like the company would lose the suit and lower when it looked like IBM might win. This would be viewed as a bad outcome: the antitrust action penalized procompetitive behavior. Petty (1986) disputes the Levy-Welzer analysis. However, although Petty disagrees with the conclusion that the litigation caused harm, he provides no argument that it provided any benefits. His analysis is therefore neutral.

Xerox: In the matter of Xerox Corp., 86 FTC 364 (1975)

In 1975, the FTC signed a consent decree with Xerox requiring licensing of all patents related to photocopying. Bresnahan (1985) has studied the copier market after this decree. Although he does not discuss the rationale for the FTC's action or the extent of anticompetitive behavior in the industry, it appears that he believes the case was justified. At any rate, he concludes that the effects were beneficial. Prices fell and there was substantial innovation in the industry. He also indicates that there is evidence that before the compulsory patent licensing, Xerox was "fat." Bresnahan indicates that because of substantial price discrimination during the "monopoly phase," Xerox had price-average cost margins of around 10 percent. Afterwards, prices fell by 30 percent, discrimination ended, and yet firms in the industry were profitable. "Xerox's accounting average cost must have overstated true marginal cost by at least 20 percent" (p. 18). Bresnahan views this as a successful and useful antitrust case.

Electrical Equipment Manufacturers

In the 1950s, more than thirty electrical equipment manufacturers conspired to fix prices for equipment sold to utilities. The conspiracies ended in about 1959, when the Department of Justice began investigating the industry. Ultimately the firms paid fines of over $1 million, and some officers served time in jail. In addition, the conspirators paid over $150 million as a result of follow-on private suits. The conspiracy affected 20 separate electrical equipment markets. Beginning in 1963, after the conspiracy ended, GE and Westinghouse adopted pricing policies for turbines that may have facilitated price coordination. Lean, Ogur, and Rogers (1985), three FTC economists, examined the impact of the conspiracy and the effectiveness of the remedy in lowering profits. They used data made available to the FTC. They examined eight of the twenty markets, concluding that

> collusion can raise rates of return. On average for eight electrical equipment markets during the 1950s, we observe significant effects on profitability of conspiratorial meetings by sellers. Further analysis suggests, however, that higher returns may have been limited to the insulator and circuit breaker markets. While conspiratorial meetings seem not to have raised turbine generator profit/sales ratios, price signaling appears to have done so. (P. 839)

Thus, this case must count as one in which antitrust policy was effective in lowering prices and stopping a profitable collusion.

Railroad Cartels: U.S. v. Trans-Missouri Freight Association et al., 166 U.S. 290 (1897) and U.S. v. Joint Traffic Association, 171 U.S. 505 (1898)

These two railroad cartel cases were the first two price-fixing decisions under the Sherman Act. Binder (1988) analyzed the effect of these cases, and particularly of *Trans-Missouri*. He shows that the decision in this case was unanticipated, so that it is acceptable to use excess stock returns to analyze the market's expectations concerning the impact of the case. Binder finds that there was a negative return to the relevant stocks, but that this return was not statistically significant. He also examines rates for shipping lard from Chicago to New York, and finds again no significant effect of the decision. He indicates that his "results are consistent with the hypothesis that the railroads responded to the rulings by replacing overt, public price fixing with private rate agreements and more concentrated markets" (p. 444). This appears to be a justified case that the government won but which had no effect.

Sealy: U.S. v. Sealy, 388 U.S. 350 (1967)

Sealy, Inc., licensed its name to several mattress manufacturers. Each was allowed to sell only in its own territory. In 1960, the Department of Justice brought an action against Sealy's geographic restraints, and in 1967 the Supreme Court found these restrictions to be illegal. Sealy replaced these prohibitions with other restrictions that had the same effect. In 1971, Ohio-Sealy brought a private action against these restrictions. In 1981, the Seventh Circuit found these restrictions also to be illegal, and there was intraband competition in many areas until 1986, when Ohio-Sealy bought out virtually all of the other Sealy companies, thus again removing intrabrand competition.

Mueller (1989) was the expert economist for Ohio-Sealy in this matter, and wrote about the case. He argues that the standard view of horizontal territorial restrictions (prevention of free riding) is incorrect and that the data in Sealy show that these restrictions reduce output and increase price. He shows that during the period when there was intrabrand competition (1981–1986), prices fell in those areas where there was competition, and output increased. We need not resolve this issue, although it appears that the increase in output and reduction in price documented by Mueller is not an equilibrium.

What is relevant is that after twenty years of litigation, both public and private, the final outcome was virtually identical to the initial position: there was no intrabrand competition among Sealy manufacturers. As Mueller indicates, the acquisition "eliminated forever intrabrand competition in Sealy brand mattresses" (p. 1321). Indeed, if production by locally owned licensees is of lower cost than production by a centrally owned firm, then the net result of the litigation would have been to increase costs. Nonetheless, no matter what cost conditions may be, Mueller views this as a justified case that the government won but which had no effect.

Discussion

The results of various analyses cited by Scherer and Ross are summarized in table 3.1, which reports for each of the forty-one authors (or co-authors) who have written about a case the author's view of the case and of the outcome.[13] Again, a "justified" case is one in which the behavior studied was seen as anticompetitive, and an "unjustified" case is one in which this is not true.

---

13. These 39 authors represent a total of 45 separate articles (including notes) cited in Scherer and Ross. Some authors wrote more than one article about a case and some articles deal with more than one case.

I report the legal outcome of the litigation (as a "win" or "loss" for the plaintiff) and also indicate those cases in which the author found no effect of the decision.

Table 3.2 is a distillation of table 3.1, so that there is one entry for each case. For most cases studied by more than one economist, authors agreed.[14] For *Standard Oil,* the case is viewed as justified since those authors evaluating the case-in-chief (Pratt; Burns) found that it was a justified case, while those who found it an unjustified case (McGee; Mariger) analyzed only the predation issue and did not discuss the overall case. Since Williamson was unable to determine the efficiency of *Pennington,* I omit it from the analysis.

There are twenty-three cases in table 3.2. Of these cases, fourteen (61 percent) are viewed as justified cases and nine as unjustified cases. Of the fourteen justified cases, the plaintiff won nine, or 64 percent. Of the nine unjustified cases, plaintiff won seven, or 78 percent. (See table 3.3.) Using a differences-in-proportions test,[15] we see that the difference in these probabilities of victory is statistically significant at the 10 percent level: plaintiffs are less likely to win a justified case. Moreover, of the nine justified cases that the plaintiff won, in four (*Standard Oil, Tobacco, the Railroad Cartels, Sealy*) the victory had no effect. Similarly, of the seven unjustified cases won by the plaintiff, two (*Brown Shoe, Addyston Pipe*) had no effect.

Table 3.4 presents essentially the same information as table 3.3, but the information is organized by authors rather than by cases. Nonetheless, approximately the same conclusions follow. This table is particularly useful in analyzing the characteristics of cases studied, since some have suggested a possibility of bias in this selection procedure.

To summarize: The view of the economists in the sample is that there are slightly more justified than unjustified cases, although in 40 percent of the cases (discussed in 44 percent of the articles) there is no anticompetitive behavior and the case is unjustified. A higher percentage of unjustified cases than of justified cases are won by plaintiff. In nine instances (discussed in fourteen articles) plaintiffs won a justified case so that anticompetitive behavior was penalized. However, in seven cases (analyzed in eleven articles) plaintiffs won an unjustified case, so that procompetitive behavior was penalized. Of those cases in which the remedy was actually judged effective (or at least not judged ineffective) there were five in which anticompetitive behavior was penalized and five in which procompetitive behavior was penalized. Based on this sample, it appears that if antitrust performs a deterrent function, it is as likely to deter efficient as inefficient behavior. Moreover, this sample is based on Scherer and Ross, which may itself impart some bias to the selection process, so that we may view the conclusion as an upper-

14. For *Cement, RealLemon,* and *IBM,* most authors viewed the case as unjustified, with one author in each case unable to reach a decision, so a rating of "unjustified" is used.
15. See Hubert M. Blalock, Jr., Social Statistics (rev. 2d ed., 1979), at 232–34.

Table 3.1 Summary of Results

Case and Author	Author Evaluation of Quality of Case	Outcome for Plaintiff
Cellophane		
Stocking and Mueller (1955)	Justified	Lost
Standard Oil		
McGee (1958)	Unjustified	Won
Mariger (1978)	Unjustified	Won
Burns (1977)	Justified	Won
		(No effect)
Pratt (1980)	Justified	Won
		(State antitrust law)
Utah Pie		
Bowman (1967)	Unjustified	Won
Pennington		
Williamson (1968b)	Uncertain	Lost
Cement		
Allen (1971)	Unjustified	Won
Meehan (1972)	Uncertain	Won
McBride (1983)	Unjustified	Won
Johnson and Parkman (1987)	Unjustified	Won
Alcoa		
Gaskins (1974)	Justified	Won
Fisher (1974)	Justified	Won
Swan (1980)	Justified	Won
Martin (1982)	Justified	Won
Suslow (1986)	Justified	Won
Brown Shoe		
Peterman (1975b)	Unjustified	Won
		(No Effect)
Interco		
Peterman (1975b)	Unjustified	Won
U.S. Steel		
Parsons and Ray (1975)	Justified	Lost
Diesel Electric Locomotive		
Marx (1975)	Unjustified	Lost
Schwinn (Discussed in article Re: Sylvania)		
Posner (1977)	Unjustified	Won
Tobacco		
Burns (1977, 1982, 1983, 1986, 1988)	Justified	Won
		(No Effect)
Cereal		
Schmalensee (1978)	Justified	Lost
Scherer (1979)	Justified	Lost
Du Pont:Titanium Dioxide		
Shepherd (1979)	Justified	Lost

Table 3.1   *continued*

Case and Author	Author Evaluation of Quality of Case	Outcome for Plaintiff
ReaLemon		
Schmalensee (1979)	Unjustified	Won (But key remedy not applied)
McCarthy (1979)	Unjustified (Licensing remedy only)	Lost
Rosenbaum (1987)	Uncertain (Pricing issue)	Won
Bread		
Block et al. (1981)	Justified	Won
Addyston Pipe		
Bittlingmayer (1982)	Unjustified	Won (No effect)
Chicago Board of Trade		
Zerbe (1983)	Justified	Lost
AT&T		
MacAvoy and Robinson (1983)	Justified	Won (But effect was harmful)
Noll (1987)	Justified	Won
IBM		
Pittman (1984)	Unjustified	Lost
Levy and Welzer (1985)	Unjustified	Lost (But harmful effects from litigation)
Petty (1986)	Uncertain	Lost (No harmful effects from litigation)
Xerox		
Bresnahan (1985)	Justified	Won
Electrical Conspiracy		
Lean et al. (1985)	Justified	Won
Railroad Cartels		
Binder (1988)	Justified	Won (No effect)
Sealy		
Mueller (1989)	Justified	Won (No effect)

Table 3.2   Results by Case

Case	Quality of Case	Outcome for Plaintiff
Cellophane	Justified	Lost
Standard Oil	Justified	Won
Utah Pie	Unjustified	Won
Cement	Unjustified	Won
Alcoa	Justified	Won
Brown Shoe	Unjustified	Won
Interco	Unjustified	Won
U.S. Steel	Justified	Lost
Diesel Electric Locomotive	Unjustified	Lost
Schwinn	Unjustified	Won
Tobacco	Justified	Won
Cereal	Justified	Lost
Du Pont:Titanium Dioxide	Justified	Lost
ReaLemon	Unjustified	Won
Bread	Justified	Won
Addyston Pipe	Unjustified	Won
Chicago Board of Trade	Justified	Lost
AT&T	Justified	Won
IBM	Unjustified	Lost
Xerox	Justified	Won
Electrical Conspiracy	Justified	Won
Railroad Cartels	Justified	Won
Sealy	Justified	Won

Table 3.3   Quality of Case and Outcome, by Case

	Justified Case	Unjustified Case	Totals
Plaintiff Victory	9 (39%)	7 (30%)	16 (69%)
Defendant Victory	5 (22%)	2 (9%)	7 (31%)
Totals	14 (61%)	9 (39%)	23 (100%)

Table 3.4   Quality of Case, by Author

	Justified Case	Unjustified Case	Totals
Plaintiff Victory	15 (40%)	11 (30%)	26 (70%)
Defendant Victory	6 (16%)	5 (14%)	11 (30%)
Totals	21 (57%)	16 (43%)	37 (100%)

bound estimate of the efficiency of antitrust. In other words, it is highly unlikely that the net effect of actual antitrust policy is to deter inefficient behavior.

The economics profession has not judged that antitrust policy as reflected in actual cases is searching for economic efficiency. This may in part explain the reduction from 1976 to 1990 in support among economists for "vigorous" antitrust enforcement—from 85 percent in favor in 1976 to 62 percent in favor in 1990—mentioned in note 1. Factors other than a search for efficiency must be driving antitrust policy.

CHAPTER FOUR

The Economic Effects
of the Antitrust Laws

GEORGE J. STIGLER

The task I have set is to form a quantitative notion of the effects of the
antitrust laws. The task is formidable. A Congress which had goodwill toward
scholars would have exempted from the Sherman Act not a collection of
special pleaders, as has been our historical practice, but a random sample of
industries. A world more favorable to scholars would have had many United
States, some of which had antitrust policies. (Our federal nation could have
been almost that favorable, but the state antitrust laws have been pushed
nearly into oblivion by the federal laws.) In our statistically inefficient world,
the investigator must somehow disentangle the effects of one battalion of an
army of forces that have been influencing the American economy in the past
seventy-five years.

Many students have undertaken our task, and diverse estimates of the
effects of our antitrust laws may be found in the literature. These estimates
have invariably been made by one procedure. The scholar studies the history
of our policy and in the light of his knowledge of our economy—and perhaps
of other economies—he makes a summary judgment. The defect of the procedure is that the link between the survey of experience and the conclusion is
not explicit, so different scholars reach different conclusions. Yet it should
be the fundamental attribute of a measurement procedure that different men
can use it to achieve similar results. Until such procedures are available,
there is no tendency for the measurements to improve—each man's work
remains independent of all others' work. The main purpose of this paper is
to seek improvable procedures.

Simple Antitrust Laws

Let us begin with an antitrust law that seems easy to assess: it is the provision
of the Panama Canal Act that no company violating the Sherman Act be
permitted to ship goods through the canal.[1] This act, we assume, has not had

This essay was previously published in the *Journal of Law and Economics* 9 (October 1966):
225–58. © 1966 by The University of Chicago. All rights reserved.
1. 37 Stat. 567 (1912), 15 U.S.C. § 31 (1964).

any effect upon the methods of shipments used by monopolists, let alone upon the extent of competition, and for several reasons:

1. An instance of enforcement would surely have received much publicity, so presumably none has occurred.
2. It is inconceivable that none of the many violators of the Sherman Act ever used the canal.
3. The Attorney General gave to the canal authorities an interpretation of the provision which implied that it could be ignored.[2]

I do not wish to quarrel with this universal presumption that the provision never influenced the movement of monopolized goods. I do wish to emphasize the fact that this presumption is a poor substitute for evidence. The provision could have frightened monopolists into using the railroads, and the only way we can eliminate this possibility is by studying the comparative shipments of firms which were and were not prosecuted under the antitrust laws. Perhaps the problem is too small to justify the extensive labor such research would entail, but until this research is done, we possess a presumption, not a finding. The central weakness of the antitrust literature has been its reliance on presumptions—and in cases vastly more important and uncertain than the trifling question with which I begin.

A slightly more significant antitrust law is that no man may serve as director of two companies if at least one has assets of $1 million or more and the two companies compete with each other.[3] The logic of the law is that joint directors could effect collusive schemes between two companies more easily than conspiring officers or directors.

As a matter of history, the law has been invoked in formal complaints on 23 occasions up to January 1965.[4] The one instance leading to a court decision concerned Sidney Weinberg who was a director of Sears, Roebuck & Co. and of B.F. Goodrich Co., both of which sold a variety of similar consumer goods at retail.[5] The economic merits of the case were negliglble.

Let me now begin the empirical study of the effects of antitrust laws. England has no such law. The number of joint directors of companies in the same industry is extraordinarily small, however (see table 4.1). I am prepared to conclude that our prohibition of interlocking directorships has not had a noticeable effect upon corporate directorates. It is therefore unnecessary to examine the more basic question: Would the existence of many interlocking directorates lead to a decrease of competition?[6]

2. 30 Ops. Att'y Gen. 355 (1915).
3. 38 Stat. 732 (1914), 15 U.S.C. § 19 (1964).
4. Staff of Subcomm. No. 5, House Comm. on the Judiciary, 89th Cong., 1st Sess., Interlocks in Corporate Management 57 (Comm. Print 1965).
5. United States v. Sears, Roebuck & Co., 111 F. Supp. 614 (D.C.N.Y. 1953).
6. Interlocking directorates are a clumsy technique, even when one desires to coordinate the activities of two firms, so I would not expect their presence or absence to have a significant relationship to the extent of competition among firms.

Table 4.1   Interlocking Directorates, Great Britain, 1964

Industry	Companies	Number of Directors	Number of Overlapping Directors
Aircraft	13	130	1
Boots and shoes	50	290	0
Rubber products: Tires	8	63	0
Cement	29	194	1

Source: The Stock Exchange Official Year-Book (1964).

The Effects upon Concentration

We turn now to the first main purpose of the antitrust laws, the prevention of monopoly. This goal was sought by two routes: the prohibition of attempts to monopolize in Section 2 of the Sherman Act; and the prohibition of mergers that tend to reduce competition.

We require both a measure of concentration and—when we consider mergers—a measure of the effects of mergers on concentration. We adopt the Herfindahl index—the sum of the squares of the shares of industry output possessed by each firm. It is a comprehensible measure of firm sizes (with a maximum value of 1 for the index with monopoly and a minimum of $1/n$ with n firms of equal size). That the Herfindahl index is suited to the study of mergers deserves a fuller explanation.

Let us consider a simple way in which the impact of a merger upon the concentration of an industry can be measured (Stigler 1956). Take, for example, the largest firm and calculate its growth, as a share of the industry, by the percentages of industry output acquired by merger at different dates. If we assume that the acquired firms would have maintained their shares of industry output in the absence of merger, we may directly calculate the contribution of internal growth and mergers to the growth of the leading firm. For example, the leading English cement producer, the Associated Portland Cement Companies, Ltd., acquired, between 1900 and 1960, approximately 125 percent of industry capacity, but had a market share of 70 percent in 1960. Internal growth would then be reckoned at −55 percent of industry output.

The sum of shares acquired by merger by all firms is unfortunately a meaningless number. There is a problem of duplication: let A have 40 percent, B 20 percent, and C 10 percent of industry output. If B acquires C (10 percent) and then A acquires B (30 percent), the sum (40 percent) is greater than if A acquired B and C directly. This duplication can of course be avoided by counting each constituent firm only once. More important, the numbers have no scale. If there are 1,000 identical firms, and each of 100 acquires 9, the sum of merged shares is 90 percent, although concentration is negligible (4 percent for the largest 4 firms). Or if two firms with shares of 10 percent and 90 percent, respectively, each acquires a firm with 10 percent, the measure of the effect of merger would be the same.

The Herfindahl index, which can be derived from general arguments on the probability of successful collusion (Stigler 1964), is a more appropriate measure of the sum of merger activity in the industry. If firms with shares p_1 and p_2 combine, the Herfindahl index rises by

$$(p_1 + p_2)^2 - p_1^2 - p_2^2 = 2p_1p_2.$$

In the 1,000-firm industry above, the Herfindahl index would rise, after the 900 firms were acquired, to .01 from its previous level of .001. If a firm with 90 percent of output acquires a firm with 10 percent, the Herfindahl index rises .18 from .82 to 1, whereas a merger of two firms, each with 10 percent, raises the index by only .02.

The basic test of the effectiveness of our policies to prevent monopoly and high concentration must of course be: has it made concentration in American industry lower than it would otherwise be? An answer is sought along three lines: comparisons of the United States with other countries which have no antitrust law; comparisons of periods before and after passage of antitrust laws; and comparisons of industries exempt from and subject to the antitrust laws.

The Comparison with England

The English economy is one source of information about an economy in which there is no public policy against concentration of control. The English economy operates in an otherwise similar legal environment and in approximately the same state of technology. Its smaller size in general tends to lead to higher concentration than we observe in the United States because the optimum size of enterprise is roughly the same in the two countries.[7] Since our economy has grown from perhaps twice the size of the British economy in 1900 to four times the British size in 1965, we should expect *national* concentration in America to be lower and to be declining relative to British concentration. However, for cement and steel, where regional data are available, we compare a region in the United States with England to reduce the bias. More work is required in this area.[8]

Comparisons have been made of the history of concentration in seven industries in the United States and England since approximately 1900. Seven industries will scarcely support any general conclusion, and the comparison

7. So, at least, argues P. S. Florence, The Logic of British and American Industry (1953), 22–29, as to relative optimum sizes in the two countries.

8. The 1954 ratios of U.S. to U.K. industry size are: automobiles, 8.8 (1955); cement, 1.0; cigarettes, 3.6; glass, 7.0; soap, 8.9; steel, 5.1; tires, 6.0.

is presented primarily for methodological purposes. The reason the sample is so small is that it has proven to be rather difficult to piece out tolerably reliable estimates for all the British and some American industries. The output of each American automobile company has long been reported by weeks, for example, but even approximate outputs began to be reported on a regular basis in England less than twenty years ago.

1. The automobile industry has been more highly concentrated in the United States than in the United Kingdom for the entire period studied.
2. The cement industry has been much more highly concentrated in the United Kingdom than in the United States (Lehigh Valley). Concentration has not risen over time in the United States.
3. The cigarette industry is concentrated in the United States, but at a much lower level since the dissolution of American Tobacco. Since 1911 the concentration in Great Britain has been much higher than in the United States.
4. The American glass industry in the 1950s was less concentrated than the British industry (which is a monopoly). Concentration has risen in the United States since the 1920s, however, to a high level.
5. The soap industry is substantially more highly concentrated in the United Kingdom than in the United States, but concentration is fairly high in the United States.
6. The steel industry (ingots) was fairly highly concentrated in the United States after U.S. Steel was formed, but it has declined steadily and substantially. Nevertheless, it is above the level in the United Kingdom.
7. The rubber tire industry is highly concentrated in the United Kingdom but concentration is declining somewhat; concentration is substantially lower in the United States, and has had no trend since the 1930s.

These instances are compatible with the hypothesis (which I presently favor) that the Sherman Act was a modest deterrent to high concentration.[9] The underlying statistical tables suggest that mergers to achieve very high concentration ($H > .3$) were more common in England than in the United States. These hypotheses can, of course, eventually be tested against a much larger body of data: the test is improvable.

The Decline of Horizontal Mergers

A second and more comprehensive set of data look to the impact of the 1950 antimerger amendment to the Clayton Act. These data concern the number

9. The industries favorable to the hypothesis that the Sherman Act has served to keep down concentration are cement and cigarettes, with glass, soap, and tires pointing more weakly the same way. The automobile and steel industries support the opposite interpretation. Since 1911, merger has not been a major source of high concentration in the United States.

of horizontal mergers engaged in by the 200 leading companies in manufacturing and mining. The basic data are presented in table 4.2.

These merger data suggest that the 1950 antimerger statute has been a
powerful discouragement to horizontal mergers. The fraction of horizontal
mergers by large companies has fallen to low levels. Even this Federal Trade
Commission count of horizontal mergers is heavily biased toward this type
of merger: two companies were considered in the same industry and market
if even a small fraction of their sales overlapped. There are also no important
mergers recorded since 1950 in the following seven American industries:
automobiles; cement; cigarettes; flat glass; soap; steel; and rubber tires and
tubes.

Unfortunately, the extent of horizontal mergers in earlier times has not
been measured—it seems incredible but it is true that all forms of merger
are combined in the standard merger series. (In our seven industries horizontal
mergers were more frequent and important before than after 1950.) The
deficiency in the statistical history of mergers is of course remediable.

The Exempt Areas

The industries exempt from the antitrust laws are still another potential source
of information, but a reluctant source. Most exempt industries are subjected
to regulation of other sorts, and presumably have economic characteristics
which distinguish them from nonexempt unregulated industries.

The insurance industry (or industries) is a fairly simple example of exempt
industries. The exemption is not unqualified, but no merger cases have been
brought against insurance companies, and the impact of the 1950 merger

Table 4.2 Distribution of Large Manufacturing and Mining Acquisitions by Type and by
Period of Acquisition

Type of Merger	1948–1953		1954–1959		1960–1964	
	Num-ber	Per-cent-age	Num-ber	Per-cent-age	Num-ber	Per-cent-age
Horizontal	18	31.0	78	24.8	42	12.0
Vertical	6	10.3	43	13.7	59	17.0
Conglomerate:						
Market Extension	4	6.9	20	6.4	24	6.9
Product Extension	27	46.6	145	46.2	184	52.9
Other	3	5.2	28	8.9	39	11.2
Total	58	100.0	314	100.0	348	100.0

Source: Bureau of Economics, Federal Trade Commission.

Table 4.3   The Impact of Mergers on Concentration
in the Fire and Casualty Insurance Industry

Year	Herfindahl Index	Contributions of Mergers from Previous Date
1945	.0163	
1953	.0164	.0000
1963	.0189	.0024

statute is presumably negligible.[10] Nevertheless, the level of concentration is low in the life and fire-and-casualty branches of the industry, and merger activity has been quite minor. The data for fire and casualty insurance companies is summarized in table 4.3. Almost as low concentration is found in a typical industrial state.[11]

The ambiguity in such evidence is that we have no standard of comparable nonexempt industries. Still, the levels of concentration and of mergers in insurance have been so low that it is virtually impossible to conceive of a pattern (of sharply falling concentration) in nonexempt industries, such that the insurance industry would corroborate our previous finding on the substantial effects of the 1950 merger act.

The Effects Upon Collusion

The main thrust of the Sherman Act was against conspiracies in restraint of trade, and the judgment of its success must rest largely on its achievements in this direction. No type of legislative endeavor, however, is harder to measure in its effects than a prohibition of actions which can be concealed.

Through 1963, there were some 957 completed antitrust cases reported in the Commerce Clearing House (CCH) Bluebooks in which some element of conspiracy was charged. Of these cases, the Department of Justice won exactly 756, or slightly over three quarters of the total. In addition, a large number of Federal Trade Commission cases involving collusion have been brought. We can equally well hail the numerous cases (and equally the victo-

10. The industry is exempt to the extent (1) that states regulate the industry, and (2) that certain forbidden acts, such as concerted boycotts, are not engaged in. The Antitrust Division believes mergers of insurance companies are exempt if the states have so-called Little Clayton Acts; see Hearings Pursuant to S. Res. 57 Before the Subcommittee on Antitrust and Monopoly of the Senate Committee on the Judiciary, The Insurance Industry, 86th Cong., 1st sess., pt. 2, at 931 (1960).

11. Thus the Herfindahl ratio in Illinois in 1963 was .0232 for fire and casualty insurance.

ries) as evidence of the beneficial effect of the Sherman Act, or as evidence of its failure. What we want, of course, is a census of collusion, detected and undetected, and a census with and without an antitrust law.

Our difficulty rests on one fundamental fact: we do not have a generally acceptable theory of oligopoly. If we had such a theory, it would tell us what the determinants of successful collusion are, and we could then investigate the effects of the Sherman Act upon these determinants. When the event we wish to study is clandestine, we cannot rely upon direct observation.

I believe that my theory of oligopoly is a useful tool for this study, precisely because it seeks to isolate the determinants and forms of successful collusion—or rather, the determinants of successful cheating and hence unsuccessful collusion. The argument turns on the problem of getting reliable information on the observance of collusive agreements: invoices, sellers, buyers, and even physical shipments may lie. And where an agreement cannot be enforced, it will not be obeyed.

In this view, certain methods of collusion are highly efficient. The most efficient is the joint sales agency, for then price cutting is impossible and any large, hidden movement of goods is also virtually impossible. This plausible position is supported by European cartel experience:

> This method (by which the cartel has access to the records of each member), no matter how rigorously it is administered, nevertheless does not give a complete guarantee against evasions of the cartel policy. Rather, it is a popular, recurring complaint that one cannot detect clever violations, especially concealed price reductions. This leads the cartels in ever rising numbers to the establishment of a *common selling agency* as the only wholly reliable protection against evasion. It is not an individual incident, but rather wholly typical, that one of the oldest and best organized Australian cartels, the plate glass syndicate, explained when a common selling bureau was established that without this device even the severest controls would not prevent price-cutting or the exceeding of quotas.[12]

It is relevant to observe that marine insurance was exempted from the antitrust laws by the Merchant Marine Act of 1920. A syndicate of domestic and some foreign companies was formed, and their business was assigned to the syndicate, in which each of the member insurance companies had a quota of participation. No member may deal directly in this market except by permission of, and at rates set by, the syndicate—a strict joint sales agency system.[13]

Somewhat less efficient collusion is achieved by the assignment of custom-

---

12. Kestner, Die Organizationszwang (1912), 153.
13. Hearings Pursuant to S. Res. 57, *supra* note 10, at pts. 2 and 9. The cartel agreement is reprinted in pt. 9 at 5555–5633.

Table 4.4   Analysis of Collusion Cases by Type and Outcome*

Type	Government Wins	Defendant Wins	Total
Efficient	9	4	13
Inefficient	9	8	17
Total	18	12	

*Cases identified by Commerce Clearing House (CCH) number are as follows (only one of a group of closely related cases is included): "Efficient" cases, Nos. 14, 18, 24, 34, 83, 239, 240, 254, 277, 282, 348, 349, and 355; "Inefficient" cases, Nos. 21, 66, 76, 215, 218, 227, 241, 243, 244, 246, 248, 265, 273, 274, 284, 331, and 343.
Source: The Federal Anti-Trust Laws, With Summary of Cases Instituted by the United States (1951); supplementary information necessary for assigning cartels to "efficient" and "inefficient" classes was obtained from U.S. Courts, Federal Anti-Trust Decisions (vols. 1–12).

ers, whether individually, by geographic area, or otherwise. There is still a possible inducement to secret price cutting: in the long run, the favored customers may grow relative to their rivals who purchase from another seller who abides by the cartel price. Actual shipments to non-assigned customers are usually detectable, as in the case of joint sales agencies.

Both the joint sales agency and the assignment of customers are obvious to the buyers and therefore they are likely to be called to the attention of the Antitrust Division and, once suspected, their existence is easily proven. No such ease of detection exists with the lesser forms of collusion, such as price agreements, but these lesser forms also are much less easily enforced.[14]

The types of collusion I call efficient (joint sales agencies and assignment of customers) are more likely found to be in violation of the antitrust laws than the other types of collusion. This is almost necessarily true, since the efficient types of collusion are per se offenses, whereas the inefficient types of collusion include a fair number of innocuous trade association activities and other uncertain extensions of the law. The hypothesis is, in fact, readily tested: in an analysis of a small sample of the two types of cases, we obtain the results in table 4.4. The sample is small so the test is weak (the results could arise by chance with probability .2), but the sample could readily be enlarged.

This line of argument may be, and I hope is, plausible, but it is not yet persuasive. Two things are needed. The first is a substantial testing of the oligopoly theory that underlies this argument. A systematic empirical test has so far eluded me. The second omission is a showing that the "nonefficient" forms of collusion are substantially less efficient than the "efficient" forms.

14. With one important exception. The government as buyer usually uses bidding techniques which make secret price cuts impossible. Hence, collusive systems usually work best against government buyers.

Table 4.5   Average Time until Detection of Efficient and Inefficient Methods of Collusion

Types of Collusion	Number	Period from Inception of Alleged Collusion to Complaint
Efficient	7	21.6 ($\pm$ 3.9) months
Inefficient	10	56.7 ($\pm$ 2.4) months

This latter defect can be partially remedied, I believe, by the following procedure.

A series of cartel cases have been brought for a variety of reasons, including the contagious property of a prominent case in a large industry eliciting parallel complaints. I hypothesize that the interval between inception of a scheme and its detection will be shorter for the more efficient techniques. If so, the act has reduced the comparative gain, and hence the comparative frequency, of these forms of collusion. A small number of cases has been analyzed, and the pattern is in keeping with the hypothesis (see table 4.5).[15] The accumulation of more such cases (many are available) and more fundamentally the rigorous testing of the underlying oligopoly theory would greatly strengthen this argument.

Conclusion

The substantive findings of this study are meager and undogmatic:

1. The Sherman Act appears to have had only a very modest effect in reducing concentration.
2. The 1950 Merger Act has had a strongly adverse effect upon horizontal mergers by large companies.
3. The Sherman Act has reduced the availability of the most efficient methods of collusion and thereby reduced the amount and effects of collusion.

Discussions of methodology are usually offered as a substitute when an author has lacked the imagination to devise strong tests and the diligence to compile a large body of evidence, and I apologetically follow this tradition. I do not claim that any reasonable man must accept the above conclusions, for even the strongest (on the effects of the antimerger statute) is not overpowering in the volume or pointedness of the evidence. I do claim that each of the findings is improvable, and the extension of this work will shrink the range of defensible conclusions.

15. The cases analyzed have Commerce Clearing House (CCH) case numbers: 18, 24, 34, 83, 277, 348, and 349 in the efficient class; 66, 76, 215, 218, 244, 265, 273, 274, 284, and 343 in the inefficient class.

CHAPTER FIVE

A Statistical Study of Antitrust Enforcement

RICHARD A. POSNER

This paper reports the results of a statistical study of antitrust enforcement by the Department of Justice, the Federal Trade Commission, state agencies, and private plaintiffs since the enactment of the Sherman Act in 1890. The purpose of the study was threefold:

1. To show by example that the collection and analysis of statistical data on the operation of legal institutions is a fruitful and practicable undertaking for students of those institutions.

2. To set forth compactly such statistics on antitrust enforcement as could be obtained without elaborate and costly field research or computer operations, and to explore their implications for issues of antitrust policy.

3. To identify gaps and deficiencies in the existing statistical sources and to suggest methods for improving antitrust statistics.

In the following pages we shall be looking at the number of cases filed by the various enforcement institutions, the length of proceedings, the record of success of antitrust claimants, the use of various civil and criminal remedies, the pattern of violations alleged, the industries involved, the possible explanatory role of politics, and some steps whereby antitrust statistics could be improved. We shall close with a discussion of the importance of statistical analyses of antitrust enforcement to effective policy planning in the antitrust field.

The Number of Cases Filed

Table 5.1 records the number of cases instituted by the Department of Justice by year (and also by five-year periods) since 1890. The source of these data, as of most of the data presented in this study, is a series of volumes published by Commerce Clearing House and known popularly as the "Bluebook."[1]

This essay was previously published in the *Journal of Law and Economics* 13 (October 1970): 365–419. © 1970 by The University of Chicago. All rights reserved.
1. CCH, The Federal Antitrust Laws, With Summary of Cases Instituted by the United States 1890–1951 (1952); 1952–1956 Supp. (1957); Trade Reg. Rep., 10th ed., Transfer Binder, New U.S. Antitrust Cases—Complaints, Indictments, Developments 1957–1961; and 5 Trade Reg. Rep. ¶ 45003–45069 (current). Hereinafter cited as Bluebook.

RICHARD A. POSNER

Table 5.1 Antitrust Cases Instituted by the Department of Justice

Year	N	Period	Year	N	Period	Year	N	Period
1890	1		1918	10		1945	20	
1891	0		1919	3		1946	37	
1892	5		1915–1919		43	1947	25	
1893	1		1920	8		1948	44	
1894	2		1921	20		1949	31	
1890–1894		9	1922	17		1945–1949		157
1895	1		1923	8		1950	48	
1896	3		1924	13		1951	42	
1897	2		1920–1924		66	1952	27	
1898	0		1925	12		1953	18	
1899	1		1926	9		1954	24	
1895–1899		7	1927	13		1950–1954		159
1900	0		1928	17		1955	34	
1901	0		1929	8		1956	30	
1902	3		1925–1929		59	1957	38	
1903	2		1930	7		1958	47	
1904	1		1931	3		1959	46	
1900–1904		6	1932	5		1955–1959		195
1905	5		1933	9		1960	35	
1906	14		1934	6		1961	47	
1907	10		1930–1934		30	1962	56	
1908	7		1935	4		1963	26	
1909	3		1936	5		1964	51	
1905–1909		39	1937	7		1960–1964		215
1910	15		1938	10		1965	35	
1911	23		1939	31		1966	36	
1912	20		1935–1939		57	1967	34	
1913	22		1940	65		1968	47	
1914	11		1941	71		1969	43	
1910–1914		91	1942	46		1965–1969		195
1915	7		1943	22				
1916	2		1944	19		Total		1551
1917	21		1940–1944		223			

Source: Computed from CCH, The Federal Antitrust Laws With Summary of Cases Instituted by the United States 1890–1951 (1952); 1952–1956 Supp. (1957). Trade Reg. Rep., 10th ed., Transfer Binder, New U.S. Antitrust Cases—Complaints, Indictments, Developments 1957–1961; 5 Trade Reg. Rep. ¶ 45003–45064 (current). Hereinafter cited as Bluebook. I have also included, in this and subsequent tables, one case that was inadvertently omitted from the Bluebook. See Hans Berger Thorelli, The Federal Antitrust Policy—Origination of an American Tradition (1955), p. 429.

The Bluebook contains brief summaries of all Department of Justice antitrust cases in the order of their filing. Although the Bluebook number of the last case filed by the Department in 1969 is 2,081, the reader will note in table 5.1 that the sum of cases through 1969 was only 1,551. The reason for this discrepancy is that, with trivial exceptions, every antitrust complaint, indictment, and information is assigned a separate Bluebook number when

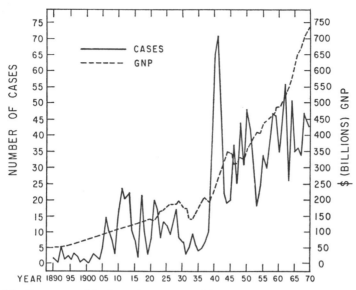

Figure 5.1 Department of Justice antitrust cases and the Gross National Product in constant 1958 dollars

Sources: Table 5.1; U.S. Bureau of the Census, Dept. of Commerce, Historical Statistics of the United States, Colonial Times to 1957; U.S. Bureau of the Census, Dept. of Commerce, Statistical Abstract[s] of the United States, 1958–1969.

it is filed, with the result that frequently what I consider a single proceeding is counted two or more times.[2]

What explains the variations in the antitrust activity, measured by number of cases brought, of the Department of Justice? A plausible hypothesis is that it is changes in the level of overall economic activity. Both the incidence of antitrust violations and the resources available to combat them could be expected to increase as the economy expanded, and decrease as the economy contracted. This hypothesis is explored in figure 5.1. It reveals a fair correlation between changes in antitrust and in overall economic activity until about 1940. Since that time, however, the number of cases brought by the Department has not increased significantly, despite the tremendous growth of the

2. Sometimes, an indictment merely supersedes an earlier one that was dismissed because it was technically defective. Often, several indictments are returned that relate to the same transactions and are disposed of in the same proceeding, the only reason for the plural indictments being a slight difference in the product or in the identity of some of the defendants. Often, too, a civil complaint will be filed solely in order to obtain an injunction against defendants in a pending or recently completed criminal proceeding arising from the same transaction. Occasionally a case is brought for contempt of a previous order; I prefer to classify the contempt proceeding as a reopening or continuation of the earlier action rather than as a separate new suit. In all of these cases, I have counted one proceeding where the Bluebook counts several.

economy. There are a number of possible explanations for this discrepancy. Cases are not fungible; perhaps the Department is bringing fewer, but bigger, cases today. This is unlikely: if the Department were bringing bigger cases one would expect the average duration of its cases to be increasing, but it is not. Another possibility is that the price of resources employed in antitrust enforcement has been rising faster than prices in general, so that the same percentage of Gross National Product devoted to antitrust enforcement buys less of it than formerly. There is some evidence to support this hypothesis. Between 1956 and 1967, the Antitrust Division's appropriations rose from $3.4 million to $7.5 million, an increase of 121 percent. Yet the personnel of the Antitrust Division rose by only 30 percent.[3] What these figures do not explain, of course, is why the 30 percent increase in the Division's personnel led to no significant increase in the number of cases brought.

Table 5.1 and figure 5.1 can be used to test two other plausible hypotheses concerning changes in the volume of antitrust activity over time. One is that such activity increases in periods of economic contraction—either because contractions are thought to be aggravated by monopoly, or because the public wants a scapegoat. The other is that antitrust activity decreases in periods of war—because economic controls are substituted for the market, because of the philosophy that underlies wartime economic controls (a distrust of economic freedom in times of national crisis), or because antitrust prosecutions are felt to be divisive or distracting at such times. The statistics support neither hypothesis.

For cases brought by the Federal Trade Commission, there is no exact counterpart to the Bluebook. Commerce Clearing House does publish an "FTC Docket of Complaints,"[4] which, like the Bluebook, contains brief summaries of each case in the order brought. But the summaries contain the barest possible description of the violation alleged. And restraint-of-trade cases are not separated from the false-advertising and mislabeling cases that constitute the major part of the Commission's docket. It is possible, however, to make the separation; and table 5.2 lists by year and by five-year periods the restraint-of-trade cases brought by the Commission since its establishment in 1915. I have excluded not only deceptive-practice cases, but also those cases involving in essence a private business tort (such as commercial bribery), and all Robinson-Patman Act cases other than those charging predatory (or, in the jargon of antitrust lawyers, "primary line") price discrimination. This last, and perhaps most questionable, exclusion is based on the view that other practices forbidden by the Robinson-Patman Act lack an arguable tendency to impair competition—the Act being in reality a price-control

3. Computed from 1964 Att'y Gen. Ann. Rep. 116; 1967 Att'y Gen. Ann. Rep. 105.
4. 3 Trade Reg. Rep. 24051, hereinafter cited as FTC Docket of Complaints. In addition, all FTC complaints are eventually published in Federal Trade Commission Decisions, the official report of the Commission's adjudicative actions.

Table 5.2   FTC Restraint-of-Trade Cases*

Year Initiated	Number		Year Initiated	Number		Year Initiated	Number	
1915	0		1935	30		1955	29	
1916	1		1936	33		1956	22	
1917	20		1937	18		1957	16	
1918	64		1938	28		1958	13	
1919	121		1939	31		1959	12	
1915–1919		206	1935–1939		140	1955–1959		92
1920	18		1940	33		1960	26	
1921	26		1941	32		1961	7	
1922	32		1942	16		1962	15	
1923	50		1943	14		1963	9	
1924	51		1944	8		1964	12	
1920–1924		177	1940–1944		103	1960–1964		69
1925	21		1945	6		1965	18	
1926	4		1946	9		1966	19	
1927	8		1947	11		1967	9	
1928	10		1948	11		1968	15	
1929	17		1949	10		1969	15	
1925–1929		60	1945–1949		47	1965–1969		76
1930	12		1950	5				
1931	4		1951	18		Total		1,061
1932	3		1952	16				
1933	4		1953	7				
1934	14		1954	11				
1930–1934		37	1950–1954		57			

Source: Computed from FTC Docket of Complaints and F.T.C. Decisions. [See text.]
*Excluding Robinson-Patman cases that do not allege predatory pricing.

rather than an antitrust statute—and on a desire to facilitate comparison with the Department of Justice. The Department has brought virtually no cases under the Robinson-Patman Act, although it has occasionally charged predatory price discrimination under the Sherman Act.

One result of this procedure is to undermine the recent assertion "that available measurements of all FTC activities, formal and informal, show a consistent and serious decline between 1961–1963 and 1969 (except in textiles and furs)."[5] Had the study separated the Commission's restraint-of-trade from its Robinson-Patman Act cases, it would have found an increase rather than a decrease in restraint-of-trade cases filed (see table 5.2).

The most striking result in table 5.2 is that the number of restraint-of-trade cases (as I have defined them) brought by the FTC in each period has shown no tendency to increase over time. Indeed, it brought more cases between 1916 and 1939 than it has in the 31 years since. Three reasons may be conjectured. The first is that the enactment of the Robinson-Patman Act in

5. ABA Comm'n to Study the Federal Trade Comm'n, Report 26 (1969).

1936, coupled with the Department's lack of interest in enforcing it, deflected the Commission's attention from the restraint-of-trade field.[6] The second is that the Commission has shifted resources from adjudicative to nonadjudicative enforcement methods such as Trade Practice Conferences and advisory opinions. The third, and probably most important, is that the screening of complaints was extremely casual in the early periods, as indicated by the very high percentage of dismissals, and that the Commission's adjudicative procedures in general were much more casual and summary than in later periods.[7] In these circumstances, it was possible to produce many more cases with the same expenditure of resources. Withal, there is plainly no reason for supposing that the Commission's level of antimonopoly activity has increased over the years; and this further undermines the hypothesis that antitrust activity is determined by overall economic activity.

Table 5.3 records the number of private antitrust cases brought since the enactment of the Sherman Act. The available data with respect to the private cases are very poor. There is no record of the private cases filed before 1938, except for those in which there is a reported decision, and to compile one would require visits to every district court in the country, none of which, to my knowledge, maintains any subject-matter index of its past cases. Since 1938, the Administrative Office of the United States Courts, in its annual reports, has recorded the number of private antitrust cases filed each year. But that is all the information it has reported about them, except that it did break out the electrical-equipment cases of the early 1960s and report their number separately. Since at least 1964, the Administrative Office has collected more information about the private antitrust cases than it publishes, but the additional information, although doubtless useful for the purposes of judicial administration for which it is collected, is of only limited interest to the student of antitrust policy.

An anonymous public benefactor, however, has catalogued all *reported* private antitrust cases,[8] and by computing the ratio of reported to initiated

6. The number of Robinson-Patman cases, not included in table 5.2, brought by the Commission since the enactment of the Act in 1936 is as follows:

1936–1939	75
1940–1944	106
1945–1949	94
1950–1954	66
1955–1959	227
1960–1964	545
1965–1969	102
Total	1,215

Source: Computed from FTC Docket of Complaints.

7. The Commission's early procedures are described in Gerald C. Henderson, The Federal Trade Commission, 49–104 (1924).

8. Nolo Contendere and Private Antitrust Enforcement, Hearings on S.2512, Before the Subcomm. on Antitrust & Monopoly of the Senate Comm. on the Judiciary, 89th Cong., 2d Sess. app. I, 180–324 (1966).

Table 5.3   Private Antitrust Cases

Period	Reported	Initiated (Excluding Electrical- Equipment Cases)	Electrical- Equipment Cases Initiated	Total Initiated
1890–1894	2	5*		5*
1895–1899	4	11*		11*
1900–1904	8	21*		21*
1905–1909	20	53*		53*
1910–1914	23	64*		64*
1915–1919	17	45*		45*
1920–1924	17	45*		45*
1925–1929	13	35*		35*
1930–1934	20	53*		53*
1935–1939	34	91*		91*
1940–1944	68	270†		270†
1945–1949	82	399		399
1950–1954	183	1,002		1,002
1955–1959	286	1,144		1,144
1960–1964	1,133	1,435	1,919	3,354
1965–1969	638	2,822	314	3,136
Total	2,548	7,495	2,233	9,728

Source: Hearings on S. 2512, Nolo Contendere and Private Antitrust Enforcement, Before the Subcomm. on Antitrust & Monopoly of the Senate Comm. on the Judiciary, 89th Cong., 2d Sess., at 180–324 (1966); United States Courts, Administrative Office, Ann. Rep.
*Estimated; see text.
†Excluding 1940, for which I have been unable to obtain information.

cases during those years in which the catalog and the records of the Administrative Office overlap, and applying it to the number of reported cases in the years prior to 1938, one can derive a very crude estimate of the number of cases brought in the earlier years. This is the estimate used in table 5.3. In no event would it be proper to add the number of private cases to the number of Department of Justice and Federal Trade Commission cases in an attempt to estimate overall levels of antitrust activity. In the first place, as shown in table 5.4, many private suits follow a government judgment, and thus arise from the same transaction. Table 5.4 probably understates this phenomenon (although one does not know by how much), since it deals only with reported cases: one would expect more controversy, and hence a higher ratio of judicial opinions, among those cases not preceded by a government action, in which action many of the important issues would have been determined. In the second place, a single antitrust violation may give rise to many private suits, for there is usually more than one victim of a monopolistic practice. The 2,233 electrical equipment cases noted in table 5.3 arose from a few indictments. One does not know how many separate violations have been attacked

Table 5.4   Reported Private Antitrust Cases Preceded by a Department of Justice Judgment

Period	Total Cases	Cases Preceded by Justice Department Judgment			
		Nolo	Consent	Other	Total
1890–1900	10			2	2
1901–1905	5				
1906–1910	23			6	6
1911–1915	22		1	5	6
1916–1920	15		2	4	6
1921–1925	15		2	4	6
1926–1930	17			1	1
1931–1935	19		1	2	3
1936–1940	43	1	7	4	12
1941–1945	71	3	1	23	27
1946–1950	99	3	8	34	45
1951–1955	199	1	20	60	81
1956–1960	278	1	19	81	101
1961–1963	880		11	748	759

Source: Computed from Hearings on S. 2512, Nolo Contendere and Private Antitrust Enforcement, Before the Subcomm. on Antitrust & Monopoly of the Senate Comm. on the Judiciary, 89th Cong., 2d Sess., at 180–324 (1966).

by private suits; it may be only a small fraction of the total number of private antitrust cases.

Figure 5.2 shows that until the 1945–1949 period, fluctuations in the number of private cases paralleled those in Department of Justice cases. This is not surprising in light of the tendency of private plaintiffs to move in the wake of government action. What is surprising is that beginning with that period the patterns diverge: the number of private suits rises in each period and the increase is proportionately greater than in the Department's activity. The reasons are not wholly clear, but it is noteworthy that the divergence coincides roughly with the decision in the *Bigelow* case,[9] which greatly simplified the proof of damages in private antitrust cases. The veritable explosion of private cases in the most recent period may similarly reflect a recent rash of procedural rulings highly favorable to antitrust plaintiffs.[10]

The data with respect to cases brought under state antitrust laws are no better, and in fact are worse, than the data regarding private cases under federal antitrust law, although better data with respect to state government cases could perhaps be obtained by inquiry of each state government. The only public source of information is *CCH Trade Cases,* which reports those state cases in which an opinion was issued by the court. A partial search of

9. Bigelow v. RKO Radio Pictures, Inc., 327 U.S. 251 (1946).
10. See, for example, Perma Life Mufflers, Inc., v. International Parts Corp., 392 U.S. 135 (1968); Hanover Shoe, Inc., v. United Shoe Machinery Corp., 392 U.S. 481 (1968); Leh v. General Petroleum Corp., 382 U.S. 54 (1965).

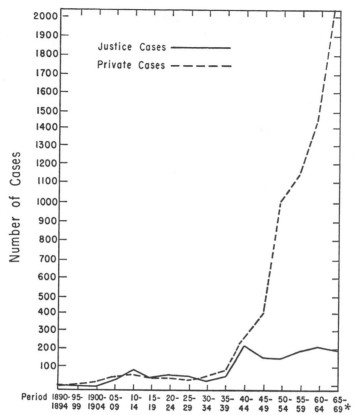

Figure 5.2   Department of Justice and private antitrust cases
Sources: Tables 5.1, 5.3.
*The total for 1965–1969 is 2,822, which is off the graph.

Trade Cases indicates that the pace of state antitrust activity has quickened in recent years, and tells something of the pattern of violations alleged. Between 1935 and 1944, only 18 state cases were reported, six of them brought by state agencies; for the shorter period 1965–1969, these numbers are 91 and 25, respectively. The number of cases instituted is doubtless larger, but since we have no information as to the actual number of cases instituted under state law in any year or period, it is impossible to estimate how much larger.

The Choice of Remedies

Federal Equitable Remedies

Table 5.5 shows the breakdown between civil and criminal antitrust cases filed by the Department of Justice in the various periods since 1890. The

Table 5.5 Breakdown Between Criminal and Civil Cases Brought by the Department of Justice

Period in Which Case Was Instituted	Total Number of Cases	Criminal	Civil	Percentage Criminal	Percentage Civil
1890–1894	9	4	5	44	56
1895–1899	7	1	6	14	86
1900–1904	6	1	5	17	83
1905–1909	39	26	13	67	33
1910–1914	91	37	54	41	59
1915–1919	43	25	18	58	42
1920–1924	66	25	41	38	62
1925–1929	59	16	43	27	73
1930–1934	30	11	19	37	63
1935–1939	57	27	30	47	53
1940–1944	223	163	60	73	27
1945–1949	157	58	99	37	63
1950–1954	159	73	86	46	54
1955–1959	195	97	98	50	50
1960–1964	215	78	137	36	64
1965–1969	195	52	143	27	73
Total	1551	694	857		

Source: Computed from the Bluebook.

proportion of civil cases has varied from 50 to 73 percent in recent years. These figures understate the government's reliance on civil remedies since they exclude cases in which civil relief is sought ancillary to a criminal proceeding. It is interesting to note that the periods of greatest increase over the previous period in the total number of cases filed (1905–1909 and 1940–1944) were periods in which the proportion of criminal to civil cases was unusually high.

The Department's civil antitrust decrees can be classified under three heads, which I shall call the "statutory language" decree, the "once-for-all" decree, and the "regulatory" decree. It is extremely common for the Department in price-fixing cases to obtain a decree that, stripped of the redundancies that are dear to lawyers, merely forbids further price fixing. Since the illegality of price fixing under the Sherman Act is well established, and directly punishable as a crime, the purpose of such an injunction is not obvious, especially in the many cases in which it is entered simultaneously with or shortly after the imposition of criminal punishment. (In other cases, in which the rule of law is not well established, a civil proceeding makes obvious good sense.) One possible explanation for the practice is that it is an attempt to increase the deterrent effect of the rule against price fixing by adding to the penalties provided by Section 1 of the Sherman Act the much heavier penalties that, in principle at least, can be imposed on a corporation that is found guilty of criminal contempt. Table 5.6, which records the criminal-contempt proceedings brought for violation of Department of Justice antitrust decrees, indicates, however, that few such proceedings have been brought, that the government's record of success in such proceedings has been poor by its usual standards, and (in conjunction with table 5.10) that the penalties imposed in such proceedings are not generally higher than those imposed in original criminal antitrust actions. I am led to question whether the "statutory language" decree serves much purpose, except in cases in which the rule of law is in doubt.

The "once-for-all" decree is one that eliminates the violation by a change in the defendant's business that, once effected, permits the Department and the court very largely to wash their hands of the case. An example would be a decree requiring the defendant to divest a firm unlawfully acquired or to dedicate its patents to the public, or a decree enjoining an acquisition. Such a decree may, of course, take some time to carry out, but once it is carried out nothing more remains to be done. Despite this attractive feature, we shall see later that divestiture, at least in monopolization cases, involves major problems of delay.

The "regulatory" decree is one whose terms are such as to establish a continuing supervisory relationship between the court in which the decree was entered and the defendant; more realistically, perhaps, between the Judgments Section of the Antitrust Division and the defendant. A good example is the old *Terminal Railroad Association* decree, which ordered the defendant association to furnish its terminal services to all seekers on reasonable and nondiscriminatory terms.[11] In effect, the decree created a little Interstate Commerce Act for the terminal association, with the court cast in the role of the ICC. The example has been followed in a large number of decrees that require defendants to grant patent licenses on nondiscriminatory and reason-able-royalty terms. Of related character are decrees that forbid the defendant to make any further acquisition, or to enter specified businesses, or to exceed a certain share of the market. The last two are manifestly anticompetitive, and all three seem highly questionable in that they implicitly grant the courts and the Department broad and lasting discretion over business decisions that may be only remotely related to the original purposes of the antitrust suit. The *Swift* decree provides a notorious example.[12]

Table 5.7 uses two methods to estimate the number of regulatory decrees

11. United States v. Terminal Railroad Ass'n of St. Louis, 224 U.S. 383, 411 (1912).

12. The most recent episode is United States v. Swift & Co., 1969 Trade Cas. ¶ 72701 (N.D. Ill. 1969). For a critical discussion of experience with the administration of a group of regulatory decrees, see Comment, An Experiment in Preventive Anti-Trust; Judicial Regulation of the Motion Picture Exhibition Market Under the *Paramount* Decrees, 74 Yale L.J. 1040 (1965).

Table 5.6 Criminal Contempt Proceedings for Violation of Department of Justice Antitrust Decrees

	1890 to 1894	1895 to 1899	1900 to 1904	1905 to 1909	1910 to 1914	1915 to 1919	1920 to 1924	1925 to 1929	1930 to 1934	1935 to 1939	1940 to 1944	1945 to 1949	1950 to 1954	1955 to 1959	1960 to 1964	1965 to 1969	Total
								Year in Which Original Action Was Brought									
Number of Criminal Contempt Proceedings Arising Out of Orders Entered in Those Actions	1			1	3			2	2	1	3	3	3	1	2		22
Number on Which Some Penalty Was Imposed	1				3			1	1		1	3	1*	1			12
Total Penalties	†				$32,500			10,000	4,000		102,500	243,700	35,000	75,003			502,703
Average Penalty	†				$10,833			10,000	4,000		102,500	81,233	35,000	75,003			45,700
								Year in Which Contempt Proceeding Was Brought									
Total Penalties	†							2,000		14,000	25,000		153,200		268,003	35,000	502,703
Average Penalty	†							2,000		7,000	25,000		76,250		89,334	35,000	45,700

Source: Computed from the Bluebook.
*One other case is pending.
†3–6 months imprisonment.

Table 5.7   "Regulatory" Decrees in Department of Justice Antitrust Cases*

Period in Which Case Was Instituted	Decrees Later Reopened or Modified (1)	Average Number of Years from Original Complaint to Latest Reopening Proceedings (2)	Reasonable-Royalty Decrees (3)	Other "Regulatory" Decrees (4)	Total of Columns 3 and 4 (5)
1890–1894					
1895–1899					
1900–1904					
1905–1909	3	17		1	1
1910–1914	15	22			
1915–1919	5	9			
1920–1924	7	16		1	1
1925–1929	5	13			
1930–1934	7	11			
1935–1939	7	20	1	1	2
1940–1944	19	9	14	2	16
1945–1949	6	15	24	17	41
1950–1954	14	9	12	12	24
1955–1959	2	5	8	11	19
1960–1964	3	3	1	4	5
1965–1969					
Total	93	13	60	49	109

Source: Computed from the Bluebook.
*There is some double counting in this table. Some regulatory decrees have been entered in cases ancillary to criminal proceedings and not counted as separate proceedings in other tables. And a few decrees containing both reasonable-royalty and other regulatory provisions have been counted twice.

that have been entered in Department of Justice antitrust cases. Column 1 reports the cases in which proceedings (other than for contempt of the original order) occurred after the termination of the original action: proceedings to reopen the case in order to modify the decree or determine its application. Since a regulatory decree, as I define it, is one that requires continuing attention after its entry, column 1 gives a partial glimpse of the importance of such decrees; it is partial because many regulatory decrees doubtless are administered without additional formal proceedings and hence do not show up in column 1. Column 2 indicates, again and for the same reason inadequately, the long span of time that often separates the original from the reopened proceeding. Columns 3 through 5 attempt a direct count of the regulatory decrees based on the Bluebook summaries. Because the summaries typically contain very scanty descriptions of the relief granted,[13] the actual number of regulatory decrees is understated, probably seriously so.

It would seem, at all events, that a significant fraction of civil antitrust decrees is regulatory in character. This finding is disturbing. First, as mentioned, such decrees are sometimes anticompetitive and often inappropriately far-reaching in their effect on future business behavior. Second, the entry of such a decree is tantamount to a confession that the antitrust action has not succeeded in restoring competitive conditions. And third, in view of persistent and serious questions that have been raised concerning the wisdom and efficacy of formal systems of regulation in the transportation, public utility, and other industries, the creation of new schemes of regulation on an ad hoc basis is a questionable expedient, especially when their administration must be left in the hands of scattered federal district courts and an obscure section in the Department of Justice.

Criminal Remedies[14]

Table 5.5 showed the breakdown between criminal and civil antitrust cases brought by the Department of Justice. Table 5.8 indicates the importance of the *nolo contendere* plea in the disposition of such cases since 1935–1939, and also that the Department's record of success in criminal cases is not significantly different from its overall record. Tables 5.9 through 5.11 and figure 5.3 record the nature and severity of the sanctions imposed in criminal antitrust cases. As table 5.9 indicates, imprisonment is a rarely used sanction; it has been imposed in fewer than 4 percent of the Department's criminal cases, and then mostly in cases involving either acts of violence or union misconduct. The first prison sentence for "pure" price fixing was imposed in the 1955–1959 period. The next was in the electrical-equipment case of 1960, in which seven company officials were given 30-day terms. Prison sentences have been imposed in two cases since then, but it is too early to tell whether the reluctance of judges to impose prison sentences in antitrust cases is diminishing significantly.

Table 5.10 and figure 5.3 indicate that the total antitrust fines imposed in cases brought in the various periods since the enactment of the Sherman Act kept at least rough pace with the growth of the economy and the decline in the purchasing power of the dollar—until the most recent period. And it is not yet clear how exceptional that period was since fines have not been assessed in all of the cases filed in the period.

13. Good summaries of most of the decrees may be found in American Enterprise Institute, Antitrust Consent Decrees 1906–1966—Compendium of Abstracts (1968), plus 1967–1968 Supp.

14. For a study of criminal antitrust cases that partially overlaps my own, see James M. Clabault and John F. Burton, Sherman Act Indictments 1955–1965—A Legal and Economic Analysis (1966), and the 1968 Cumulative Statistical Supp.

Table 5.8 Criminal Convictions

Period in Which Case Was Instituted	Disposed of on Nolo Contendere Plea	Other Convictions	Total Convictions	Acquittals and Dismissals	Percentage of Convictions
1890–1894	0	0	0	4	0
1895–1899	0	0	0	1	0
1900–1904	0	1	1	0	100
1905–1909	0	11	11	14	44
1910–1914	9	12	21	16	57
1915–1919	5	8	13	10	57
1920–1924	1	14	15	10	60
1925–1929	4	10	14	2	88
1930–1934	2	6	8	3	73
1935–1939	13	6	19	8	70
1940–1944	110	13	123	40	75
1945–1949	41	9	50	8	86
1950–1954	55	10	65	8	89
1955–1959	65	21	86	11	89
1960–1964	47	17	64	14	82
1965–1969	40	6	46	1	98
Total	395	143	538	150	

Source: Computed from the Bluebook.

Table 5.10 indicates that the amendment to the Sherman Act in 1955 raising the maximum penalty from $5,000 to $50,000[15] has had some impact on the aggregate, and even more on the average, antitrust fines imposed. But the impact was neither immediate—the average fine in the 1955–1959 period, while considerably higher than the average fine in the immediately preceding period, was lower than the average fine in several earlier periods—nor anything like tenfold in magnitude. The average fine for the period 1890–1954 was $38,479; the average fine for the period 1960–1969 was $122,326, less than a fourfold increase. The explanation for the lagged effect of the penalty increase is obvious. The new penalties could be imposed, consistently with constitutional requirements, only on conspiracies begun or continued after 1955, when the amendment became effective. The explanation of why the amendment has thus far effected less than a fourfold increase in the average fine imposed should be obvious too: the amendment simply raised the maximum fine, and a judge is not required to impose the maximum. Judges apparently took the congressional action as a signal for increasing fines somewhat, but not by a factor of ten.

In view of the recent proposal of the Department of Justice to increase the

15. Act of 7 July 1955, ch. 281, 69 Stat. 282, amending 15 U.S.C. secs. 1–3 (1952).

Table 5.9 Criminal Sanctions—Imprisonment

Period in Which Case Was Instituted	Total Number of Criminal Cases	Total Number of Convictions	Prison Sentence Imposed*	Length of Sentence	Characteristics of Case
1890–1894	4	0	0		
1895–1899	1	0	0		
1900–1904	1	1	0		
1905–1909	26	11	0		
1910–1914	37	21	1	4 hours	labor
				4 hours	labor
1915–1919	25	13	3	1 year	labor-sabotage
				1 year	labor
				N.A.	price fixing-labor
				10 days	labor
1920–1924	25	15	5	10 months	labor
				8 months	
				1 year	labor
				6 months	labor
1925–1929	16	14	3	N.A.	price fixing-labor
				10 days	price fixing-violence
				3 months	monopolization-
				6 months	violence
1930–1934	11	8	6	6 months- 2 years	price fixing-violence
				2 years	price fixing-violence
				2–5 months	price fixing-labor violence
				3–6 months	labor-violence
1935–1939	27	19	1	1 year	labor-violence
1940–1944	163	123	0		
1945–1949	58	50	0		
1950–1954	73	65	2	6 months	price fixing-labor
				9 months	price fixing-labor
1955–1959	97	86	2	90 days	price fixing-labor
				1 year	
1960–1964	78	64	2	30 days	price fixing
				N.A.	price fixing
1965–1969	51	46	1	24 hours- 60 days	price fixing
TOTAL	693	536	26		

Source: Computed from the Bluebook.
*Suspended and remitted prison sentences and probation are excluded.

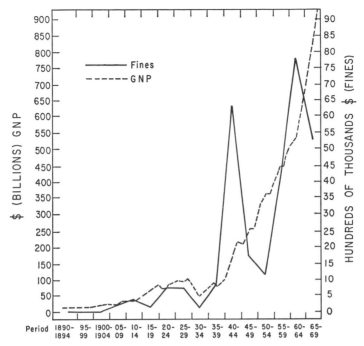

Figure 5.3 Aggregate antitrust fines and the Gross National Product (in current dollars)
Sources: Table 5.10; U.S. Bureau of the Census, Dept. of Commerce, Historical Statistics of
the United States, Colonial Times to 1957; U.S. Bureau of the Census, Dept. of Commerce,
Statistical Abstract[s] of the United States, 1958–1969.

maximum fine in the Sherman Act from $50,000 to $500,000,[16] it bears
emphasizing that a change in maximum penalties is an indirect, and in magnitude uncertain, method of changing the actual penalties. Another tenfold
increase in the maximum today might have even a smaller effect than the
last. In 1955, the maximum penalty under the Sherman Act had remained
unchanged since its enactment in 1890, a period that had seen a tremendous
growth in economic activity and a large decline in the purchasing power of
the dollar. Judges would be less likely to consider the 1955 penalty structure
so soon obsolete.

One would most like to know whether the antitrust criminal remedies, as
they are actually applied, effectively deter price fixing and other concealable
antitrust violations, wherein the need for punitive rather than merely remedial
sanctions is evident (Becker 1968; Posner 1969b). The question cannot be
answered directly. Not only is the incidence of undetected antitrust violations
unknown, but there is another punitive sanction besides the criminal—the

16. See 429 BNA Antitrust & Trade Reg. Rep. (30 Sept. 1969); S.3036, 91st Cong., 1st
Sess. (1969); H.R. 14116, 91st Cong. 1st Sess. (1969).

Table 5.10   Criminal Sanctions—Fines

Period in Which Case Was Instituted (1)	Total Criminal Convictions (2)	Number of Cases in Which Fine Was Imposed (3)	Aggregate Amount of Fines Imposed in Period (4)	Average Fine per Case (Col. 4 ÷ Col. 3)
1890–1894	0	0		
1895–1899	0	0		
1900–1904	1	1	1,000	1,000
1905–1909	11	10	218,875	21,876
1910–1914	21	19	400,090	21,057
1915–1919	13	13	145,857	11,220
1920–1924	15	13	764,850	58,835
1925–1929	14	12	796,510	66,376
1930–1934	8	7	142,444	20,349
1935–1939	19	17	882,914	51,936
1940–1944	123	123	6,319,506	51,378
1945–1949	50	50	1,790,123	35,802
1950–1954	65	64	1,197,537	18,711
1955–1959	86	86	4,306,375	50,074
1960–1964	64	62	7,846,552	126,557
1965–1969	46	46	5,364,633	116,622

Source: Computed from the Bluebook.

penalty component of the treble-damage awards in private antitrust cases—and it would be difficult to disentangle the deterrent effects of each. As a first step, it would be worthwhile to determine the frequency of successful private suits following government price-fixing actions and the magnitude of the awards decreed (or negotiated) in such suits. I have been unable to make this determination because of the statistical deficiencies in the recording of private antitrust actions noted earlier.

Another possibly fruitful and somewhat easier line of attack is to consider the incidence of repeated violations of antitrust law and the punishments meted out to the recidivist. Two obstacles are that the Bluebook, in cases brought before 1952, frequently fails to identify all of the defendants and that it rarely indicates when one defendant, due to a change of name or merger, is the same corporation as, or a predecessor (or successor) to, a defendant in another case. It is possible to ascertain from the Bluebook that 46 of the 320 corporations that were convicted of a criminal violation of the antitrust laws in cases brought between 1964 and 1968 had previously been convicted, in either a civil or criminal case (or several cases), of the same offense (usually price fixing); and in view of the deficiencies just mentioned, the true percentage of recidivists is undoubtedly higher. Ten of the 46 firms had three or more prior convictions.

The courts appear to take a rather lenient attitude toward the antitrust

Table 5.11 Frequency Distribution of Antitrust Fines

Period in Which Case Was Instituted	Percentage of Fines in Various Size Classes									
	$0–10,000	$10,001–25,000	$25,001–50,000	$50,001–75,000	$75,001–125,000	$125,001–200,000	$200,001–300,000	$300,001–500,000	$500,001–1,000,000	$1,000,001–2,000,000
1890–1894										
1895–1899										
1900–1904	100									
1905–1909	50	10	20	20						
1910–1914	63	21		5	5	5				
1915–1919	54	38	8							
1920–1924	23	15	23	15	8	8	8			
1925–1929	25	17	25	8	8	8		8		
1930–1934	57	29	14	6	6					
1935–1939	41	18	24						6	
1940–1944	19	20	27	10	14	7	2	1		
1945–1949	18	30	34	6	10	2				
1950–1954	45	38	18	2	2	2	1			
1955–1959	31	28	20	3	6	7		5		
1960–1964	11	6	27	11	17	11	11	2		
1965–1969	19	24	13	2	13	9	15		7	3

Source: Computed from the Bluebook.

recidivist. The forty-six recidivists were not punished more severely than other defendants in the same case who had a clean record; nor were their officers, in cases in which individuals as well as corporations were charged. These results cannot be explained by the limitations on the judge's sentencing discretion imposed by the statutory maximum, because in only fifteen of the forty-six cases was the maximum penalty imposed in the latest conviction, and in no case was an officer fined more than one-half the maximum. Even in the ten cases in which the corporation had three prior convictions, the maximum penalty was not imposed on the corporation in three. Perhaps the explanation for the courts' lenience is that the concept of corporate, as opposed to individual, recidivism is felt to be unsatisfactory. A widely diversified corporation is quite likely to commit more antitrust violations than one that operates in a single market: Should the first be punished more severely on that account? Should a corporation be charged with the old antitrust violations of a recently acquired division, or with the violations of a previous generation of officers?

Considering the virtual nonuse of imprisonment as a sanction, the rather low average fine in price-fixing cases even in the period since the maximum fine was increased, the high incidence of repeat offenses, and the lenient attitude of the courts toward the repeat offender, I am inclined to question the adequacy of the criminal antitrust remedies, standing alone, as a deterrent to concealable violations, especially price fixing. The long average duration of those conspiracies that are detected adds to one's sense of uneasiness concerning the deterrent adequacy of the present system.

Politics as an Explanatory Factor

I have not attempted to account systematically for most of the variations in the various quantitative indicia of antitrust enforcement presented in this study, although I suggested earlier that changes in the level of overall economic activity could not explain changes in the overall level of antitrust activity. One factor of potentially great explanatory power is politics, the identity of the party in the White House. The parties have, or at least avow, different economic philosophies and antitrust has always been—or seemed—politically controversial (e.g., Hofstadter 1966). The possibility that the politics of the administration affects the quantity or quality of antitrust activity is explored, with negative results, in table 5.12 and figure 5.4. If we exclude the period before 1905, when antitrust activity was quantitatively negligible, Democratic administrations have brought 979 antitrust cases and Republican administrations 550. During this period the Democrats have occupied the White House 58.2 percent of the time. If their share of the cases were proportional to their occupancy of the White House, they would have brought 890 cases; and they have thus exceeded their quota. But this method of measure-

Table 5.12 Department of Justice Antitrust Cases by Presidential Term

Term in Which Instituted	Party in White House	Number Instituted
1890–1893	R	6
1893–1897	D	7
1897–1901	R	3
1901–1905	R	6
1905–1909	R	36
1909–1913	R	74
1913–1917	D	31
1917–1921	D	48
1921–1925	R	51
1925–1929	R	54
1929–1933	R	19
1933–1937	D	24
1937–1941	D	115
1941–1945	D	157
1945–1949	D	126
1949–1953	D	148
1953–1957	R	106
1957–1961	R	171
1961–1965	D	176
1965–1969	D	154
1969	R	39

Source: Computed from the Bluebook.

ment is obviously unfair to the Republicans, whose presidential terms are bunched in the early part of the period when the level of antitrust activity, regardless of the party in power, was much lower than later. Let us therefore split the period since the enactment of the Sherman Act into two parts, an earlier and a later period. A natural break between them comes at the end of Franklin D. Roosevelt's first term, in which 24 cases were filed; his next term the figure jumped to 115. In the earlier period, the Democrats occupied the White House 40.1 percent of the time and if their share of cases were the same they would have brought 144; they brought only 110. In the later period the Democrats occupied the White House 72.8 percent of the time and "should" have brought 868. They exceeded this quota very slightly, bringing 876.

A further refinement is to compare Republican and Democratic antitrust enforcement (for the period since 1936) eliminating those years in which the economy was in recession (GNP declined). The results are as before. The total number of cases brought in nonrecession years since 1936 is 1,008. Based on the number of nonrecession years in which they occupied the White House during this period, the Democrats "should" have brought 747; they in fact exceeded this quota very slightly, bringing 763. An additional test of the impact of politics on antitrust enforcement is whether the number of cases

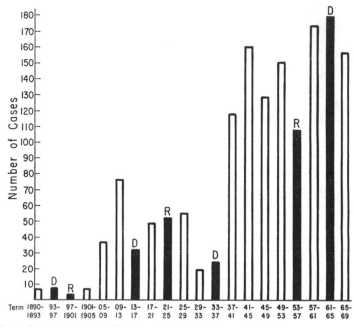

Figure 5.4   Department of Justice cases initiated by presidential term
Source: Table 5.12
*Terms in which the party in the White House changed are indicated by a solid bar.

brought in presidential election years is above or below average. If politics had no effect, we would expect that 25 percent of all Department of Justice antitrust cases would have been initiated in such years; in fact 26.7 percent have been initiated in such years. Finally, as shown in figure 5.4, in which the solid bars indicate the number of cases brought in the first term after a change of parties, no systematic tendency of one party to increase or decrease antitrust activity upon taking office appears.

Since the enactment of the Sherman Act the Democrats have been in the White House 48.1 percent of the time and their "quota" of landmark cases is therefore 22.8. They have modestly exceeded this, bringing a total of 24.2, in fact.

On such evidence as I have been able to gather, it does not appear that the identity of the party in power has much influence on the quantity or quality of the Justice Department's antitrust activity.

CHAPTER SIX

The Economic Determinants of
Antitrust Activity

WILLIAM F. LONG, RICHARD SCHRAMM,
AND ROBERT D. TOLLISON

The literature on the welfare costs of monopoly and the estimated consumer gains from its elimination[1] provides at least an implicit basis for formulating antitrust policy in cost-benefit terms. In principle, antitrust agencies can use welfare-loss models to measure the benefits of bringing particular cases and other actions against firms. Then weighing these benefits against the associated costs of bringing antitrust actions, the agencies can determine their optimal resource allocation strategy.

But while they are easily formulated, what do these normative prescriptions for antitrust policy have to do with the actual behavior of antitrust agencies? And what role (if any) do economic measures of the costs and pervasiveness of monopoly power play in the conduct of the affairs of the government overseers of competition?

This study derives and tests linkages between the prescriptions of economists and the actual case-bringing activity of the Antitrust Division of the Justice Department over the last twenty-five years. We draw on the recently published data of Posner (1970) on how antitrust activities have in fact been conducted in the past and compare a benefit-cost model of desirable antitrust behavior with actual antitrust activity to assess the role of economic factors in the conduct of antitrust policy. In effect we draw on the prescriptive studies of economics to see to what extent industry welfare losses, and the components of welfare losses which measure the price impact of monopoly and the industry size, explain the historical distribution of antitrust cases across different manufacturing industries.

The first section presents the traditional welfare-loss triangle model and relates these losses to the case allocation problem faced by the Antitrust Division. The second section uses the welfare-loss model to try to explain the actual allocation of antitrust cases across industries and the sensitivity of these results to several important underlying assumptions. The third section reviews some qualifications that are important in interpreting the results.

This essay was previously published in the *Journal of Law and Economics* 16 (October 1973): 351–64. © 1973 by The University of Chicago. All rights reserved.
1. The empirical literature on this subject dates from Arnold C. Harberger's (1954) classic paper.

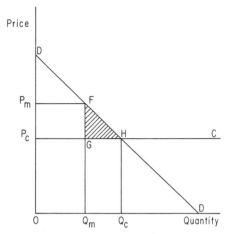

Figure 6.1   Welfare losses due to resource misallocation resulting from monopoly

Finally, the fourth section summarizes the results and discusses the implications of this study for antitrust policy.

The Economic Benefits and Costs of Antitrust Activity

As a basic model to explain the case-bringing behavior of the Antitrust Division, we assume the Division rationally weighs the economic benefits and costs of bringing individual cases and proceeds most frequently in industries in which the benefits most exceed the costs. We also assume initially that this benefit-cost approach is unconstrained by legal or other factors. These factors are clearly very important determinants of Antitrust Division behavior, but we wish to focus this study primarily on economic factors. Later we consider some of the qualifying effects that these constraints may have on our model and results.

The Basic Welfare-Loss Model

The economic benefits from antitrust cases are most simply represented by an extension of the welfare-loss procedure as presented by Harberger (1954). The welfare losses due to resource misallocation resulting from monopoly are shown in figure 6.1. D–D is the linear long-run demand curve for a given product; P_c–C is the long-run average and marginal cost curve, assumed constant and equal for all firms. In long-run competitive equilibrium the price, P_c, would prevail, and the quantity, Q_c, would be sold. Under monopoly the product would be priced at P_m as the monopolist produces less (Q_m) to secure the higher price and profits. The triangle of F–G–H represents the net welfare loss resulting from monopoly, assuming the stockholders gaining income from the increased price have the same marginal utility of income as the consumers losing income by paying the higher price charged by the monopolist and assuming that P_c–C is the competitive cost function after dissolution of the monopoly. Under these conditions triangle F–G–H represents the lost consumer surplus due to the existence of monopoly power.

The welfare-loss triangle provides a simple measure of the net economic gains from the reallocation of resources arising from de-monopolization of industries. If we equate the potential total benefits from antitrust action with this welfare measure, then, other things being equal, antitrust activity against firms in industries should be positively correlated with the relative magnitude of the industry welfare-loss triangle.

An alternative measure of benefits, which includes the redistributive effects of monopoly, is a weighted average of the welfare-loss triangle F–G–H and the excess profits rectangle P_m–P_c–F–G. This can be viewed as the returns from antitrust action if the loss of income from consumers due to higher prices is weighed more heavily by antitrust officials than the increase in utility to stockholders enjoying the higher profits. The weights placed on the two components would reflect the relative concern for deadweight welfare losses versus income redistribution from consumers to monopoly shareholders.

Measuring the Benefits and Costs of Antitrust Activity

From figure 6.1 the area of the welfare-loss triangle can be measured as $\frac{1}{2}(\pi/S)^2$ S E, where π is excess profits, S is sales, and E is the price elasticity of demand.[2] While profit and sales estimates are available, measurements of the price elasticity of demand are much more difficult to obtain. In the absence of more precise elasticity estimates, we assume in the basic model that the elasticity is the same in all industries considered. This follows Harberger's approach which used the unit elasticity of 1.0 for computing welfare losses in different industry groups. Since we are interested in relative benefits, if we assume constant elasticity across industries, we can choose any value for this constant. For simplicity we use a value of 1.0. Benefits under this assumption, B_H, become

(1) $$B_H = \frac{1}{2}(\pi/S)^2 S$$

An alternative assumption about elasticity is that used by Kamerschen

---

2. The proof for linear demand and cost conditions is available in most price theory textbooks. See, for example, F. M. Scherer, Industrial Market Structure and Economic Performance (1970), at 401–2. This proof is strictly for the case of a movement from monopoly to competition. The same formula holds for movement down the demand curve to competition from any point between F and H. If P_o, Q_o, S_o, and E_o are price, quantity, sales, and elasticity at some point between F and H, then $\frac{1}{2} (\pi/S)^2$ S E at that point is equal to $\frac{1}{2} [(P_o\text{-}P_c)/P_o]^2 (P_oQ_o) [(Q_c\text{-}Q_o)/(P_o\text{-}P_c)]/(Q_o/P_o)$. Simplification of this term gives $\frac{1}{2} [(P_o\text{-}P_c)/(Q_c\text{-}Q_o)]$, which is the area of the appropriate triangle.

(1966) who employed Lerner's measure of monopoly power (price minus marginal cost all divided by price) to derive S/π as an estimate of elasticity. Under this assumption benefits, B_K, are

$$(2) \qquad B_K = \frac{1}{2}(\pi/S)^2 S \, (S/\pi) = (\frac{1}{2})\pi$$

The Harberger and Kamerschen welfare-loss measures utilize the performance measure, π/S, directly. An alternative approach to measuring welfare losses is to specify welfare losses in terms of the structural variables that determine π/S. Assuming π/S is positively related to concentration, we can substitute this relationship into equations (1) and (2), so that welfare benefits from antitrust action depend on concentration, sales, and elasticity. Measures of barriers to entry could also be introduced in a similar fashion. However, since the entry-barrier approach involves especially difficult theoretical and measurement problems, it will not be employed in the empirical analysis to follow.

The costs of bringing antitrust cases are more difficult to represent. Basically, they are the economic costs involved in bringing cases to successful completion, including investigation and courtroom expense for both the Antitrust Division and the company, and any indirect costs of the case. One way to measure such costs would be to estimate the actual outlays of time and money on past cases, using information such as the internal records of the Antitrust Division and the firm against which cases were brought. Since this information is not readily available, we have no method of directly measuring costs of bringing cases. Thus, we initially make the assumption that it is equally costly for the Antitrust Division to bring cases against all industries. Later, we test this assumption by introducing an indirect measure of costs which differs across industries.

The various measures of benefits and costs could be used to help guide antitrust case-bringing activity at different levels of industry aggregation, with or without estimates of demand elasticity, and with measures of performance and/or structural variables. What influence these measures, or their component variables, have had on actual antitrust activity in the past is the question discussed in the next section.

Economic Models and Actual Antitrust Activity

The basic model presented in the first section provides a simple economic basis for guiding the Antitrust Division's allocation of resources in reducing monopoly power in different industries. The benefit-cost model developed in that same section is not expected to fully explain actual antitrust activity which is, of course, subject to a wide variety of forces other than those incorporated in this model. The model and its economic ingredients, however, provide a useful starting point in explaining actual antitrust activity and, of equal interest, a basis for estimating the role and importance of welfare-loss considerations in the Antitrust Division's behavior.

We should note that while we are trying to use a model of benefit-cost analysis to explain differences in the number of antitrust cases brought against different industries, we are not requiring that all cases be brought against the industries in which the highest benefits could be secured. To maximize the benefits possible from a fixed budget, one would want to bring cases against the industry with the highest benefit-cost ratio until the point at which the ratio in the highest industry equals the ratio in the next highest. Then cases should be brought against two industries, and so forth. We are making the weaker assumption that if the Division follows the approach suggested here, it will tend to bring more cases against industries with high benefit-cost ratios than against industries with low ratios.

In this section we are essentially comparing alternative economic explanations of antitrust case-bringing behavior, based on the welfare-loss triangle model. First, we test the effects of aggregate welfare losses. For a given elasticity assumption, however, welfare losses can be broken down into two main ingredients: monopoly price effects measured by industry concentration or excess profit rate on sales, and industry size as measured by industry sales. These ingredients provide two additional hypotheses of the determinants of antitrust activity—monopoly power and industry size—which we subject to empirical analysis. Finally, we test some of the critical assumptions of the model.

Our data were all the cases brought by the Antitrust Division against two-digit SIC manufacturing industries during the period 1945–1970. We collected data on average profits and sales over the same period and computed excess profits from rates of return on capital in different industries using total assets in 1956 as a base.[3]

Cases Brought and Aggregate Welfare Benefits

To examine the relationship between cases brought and aggregate welfare benefits, we first ran ordinary least squares regressions of cases brought, N, on industry welfare losses as measured in the first section. The results are presented in table 6.1.

Equations 1a and 1b indicate that there is a positive relationship between cases brought and B_H and B_K, although the benefit measures explain a very

3. Excess profits in each industry were computed from the excess rate of return in that industry relative to the lowest rate of return industry in the manufacturing sector. Alternatively, we could have computed excess profit rates relative to the "average" rate of return in manufacturing, but this would have produced negative rates of return for some industries. In either case, we are measuring relative rather than absolute potential benefits from antitrust action.

Table 6.1   Antitrust Cases and Aggregate
Welfare Losses

		$\overline{R}^2$
1a	N = 20.70 + .308 B_H	.013
	(5.05) (1.12)	
1b	N = 16.82 + .029 B_K	.164
	(3.88) (2.17)	
1c	N = 12.78 + .047π − 1.35B_H	.320
	(2.97) (3.02) (2.27)	

$\overline{R}^2$ = Coefficient of multiple determination adjusted
for degrees of freedom.
"t" statistics in parentheses.

small fraction of antitrust activity against manufacturing industries. Equation 1c, which relates cases brought to both deadweight welfare loss, B_H, and the magnitude of income redistribution, π, explains case-bringing behavior somewhat better, but the sign on B_H is wrong. This result is probably due to multicollinearity between B_H and π; the simple correlation coefficient between them is .92. All in all, aggregate benefit measures do a poor job of explaining the distribution of antitrust cases across manufacturing industry groups.

Cases Brought and Components of Welfare Benefits

Table 6.2 shows the empirical relation between cases brought and the component variables of B_H and B_K, treating welfare loss as simple linear functions of the square of the profit rate and sales, for B_H, and the profit rate and sales, for B_K.[4] Both equations 2a and 2b reveal a very important role for industry sales in explaining cases brought, but little importance for profit rate in this

Table 6.2   Antitrust Cases, Profit Rates, Sales,
and Elasticity

		$\overline{R}^2$
2a	N = 8.54 + 1075.3$(\pi/S)^2$ + .0007 S	.438
	(1.89) (.339) (3.90)	
2b	N = 7.81 − 85.74(π/S) + .00073 S	.442
	(1.58) (.48) (3.77)	

$\overline{R}^2$ = Coefficient of multiple determination adjusted
for degrees of freedom.
"t" statistics in parentheses.

4. While a logarithmic form would be more appropriate (since the variables enter multiplicatively), the existence of zero values in the data precluded its use.

Table 6.3   Antitrust Cases, Concentration Ratios, and Sales

		$\bar{R}^2$
3a	$N = 12.57 - .123\,C + .00080\,S$	.451
	(1.91) (.729) (4.17)	
3b	$N = -4.37 + 1.08\,C - .015\,C^2 + .00066\,S$	.495
	(.35) (1.38) (1.57) (3.22)	

$\bar{R}^2$ = Coefficient of multiple determination adjusted for degrees of
freedom.
"t" statistics in parentheses.

form of the model. Since 2b, which is based on the Kamerschen measure, is not markedly better than 2a, and since the elasticity assumption is subject to substantially more criticism, we will drop the S/π elasticity estimate for the balance of our empirical analysis.

Cases Brought and Concentration

The above results measure monopoly power using a performance variable, profit rate on sales. An alternative measure for monopoly power is to use a structural variable such as concentration in place of the profit rate, as discussed in the first section. Table 6.3 presents the regression results, substituting an industry concentration measure, C, for $(\pi/S)^2$. We used both a linear and a quadratic relationship between C and $(\pi/S)^2$ when making the substitution.

Equation 3a reveals that there is no statistically significant relationship between concentration and cases brought, essentially replicating the findings of Posner (1970). However, when concentration enters quadratically, the influence of concentration on cases brought increases (although neither coefficient is statistically significant) with a slight increase in the explanatory power of the equation. These results suggest that as industry concentration increases, more cases are brought against that industry. However, the cases brought do not increase in proportion to the increase in concentration and, beyond some point, may actually begin to decrease.

An Indirect Measure of Antitrust Costs

To this point we have focused on the role of benefits from bringing antitrust cases and treated the costs as constant across industries. In the absence of a direct estimate of the costs of case-bringing activity, it is necessary to introduce an indirect measure to test the importance of costs on antitrust activity. One way to estimate the costs to the Antitrust Division indirectly is to estimate the industry resources available to fight or prolong antitrust action against the industry. While industry economic and political power, and the resulting

Table 6.4   Antitrust Cases, Profit Rate or Concentration, Sales and Total Assets

		$\overline{R^2}$
4a	$N = 8.87 + 2836.5\,(\pi/S)^2 + .00097\,S - .00055\,TA$	.416
	(1.91) (.65) (2.28) (.60)	
4b	$N = -5.05 + 1.17\,C - .0161\,C^2 + .00080\,S - .00034\,TA$	.471
	(.39) (1.43) (1.61) (2.30) (.52)	

$\overline{R^2}$ = Coefficient of multiple determination adjusted for degrees of freedom.
"t" statistics in parentheses.

case-bringing costs, may already be represented in part by profit rate, concentration, or sales, we surmise that the main effect of these variables would be on the benefits rather than the cost side, since they enter the welfare-benefits measure. Another measure of industry power which does not enter the welfare-benefits measure, however, is industry capitalization. Thus, we use industry total assets, TA, as a surrogate for costs and predict a negative influence of total assets on antitrust cases brought.

Equations 4a and 4b of Table 6.4 indicate that total assets have a negative but not statistically significant influence on antitrust cases when added to the disaggregated welfare-benefit equation. The explanatory power of the equations, furthermore, is reduced through the addition of this variable.

Aggregation Problems

A final concern of our empirical analysis is the effect of industry aggregation on the results. The two-digit industry groups in manufacturing are highly aggregated, as is well known. If all the subgroups of a two-digit industry are very similar, then the use of aggregated measures of profit rate, concentration, sales and total assets probably does not introduce a great deal of bias in our results. For a very heterogenous two-digit industry, however, aggregation and the resulting average values for industry variables probably biases the effects of these variables on antitrust cases in a downward direction.

In an attempt to correct for the bias of industry diversity, we used the number of four-digit subgroups within the two-digit aggregates as a measure of diversity, DIV. We predict a positive influence of diversity on antitrust cases brought.

Table 6.5 shows the effects of adding the diversity variable. Introduction of the correction for diversity substantially improves both the profit rate (equations 5a and 5b) and the concentration (equations 5c and 5d) forms of the model. In the profit rate version, not only is diversity highly significant, but the effect of profitability is also improved. The coefficient of $(\pi/S)^2$ in equation 5a is greater than in equation 2a, and is now significantly greater than zero. Some of this improvement appears to be at the expense of sales, with both the coefficient and the t-statistic falling.

Table 6.5   The Effects of Industry Diversity on Antitrust Cases

		$\bar{R}^2$
5a	$N = -3.82 + 5397.0(\pi/S)^2 + .00037\,S + .78\,DIV$ (.72) (1.87) (1.91) (3.19)	.635
5b	$N = -3.44 + 6692.2(\pi/S)^2 + .00055\,S + .77\,DIV - .00042\,TA$ (.63) (1.79) (1.48) (3.08) (.565)	.619
5c	$N = -13.66 + 1.03\,C - .0124\,C^2 + .00041\,S + .55\,DIV$ (1.12) (1.45) (1.42) (1.85) (2.10)	.584
5d	$N = 13.88 + .975\,C - .0117\,C^2 + .00031\,S + .59\,DIV + .00020\,TA$ (1.10) (1.30) (1.24) (.756) (1.98) (.30)	.558

$\bar{R}^2$ = Coefficient of multiple determination adjusted for degrees of freedom.
"t" statistics in parentheses.

The overall effect on the concentration version of the model is also striking. The level of significance of the diversity variable is not as great, however, and the impact of concentration is essentially unaltered.

Some Qualifications

In practice, there are many reasons why the Antitrust Division brings cases against different industries and why the welfare-loss model and the assumption of equal costs for case-bringing activity against all industries may not "fit" antitrust behavior. The Division may respond to complaints brought to it; it may seek out cases in which there is a high probability of winning; it may try to establish precedents; and so on. We are basically interested in this paper in the empirical issue of whether cases are brought where they could have the most impact on economic welfare. It is useful, however, to mention briefly some general reasons why the welfare-loss model would have to be adapted considerably in practice to describe an optimal antitrust strategy.

The data on antitrust cases brought compiled by Posner do not allow us to distinguish between conduct cases and monopoly cases in which dissolution is sought. Conduct cases (for example, *American Tobacco*) are intended to show that tacit collusion or certain business activities are illegal and only indirectly seek to increase competition in an industry. On the other hand, it obviously makes sense to attack high-profit firms (for example, Alcoa) when dissolution is sought..However, we would note that there is some justification in including both conduct and monopoly cases in our tests. When welfare gains from conduct cases can be adequately defined, then such cases should be brought where welfare gains are high.

Problems of legal strategy are not considered in the simple welfare-loss model. These problems are important in antitrust policy. Once the economic data on which antitrust cases should be brought is developed, legal strategy would dictate that estimates be made of the probabilities of winning cases and that perhaps expected value estimates of the benefits from antitrust policy be developed. Thus, one may find examples in practice in which local or regional cartels that are inherently unstable are prosecuted because the probability of winning the case and establishing a precedent for use against all firms may outweigh the small direct economic benefits from such cases.[5]

The welfare-loss model does not directly provide for preventive antitrust action to stop monopoly before it comes into existence. For example, in the food and beverage industry many of the cases brought were merger cases which helped to avert an increase in welfare losses. However, merger cases could be ranked ex ante by potential welfare losses and gains, compared to the costs of litigation, and antitrust policy devised accordingly. In this way an element of preventive antitrust policy can be addressed in the welfare-loss model.

Finally, the Antitrust Division would have to sort out which are legal monopoly returns (for example, patents) and which are illegal. The welfare loss data picks up both types and thus biases the outcomes to some extent against the Antitrust Division. A similar problem exists when the excess profits and welfare losses are due to entry barriers. One might argue here that the Antitrust Division cannot bring a case if competition does not emerge and the oligopolists do not engage in collusive activities. However, this is not a foregone conclusion since the welfare-loss model may imply dissolution and structural remedies. In effect we are discussing antitrust policy in a simple cost-benefit sense and not with respect to whether it is possible to implement such an approach under existing U.S. antitrust law.

Summary and Conclusions

We have presented an economic model for the allocation of antitrust resources stressing welfare-loss measures and the economic variables that underlie the welfare-loss measures. We then tested the model's ability to yield qualified explanations of past antitrust behavior on the assumption that it costs the same for the Antitrust Division to bring a case against any industry. We stress that our empirical results are tentative and suggestive of the need for additional research in this area.

The composite measures of the potential benefits from antitrust action that we tested—the welfare-loss triangle alone or together with excess profits—appear to play a minor role in explaining antitrust activity. However, in models in which component economic variables are separated out, industry sales appear as a strong explanatory variable throughout. Furthermore, profit rate and concentration variables increase the explanatory power of the models but appear to play a secondary role to industry sales. Adding industry assets

5. Richard A. Posner (1970) presents evidence on this type of behavior by the Antitrust Division.

to correct for the costs of bringing cases does not change these results, although a possible negative influence of this variable on antitrust activity is worth further study. Including a variable to correct for suspected aggregation bias substantially improves the results, with the apparent additional effect of increasing the relative importance of the profit rate on sales.

The empirical analysis suggests that industry size, as measured by sales, is the most important industry economic characteristic determining antitrust case-bringing activities. Variables more closely measuring monopoly actual or potential performance, such as profit rate on sales, concentration, and aggregate welfare losses play a less important role in explaining antitrust activity.

While economic variables may influence antitrust decisions, we should stress that all the models tested explain at best about 60 percent of the variance in cases brought across industries. Much of the explanation of antitrust activity clearly lies outside our model. This indicates the need for additional work in specifying and testing models such as those we have presented. Such work should be aimed at approximating an optimal allocation of existing antitrust resources and, with the development of proper cost data, perhaps even extended to derive an optimal size antitrust budget. These are important extensions worth further research, and they blend nicely with Posner's (1970) call for greater efforts by the Antitrust Division to develop statistical information on its activities.

CHAPTER SEVEN

Is Collusion Profitable?

PETER ASCH AND JOSEPH J. SENECA

This paper reports on an empirical examination of the role of collusion in the profitability of American manufacturing corporations during the period 1958–1967. The study attempts to determine (a) whether the profit rates of collusive firms differ from those of noncolluders, and (b) whether the incidence of collusion can itself be explained on the basis of the structure and performance patterns of affected firms and markets. The results reported below indicate that collusive firms are consistently less profitable than noncolluders, and that important structural differences exist between the two groups.

The meaning of these results is not fully obvious, for collusion and profitability may be linked in a number of ways. Even under alternative causality hypotheses, however, the findings raise some question about the effects both of collusive conduct and of public policies to restrict such conduct.

Background

A substantial interest in the theory and consequences of collusion is reflected in the literature of the past thirty years. At the same time, public policies against conspiracy, pursued under Section 1 of the Sherman Act, have consumed a major portion of antitrust resources. Yet, despite these apparent incentives, empirical investigation of collusion has been limited.

The paucity of evidence may be attributed in part to two factors. First is the theoretical and definitional ambiguity that surrounds the subject. Collusive oligopoly[1] is often treated as a special case of monopoly in which the market outcome may be subject to significant qualification. A rational collusive group striving to maximize joint profits may be prevented from doing so by the prisoner's-dilemma nature of the pricing problem. Further, the fact that conspirators are unlikely to hold identical preferences about group policies may

This essay was previously published in the *Review of Economics and Statistics* 58 (February 1976): 1–12.

1. Since the incentive to collude presupposes interdependence among firms, collusion is, almost by definition, an oligopolistic phenomenon.

suggest the necessity for side payments and/or the existence of a bargaining problem in the determination of prices and outputs.

These difficulties or costs of collusion point to the possible instability of such arrangements, and to the probability of imperfection in attaining group goals while agreements are in force. Profit performance expectations are, accordingly, imprecise. Collusive markets may demonstrate "tendencies" toward the monopolistic result (Fellner 1949), but neither the strength nor the consistency of such tendencies is easily characterized.

An associated problem of definition adds a further difficulty. If by collusion one means an explicit, cartel-type agreement, it is not clear that performance will differ consistently from that which occurs under equally rational but less formal kinds of coordination.[2] If, on the other hand, one joins Machlup (1952, 432ff.) in the view that virtually all oligopolistic behavior is collusive to some degree (see also Bain 1968, 306ff.), it is difficult to discuss the effects of such conduct, for there is no longer a noncollusive point of comparison.

Any study of collusion must therefore confront not only somewhat uncertain performance expectations, but also the direct dependence of these expectations upon the definition of collusion that is adopted. Given such circumstances, it is not surprising to observe that beneath the widely shared opinion that collusion is undesirable, there is considerable disagreement as to how serious a public problem it may pose.[3]

A second major obstacle to the empirical study of collusion is the existence of formidable data problems. Collusive activity is usually illegal and therefore surreptitious. Furthermore, when such activity has been discovered, antitrust adherence to a rule of per se illegality has discouraged exploration of its market consequences.

For purposes of statistical examination, the resolution of both these difficulties is in effect dictated by data availability. In identifying "collusive" firms and thereby defining collusion, there is no ready alternative to the use of legal criteria. In addition, structure and performance patterns can be observed for large samples only at the firm and industry levels rather than on narrower product-line bases which would undoubtedly be more appropriate in some cases.

2. It might be hypothesized that, *ceteris paribus,* explicit agreements will be more effective than tacit understandings. But in a legal environment that is far more likely to penalize explicitness, such behavior may be undertaken only when circumstances (e.g., poor performance) dictate relatively desperate measures. The conditions surrounding overt and covert agreements may thus tend to be noncomparable. For an interesting theoretical treatment, see Williamson (1965).

3. Indeed, the possibility of beneficial effects has been suggested by Phillips (1962) and Downie (1958) among others and is explicitly recognized in the laws of most industrialized Western nations. McGee (1971), conceding that cartels may be "hurtful," nevertheless states that "most of them probably do not accomplish much for very long" (p. 133). F. M. Scherer,

Approach to the Problem

Although it is reasonable to suppose that firms collude in order to increase their profits, expectations concerning the relationship between observable (i.e., illegal) collusion and profitability are by no means clear. Collusion in the general sense may tend to raise profits, *ceteris paribus*,[4] but the law focuses on a narrower subset of all collusive events.

Without becoming enmeshed in the question of what the courts may mean by collusion or conspiracy, it should be obvious that agreements to fix prices or divide markets can be prosecuted only when they became visible; and that this in itself implies some tendency for litigation to center on overt (or even flagrant) collusive episodes (Posner 1970). Whether these relatively formal manifestations of collusion will be profitable vis-à-vis alternative forms of rational oligopoly behavior is not clear.

In attempting to isolate the collusion-profitability relationship, it is obviously necessary to take account of other influences on firm profits. Variables that have been found significant in past profit studies are therefore examined. These include, at the industry level, concentration, which has tended to show a positive effect in numerous studies. Also, industry advertising intensity is expected to have a direct impact on profits, both because of its role in raising entry barriers through product differentiation and because economies of scale may exist in promotional activity.

At the firm level the growth rate of sales reflects variations in demand over the period and is expected to exert a positive effect on profit rates. Firm asset size is included on the ground that it may be indicative of entry barriers; however, the expected direction of its influence on profits is, on balance, unclear, and findings reported in the literature have been mixed. In addition, firm-temporal measures of risk are introduced to take account of the possibility that observed profit variations may in part represent differences in the degree of risk exposure.

The measure of firm profitability is the rate of return to stockholders' equity. This profit rate was chosen as theoretically appropriate and is in any case highly correlated with alternative measures. Collusion is introduced in the form of a binary variable.

Equations incorporating these variables are first examined for a sample of 101 firms. A binary variable indicating whether firms are primarily in pro-

Industrial Market Structure and Economic Performance (1970), although cognizant of the obstacles to effective collusion, appears more troubled by potential effects (pp. 161–62). The dimmest view of all has been taken by the American courts, which have long held that collusive agreements lead consistently to inferior market performance and are to be prohibited without case-by-case examination of their consequences (e.g., United States v. Trenton Potteries Co.).

4. In fact, empirical studies of profitability usually include market concentration as an explanatory variable on the ground that high levels of concentration are conducive to effective collusion and lead to higher profit rates.

ducer or consumer goods industries is also introduced. The sample is then divided according to this classification and each subsample is examined separately.

The purpose of this dichotomy is twofold. First, there is some presumption that producer goods industries are more (product) homogeneous, or at least less vulnerable to "artificial" product differentiation. This suggests that certain variables, most notably advertising, may perform differently within each group.[5] Secondly, there are plausible reasons to think that collusion may be more effective (or less costly and hence more likely) in the more standardized product markets.[6] The implication of the dichotomy with respect to the latter point is contestable, however. It also may be argued that if buyers' markets for consumer goods are relatively atomistic, price cuts to individual buyers are relatively unprofitable, cheating is less of a problem, and the prospects for collusion are thereby enhanced.

Following the analysis of firm profit rates, an attempt is made to explain the incidence of collusion in terms of several firm and market structure-performance elements. This procedure reflects awareness of the difficulty encountered in assessing the direction of causality between collusion and profitability.

Data

The study employs a sample of large manufacturing corporations, most of which appear on the *Fortune 500* lists, and all of which are reported in *Moody's Industrial Manual* during the period 1958–1967. The sample of 51 collusive firms consists of companies that were found guilty or entered pleas of *nolo contendere* in response to Sherman Act conspiracy charges during the period.[7] Firms were excluded if comprehensive data (including Standard Industrial Classification [S.I.C.] industry groupings)[8] were unavailable. The sample of 50 noncollusive firms was drawn randomly from *Moody's*, subject to similar data availability.

Firm Variables

The profit rate is the mean value of the ratio of net income after taxes to stockholders' equity for the period. Firm size is measured by the logarithm

5. In addition, the subsamples avoid the relatively high collinearity of advertising with the output classification measure which is present in the full sample.

6. The usual argument is that the task of collusion is simpler in such a setting. This may be true even if producer goods are *not* "more" homogeneous, so long as the product differences are themselves subject to relatively objective interpretation.

7. Reported in Commerce Clearing House, Trade Regulation Reporter, summaries of antitrust cases.

8. Companies were assigned to four-digit S.I.C. groupings on the basis of descriptions in Moody's and Poor's Register of Corporations, Directors and Executives. In some cases concentration was calculated on the basis of a weighted average of more than one grouping.

of mean total assets. The compound annual growth rate of sales revenue for 1958 1967 is used to reflect firm growth. These data are derived from *Moody's*.

In order to examine risk, a trend regression is estimated to the profit rates of each firm over the time period. Risk is then measured by the standard deviation and skewness of the residuals about this trend. The standard deviation of the residuals captures the range of profit variation, and higher risk is reflected in greater variability. Increased risk exposure is also associated with positive skewness.[9] Therefore, both measures of risk have a positive a priori relation with firm profitability.

Industry Variables

Concentration is measured by the four-firm value-of-shipments ratios compiled by the Bureau of the Census, as adjusted by Shepherd (1970, appendix tab. 8).[10] Industry advertising intensity is measured by the ratio of advertising expenditures to business receipts as reported by the Internal Revenue Service (I.R.S.).[11] The breakdown of the complete sample of firms into consumer and producer goods categories is based on classifications employed in the Index of Industrial Production.[12] The ratio of firm to industry profitability over the period is also used to provide a measure of relative performance.

Empirical Results

An extension of the large literature analyzing firm profitability offers an initial test of the association between collusive behavior and profit rates. Table 7.1 presents regression equations for the entire sample of firms and for the two subsamples classified by type of primary output: consumer or producer goods.

---

9. Pearsonian skewness is the measure used, viz., Skewness = 3 (Mean–Median)/Standard Deviation. This measure provides an intuitive interpretation of skewness as a risk variable. A positive median implies most of the actual values of profitability exceed the trend prediction. Since the mean of the trend residuals is always zero, a positive median results in negative skewness; thus as skewness becomes more negative, risk declines. Alternatively, a negative median indicates most of the actual profit rates are below the trend predictions. A negative median yields a positive measure of skewness. As skewness becomes more positive, exposure to risk increases.

10. Adjustments are for over- and under-inclusiveness of market definitions, the regional or local nature of some markets, and exclusion of significant imports. The unadjusted concentration ratio, highly collinear with the adjusted, was also used. A measure of economies of scale—the proportion of industry value added originating in plants over a specified employment size—was also highly collinear with the concentration measures.

11. Matching of Census Industries (S.I.C.) and I.R.S. Industries (Standard Enterprise Classification) is based on Statistics of Income, Corporation Income Tax Returns (1963), table 3. Advertising intensity is measured for 1965, although it is highly collinear ($r = .99$) with the average intensity over the full period for which data are available (1964–1967).

12. Of the 101 firms examined, 45 were classified as consumer goods; of these, 19 were colluders.

Table 7.1   Firm Profitability Analysis (dependent variable = net income/equity)

Sample and Equation	Concentration Ratio	Advertising-Sales Ratio	Compound Annual Growth in Sales	Collusion Binary Variable	Log of Firm Assets	Standard Deviation of Residuals	Skewness of Residuals	Consumer-Producer Goods Binary Variable	Constant	R^2
I. All Firms										
1	4.296	.3961	236.920	−26.033	3.3171	.1487	10.496	4.635	41.977	.282
	(1.65)	(2.16)	(3.03)	(3.09)	(0.91)	(0.75)	(1.78)	(0.50)	(1.79)	
2	5.217	.4159	235.643	−23.612	—	—	9.975	—	59.288	.294
	(2.26)	(2.74)	(3.05)	(2.96)			(1.75)		(3.45)	
II. Consumer Goods										
3	4.699	.3579	246.345	−26.407	.4487	.1105	18.503	—	61.019	.168
	(0.85)	(1.38)	(1.44)	(1.64)	(0.06)	(0.27)	(1.76)		(1.20)	
4	5.306	.3464	254.952	−26.088	—	—	17.835	—	62.297	.208
	(1.16)	(1.50)	(1.55)	(1.72)			(1.79)		(1.93)	
III. Producer Goods										
5	3.540	−.1630	245.568	−29.754	4.925	.1271	1.381	—	43.967	.263
	(1.15)	(0.20)	(2.97)	(2.88)	(1.29)	(0.59)	(0.19)		(1.55)	
6	4.083	—	245.039	−28.567	4.276	—	—	—	45.914	.300
	(1.44)		(3.05)	(3.05)	(1.22)				(1.99)	

Figures in parentheses are t-statistics.

In addition to the explanatory variables conventionally used in studies of firm profitability, a binary variable indicating the presence of firm collusion is included in the data set (coded 1 for firms convicted of collusion during the period).

The major finding seen in table 7.1 is that after accounting for other basic influences, the presence of collusive behavior is negatively associated with firm profitability in all three samples. Within the two subsamples, however, this relation is somewhat more significant for producer goods firms (e.g., the t-statistic for collusion is 1.64 in equation 3 compared with $t = 2.88$ in the comparable equation 5). The performance of the traditional explanatory variables of firm profit rates generally supports previous findings and provides reasonable *ceteris paribus* conditions for this conclusion.

Equations 1 and 2 summarize the results for the full sample. Firm profitability is related positively to industry concentration and advertising intensity. The positive relation of concentration continues in both the consumer and producer goods subsamples (equations 3 through 6) although advertising intensity becomes insignificant (and negative) for the relatively output-homogeneous producer goods firms (equation 5).[13]

The change in the demand for the firm's products as measured by the compound annual growth rate in sales is positive throughout the equations and exerts an important effect on firm profitability (e.g., an elasticity at the means of 1.6 in equation 2). The importance of such a growth variable agrees with some but not with all previous empirical work.

13. Shepherd (1972) also records a decrease in the size of the advertising coefficient and its significance, although it remains positive in both his producer and consumer goods samples.

The risk environment of the firm, proxied by the standard deviation and skewness of the residuals of the trend regression on firm profit rates, has the expected positive relation with profitability (equations 1, 3, and 5). However, the standard deviation variable is insignificant at conventional confidence levels for all three samples. The skewness measure is significant for both the full sample and the consumer goods sample but insignificant and much smaller in magnitude in the producer goods sample, indicating that this characteristic of the firm's earnings distribution has a relatively greater impact on consumer goods firms.[14]

Firm size is positively, although only weakly, related to profitability. This positive effect is consistent with some previous studies although opposite results have also been found. However, the generally weak relation (possibly due to multicollinearity) suggests that little reliance can be placed on this result.[15]

A binary variable classifying firms by the type of primary output (consumer goods = 1) was introduced into the full sample of firms. The positive sign of this variable (equation 1) supports the expectation that consumer goods firms, because of greater perceived differentiation of product, have relatively higher profitability. The high variance of the estimator of this variable ($t =$ .5) is due to collinearity with advertising intensity ($r = .52$). In order to avoid this, the sample was divided into the two subgroups explained above, and equations 3 through 6 report the results. However, tests for structural differences between the two revealed no significant differences in coefficients for any of the explanatory variables except the skewness of the residuals.[16]

Tests on the residuals for a typical equation indicated that heteroscedasticity was not a problem.[17]

14. Producer goods firms had much less skewness than the consumer goods group. Tests of significant differences between coefficients in the two samples revealed that the coefficient of skewness is significantly lower in the producer goods equations. The test used included a binary slope variable for each of explanatory variables. These slope variables were formed by multiplying each explanatory variable by the binary output classification variable and including the variables and their slope dummies in the equation. Equations 2, 4, and 6 eliminate the insignificant risk variables.

15. Size is related to concentration, advertising, and collusion. The simple r between size and profitability is -0.06 for the full sample, but -0.21 for consumer goods firms and $+0.08$ for producer goods firms. These results support previous work which concludes that size exerts little independent effect on profitability.

16. Although the asset coefficient differs markedly between the two groups, its relatively high variance *within* each group leads to a test result of no significant difference *between* groups.

17. The residuals (e_i) of equation 2 were squared and the following function

$$e_i^2 = AX_i^\beta u$$

was fitted, in turn, to each of the explanatory variables (X). In all cases, the β estimators proved not significantly different from zero. However, the diversification of firms and the firm-industry basis of the explanatory variables may result in other estimation problems.

Table 7.2   Incidence of Collusion (dependent variable = presence of collusion)

Sample and Equation	Relative Profit Rate (firm/industry)	Advertising- Sales Ratio	Log of Firm Assets	Concentration Ratio	Consumer-Producer Goods Binary Variable	Constant	R^2
I. All Firms							
1	−.37636	−.00337	.10489	−.002388	−.02010	.50951	.199
	(3.21)	(1.60)	(2.81)	(0.84)	(0.19)	(1.93)	
II. Consumer Goods							
2	−.27464	−.00370	.07691	.004824	—	.13149	.221
	(1.91)	(1.64)	(1.27)	(1.12)		(0.31)	
III. Producer Goods							
3	−.51416	−.02642	.11430	−.008742	—	1.13880	.262
	(2.58)	(2.67)	(2.54)	(2.33)		(3.25)	
All Firms							
4	−.51035	−.02686	.10051	−.008480	−1.18425	1.19864	.260
	(2.54)	(2.71)	(2.79)	(2.27)	(2.82)	(3.60)	
Binary Slope Variables	.23960	.02352		.012774			
	(0.97)	(2.33)		(2.34)			

Figures in parentheses are t-statistics.

The Issue of Causality

Empirical analysis of firm profitability necessarily raises the question of causality. Conventional studies have argued that the cross-section basis of the underlying data reveals long-run firm and industry differences and therefore that causality runs from the explanatory variables to profit rates. While this is a reasonable argument it does not necessarily extend to the relationship between collusive behavior and firm profit rates.

Is collusion a determinant of firm profitability as the specifications of table 7.1 imply, with the resulting empirical conclusion that collusive behavior leads to lower profit rates? An interesting alternative suggested by the non-profit-maximization literature is that an unsatisfactory profit performance by the firm will provide an incentive to collude. This possibility raises the issue of bias of the estimated coefficients in table 7.1 and it seems appropriate, therefore, to investigate the characteristics of collusive firms from an alternative hypothesis of causality. Accordingly, the specification of the equations is changed, with the binary variable for the presence of collusion serving as the dependent variable.[18] In addition, a measure of relative profit rates—the *ratio* of firm to industry profits over the period—replaces the absolute profit variable in order to reflect the firm's position within its immediate competitive environment.

Table 7.2 reports equations examining the incidence of collusion for the three samples. Collusion is negatively related to the relative profitability

18. Such equations can be interpreted as explaining the probability of collusion. It is well known that least squares applied to qualitative dependent variables produce inefficient estimators. Also, the R^2s of such equations do not have the conventional interpretation.

throughout the samples and in terms of the alternative hypothesis of this specification, a poor profit performance by the firm vis-à-vis its industry, increases the probability of collusion.[19]

For the entire sample (equation 1) firm size is positive and significant, indicating an increasing probability of collusion for larger firms. This result holds in both subsamples although it is somewhat weaker in the consumer goods group. Industry concentration is negative and only marginally significant in the full sample but surprisingly has opposite signs and considerably improved statistical significance in the two subsamples. The risk variables proved insignificant throughout and are not reported.

In equation 1 the binary classification of the firm by type of output has a negative sign, supporting the hypothesis that collusion is more likely to occur in the relatively homogeneous producer goods firms, although the collinearity between this variable and advertising intensity again causes this estimator to be imprecise. Statistically, the positive association between firm output classification and advertising may lead to the observed negative effect of advertising on the probability of collusion. The sample was divided by output classification in order to determine whether advertising merely reflects this collinearity or has a more independent effect. In addition, tests for structural differences between output groupings were also made.

The subgroup results appear in equations 2 and 3. Both the relative profit measure and advertising retain their negative signs in each subsample. It appears, therefore, that advertising does exert an effect within each subgroup, independent of its association with output classification. High advertising intensity may mean that collusion is difficult because of substantial product differentiation. Industry concentration, which was only marginally significant and negative in the full sample, exerts a positive influence for consumer goods but is negative for producer goods.

Finally, tests for differences in slope reveal that the coefficients of relative profitability, advertising intensity, and concentration are significantly different between the two groups of firms.[20] No significant difference was detected for asset size. Equation 4 reports this result by giving the coefficients and t-statistics for the slope binary variables directly below the results for the explanatory variables. The equation indicates that producer goods firms are more likely to collude (reflecting the significant negative effect of the output classification).[21] However, depending on their output classification, the prob-

---

19. Industry profit rates, obtained from Federal Trade Commission and Securities and Exchange Commission reports, are at relatively broad two- and three-digit levels. Four-digit rates, which would also be of interest, are unavailable. Similar (negative and significant) relationships between profitability and collusion are found when the absolute firm profit rate on equity replaces relative profits.

20. Although the slope test for relative profitability is significant at the 80 percent level.

21. The use of slope variables improves the significance of the binary output classification variable (equation 2 vs. 4) by separating the differences in slope from the intercept effect.

ability of collusion differs with respect to changes in relative profit rates, advertising intensity, and concentration across firms.

Thus, any given increase in relative profitability or advertising intensity decreases the probability of collusion more in producer than in consumer goods firms.[22] Concentration, however, increases the probability of collusion in consumer goods firms while decreasing it in producer goods firms. There is no obvious a priori reason for this last distinction; it may suggest an institutional explanation in terms of differential public propensities to challenge collusion across industry settings.

In general the variables commonly employed in studies of profitability perform much as expected in the above analyses. A number of relationships between collusion and other structure and performance factors are also of interest although they are not the primary concern of this study.

The major finding of this paper is the consistently negative and significant relationship between firm profitability and the presence of collusion. This result may indicate the inappropriateness of some common notions about the role of collusion and about the economic impact of public policies to prohibit collusion.

Conclusions

The finding that collusion and firm profitability are negatively related is, at least superficially, surprising. As the specifications in the preceding section indicate, the interpretation of causality is not clear and initially at least three distinct possibilities appear obvious.

1. Collusion may consistently lead to lower profitability. This, however, does not seem to be a satisfactory explanation. Even if one were to hypothesize, e.g., that collusive firms give up profits in order to increase their "stability" or "security," the observed results would not be adequately explained. Moreover, there is no indication in terms of the measures employed that collusion is significantly associated with reduced risk exposure.
2. Unsatisfactory profit performances may motivate firms to collude. The significance of relative profitability agrees with this hypothesis. What the observed relationship reflects, then, may be the effect of profitability on collusion, and the equation specifications of table 7.2 therefore embody the correct causality.
3. It may be that, within the range of firm and market structures examined, broadly collusive behavior is the rule, but that antitrust prosecution centers largely on the *unsuccessful* manifestations. Such a contingency is suggested by: (a) the possibility that overt agreement, which is clearly more vulnerable to prosecution, is itself a response to conditions that are not

22. Alternatively, given decreases in relative profit rates raise the probability of collusion more in producer than in consumer goods firms.

conducive to the success of collusion; and (b) the fact that government action is often based on information provided by disaffected conspirators. Most truly successful arrangements probably remain invisible. Accordingly, the relationship that is observed may reflect a bias in the enforcement of the law. Simply put, poor collusive performances are more likely to be discovered.

Alternatives 2 and 3 seem the most plausible, and may in fact reinforce each other. That is, relatively unfavorable profit performances may induce overt collusive agreements, which then proceed under conditions that are frequently discouraging to their success.

Any definitive choice among these explanations (or others) cannot be based directly on the results of this study. Indeed, it seems probable that the question of causality will remain empirically difficult, if not intractable. As noted at several points, the problem arises in some measure from the confinement of observations to *legally defined* collusion. The interpretation of results is complicated by the resulting mixture of economic and legal phenomena that comprise the data base.

These findings nevertheless provide some support for observers such as Phillips (1962) and Williamson (1965) who have stressed certain complexities of interfirm behavior. They further suggest the possibility of a bias in antitrust policy that reduces the economic impact of legal restrictions on collusion. Finally, it appears that further research may fruitfully center on longitudinal studies of firms on a case-by-case basis.

PART TWO
The Positive Economics of Antitrust Enforcement

BRUCE YANDLE

K21

The Sherman, Clayton, and Federal Trade Commission Acts seem so logical. Any competent first-year economics student can recite from memory the structural definition of perfect competition: "many buyers and sellers, none of whom is large enough to affect the market price." Monopoly is easily understood as well. Monopolies are large, can establish prices to their liking, and in doing so restrict output, convert consumer surplus into profit, and impose deadweight losses on society. Horizontal mergers, which by definition result in the disappearance of a formerly independent competitor, seem to offer an attractive way of creating a monopoly.

The conventional discussion of antitrust rarely dives beneath this surface. Little more than lip-service is typically paid to the possibility that mergers can reduce the costs of discovering improved products and marketing techniques, or that the openness of post-merger markets safeguards consumers from any resulting market power. Even less attention is devoted to the possibility that firms might use the antitrust laws themselves for anticompetitive purposes. The problem of achieving long-run equilibrium in industries with marginal costs below average costs almost certainly goes unnoticed. The possibility that antitrust might be valuable to politicians in stifling politically undesirable competition is never raised. There is obviously more to the antitrust story.

The End of Innocence: Welfare Tradeoffs

Although many commentators refer to the Sherman Act as a *magna carta* of free enterprise, there is no persuasive evidence that its passage was inspired by any intent to enhance economic efficiency. To the contrary, as discussed in Part Four of this book, economic historians increasingly conclude that the Sherman Act and later antitrust statutes had more to do with appeasing special interests than with correcting a perceived source of market failure. But regardless of origins and motives, there would be serious reason to question the efficacy of antitrust.

A government with authority to combat collusion and monopoly admittedly has the power to serve the public interest. If antitrust enforcers were all-knowing, the public interest might systematically be advanced. Potential consumer welfare gains would be measured against possible costs, both appropriately discounted for time and uncertainty. Eagerness to do good by purging markets of monopoly would be weighed against the equally compelling desire to do no harm. But as reported in Part One of this book, once economists began their empirical study of antitrust enforcement, they found no evidence that antitrust was systematically attacking true problems of collusion and monopoly that resulted in important welfare losses. The question remained, why?

Antitrust officials face an immense knowledge problem. Even with the best of intentions, they will inevitably make mistakes. The ratio of meritorious cases to mistaken ones is a function of the amount of information necessary to distinguish between the two. Consider the kinds of cases discussed in the first two chapters in this section, horizontal mergers. A merger between two competing firms (like a collusive agreement on prices) can impair *allocative efficiency* by restricting output and raising price. But the same events can increase *productive efficiency* by reducing costs. The tradeoff between allocative inefficiency and productive efficiency places a heavy analytical burden on the antitrust authorities. How are they to know in any particular case whether consumers are on net better off or worse off following a merger? And what are the safeguards for consumers if the antitrust authorities, seeking to do no harm, take a cautious enforcement approach?

Oliver Williamson (1968a) sought to specify the conditions under which mergers between competitors would on balance increase consumer welfare. He identified as key factors the demand elasticity of the final product, the cost savings from the merger, and the initial degree of and subsequent increase in market power. Williamson then worked out a series of numerical examples with various combinations of assumed parameter values. Overall, Williamson found that the production-cost efficiencies associated with merger were usually larger than the consumer-welfare losses from increased market power. He showed that a relatively large percentage increase in price is usually required to offset the benefits resulting from relatively small production cost savings. Thus, Williamson (p. 34) concluded, the welfare tradeoffs posed by the typical merger should "give the antitrust authorities pause" before they challenge it.[1]

---

1. The basic treatment of the welfare tradeoffs from horizontal mergers can of course be extended to single-firm monopolies. Bork's (1978) analysis of two landmark antitrust cases illustrates the tradeoffs between production cost savings and market power. Both United States v. Aluminum Co. of America, 148 F.2d 416 (2d Cir. 1945) and United States v. United Shoe Machinery Corp., 110 F.Supp. 295 (D.Mass. 1953), aff'd *per curiam*, 347 U.S. 521 (1954), stand out as cases in which the Supreme Court saw the defendant firms as having gained their virtual monopoly status by dint of technology development and cost efficiency. Yet in both cases the firm's market dominance caused it to be held in violation of the antitrust laws.

Should the antitrust authorities follow Williamson's advice? Other factors argue for even greater caution than he urged in the merger context. Even if the price rise from a merger is sufficient to outweigh the production-cost savings from the combination of two previously independent firms, it still does not follow that an antitrust challenge would increase consumer welfare. First, Williamson's analysis ignores the fact that pre-merger technologies remain available to actual or potential competitors. Any short-run increase in market price cannot be sustained as long as entry is not blocked.[2] Entry is the relevant factor to consider. With open markets, no Williamsonian tradeoff exists in the long run; any merger that results in cost efficiencies should go unchallenged. The relevant data required for informed antitrust enforcement thus include accurate predictions about future entry conditions.

Second, antitrust enforcement pays only if the expected benefits to consumers from preventing the increase of market concentration are greater than the value of the resources consumed by the antitrust enforcement process. The cost of antitrust includes not only the budgets of the public law-enforcement agencies, but the direct and indirect expenses incurred by current and prospective merger partners themselves in responding to a charge of unlawful monopolization (McWilliams, Turk, and Zardkoohi 1993).

Third, even if expected price rises from a merger are both substantial enough to outweigh efficiencies *and* sustainable in the long run despite new entry, effective antitrust enforcement requires fashioning effective remedies. This has been a notorious problem in merger cases, particularly in instances in which an already-consummated merger is challenged (Elzinga 1969; Rogowsky 1987).[3] Passage of the Hart-Scott-Rodino Act in 1976 now facilitates government scrutiny of mergers before completion, but has resulted in antitrust authorities' functioning essentially as regulatory agencies. Mergers routinely are cleared only after forced divestitures, dictated by product- or geographic-market overlaps. Obviously, such a micro-management approach to merger policy greatly increases the information burden on antitrust enforcers.

2. See Richard S. Higgins and William F. Shughart II, Economies as an Antitrust Defense Once Again (manuscript).

3. It is a serious problem also in monopoly cases under Section 2 of the Sherman Act. For example, in the United Shoe case, cited in note 1 above, the defendant firm was essentially ordered not to compete in certain ways that had been successful with the firm's customers. Long-term leases and free machinery repair offered by United Shoe were barred by the court. The remedy was particularly bizarre, given that all of United Shoe's competitors also used the type of long-term lease system that United Shoe was prohibited from continuing. In the Alcoa case, also discussed in note 1, Alcoa was essentially forced to restrict output in order to make room for new competition. The resulting loss of scale economies left Alcoa little choice but to raise price. Even then, entry by new competition was facilitated by heavy government subsidies. For details on the effects of the Alcoa decision and the government subsidies, see Robert A. Solo, The Political Authority and the Market System (1974).

The Papers in This Section

As discussed by Fred McChesney in the introduction to Part One of this volume, serious economic analysis of antitrust's empirical record began with studies of individual cases. It then turned to measuring the more systematic effects of antitrust enforcement. Data limitations which initially hampered that effort gradually abated. By the middle 1970s, it was becoming clearer that the supposed goals of antitrust were not being realized. The inferences were largely negative: Antitrust was *not* focused on the industries in which welfare gains were most evident, and was *not* (at least in price-fixing cases) even targeting firms that were successfully raising prices. The obvious affirmative question remained, what then *have* the results of antitrust been? This section's chapters illustrate research on this question.

The first paper, by George Bittlingmayer, examines the great merger wave of the late nineteenth century, whose structural imprint on industries remains visible today.[4] As Bittlingmayer points out, close to 50 percent of U.S. manufacturing capacity became involved in mergers in the brief period 1898–1902. He asks whether antitrust itself might actually have *caused* the wave of mergers, and thus have increased the very concentration it was supposed to reduce. The question is important because the higher levels of concentration that resulted later became arguments for more vigorous antitrust enforcement to break up the new industrial giants.

Bittlingmayer tells a rich story. In expanding industries with relatively high fixed costs and sharply declining marginal costs that lie below average costs over the relevant range of production, competition leading to price-equals-marginal-cost cannot be sustained. Marginal-cost pricing will, by definition, be "ruinous," because the resulting revenue will not be sufficient to replenish fixed-cost assets as they depreciate. With price competition ruinous, firms must somehow cooperate, either by fixing prices or by merging. Cooperation under the conditions specified is required for survival, and it facilitates the investments necessary to replace depreciating fixed capital. Given the alternatives of temporarily cooperating across the ownership boundaries of firms or arranging more durable mergers, consumers are generally better off with cooperation because it is less costly than consolidation.

Under the conventional antitrust approach, mergers are eyed with suspicion as possible monopolizing devices having nothing to do with shape of cost curves. But surely, if monopoly profits from mergers were available from merger before passage of the Sherman Act in 1890, firms would have cap-

---

4. Economists have come to believe that four "merger waves" have washed over the economy since passage of the Sherman Act. Whether this has in fact been true is debatable. See William F. Shughart II and Robert D. Tollison, "The Random Character of Merger Activity," 15 Rand J. Econ. 500 (1984). It is clear, however, that the period analyzed by Bittlingmayer did amount to a truly discontinuous jump in the historical time series of merger activity.

tured those rents long before. Monopoly profit seems an unlikely explanation for the sudden four-year spate of mergers, within a decade of the Sherman Act's passage, involving fully half of American manufacturing.

As Bittlingmayer discusses, it was the Sherman Act itself and its attack on beneficial cooperative arrangements that sparked the merger wave. Previously, firms had been free to coordinate in ways that minimized long-run costs and generated a competitive equilibrium. All along, expanding markets and emerging rivalry limited the potential abuses of monopoly power. The loose cooperative arrangements that resulted were superior to more permanent mergers, which tended to solidify particular management structures and eliminate financial incentives found in independent, competing firms. But following the Sherman Act, with the Supreme Court's categorical rejection of the defense that price competition would be ruinous,[5] prior cooperative arrangements in high-fixed-cost industries became untenable. The relative attraction of mergers increased.

Bittlingmayer reviews the evolution of antitrust policy in light of the contrasting hypotheses, compares the American merger record with that of the United Kingdom, and then examines several industries in detail. The two merger models—one about cooperative efficiency and the other about monopolization—guide Bittlingmayer's statistical tests. In light of the evidence presented, even staunch supporters of the merger-to-monopoly theory must reconsider their position. Bittlingmayer draws a parallel between the pre-1890 informal cartels and modern franchise agreements in which contracts specify modes of production and distribution. We are left to consider the effects on the economy today if all franchise agreements suddenly become the target of antitrust actions.

The second chapter in this section carries us later into the twentieth century, with a focus on merger enforcement under the 1976 Hart-Scott-Rodino (HSR) Antitrust Improvements Act. Espen Eckbo and Peggy Wier present the public-interest explanation of HSR, which requires merging firms to notify the antitrust authorities of their plans. Thereafter, the antitrust enforcers analyze the information submitted by the prospective merger partners, consider the effects of the proposed transaction, and ultimately disapprove or approve the plans (often with such major modifications as selective divestitures being required).

As explained above, HSR enables the government to avoid problems of fashioning effective remedies for anticompetitive mergers after the fact by simply disallowing mergers before they are consummated. But HSR also places greater informational burdens on the government. Rather than observing the results of mergers and then undoing those mergers with demonstrated anticompetitive effects (assuming that these can be accurately identified and

5. United States v. Trans-Missouri Freight Ass'n, 166 U.S. 290 (1897).

the costs correctly weighed against the efficiency benefits), the antitrust authorities now must prognosticate which mergers are *likely* to have anticompetitive effects outweighing expected benefits.

How, Eckbo and Wier ask, have the authorities performed in the post-HSR world? The authors use financial market analysis to examine data on contested mergers before and after passage of HSR, to see how investors reacted to pre-notification requirements. Efficiency-enhancing mergers would be hard on the portfolios of rival firms—old firms in an industry would face a new lower-cost competitor—but good for investors in the merging firms. On the other hand, mergers leading to monopoly power and higher prices would be good for all parties—even the fringe firms would have the advantage of operating under the new monopolist's protective price umbrella.

The results of the Eckbo-Wier tests engender no enthusiasm for pre-merger screening and approval. Government actions to modify or deny post-HSR mergers are associated with *positive* returns for competing firms, while the portfolios of the merging firms experience negative returns. The HSR pre-notification regime thus is seen as a policy that allows rival firms to gain when the creation of a more efficient competitor is blocked. Meanwhile, the punished firms sustain heavy losses. As Eckbo and Wier put it, "while it is possible that the government's merger policy has deterred some anticompetitive mergers, the results indicate that it has also protected rival producers from facing increased competition due to efficient mergers."

The third chapter, by William Shughart and Robert Tollison, moves to an area that has been studied relatively little, the more general impact of antitrust enforcement on overall economic performance. In the traditional model of antitrust, higher concentration facilitates collusion and other forms of anticompetitive conduct. Reduced output and higher prices ensue. All else equal, then, accelerated antitrust activity should be associated with economic expansion, measurable in terms of output, investment, employment, and other familiar indicators of macroeconomic performance. But of course, if antitrust targets efficiency-increasing rather than welfare-decreasing arrangements, the macroeconomic results would be precisely the reverse: lower output and therefore lower employment.

The chapter by Shughart and Tollison takes what they describe as the first step toward linking antitrust enforcement to macroeconomic welfare. They focus on antitrust and total employment, and demonstrate a kind of antitrust "Phillips Curve" in which vigor of antitrust enforcement is traded off against employment. For this inverse relationship to hold, the actions taken by antitrust authorities must be unpredictable. Otherwise, the expectations of employers and employees would adjust over time to anticipated regulatory interventions and there would consequently be no real effects from tighter or looser antitrust enforcement. As Shughart and Tollison model the process, random antitrust shocks hit a selected industry, and in that industry employment declines. Observing the event, managers in other industries alter their plans and adjust production to avoid an antitrust encounter. The antitrust shock has its ripple effects.

Using data for Antitrust Division cases from 1932 to 1981, Shughart and Tollison use time series analysis to separate antitrust into its anticipated and unanticipated components, and then test the relationship between changes in the nation's unemployment rate and the unanticipated level of antitrust activity. They use various tests for causality and different model specifications as they seek the antitrust-employment relationship over time. Their findings fail to refute the Phillips Curve relationship. With a 1 percent increase in unanticipated antitrust activity comes a .15 percent increase in unemployment, all other things being equal. The tests force rejection of the notion that antitrust actually generates more production and more employment, as it should under the traditional view.

The Shughart-Tollison results parallel those of Bittlingmayer (1990), who also examined the historical record on antitrust's macro-effects. Measured by different performance aggregates, the effects of antitrust enforcement have been negative, controlling for other variables. As Shughart and Tollison find on the question of employment, Bittlingmayer's evidence indicates that at the margin additional antitrust cases have lowered real income, real output, stock prices, and other measures of macroeconomic performance.

Bridging the Gap: Mistaken or Purposeful Behavior?

As economists progressively discovered, by examining antitrust's actual performance, that the law did not achieve its stated goals (see Part One of this book), they asked the next logical question. If antitrust has not produced the intended results, what effects has it had? The first three chapters of this section illustrate how the discipline approached and answered this second question. The answers from all three chapters are analogous: Antitrust has forced firms into less efficient modes of organization (Bittlingmayer); targeted competing rather than monopolizing firms, to the benefit of their less efficient rivals (Eckbo and Wier); and—not surprisingly, given the first two empirical studies—lowered overall economic performance (Shughart and Tollison).

An obvious issue raised by such scholarship is why antitrust has performed so perversely. One possible explanation is outlined above, namely that the informational demands made on them by an increasingly regulatory system make it impossible for mere bureaucratic mortals systematically to promote economic efficiency. Surely, at least some of antitrust's failures can plausibly be attributed to mistakes.

But social scientists are properly skeptical of models that rely principally on mistake, particularly on repeated mistakes (as further discussed by Fred McChesney in chapter 18 of this book). Not only can one explain anything—

and therefore nothing—by mistake, but the notion that a century-old policy can still be explained as the result of uncorrected error and not of purposeful behavior is hardly credible. Identifying the informational barriers helping to explain why antitrust cannot possibly produce the desired goals, and demonstrating that in fact it has not, is obviously important. The next task then becomes modeling and testing a positive model of purposeful antitrust behavior.

That is essentially the goal of the chapters presented later in Part Three of this book. However, the final chapter in this section, by William Shughart, Jon Silverman, and Robert Tollison, begins to bridge the gap. As discussed above and by Shughart et al., the need for antitrust to safeguard competition is a function of the ease of entry into markets. The vigor of competition from imports should thus be a substitute for spending domestic resources on antitrust enforcement. On the other hand, if antitrust is itself anticompetitive, increased import competition should *increase* the resources voted for antitrust.

Shughart, Silverman, and Tollison examine variations in the budgets of the Federal Trade Commission (FTC) and the Department of Justice's Antitrust Division for the years 1932 through 1981, adjusting for other variables including the share of GNP accounted for by imports. If the antitrust authorities and Congress recognize the spur to competition brought by imports, their actions belie it. The three authors find that enforcement budgets rise and decline directly with import competition. Tough competition from imports is associated with tough antitrust activity; when imports fall, so do the budgets of the antitrust enforcers.

Have Congress and antitrust officials merely been mistaken in treating import competition and budgets as complements rather than substitutes for fifty years? Or does the long-run complementary relationship indicate more conscious intent than mistake? The suggestion is raised that the latter is more likely true. The findings indicate the FTC is the principal winner in the budget game, and that agency has a long-standing reputation as a protector of small business. And smaller businesses are more vulnerable than larger ones to import competition.[6] With systematic long-term winners and losers from antitrust identified, the suspicion grows that politics more than welfare economics drives antitrust.

6. This point also supports the notion that mergers allow for stronger U.S. competition in international markets. See William F. Chappell and Bruce Yandle, The Competitive Role of Import Penetration, 37 Antitrust Bull. 957 (1992).

127-45

[1985]

G 34

U.S

L 40

N 42

N 62

N 61

CHAPTER EIGHT

Did Antitrust Policy Cause the Great Merger Wave?

GEORGE BITTLINGMAYER

Introduction

Perhaps as much as one-half of U.S. manufacturing capacity took part in mergers during the years 1898 to 1902. These mergers frequently included most of the firms in an industry and often involved firms that had been fixing prices or that had been operated jointly through the legal mechanism of an industrial trust. The histories of Standard Oil and U.S. Steel provide well-known instances in which merger followed looser forms of organization in what has come to be known as the Great Merger Wave. What caused this rapid change of industry structure? The Sherman Antitrust Act was passed in 1890, and the first crucial decisions making price fixing illegal—*Trans-Missouri* (1897), *Joint Traffic* (1898), and *Addyston Pipe* (1899)—occurred just before or during the first stages of the merger wave.[1] Merger of competing firms remained unchallenged until 1904.

Although it certainly seems plausible that antitrust policy caused the Great Merger Wave, the question has never been looked into at length, and some influential studies of the mergers and of early antitrust policy play down the possibility of a connection. This is puzzling because the search for alternatives has not borne fruit. One reason that economists may be inclined to dismiss the influence of cartel policy, and that the possibility has never been pressed, comes from the presumption that firms would choose merger over price fixing if they could because merger avoids a host of problems that cartels face. Why should monopoly-minded firms have to be forced to merge at the point of a bayonet? The answer, of course, is that firms will prefer cartels to mergers if the gains are greater. If there are diseconomies from merger and if the available monopoly gains are not large, the preferred choice may very well be cartelization, making it at least conceivable that the introduction of a law against price fixing swung the balance in favor of merger.

This essay was previously published in the *Journal of Law and Economics* 28 (April 1985): 77–118. © 1985 by The University of Chicago. All rights reserved.

1. United States v. Trans-Missouri Freight Ass'n, 166 U.S. 290 (1897); United States v. Joint Traffic Ass'n, 171 U.S. 505 (1898); and United States v. Addyston Pipe & Steel Co., 175 U.S. 211 (1899). Judge William Howard Taft's Court of Appeals opinion, U.S. v. Addyston Pipe, 85 Fed. 271 (6th Cir. 1898), aff'd, was also influential.

This argument assumes that the motive for both cartels and mergers is monopoly gain. However, the idea that the motive may not be monopoly at all also seems worth exploring, especially since many firms seemed to prefer the vagaries of a cartel agreement to the more secure coordination of a merged existence. For example, cartels and mergers may be cooperative attempts to solve market problems that do not have a noncooperative solution. One focus of such an explanation, and the one that I will emphasize, is the integer or fixed-cost problem. This is a well-known instance in which there is no competitive equilibrium. As always, the choice between two theories should be governed by their ability to explain the facts, and I hope to show that an explanation based on the desire to remedy the problems posed by fixed costs has at least as much going for it in the case of the Great Merger Wave as an explanation based on simple greed.

I should emphasize that these two explanations, alone or together, do not provide a general theory of merger; there are certainly reasons other than a desire for monopoly gain or a desire to remedy market failure stemming from fixed costs why firms might merge. My primary aim is to see whether a reasonable theoretical foundation can be constructed for the view that changes in antitrust policy caused the large year-to-year variations in merger activity that took place in the late nineteenth and early twentieth centuries and that converted many cartels to single-firm organization. This essay is not an attempt to explain horizontal mergers in general, and I do not rule out the possibility that something like U.S. Steel would have been formed eventually even if the antitrust laws had never been passed.

Mergers in the United States and United Kingdom, 1890–1905

Four points about developments in antitrust policy[2] deserve emphasis: *E. C. Knight* made merger legal, at least in the minds of many lawyers;[3] judicial policy after *Knight* was directed at cartels and not at merger; public agitation against the cartels may have added extra impetus to the merger wave through the many new state laws and federal legislative initiatives directed at the

2. For general background on this topic see Hans B. Thorelli (1955); and William Letwin (1965). Lester G. Telser, Genesis of the Sherman Act (December 1982) (Working Paper No. 24, Center Stud. Econ. and State, Univ. Chicago), presents an economic analysis of the origins of antitrust policy and railroad regulation.

3. United States v. E. C. Knight, 156 U.S. 1 (1898). The case involved the acquisition of four Philadelphia refineries by the American Sugar Refining Company (the ''Sugar Trust''), which owned about 60 percent of sugar refining capacity nationwide. The history of the Sugar Trust is treated in Alfred S. Eichner, The Emergence of Oligopoly (1969). I thank Lester Telser for calling my attention to this book and to the emphasis it places on *Knight* as a cause of the merger wave.

trusts in the years 1896–1900; and the nature of the assault on the trusts in the courts and legislatures was clear to the press and the legal profession.

Table 8.1 shows the remarkable increase in mergers that occurred in the late 1890s. The number of firms absorbed by merger in manufacturing and mining rose from 69 to 303 between 1897 and 1898, and rose further to 1,208 in 1899. Merger disappearances in primary metals and metal products rose even more sharply over the same period. Another important point is that consolidation of several firms, rather than piecemeal acquisition, accounted for roughly 90 percent of all firm disappearances until 1902.

Firm disappearances count large and small firms alike. A better way to get an idea of the scope of the merger wave is to look at total merger capitalizations, although this involves substantial double counting when firms are formed in a series of mergers. Based on capitalization values, more than half of the merger movement in mining and manufacturing during the peak years 1899–1901 can be accounted for by mergers in metal industries. The merger movement as a whole seems to have encompassed between one-fourth and one-half of U.S. industry.[4]

One issue that arises in connection with the U.S. mergers at the turn of the century is that Great Britain had a merger wave at about the same time. In fact, it is possible to show that the two are related statistically. This suggests the possibility of a joint cause, apparently confined to the United States and United Kingdom. It is not clear though if the two merger movements are in fact part of the same phenomenon since there are some noteworthy differences and since statistical correlations are never enough to establish causation. A plausible joint cause has so far proved elusive.

Table 8.2 presents comparable data for U.S. and British mergers for the years 1895–1905. Comprehensive U.S. data go back only to 1895. Although it is clear that there was an increase in mergers in both countries in the late 1890s, there are several notable differences. First, the United States seems to have had a larger wave, and a sharper increase. (Although the U.S. data go back only to 1895, I will extend my range for the U.K. data to 1890 in the comparisons of U.S. and U.K. data that follow to allow for the possibility that the U.K. "wave" started earlier.) The peak U.K. value for mergers (73) is 10 times the lowest value (7 in 1892), while the U.S. peak (191) is

4. The 1898–1902 capitalizations amounted to 53 percent of the value of all manufacturing and mining operations. However, this probably overstates the extent of the merger movement because the same property was often involved in several successive mergers. See Yale Brozen, Mergers in Perspective 6–8 (1982). According to one estimate based on incomplete merger data, about 15 percent of the total number of plants and employees in manufacturing in 1900 were involved in mergers over the years 1887–1904. See Jesse W. Markham, Survey of the Evidence and Findings on Mergers, in Business Concentration and Price Policy: A Report of the National Bureau of Economic Research (1955), at 141, 152. According to another estimate, 318 industrial combinations formed in the years 1897–1904 controlled 40 percent of U.S. manufacturing capital. See Donald Dewey, Monopoly in Economics and Law 49 (1959).

Table 8.1 Firm Disappearances and Capitalizations through Consolidation and Acquisition, 1895–1905

	Firm Disappearances			Capitalizations		
	Total Manufacturing and Mining	Primary Metals and Metal Products as Percentage of Total	Consolidation as Percentage of Total	Total Manufacturing and Mining ($1,000s)	Primary Metals and Metal Products as Percentage of Total	Consolidations as Percentage of Total
1895	43	2.3	86.1	40,770	10.0	84.6
1896	26	7.7	84.6	24,691	4.1	89.1
1897	69	17.4	89.9	119,651	15.9	92.4
1898	303	18.5	93.1	650,569	44.8	94.6
1899	1,208	23.1	91.7	2,262,695	33.6	92.1
1900	340	25.3	89.9	442,204	44.4	88.1
1901	423	24.6	83.2	2,053,924	77.6	92.4
1902	379	19.0	70.7	910,807	29.5	76.2
1903	142	9.9	39.4	297,600	14.8	49.5
1904	79	19.0	45.6	110,533	45.6	28.1
1905	226	9.7	63.7	242,996	19.5	43.4
Average 1905–1914	67	12.0	52.6	163,405	21.3	53.7

Source: Constructed from Ralph L. Nelson, Merger Movements in American Industry, 1895–1956 (1959), at 60, 144–45, 152–53. Capitalization values correspond roughly to the value of firms formed through merger plus the value of firms absorbed through acquisition.

Table 8.2   United Kingdom and United States Manufacturing Mergers, 1895–1905

	Number of Mergers		Firm Disappearances by Merger*		Merger Capitalizations ($ Millions)	
	United Kingdom	United States†	United Kingdom	United States	United Kingdom‡	United States
1895	26	10	32(1.2)	34(3.4)	4.4	30.8
1896	44	9	69(1.7)	26(2.8)	28.2	24.7
1897	52	14	83(1.6)	67(4.8)	20.9	115.0
1898	73	44	151(2.1)	271(6.2)	40.4	647.6
1899	62	191	255(4.1)	979(5.1)	56.0	2,063.6
1900	63	75	244(4.1)	306(5.1)	106.7	417.0
1901	29	94	49(1.7)	284(3.0)	34.1	1,963.1
1902	53	125	76(1.4)	285(2.3)	46.8	725.3
1903	41	84	53(1.3)	120(1.4)	20.5	190.1
1904	24	46	32(1.3)	68(1.5)	7.3	91.6
1905	35	78	39(1.1)	120(1.5)	12.2	160.4

Source: Leslie Hannah, Mergers in British Manufacturing Industry, 1880–1918, 26 Oxford Econ. Papers 1 (1974), at 18 Table 4; and Ralph L. Nelson, Merger Movements in American Industry, 1895–1956 (1959), at 144–45 table B-3, at 150–51 table B-6, and at 152–53 table B-7. U.K. figures in pounds sterling were multiplied by 4.87 to arrive at the U.S. dollar price. See Milton Friedman and Anna Jacobson Schwartz, A Monetary History of the United States, 1860–1960 (1963), at 772.

*The figures in parentheses give firm disappearances per merger.

†The U.S. figure is the sum of consolidations plus firm disappearances by acquisition. Nelson does not give merger figures comparable to Hannah's. This amounts to assuming that all U.S. mergers through acquisition involved only one firm. This may bias the U.S. merger series upward. Since a chief concern is whether U.S. mergers involved more firm disappearances per merger, the reader can easily see that this is a safe procedure.

‡This figure reflects an upward adjustment made by Hannah to account for the value of smaller mergers not reported in the trade press.

20 times the lowest value (9). Similarly, the highest value for U.K. firm disappearances, which occurs in 1899, is 23 times the lowest value of 11, which occurred in 1893; in the U.S. the highest and lowest values are 979 and 26, implying a 38-fold increase. Since the U.S. series is truncated at 1895, these comparisons probably understate the differences. Only in capitalizations are the British increases greater than those for the United States: an increase of 109-fold from 1893 to 1900, compared to a U.S. increase by a factor of 66 from 1896 to 1899. Note though that the average yearly increase is about the same. Second, U.S. mergers involved more firms per merger, although this difference narrowed after the *Northern Securities* case was filed. Third, the U.S. mergers, although roughly equal in number to U.K. mergers, apparently involved much larger firms and quite likely more successive mergers in the same industry. Cumulative capitalizations in the U.S. were seventeen times U.K. capitalizations. In one year, 1901, capitalizations were 58 times as great. One reason for this may be that U.S. mergers were concentrated in metal and metal fabricating, where average plant size tends to be greater. Twenty-six percent of the 2,782 U.S. firm disappearances from 1895 to 1909 occurred in this industry, while only 11 percent of the 1,428 U.K. disappearances took place there. Nearly 30 percent of the U.K. disappearances took place in textiles, and another 28 percent took place in food and drink manufacture (chiefly brewing), together accounting for nearly 60 percent of British firm disappearances. In contrast, 22 percent of U.S. mergers took place in textiles, and less than 4 percent took place in food (and drink) products. Although comparable U.K. data are unavailable, it should be noted that textile capitalizations account for less than 1 percent of total U.S. manufacturing capitalizations for 1895–1904, while primary metals alone account for 41 percent.[5]

Although these comparisons suggest that the U.S. merger wave was larger and more pronounced, and that it tended to be stronger in certain industries, there is still the question why mergers occurred in both countries. It can be shown that merger time series data for the years 1895–1918 for the United States and United Kingdom are related.[6] For example, there is a correlation between year-to-year changes of U.K. firm disappearances and year-to-year changes of U.S. firm disappearances by consolidation ($r = .38$, which is significant at the 10 percent level for 23 observations). But what should be done with this empirical finding? Granting the fact of a statistical relationship, I would not want to insist on a single explanation. Well-worn but valid

5. Data are from Leslie Hannah, Mergers in British Manufacturing Industry, 1880–1918, 26 Oxford Econ. Papers 1, 18 (1974); and Ralph L. Nelson, Merger Movements in American Industry, 1895–1956 (1959), at 144–53. These comparisons are meant only to suggest the differences involved. A more formal investigation would require information on the assets and numbers of firms in various British and U.S. industries.

6. These are the years for which the data cited *supra* note 5 overlap.

arguments force me to observe that such results could be spurious,[7] and we have precious little in the way of a plausible common explanation. Under these circumstances, investigating the two movements one at a time strikes me as a defensible research strategy.

In examining the data we should also look to see whether merger activity is inconsistent with the timing of key antitrust decisions. Table 8.3 presents quarterly merger figures and some key events in antitrust history for the years 1895–1900. Bold-face numbers show where the quarterly merger figures reached a new high (beginning with the third quarter of 1895). Thus *E. C. Knight* was followed by three successive quarters of increased merger activity, consistent with the view that it did signal that merger was legal under the Sherman Act. Only twelve firm disappearances occurred between this mini-wave and the first quarter of 1897, when *Trans-Missouri* was announced and many state antitrust laws were passed. After a one quarter lull, merger activity increased to unprecedented levels, then decreased just before the *Addyston* appeals decision, only to increase when the decision was announced. After another one-quarter lull, merger activity increased steadily until early 1899, and remained above pre-1897 levels until the end of 1900.

It would be unrealistic to expect data of this kind to show unambiguously that Supreme Court cases caused mergers, since the lags could be variable and the cases are only a proxy for actual expected policy. Interpretations of court doctrine by prominent authorities, initiatives to amend legislation, and declarations of war are all factors that could make mergers occur one or two quarters sooner or later. However, I would emphasize that increases in mergers occurred within one or two quarters or at the same time as the crucial cases, and not before or after very long delays. Statistical tests reported below, which use a longer time series for mergers, confirm the empirical connection between changes in antitrust policy and merger in a more formal way.

Some Case Studies of Merger

Two well-studied industries, railroading and iron and steel, provide concrete instances in which merger followed extensive cartelization after the court

---

7. For example, antitrust enforcement may be procyclical. This seems reasonable since landmarks in more stringent antitrust policy such as the passage of the Sherman Act (1890), the per se rule (1897–99), *Northern Securities,* the tobacco and oil dissolutions (1911), and the reestablishment of the per se rule in United States v. Trenton Potteries, 273 U.S. 392 (1927), occurred during periods of expansion. Backsliding, as in *E. C. Knight,* United States v. United States Steel, 251 U.S. 417 (1920), Appalachian Coals v. United States, 288 U.S. 344 (1933), and the NRA cartelizations, occurred in periods of contraction. The less volatile U.K. series may have been the response to other developments that were also related to business activity. The business cycles of the United States and the United Kingdom were of course related, in part because both were on the gold standard.

Table 8.3   Quarterly Merger Statistics and Antitrust Policy, 1895–1900

Year and Quarter	Manufacturing Merger Capitalizations ($ Millions)	Quarterly Firm Disappearances	Events
1895: I	1.0	3	*E. C. Knight*
II	10.4	14	
III	**14.5**	**24**	
IV	.6	1	
1896: I	6.1	3	
II	4.5	7	
III	0	0	Election campaign of 1896
IV	1.3	1	
1897: I	10.0	8	State Laws and *Trans-*
II	0	0	*Missouri*
III	**81.6**	**38**	
IV	10.3	17	
1898: I	**167.6**	**132**	*Addyston* (Appeals Court)
II	44.7	64	Spanish-American War
III	**209.3**	19	
IV	**212.3**	76	*Joint Traffic*
1899: I	**862.4**	**410**	
II	522.4	271	
III	373.4	316	
IV	112.9	128	*Addyston* (Supreme Court)
1900: I	149.9	147	
II	126.9	55	
III	98.3	60	
IV	11.8	53	

Source: Ralph L. Nelson, Merger Movements in American Industry, 1895–1956 (1959), at 139 tables B-1, 164 C-7; and 1 U.S. Courts, Federal Antitrust Decisions (1912).

Note: These figures do not agree with Nelson's annual statistics because he could not assign all mergers to a specific quarter. Beginning with 1895:III, boldface numerals indicate a new high.

decisions of 1897 and 1898. In several industries antitrust charges preceded merger, and in at least two cases we know of, the firms merged after looser arrangements were ruled out on the basis of legal advice.

Iron and Steel

Cartel agreements in iron and steel existed in pig iron, steel billets, steel rails, structural steel, steel plate, nails and wire, and numerous other products.[8] U.S. Steel was formed in 1901 as a holding company organized under

8. This sketch of developments in iron and steel is based on Eliot Jones, The Trust Problem in the United States 186 (1921). Charles Schwab, who had been Andrew Carnegie's protégé, and who was later president of U.S. Steel and Bethlehem Steel, was asked while testifying before the Industrial Commission whether pooling arrangements had existed before the formation

the laws of New Jersey. Its three major components were the three largest iron and steel producers in the United States: the Carnegic Company, the Federal Steel Company, and the National Steel Company. U.S. Steel also assumed control of a number of producers of finished goods that dominated their fields, including the American Tin Plate Company, the American Steel and Wire Company, and the National Tube Company, and it absorbed substantial transportation and mining facilities that had previously been independent firms. In turn, two of the major steel companies that became part of U.S. Steel, Federal and National Steel, were themselves formed through mergers in 1898, as were many of the producers of finished products. For example, the American Steel and Wire Company was organized in April of 1898 out of fourteen mills, and the successor consolidation, with twenty-nine plants in 1900, owned nearly every wire, wire rod, and wire nail plant in the United States. The Wire Nail Association had cartelized this industry in the mid-1890s.[9]

The connection between price fixing and merger in the steel industry can probably be explored at greater length, but the major developments in this industry certainly make it reasonable to infer that merger performed some of the function of the abandoned cartels. The mergers also occurred at just the right time to raise the suspicion that they were a response to legal developments. In addition, iron and steel provides a classic example of an industry in which production takes place under fixed costs and in which transportation costs were probably high enough to create regional markets with small numbers of competitors.[10]

Railroading

Railroading provides another instance in which production is carried out with substantial fixed expenses, and in which the relevant market (transportation between two points) frequently has few competitors. In addition, railroad cartels were the focus of the first two significant cartel cases to reach the Supreme Court.[11]

Railroads had passed through trying times in the early and mid-1890s.

---

of U.S. Steel in 1901. "Yes," he replied, "in all lines of business, not only in steel, but in everything else. There were similar agreements, known as joint arrangements to maintain prices. They have existed in all lines of business as long as I can remember." Quoted in Lewis Haney, Business Organization and Combination (1913), at 146.

9. Nails and Wire in 1898, Iron Age, January 5, 1899, at 41.

10. This is illustrated in Bittlingmayer (1982, 70–72). Cast iron pipe was transported at the same rate as pig iron. The f.o.b. price of pig iron varied between $6.00 and $12.00 per ton in the 1890s, and the cost of transportation in 1893 from the southern producing district in Alabama to Cincinnati (400 miles) was $2.75 per ton, or as much as 31 percent of the delivered price.

11. I thank Lester Telser for asking, after reading the first draft of this paper, what happened in railroading.

Although the 1887 Act to Regulate Commerce had prohibited pooling (apparently to satisfy one senator and on an experimental basis),[12] pooling agreements continued to be prevalent. These agreements faltered in the mid-1890s, however, possibly because of their shadowy legal status. Two major recessions also occurred in that decade, and some combination of low freight rates and low freight volume caused railroads to go into receivership. Although some railroad consolidations had been undertaken in the mid-1890s, their number increased sharply after the *Trans-Missouri* and *Joint Traffic* decisions. This is evident in the data on mergers for twelve-month periods ending in June that are displayed in table 8.4. Mergers increased substantially in 1897, following *Trans-Missouri,* and declined while *Joint Traffic* wound its way to the Supreme Court. This case was decided in October of 1898, and mergers and consolidations increased for the period July 1898–1899. Over the next twelve months, ending June 1900, mergers increased to a new high.

The effect of these mergers is also reflected in the growth of class 1 railroads—those with 1,000 miles or more of track, also shown in table 8.4. The number of class 1 railroads increased from forty-four to fifty-one (or 16 percent) between June 1899 and June 1902. In addition, the larger 23 percent increase in class 1 mileage suggests that a good deal of the overall growth came from existing class 1 roads. The percentage of railroad mileage under class 1 control increased from 57 percent in 1899 to 65 percent in 1902.

Merger was only one way of achieving coordinated operation of different railroads. Another method, pioneered by Standard Oil and adopted by the railroads in 1899, was the "community of interest," which formed the basis for the "great systems" associated with Morgan, Gould, Harriman, and others.[13]

These developments are consistent with the view that the Supreme Court drove railroads to other forms of joint control, although not always merger. Writing in 1902 for the Industrial Commission, William Ripley claimed that a less formal organization took the place of the Joint Traffic Association. "It continues to perform many functions of a cooperative character, and has not occasioned serious complaints on the part of shippers. There seems to be some sort of agreement between the lines by which harmony is engen-

12. 19 U.S. Industrial Commission, Final Report, House Doc. No. 380, 57th Cong., 2d Sess. (1902), at 337–38. (This volume bears the title Transportation and was written by William Z. Ripley.)

13. Lewis Haney, Business Organization and Combination, 205–7 (1913). Haney, ibid., at 246–48, claims that leasing was yet another method used to obtain control of a railroad. For more recent accounts of the development of the "great systems," see Alfred D. Chandler, The Visible Hand 172–74 (1977), and id., The United States: Seedbed of Managerial Capitalism 27, 38 (1980). According to a table compiled in 1901 by the Common Carrier, a trade journal, more than half of U.S. mileage was under the control of six "financial interests," of which four had at least 18,000 miles of track each. U.S. Industrial Commission, supra note 12, at 307–8. The United States had approximately 200,000 miles of railway in 1900.

Table 8.4 Railroad Mergers and Consolidations and Number and Mileage of Class 1 Railroads, 1890–1907

Year Ending	Merged		Consolidated		Number of Class 1 Railroads	Mileage of Class 1 Railroads	Percentage of Total Mileage
	Number	Miles	Number	Miles			
1890	13	599	50	6,196	40	77,873	47.5
1891	35	4,436	39	3,184	41	94,265	56.0
1892	19	1,143	16	323	43	99,232	57.9
1893	28	750	16	1,469	42	98,386	55.8
1894	15	1,735	14	1,590	44	100,547	56.3
1895	9	1,986	28	1,591	42	100,715	55.7
1896	22	1,505	18	718	44	103,346	56.9
1897	57	3,180	19	1,197	44	103,566	56.3
1898	22	1,234	14	1,310	44	105,372	56.6
1899	42	1,938	20	713	44	109,405	56.3
1900	89	4,490	36	5,762	48	117,880	59.2
1901	55	3,827	28	3,080	49	127,489	63.0
1902	62	2,228	46	2,628	51	134,090	64.7
1903	66	4,762	28	4,930	50	139,858	65.5
1904	47	3,046	32	1,913	48	143,952	65.4
1905	30	1,218	22	1,438	49	147,299	65.4
1906	28	1,274	24	2,157	50	150,927	65.4
1907	20	996	25	1,740	51	155,101	65.5
Total		40,347		41,939			

Source: U.S. Interstate Commerce Commission, Annual Report on Statistics of the Railways of the United States, various issues.
Note: "Miles" refers to miles of rail line owned, not to miles operated.

dered."[14] Harmony among members of the Trans-Missouri Freight Association was apparently sought by a community of interest.[15]

There seem to be two factors that offset the influence of the 1897 and 1898 decisions. The prohibition of pooling and the erosion of Interstate Commerce Commission powers in the early 1890s[16] probably stimulated some consolidations among railroads even before these court decisions were made. Consistent with this, table 8.4 shows that an annual average of about 2 percent of U.S. mileage was merged or consolidated over the years 1890–1896. However, serious legislative efforts were made to permit pooling and to reform the regulation of railroads in other ways in the late 1890s and ensuing years.[17] The overall effect of these two influences was probably to soften the impact of the two railroad cases.

An Econometric Study of Antitrust Policy and Mergers

There were several swings in merger and cartel policy following the 1904 *Northern Securities* decision. Standard Oil and American Tobacco were broken up, and tougher antitrust standards were written into the Clayton and Federal Trade Commission Acts. The Taft and Wilson administrations, during which these two pieces of legislation were considered and passed, had a particularly strong antimerger policy. This is reflected in the large number of "monopolization" cases filed in the years 1910–1914.[18]

At other times antitrust was more of a paper tiger. The government tried but failed to break up U.S. Steel, and merger policy was very lax in the 1920s. The per se rule against price fixing was scuttled in 1911 in *Standard Oil* and not firmly reestablished until 1927 in *Trenton Potteries*.[19] Throughout the intervening years, cases involving trade associations added to the uncertainty about what the Sherman Act did and did not prohibit.[20] Strenuous efforts were made during Theodore Roosevelt's second term, in the years before the Clayton Act was passed, and in the late 1920s and early 1930s to rewrite the antitrust laws to allow at least regulated price fixing.[21] This end

14. U.S. Industrial Commission, *supra* note 12, at 335.
15. Ibid., at 336.
16. Gabriel Kolko, Railroads and Regulation, 1877–1916 (1965), ch. 4.
17. Ibid., ch. 5.
18. Posner (1970, 398).
19. Standard Oil v. United States, 221 U.S. 1 (1911); and United States v. Trenton Potteries, 273 U.S. 392 (1927). See the commentary in Richard A. Posner and Frank H. Easterbrook, Antitrust 114 (2d ed. 1981).
20. Charles S. Tippets and Shaw Livermore, Business Organization and Public Control, 297–310 (1941) review this development. They credit Arthur J. Eddy, The New Competition (1911), with stimulating the formation of these associations, which were known until the 1920s as open price associations. Posner (1970, 398) reports a sharp increase in the number of trade association and information exchange cases for the years 1920–1924.
21. See J. D. Clark, The Federal Antitrust Policy (1931), chs. 6–11; and Robert F. Himmelberg, The Origins of the National Recovery Administration (1976).

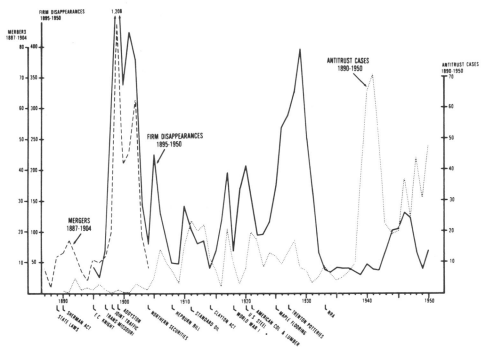

Figure 8.1 Antitrust cases instituted by the Justice Department and merger activity, 1887–1950. (Antitrust cases instituted by the Department of Justice are from Richard A. Posner, A Statistical Study of Antitrust Enforcement, 13 J. Law & Econ. 365, 366 [1970]. Mergers, 1887–1904, come from Jesse W. Markham, Survey of the Evidence and Findings on Mergers, in Business Concentration and Price Policy, 141, 149 [1955]. Firm disappearances, 1895–1970 and 1919–1950, are from Ralph L. Nelson, Merger Movements in American Industry, 1895–1956 [1959], table C-7 at 164–69.)

was briefly achieved with the National Recovery Act cartelizations. Even the Supreme Court's resolve sagged in *Appalachian Coals*.[22] Finally, the Roosevelt administration reversed its course and adopted a stringent antitrust policy in the late 1930s and early 1940s.[23]

Figure 8.1 shows the number of antitrust cases instituted by the Department of Justice for the years 1890–1950. It also shows several merger series that jointly cover the same period. The number of cases is a poor measure of antitrust policy, in part because this aggregate lumps together price fixing and other types of cases. But we have to make do. Important developments for antitrust, which should also have an effect on merger, are marked below the graph.

Beginning in 1904 and up to the late 1940s, there seems to have been a connection between the two series. This covers the period between *Northern Securities* and the Celler-Kefauver Amendment. Between 1904 and the early 1920s there are four cycles of antitrust enforcement matched by four cycles

22. Appalachian Coals v. United States, 288 U.S. 344 (1933).
23. Ellis W. Hawley (1966).

of merger activity. The first ended in 1908, when the Hepburn Bill—a legislative proposal that would have allowed price fixing—was being considered. That effort failed, and mergers increased sharply and then decreased during the years when reform of the antitrust laws was being considered again, hitting their lowest point for the years 1900–1920 in 1914, when the legislative labor gave birth to the FTC and Clayton Acts. The third and fourth cycles are really one, interrupted by the First World War, when industry was cartelized by government.

One feature of these data, confirmed below in econometric results, is the tendency for changes in merger activity to lead changes in case filings. This can mean either that merger caused more cases to be filed or that case filings represented earlier changes in policy. Although yearly data on the number of merger and price-fixing cases are not available, five-year averages of charges filed from 1904 through 1925 indicate that only 18 percent of all cases involved monopolization charges, while 71 percent involved horizontal agreements.[24] Note also that the number of cases filed underwent fairly dramatic swings, making it unlikely that budget cutbacks due to business cycles or other extraneous factors caused the periodic declines in case filings if the Department of Justice operated under roughly constant returns to scale.

The 1920s merger wave is usually considered to be the second important one after the 1898–1902 movement. The actual "wave" can probably be dated at 1925–1929. Carl Eis emphasizes the lax merger policies in his study of these mergers.[25] This is consistent with the evidence from the earlier merger wave, but the two periods may have had an increasingly stringent cartel policy in common as well. Not only did the Supreme Court reestablish the per se rule in 1927 in *Trenton Potteries,* but the number of horizontal conspiracy cases filed in 1920–1924 (fifty cases) and 1925–1929 (thirty-six cases) was greater than in all preceding five-year periods except 1910–1914. It was also greater than in the next two five-year periods.[26] A renewed effort to change the antitrust laws followed the 1927 case, and case filings also decreased. The number of mergers decreased at the same time, remaining low through the first two terms of the Roosevelt administration. However, case filings increased substantially in the late 1930s and early 1940s, and the number of mergers increased directly after this 180-degree change in policy. This sort of graph reading certainly does not prove a connection, but it does provide the outlines of one explanation for large swings in merger activity before passage of the Celler-Kefauver Amendment and before price fixing had become illegal permanently and beyond all doubt.

24. Posner (1970, 398).

25. Carl Eis, The 1919–1930 Merger Movement in American Industry, 12 J. Law & Econ. 267, 284–92 (1969).

26. Posner (1970, 398). Himmelberg, *supra* note 21, at 54–57, argues that Republican policy in the mid-1920s, although lenient toward trade association activities, was severe with regard to out-and-out price fixing.

Some statistical results support the likelihood of a link between mergers and case filings. In the results that follow, annual merger activity for the years 1895–1920 is regressed on case filings, stock price changes, and dummy variables covering periods when antitrust policy underwent changes. Stock price changes are included because the weak statistical association between stock prices and merger is one explanation—although an explanation without a theory—that has often been proposed as a cause of cycles in merger activity. The dummy variables are a necessary evil because they are the only way of taking into account the key policy changes. The problem with using dummies, of course, is that the data are made up, so to speak, and given enough dummies, it would be possible to explain just about any time series. I will define three: one for 1898–1902 (the period between *Trans-Missouri* and the initiation of *Northern Securities*); 1899 (the year following *Joint Traffic* and the *Addyston* Court of Appeals decision); and 1896 and 1908–1916 (the period covering the Hepburn Bill, the monopolization prosecutions of the Taft administration, the FTC and Clayton Acts, and the creation of exempt industries, as well as the political uncertainty of 1896).

The most striking feature of table 8.5 is that the dummy variables for 1898 and 1898–1902 provide strong and consistent support for the view that those years were special, even taking into account the influence of stock prices. The dummy for policy uncertainty (1896, 1908–1916), on the other hand, shows a strong negative effect. Also of interest, the number of antitrust cases has as much explanatory power as stock returns. Current stock returns are more strongly related than either lagged or leading stock returns. In contrast, antitrust cases from past years are negatively related and from future years positively related to merger. Since case filings represent policy initiatives that had their origins before a given case was filed, the negative association of earlier case filings with current mergers suggests at first glance the perverse inference that mergers in the current period are stimulated by a lax price-fixing policy initiated more than a year ago. This is probably a statistical fluke that comes from the see-saw nature of antitrust enforcement. The positive association of next year's case filings with current merger activity comes closer to capturing an intelligible relationship since it takes time to prepare cases and since an administration will usually reveal before case filings are made what its stance on antitrust issues will be.[27]

The last two columns of table 8.5 show that when filings are used as

27. My results contrast with those of Michael S. Lewis-Beck, Maintaining Economic Competition: The Causes and Consequences of Antitrust, 41 J. Pol. 169 (1979), who finds no relation between antitrust enforcement and mergers. He uses Department of Justice case filings as the dependent variable and mergers as the independent variable to assess whether "less competition" (more mergers) causes a change in antitrust enforcement for the years 1895–1973. This raises the question why increased merger activity should cause more price-fixing cases to be filed if mergers and price fixing are substitutes. In addition, Lewis-Beck uses one regression equation for the entire period, uses no trend or trendlike variable, and makes no attempt to incorporate the possible effects of court cases.

Table 8.5 Regressions of Yearly Firm Disappearances through Mergers, 1896–1920

Variable	Regressions Using Stock Returns		Regressions Using Antitrust Cases		Regressions Using Stock Returns and Antitrust Cases			
	(1)	(2)	(3)	(4)	(5)	(6)	(7)	(8)
Constant	107.1	139.1	103.8	123.1	93.8	112.7	78.0	115.6
	(9.32)	(9.82)	(4.74)	(7.31)	(4.26)	(6.39)	(3.68)	(6.95)
Stock return:								
$t-1$	112.7	96.8	...	...	140.9	38.2	...	...
	(.92)	(.96)			(1.41)	(.47)		
t	125.5	159.0	...	...	...	...	45.89	87.25
	(1.29)	(1.97)					(.96)	(1.24)
$t+1$	−90.1	−80.9	...	...	...	...	...	...
	(.82)	(.90)						
Antitrust cases:								
$t-1$	...	...	−4.50	−3.02	...	...	...	...
			(2.68)	(2.34)				
t	...	...	1.87	1.45	...	...	...	...
			(.98)	(1.03)				
$t+1$	...	...	2.61	3.52	1.60	3.59	2.85	3.67
			(1.62)	(2.92)	(.91)	(2.49)	(1.69)	(3.11)
Dummy, 1899	821.3	818.6	846.8	849.4	848.6	852.0	845.7	842.2
	(14.71)	(17.85)	(15.81)	(21.48)	(14.57)	(19.04)	(13.57)	(19.55)
Dummy, 1898–1902	235.8	201.3	255.5	234.1	247.8	238.4	274.15	231.0
	(6.04)	(5.92)	(8.18)	(9.91)	(6.68)	(8.33)	(7.55)	(8.67)
Dummy, 1896–1897 and 1908–16	...	−58.37	...	−69.28	...	−75.8	...	−83.20
		(3.03)		(4.11)		(3.76)		(4.78)
SSR	39,940	25,358	43,456	22,438	51,420	28,766	59,674	27,075
R^2	.970	.981	.968	.984	.961	.978	.956	.980
D-W	1.92	2.68	1.20	2.48	1.65	2.76	1.47	2.83
N	23	23	23	23	24	24	25	25

Source: Yearly firm disappearances are from Ralph L. Nelson, Merger Movements in American Industry, 1895–1956 (1959), at 152–53, table B-7; stock returns are from U.S. Bureau of the Census, Historical Statistics of the United States (1975), Ser. X479, at 1003; antitrust cases are from Richard A. Posner, A Statistical Study of Antitrust Enforcement, 13 J. Law & Econ. 365 (1970), at 366, table 1.
Note: Parentheses indicate t-statistics.

explanatory variables the effect that can be credited to stock returns falls off. My guess about this is that stock prices changed partly in response to developments in antitrust. The Dow-Jones average used in these regressions was composed chiefly of railroad stocks and stocks of corporations that had been formed in the 1898–1902 merger wave, and these are precisely the firms that had an interest in the interpretation and enforcement of the Sherman Act. As each of several crises in antitrust policy came and went (the years 1904, 1908, and 1914 provide examples), stock prices may have dropped and then risen as it became clear that more radical solutions to the trust problem—such as dissolution of firms that happened also to be in the Dow-Jones index—were being passed up in favor of renewed dedication to catching price fixers.[28] Similar arguments would hold for more broadly defined indexes, since a large fraction of industrial stocks were issued by firms formed in the Great Merger Wave.

The results so far have used firm disappearances through merger in mining and manufacturing as the dependent variable. Examination of the data revealed that mining disappearances, chiefly in coal mining, accounted for a large fraction of disappearances (17 percent for the years 1895–1920) and were very variable. For example, they accounted for 43 percent of the total in 1905. In addition, it seemed desirable to break down the regressions by the two types of merger, consolidation and acquisition. The regression results in table 8.6 show an even weaker effect of stock returns on manufacturing disappearances than on manufacturing and mining disappearances. They also show a much stronger relation between antitrust case filings and acquisition than between antitrust case filings and consolidation. On the other hand, consolidation seems largely to have been a response to events in 1898–1902 and does not appear to have been affected at all by the periods of "policy uncertainty" (1896, 1908–1916) or by case filings. One possibility is that acquisition was more sensitive to the antitrust climate, but it seems more likely that the large number of consolidations in the years 1898–1902 imparted so much variability to the data over those years that the more subtle effects of case filings and the periods of policy uncertainty are lost.

Conclusion

Did antitrust policy cause the merger wave that began in the late 1890s? An assessment of what the key court decisions said and how they were interpreted makes it reasonable to suppose that merger was legal while cartels were not. This was at least a widespread view, and these decisions (*Knight, Trans-*

28. From the Wall Street Journal, 6 January 1909, at 8, it can be established that six of the twelve industrials in the Dow-Jones index are in a list of consolidations in Thorelli, *supra* note 2, at 294–303. A study based on stock market data by Malcom R. Burns (1977) finds that the dissolution ordered for Standard Oil was not as severe as expected.

144   GEORGE BITTLINGMAYER

Table 8.6   Regressions of Manufacturing Firm Disappearances Broken Down by
Consolidations and Acquisitions, 1896–1920

Variable	Consolidation and Acquisition	Consolidation Only	Acquisition Only
	Dependent Variable: Manufacturing Disappearances by:		
Constant	86.5	37.47	49.08
	(6.88)	(3.95)	(5.14)
Stock return t	−8.78	8.09	−16.87
	(.17)	(.20)	(.42)
Antitrust cases $t + 1$	2.49	.23	2.26
	(2.78)	(.33)	(3.33)
Dummy, 1899	696.0	646.7	49.33
	(21.33)	(26.31)	(1.99)
Dummy, 1898–1902	198.4	198.1	.29
	(9.82)	(13.03)	(.19)
Dummy, 1896–97	−52.71	−9.20	−43.51
and 1908–16	(4.00)	(.93)	(4.35)
R^2	.982	.989	.619
D-W	1.98	2.43	1.36
N	25	25	25

Source: Same as table 8.5.

Missouri, Joint Traffic, and Taft's *Addyston Pipe* opinion) enjoyed prominent play in newspapers and legal publications.

The timing of the mergers is consistent with this story. There was a brief flurry of mergers in the late 1880s—around the time the first antitrust laws were passed and the trusts were first brought into the courts. There was another increase after *E. C. Knight,* and finally an unprecedented number of mergers in 1898 following a new outcry against the trusts and a series of court cases that held price fixing to be illegal. Merger activity decreased substantially while *Northern Securities* was litigated.

Other evidence comes from particular industries. The mergers in several industries—cotton oil, sugar, cast iron pipe, oil, and meat packing—appear to have been the result of antitrust action taken against cartels in those industries. In other cases—shoe machinery and explosives—merger was apparently undertaken on the advice of attorneys worried about the antitrust laws. Steel and railroading, two heavily cartelized industries, resorted to merger at a substantially greater pace beginning in 1898, and a major promoter of consolidations claimed that the antitrust laws increased the number of U.S. mergers. In addition to merger, another device, the community of interest, seems also to have sprung up in the late 1890s in railroading as a substitute for cartel agreements.

Data from later years suggest that antitrust policy continued to influence the number of mergers. *Northern Securities* resulted in fewer consolidations and more acquisitions. There is a strong, positive statistical relationship between merger and the number of antitrust case filings during the years 1904 to 1920, and a more casual investigation suggests that the merger wave of the late 1920s may have been related to increased case filings and the reestablishment of the per se rule, and that the merger wave of the 1940s may have been a response to the antimonopoly campaign of 1939–1942.

Any explanation has to be evaluated against the alternatives. The mergers grew so rapidly and encompassed so many different industries that it seems reasonable to look first at policy intervention—a change in corporation laws or a change in cartel policy, for example. The obvious difficulty with the corporation law argument is that the laws were changed a decade before the mergers took place. It also begs the question, Why was the law changed? It seems more reasonable, I think, that mergers in 1898 and 1899 were caused by court cases decided in 1897 and 1898. While the British mergers of the 1880s and 1890s represent a challenge to this seemingly straightforward interpretation of the evidence, it seems defensible at the very least to say that the U.S. merger movement was larger and more pronounced by a great enough margin to merit special attention.

I have also tried to revive an old controversy that the evidence seems to invite. Were the cartels and mergers caused by the desire for monopoly or by the desire to prevent ruinous competition? Both explanations are consistent with the notion that the 1898–1902 mergers were caused by the court cases of 1897 and 1898. However, many firms apparently preferred the less secure collusion of a cartel until the late 1890s, suggesting that the monopoly gains from merger may not have been very great. So it certainly seems worthwhile to consider explanations that do not posit monopoly gain as the reason for collusion and for merger induced by a law against price fixing.

The view that collusion and merger were both responses to unavoidable market imperfections stemming from fixed costs has some advantages considered purely as theory, and it also receives some support from the disproportionate representation of the iron and steel industry in the peak years of 1898–1902, as well as from the prominent cartelization, merger, and development of communities of interest in railroading. The implication, only thinly sketched here, that there can be too much competition is also in harmony with the view of turn-of-the-century businessmen and economists, which seems to me to be a happy result if it can be achieved on an economically defensible basis. But, while I hope to have aided in the rehabilitation of a way of looking at competition and monopoly, much remains to be done.

CHAPTER NINE

Antimerger Policy under the Hart-Scott-Rodino Act: A Reexamination of the Market-Power Hypothesis

B. Espen Eckbo and Peggy Wier

Introduction

Since 1950 the Department of Justice and the Federal Trade Commission have filed more than 500 antitrust complaints against firms involved in mergers, on the grounds that these mergers would "substantially lessen competition" and thus violate Section 7 of the Clayton Act.[1] Approximately 85 percent of the complaints were filed against horizontal combinations, and most resulted in divestiture or cancellation of the merger. Stigler (1966) perceives another consequence of these prosecutions; he attributes the decline in the relative frequency of horizontal mergers in the United States since 1950 to the deterrent effect of vigorous Section 7 enforcement (see chapter 4 of this volume).

In theory, mergers between competitors—horizontal mergers—can lead to accumulations of market power.[2] However, recent empirical evidence devel-

This essay was previously published in the *Journal of Law and Economics* 28 (April 1985): 119–49. © 1985 by The University of Chicago. All rights reserved.

1. With the Celler-Kefauver amendment in 1950, Section 7 of the Clayton Act of 1914 replaced Section 2 of the Sherman Act of 1890 as the principal federal antitrust law regulating corporate mergers and acquisitions. A potential threat to competition constitutes an offense under this law, and it is not necessary to prove a horizontal relationship between the combining firms. Furthermore, anticipated or demonstrated economic efficiencies are not a defense against the illegality of a merger that may lessen competition. United States v. Procter and Gamble, 386 U.S. 568, 580 (1967). Prior to the Celler-Kefauver amendment, Section 7 applied to the transfer of corporate stock only and was applied exclusively to horizontal mergers.

2. Oligopoly models in the tradition of Augustin Cournot, Recherches sur les principes mathématiques de la théorie des richesses (1938), and the information-based oligopoly model of George J. Stigler. A Theory of Oligopoly, 72 J. Pol. Econ. 44 (1964), imply that the difference between the actual and competitive price level is inversely related to the number of independent producers in the industry. Since a horizontal merger by definition reduces the number of firms by one, the potential anticompetitive effects of such mergers are typically analyzed in terms of these oligopoly models. See also idem, Monopoly and Oligopoly by Merger, 40 Amer. Econ. Rev. 23 (1950).

oped by Eckbo (1983) and Stillman (1983) indicates that the mergers challenged by the government between 1963 and 1978 were not, in general, anticompetitive. Both authors use stock price data to test the hypothesis that these mergers would have promoted profitable collusion in the defendants' industries. Collusive mergers generate increased net cash flows for the combining firms and their industry rivals. In an efficient stock market, the present value of increments to expected future cash flows will be reflected in positive abnormal stock returns for industry members when collusive mergers are announced. Subsequent Section 7 challenges will induce negative abnormal stock returns if investors expect the government to eliminate collusive behavior in the merging firms' industries. Eckbo and Stillman do not observe the stock price patterns predicted by the collusion hypothesis. In fact, Eckbo's data suggest that, had they survived, the challenged mergers in his sample would have been economically efficient on average rather than anticompetitive.

How can the government's apparent failure to prosecute anticompetitive mergers be explained? In this paper we test the proposition that legal constraints in effect during the Eckbo and Stillman sample periods prevented the agencies from obtaining the information needed for judging a merger's competitive impact before filing a complaint. The implementation of the Hart-Scott-Rodino (HSR) Antitrust Improvements Act in September 1978 significantly relaxed those constraints. A major purpose of the HSR Act was to increase the precision with which defendants are chosen by providing the agencies with more information about potential Section 7 violations and more time to analyze that information before they take legal action. We examine a sample of Section 7 cases filed after 1978 for evidence that HSR has enhanced the agencies' ability to select anticompetitive mergers for prosecution, but we find no such evidence. Our study indicates that the government's tendency to challenge efficient mergers cannot be explained by constraints on the enforcement process.

Our empirical analysis addresses two additional issues of central importance for drawing public policy inferences from a study of this type.[3] First, we discuss a conclusion reached by Elzinga (1969), by Pfunder, Plaine, and Whittemore (1972), and by Ellert (1976). They argue that the government's successes in Section 7 cases represent "paper victories" because the relief imposes no significant economic constraints on the firms' behavior. Their argument implies that if mergers provide opportunities for anticompetitive activity, these opportunities are undisturbed by judgments against the merg-

3. Recently, the law enforcement agencies have shown an interest in using the Eckbo-Stillman test to diagnose anticompetitive mergers: " '[One] tool that might be considered [for detecting price fixing],' an Antitrust Division lawyer said, 'would be a study of stock prices of companies involved in a merger and their competitors. . . .' '' Wall Street Journal, 10 January 1984, at 3.

ers. If this is a valid contention, Section 7 suits are unlikely to affect industry rivals' share prices whether or not the prosecuted mergers are anticompetitive. Thus, the Eckbo-Stillman methodology cannot reliably discriminate between hypotheses about the mergers' competitive effects. We reject the "paper victory hypothesis" for the defendant firms in our sample. Furthermore, results obtained from tests in which rival firms are grouped according to the outcome of the cases support the conclusion that the challenged mergers would have been efficient rather than anticompetitive. Finally, we test whether the earlier conclusions concerning the market-power hypothesis depend on the method used to select economically relevant rival firms. Eckbo and Stillman use different selection procedures, and for the purpose of our last test we use both. We find that share price performance is similar across the two sets of rival firms and uniformly inconsistent with the market-power hypothesis.

In sum, our results do not support the contention that enforcement of Section 7 has served the public interest. While it is possible that the government's merger policy has deterred some anticompetitive mergers, the results indicate that it has also protected rival producers from facing increased competition due to efficient mergers. The additional enforcement powers granted under the HSR Act apparently have not led the agencies to pick cases better.

Market Power and Efficiency Hypotheses: Review of Predictions

Table 9.1 summarizes the implications of alternative market-power and economic-efficiency hypotheses for the behavior of the stock prices of bidders, targets, and their competitors. The predictions are based on the presumption that stock prices are unbiased estimates of the present value of stockholders' claims to firms' future cash flows.[4] Changes in these cash flow estimates caused by merger-related events will induce changes in stock prices when the events are announced. We assume for all of the predictions outlined in table 9.1 that mergers are value-enhancing investments for the merging firms (an assumption that will be supported by the data reported in Table 9.2). Thus, events increasing the probability that a merger will occur or, once completed, will survive (merger proposals and prodefendant decisions) will be associated with positive abnormal returns for merging firms. Probability-decreasing events (complaints and progovernment decisions) will have a negative effect on merger partners' prices. The merger-related price effects on

4. This efficient-markets/rational-expectations assumption underlies numerous empirical studies in the finance and industrial economics literature. For a methodological survey, see G. William Schwert, Using Financial Data to Measure Effects of Regulation, 24 J. Law & Econ. 121 (1981).

Table 9.1   Abnormal Returns to the Merging Firms and Their Rivals as Predicted under the Market-Power and Economic-Efficiency Hypotheses

A. Probability-increasing Events: Merger Proposal or Prodefendant Decision

Theory Predicting the Source of the Merger Gains*	Abnormal Returns to Merging Firms	Abnormal Returns to Rival Firms
Market power:		
Collusion, Cournot model	Positive (monopoly rents)	Positive (monopoly rents)
Predatory-pricing model	Positive (monopoly rents)	Negative (costs of price war)
Economic efficiency:		
Productivity increases (synergy)	Positive (cost savings)	Negative (competitive disadvantage)
Information†	Positive (undervalued resources)	Zero or positive (undervalued resources, and/or possible productivity increases)

B. Probability-decreasing Events: Antitrust Complaint or Progovernment Decision

Market power:		
Collusion, Cournot model	Negative (loss of monopoly rents)	Negative (loss of monopoly rents)
Predatory pricing model	Negative (loss of monopoly rents)	Positive (avoiding price war)
Economic efficiency:		
Productivity increases (synergy)	Negative (loss of cost savings)	Positive (avoiding competitive disadvantage)
Information‡	Zero	Zero

*Under the assumption of managerial value maximization, the sum of the gains to the *merging* firms will be positive, regardless of the sources of the gains.
†Examples of positive information effects on rival firms are the case when the merger announcement reveals possibilities for efficiency gains also available to nonmerging firms and the case when the merger signals an increase in demand for resources generally owned throughout the industry of the merging firms. In these cases there will be no additional information effect of a subsequent prodefendant decision.
‡The information effect on rival firms is negative if the complaint or case outcome also signals a restriction on the future merger opportunities of the rival firms (such as in "landmark" cases).

rival firms will depend on the competitive effect of the merger and can therefore be used to discriminate among alternative hypotheses.

Market-Power Hypotheses

The collusion hypothesis is that challenged mergers would have promoted tacit or explicit cooperation among the members of the merger partners' industries. Under this hypothesis, events that make the merger more likely will cause rivals' share prices to rise to reflect increases in expected future cash flows, and events that make the merger less likely will be associated with share price declines for rivals. Mergers also could help the new, larger firm engage in predatory conduct. The merging firms could gain by waging price wars against their competitors. Rivals' stock prices will fall as survival of a merger becomes more likely and will rise in response to probability-decreasing events.[5]

Efficiency Hypotheses

The predictions of the efficiency hypotheses are more complex. For example, suppose that two merged firms can employ a scale-increasing technological innovation that reduces their average cost. In a competitive industry this cost reduction will put downward pressure on product prices (and upward pressure on factor prices). Other things equal, this reduces the market value of the rivals. This is the "productivity increases" hypothesis of table 9.1. Now suppose that the merged firms cannot costlessly exclude rivals from using the same technology. Then the merger announcement can signal the availability to the rival producers of the cost-reducing technology. As a result, share prices of rival firms could rise to reflect expected gains from exploitation of the technology, perhaps through mergers of their own.[6] Alternatively, a merger can signal an increase in the demand for certain resources owned by the rival firms as well as by the target, so that the merger announcement contains good news for rival firms' shareholders. These signaling scenarios are collectively called the "information" hypothesis in table 9.1.

Efficient mergers can have simultaneous productivity and information effects. Therefore, either positive or negative abnormal returns to rivals are consistent with the efficiency hypothesis. However, events such as Section 7 complaints, which threaten the survival of efficient mergers, will not, in

---

5. In Stigler's oligopoly theory, *supra* note 2, the costs of monitoring a tacit, industrywide collusive agreement are inversely related to the number of firms in the industry. A horizontal merger increases the short-term profitability of a collusive agreement by lowering the costs of policing individual cartel members' attempts to free ride on the supracompetitive product price supported by the cartel's policy. In the classical dominant firm model, the acquisition of a "fringe" firm by the price leader reduces his profit-maximizing level of output, assuming no efficiency or cost savings are involved. See, for example, William M. Landes and Richard A. Posner, Market Power in Antitrust Cases (1981), for an exposition of the dominant firm model. The controversial predation model is reviewed by John S. McGee, Predatory Pricing Revisited, 23 J. Law & Econ. 289 (1980). Evidently the enforcement agencies regard predation as highly unlikely and focus on collusive effects in Section 7 investigations. See Gregory Werden, Market Delineation and the Justice Department's Merger Guidelines, 1983 Duke L. J. 517.

6. A similar argument is made by Gregg A. Jarrell and Michael Bradley, The Economic Effects of Federal and State Regulations of Cash Tender Offers, 23 J. Law & Econ. 371 (1980).

most cases, harm rival firms.[7] Complaints lessen the danger to rivals of increased competition due to the merger, but do not devalue the information released earlier.

Thus the only pattern of abnormal returns to rival firms at once inconsistent with the market-power hypotheses and consistent with the efficiency hypothesis is one in which rivals experience nonnegative returns when *both* probability-increasing and probability-decreasing events occur. This is essentially the result reported by Eckbo and Stillman. Eckbo found that in his sample of sixty-five horizontal Section 7 cases filed between 1963 and 1978, the rivals, on average, earned statistically significant positive abnormal returns relative to the merger proposal announcement and zero or positive returns relative to the subsequent announcement of the government's suit. Stillman found that rivals earned zero abnormal returns relative to the merger and case announcements in nine of eleven cases filed between 1964 and 1972.

It may be that a merger is not an appropriate candidate for prosecution even if the abnormal returns to rival firms are consistent with the market-power hypothesis. A merger with anticompetitive effects could also have compensating efficiency effects.[8] The Eckbo-Stillman test does not reveal the relative magnitudes of the welfare gains and losses. But when the test rejects the market-power hypothesis, it follows that disallowing the merger will reduce social welfare.

Sample Design and Methodology

Our sample consists of eighty-two horizontal mergers challenged under Section 7 of the Clayton Act between January 1963 and December 1981. It includes the sixty-five challenged horizontal mergers compiled by Eckbo and the eleven horizontal mergers examined by Stillman. Of the eighty-two mergers, seventeen were challenged after 5 September 1978. Each merger satisfies the following seven criteria:

1. The merger was alleged by the DOJ or the FTC to violate Section 7 of the Clayton Act.
2. The merger proposal took place between January 1963 and December 1981 and was announced in the *Wall Street Journal*.
3. The bidder or the target firm was listed on the New York Stock Exchange (NYSE) or the American Stock Exchange (ASE) at the time of the merger proposal.
4. The government's complaint alleged that the merger endangered competition in a mining or manufacturing industry.

7. An exception is the filing of a "landmark" case that signals a change in enforcement policy. Such a change can reduce the value of the rivals even though the merger is efficient. In this case, the stock price test does not have the power to reject the efficiency hypothesis. However, it can be used to reject the market-power hypothesis.
8. Williamson (1968a).

5. This endangered product market belongs to one of the four-digit SIC industries listed in the Standard Industrial Classification Manual of 1972 and its supplements.
6. The relevant geographic market was listed in the antitrust complaint as "nationwide" or represented a major part of the United States.
7. It was possible to identify (using the algorithm described below) at least one rival firm listed on either the NYSE or the ASE at the time of the merger proposal.

The suits were terminated in several ways. Nineteen mergers were canceled following the complaint. Consent decrees were issued in thirty-eight cases, thirty-four requiring divestiture and four imposing other remedies. In eight cases the government prevailed in court.[9] Twelve complaints were dismissed or dropped, and five cases were still pending as of December 1983.

Selection of Rival Firms

For each case not already included in Eckbo's sample, we collected rival firms using Eckbo's algorithm, which can be summarized as follows:

1. Select the product market by a five-digit code consisting of a four-digit SIC code, and a fifth digit assigned using the product-specific information in the 1972 SIC Manual and its 1977 supplement.
2. Generate a list of all firms on the University of Chicago Center for Research in Security Prices (CRSP) stock returns tape that CRSP associates with the first four digits of this five-digit code.[10]
3. Use information on product lines in the Standard and Poor's Registry of Corporations to delete from the CRSP list all firms for which it cannot be confirmed that the company belongs to the relevant five-digit industry.
4. Eliminate firms that do not have stock returns available during the estimation period (defined below). We call the remaining firms "five-digit SIC rivals."

Next, we searched for a second set of companies identified by the prosecuting agencies as rivals of the defendant firms. This selection process involved reading the case summaries in the Merger Case Digests and the Trade Regulation Reporter. When no rivals were mentioned we pursued the references

9. A wide variety of requirements in addition to, or instead of, divestiture have been imposed on Section 7 defendants. Examples of such requirements are the prohibition of future acquisitions or clearance of such acquisitions with the complaining agency, and mandatory patent licensing. Defendants have also been ordered to purchase a specified quality of inputs from manufacturers other than the merger partner: to refrain from producing inputs for their own use; and to avoid tie-in sales, market allocation, and discriminatory pricing. See 1963–74 A.B.A. Merger Case Dig. for a summary of ancillary relief granted.

10. The Center for Research in Security Prices (CRSP) assigns to each firm one four-digit SIC code, and the date on which the code became effective. This single code is intended to represent the major four-digit SIC industry of the firm.

given in the summaries to actual published reports of the cases.[11] All rivals mentioned in these sources and listed on the NYSE or ASE during the relevant period are included in our second set of rivals. This search, and information supplied by the agencies themselves, provided agency-based rival portfolios for thirty-six of the eighty-two cases. The number of agency-based rivals per case ranges from one to seven, with a mean of three, while the number of five-digit SIC rivals ranges from one to twenty-nine, with a mean of five. For the cases in which both sets of rivals are available, on average 38 percent of the agency-based rivals also appear in the portfolio of five-digit SIC rivals for a given case, while 21 percent of the five-digit SIC rivals also appear as agency-based rivals.

Estimation and Test Methodology

For the ith merger in our sample, we compute abnormal share price performance relative to a specific event (the merger proposal, the antitrust complaint, or the case outcome) by estimating the coefficients of the following regression equation:

$$(1) \qquad \tilde{\mathbf{r}}_i = \alpha_i + \beta_i \tilde{\mathbf{r}}_m + \gamma_i \mathbf{d} + \tilde{\boldsymbol{\epsilon}}_{i'}$$

where $\tilde{\mathbf{r}}_i$ = a $T \times 1$ vector of the daily, continuously compounded returns to the bidder firm, the target firm, or an equal-weighted portfolio of the rival firms.

$\tilde{\mathbf{r}}_m$ = a $T \times 1$ vector of daily, continuously compounded returns to the value-weighted CRSP market index.

$\mathbf{d}$ = a $T \times 1$ vector containing values of one for days in the event period (defined below) and of zero otherwise.

$\tilde{\boldsymbol{\epsilon}}_i$ = a $T \times 1$ vector of daily random disturbances, assumed to be independent of $\tilde{\mathbf{r}}_m$ and $\mathbf{d}$, serially uncorrelated and distributed multivariate normal with zero mean and constant variance.

In order to account for any contemporaneous correlation of returns across firms in the same industry, returns of the rival firms associated with a given merger are pooled into one equal-weighted industry portfolio before estimating the coefficients of equation (1). The coefficient β_i extracts the marketwide influence on security returns, while the coefficient γ_i represents the average one-day abnormal return to the ith bidder, target, or portfolio of rivals during the event period. The estimation period T is always two hundred trading days before the event day (day 0) through ten trading days after the event day. Day 0 is defined as the day of the *Wall Street Journal* publication of the actual merger-related announcement. To capture any prepublication leakage of relevant information, which can be caused by a delay in the *Wall Street*

11. Notes in the summaries refer to reports in various issues of Trade Cases (CCH); FTC Decisions; Federal Reporter (F.2d); and Federal Supplement (F. Supp.).

Journal publication of the announcement, as well as any immediate post-announcement developments, we focus on a maximum event period of thirty-one trading days (day -20 through 10) surrounding the event day.[12] We summarize the abnormal performance over various intervals within these thirty-one days by estimating equation (1) for five different window lengths (-20 through 10, -10 through 5, -3 through 3, -1 through 1, and day 0). Our dummy variable d takes on the value of one for each day in the window. When we estimate γ_i for a window inside the period -20 through 10, we delete the returns which fall outside the window but inside (-20, 10). Thus, the normal or comparison period for, say, window (-1, 1) is the same as that for window (-20, 10), namely the period -200 through -21.

To summarize samplewide abnormal performance we pool the information across the N mergers in the sample by forming the cumulative average abnormal return (CAAR) relative to an event period of length D days:

$$\text{CAAR}_D = \frac{D}{N} \sum_{i=1}^{N} \hat{\gamma}_i.$$

CAAR_D cumulates $\hat{\gamma}_i$ (the OLS estimate of γ_i) over the D event days used to estimate γ_i and averages this number across the sample of N mergers. It will be clear from the context whether CAAR_D refers to bidder firms, target firms, or to portfolios of rival firms. Under the hypothesis of zero abnormal returns ($\text{CAAR}_D = 0$), and assuming that the N mergers are independent events, the following Z-statistic is a standard normal variate for large N:

$$Z_D \equiv \frac{1}{\sqrt{N}} \sum_{i=1}^{N} \left(\frac{\hat{\gamma}_i}{SE_i} \right),$$

where SE_i is the standard error of $\hat{\gamma}_i$ produced by the OLS regression.

Empirical Results

Preliminaries: Abnormal Performance of the Merging Firms

Before reporting the results of tests of the hypotheses in table 9.1 we provide empirical support for two assumptions underlying the predictions of the hypotheses. The first is that the mergers examined here are value-increasing investments for the merging firms. Positive abnormal returns to bidders and

---

12. In our three-event study (merger proposal, complaint, and outcome), the estimation period of one event sometimes incorporates days close to one or both of the two other events. In order not to confound the results for such cases, we exclude twenty-one days (-20 through 1) surrounding each of these other events from the estimation period of the event in focus.

Table 9.2   Percentage Cumulative Average Abnormal Returns (CAAR) to Bidder and Target Firms in Challenged Horizontal Mergers Relative to the *Wall Street Journal* Announcement of the Merger Proposal, the Antitrust Complaint, and the Final Case Outcome, 1963–1981 (Z-value; Percentage Positive)

Wall Street Journal Announcement	Sample size	Days Relative to the *Wall Street Journal* Announcement (Day 0)				
		−20 through 10	−10 through 5	−3 through 3	−1 through 1	0
A. Bidder firms:						
Merger proposal	68	3.0* (1.8, 60)	1.1 (.7, 46)	1.0* (1.9, 62)	.8† (2.3, 60)	.1 (.2, 44)
Antitrust complaint	55	−1.8 (−1.5, 45)	−2.4‡ (−2.4, 43)	−1.2 (−1.5, 40)	−1.4‡ (−3.0, 38)	−1.0‡ (−4.4, 35)
Case outcome:						
1. Cancellation or divestiture	50	−1.2 (−1.0, 42)	−1.7† (−2.0, 46)	−0.9 (−1.0, 40)	−.6† (−2.1, 42)	−.40‡ (−2.4, 46)
2. Dismissal or no divestiture	13	−.5 (−.2, 40)	−.9 (−1.0, 46)	−.2 (−.7, 38)	−.5 (−.4, 40)	−.3 (−.5, 54)
B. Target firms:						
Merger proposal	38	25.7‡ (10.7, 87)	20.8‡ (12.4, 84)	13.5‡ (12.8, 76)	10.5‡ (15.0, 76)	4.4‡ (13.1, 61)
Antitrust complaint	22	−6.5‡ (−2.4, 23)	−7.4 (−3.1, 32)	−8.2‡ (−5.8, 9)	−7.6‡ (−7.9, 9)	−4.6‡ (−8.7, 14)
Case outcome:						
Cancellation or divestiture	15	−1.2 (−.5, 40)	−4.6† (−2.0, 33)	−4.9‡ (−2.6, 40)	−6.1‡ (−4.7, 33)	−1.1 (−1.5, 40)

Note: In this table, the number of bidders is the total number of listed bidders in the sample, and the number of targets is the number of listed target firms given that the bidder is also listed. The complaint announcement sample excludes thirteen cases in which the complaint and final outcome were announced simultaneously. The "dismissed or no divestiture" group is ignored for the target firms as it contained only three targets that were still listed at the time of the outcome announcement. The delisting of the target firms in this group reflects the relatively long delay (on average more than nine hundred trading days) between complaint and case outcome: the merger is frequently consummated during this interim period.

*Hypothesis of zero abnormal returns (CAAR = 0 percent) rejected at the 10-percent level of significance.

†Hypothesis rejected at the 5-percent level of significance.

‡Hypothesis rejected at the 1-percent level of significance.

targets during the merger proposal period are consistent with this assumption. Second, we assume that relief secured by the government in challenged merger cases is costly to defendants. Thus, we expect that on average defendant firms will earn negative abnormal returns when complaints are announced and that losing defendants will earn negative abnormal returns at the conclusion of their cases.

The results reported in table 9.2 support both assumptions. Bidder firms on average earn significantly positive abnormal returns relative to the merger proposal date, with CAAR of 0.8 percent (Z-value of 2.3) over the three-day period -1 through 1. Sixty percent of the individual bidder firms show positive abnormal performance over this event period. Target firms show large gains over all five event periods relative to the proposal date, with CAAR of 10.5 percent (Z-value of 15.0) over the -1 through 1 period and 4.4 percent (Z-value of 13.1) on the day of the proposal announcement. Over the thirty-one-day period -20 through 10, bidder firms earn CAAR of 3.0 percent (which is only weakly significant according to the Z-test) while target firms earn on average 25.7 percent abnormal returns. The latter CAAR is more than ten standard deviations from zero and 87 percent of the targets show positive abnormal performance. These results are similar to the proposal-related gains to bidder and target firms reported elsewhere in the merger literature.[13]

Second, antitrust complaints are associated with negative abnormal returns to bidders and to targets that are still listed at the complaint date. For example, over the three-day period -1 through 1 relative to the complaint announcement the CAAR is -1.4 percent (Z-value of -3.0) for bidder firms and -7.6 percent (Z-value of -7.9) for target firms. On the day of the complaint, the abnormal returns are -1.0 percent and -4.6 percent, respectively; both are strongly significant. These negative abnormal returns are presumed to reflect a combination of costs that investors expect will be borne by the defendant firms, such as legal expenses, interruptions of productive activity, costs of regulatory constraints frequently imposed on convicted (or settling) firms, and direct loss of merger gains should the suit eventually result in cancellation of the merger or divestiture of some of the acquired assets.[14]

13. See, for example, Michael C. Jensen and Richard Ruback, The Market for Corporate Control: The Scientific Evidence, 11 J. Fin. Econ. 5 (1983), for a review. While this literature uniformly shows large gains to target firms involved in mergers, whether bidder firms on average gain, lose, or break even from merger activity is not clear. Note that the estimates of proposal-induced gains to the merging firms in our sample are biased toward zero if the market to some extent anticipates antitrust problems.

14. Significant case-related abnormal losses to bidder and target firms are also reported by Eckbo (1985); and by Peggy Wier, The Costs of Antimerger Lawsuits: Evidence from the Stock Market, 11 J. Fin. Econ. 207 (1983). Data in table 9.2 suggest that losses to bidders at complaint announcements exceed proposal-related gains. One possible explanation for this result is that

The results in table 9.2 indicate that the magnitude of the abnormal losses to bidder firms relative to the final outcome announcement depends on the nature of the outcome. Cases in which the merger is canceled or in which divestiture is ordered are associated with significant abnormal losses to defendant firms. On the other hand, dismissals or final decisions not involving divestiture do not cause any apparent abnormal movements in the stock prices of the defendants. Evidently the government is able to impose significant economic constraints on unsuccessful defendants. Therefore we can reasonably expect the announcement of a Section 7 complaint or a progovernment final decision against a truly anticompetitive merger to have a significant effect on the rival firms as well.

Tests of the Market-Power Hypotheses

As shown in table 9.3, first row, the five-digit SIC rivals in our data base on average earn significantly positive abnormal returns relative to the merger proposal announcement. Rivals of defendants that were challenged prior to the HSR Act on average earn 2.4 percent abnormal returns over the thirty-one-day period −20 through 10 (Z-value of 2.6, 64 percent positive) and 0.8 percent over the seven-day period −3 through 3 (Z-value of 2.0, 52 percent positive). These numbers are roughly equivalent to those generated by Eckbo, using a slightly different estimation procedure, for the same sixty-five cases. Rival firms also show positive proposal-related abnormal performance in the sample of mergers which were challenged after August 1978, with 2.4 percent abnormal returns over the thirty-one-day period −20 through 10 (Z-value of 1.9, 59 percent positive).

The positive proposal-induced abnormal returns to rival firms contradicts the predation hypothesis. Apparently the market does not expect that the typical merger in the sample will result in a price war that is costly for the rival firms. Furthermore, the evidence of the table contradicts the proposition that the proposal-related gains to the rivals represent expected monopoly profits from a postmerger collusive agreement. There is no evidence that the typical antitrust complaint or progovernment final outcome announcement, which significantly reduce the probability that a merger (and any merger-related collusive agreement) will survive, cause the share prices of the rival firms to fall. Indeed, for the sample of mergers challenged after the effective date of the HSR Act, a progovernment decision is on average associated with

abnormal returns measure only deviations from prior expectations. Other things equal, the less likely an event is considered by investors the larger the abnormal returns (in absolute value) associated with the announcement that the event has in fact occurred. The mergers in our sample could have been anticipated to a greater extent than the complaints that followed. A second possible reason for the result is that the merger proposal portfolio and the complaint portfolio do not contain exactly the same firms, as explained in the note to table 9.2.

Table 9.3 Percentage Cumulative Average Abnormal Returns (CAAR) to Five-Digit SIC Rivals of the Merging Firms Relative to the *Wall Street Journal* Announcement of the Merger Proposal, the Antitrust Complaint, and the Final Outcome (Z-value; Percentage Positive)

Sample Period	Number of Cases (DOJ, FTC)	Days Relative to the *Wall Street Journal* Announcement (Day 0)				
		−20 through 10	−10 through 5	−3 through 3	−1 through 1	0
Merger proposal announcement:						
Jan. 63–Aug. 78	65 (40, 25)	2.4‡ (2.6, 64)	.7 (1.7, 50)	.8† (2.0, 52)	.2 (.4, 46)	.1 (−.4, 48)
Sept. 78–Dec. 81	17 (7, 10)	2.4* (1.9, 59)	.7 (1.2, 59)	.1 (.2, 65)	.3 (−.4, 49)	.2 (.9, 59)
Antitrust complaint announcement:						
Jan. 63–Aug. 78	56 (37, 19)	.8 (.5, 54)	.4 (.6, 48)	−.1 (−.5, 48)	.1 (.7, 48)	−.1 (−.3, 55)
Sept. 78–Dec. 81	10 (5, 5)	−.5 (−.1, 40)	1.9 (1.2, 60)	.8 (1.1, 40)	.6 (1.5, 40)	−.6 (−1.1, 50)
Case outcome announcement (cancellation or divestiture):						
Jan. 63–Aug. 78	48 (32, 16)	.1 (−.6, 44)	−.6 (−1.5, 42)	−.4 (−1.4, 36)	−.4 (−1.3, 42)	−.4 (−1.4, 42)
Sept. 78–Dec. 81	10 (3, 7)	.4 (.5, 60)	3.5† (2.0, 70)	−.1 (.3, 60)	−.5 (.2, 50)	.7 (1.1, 70)
Case outcome announcement (dismissal or no divestiture):						
Jan. 63–Aug. 78	12 (9, 3)	−1.7 (−.4, 42)	.8 (.3, 57)	−2.2 (−1.2, 33)	−1.0 (−.5, 25)	−.7 (−.5, 25)

Note: The two subsamples relative to the complaint announcement exclude nine cases before September 1978 and seven cases after August 1978 in which the complaint and final case outcome were announced simultaneously in the *Wall Street Journal.* Of these sixteen mergers, twelve were canceled or divested, two were convicted but no divestiture was ordered, and two were dismissed. Of the sixty-five mergers relative to the proposal announcement before September 1978, two are pending in court (as of December 1983) and three had rival firms with insufficient return data at the time of the final outcome announcement: hence the sample relative to the outcome announcement before September 1978 contains only sixty cases. Of the seventeen mergers relative to the proposal announcement after August 1978, three are pending, one was dismissed, and three had insufficient rival return data at the time of the final outcome announcement. Thus, the "dismissal or no divestiture" group is available only for the pre-September 1978 sample.
*Hypothesis of zero abnormal returns (CAAR = 0 percent) rejected at the 10-percent level of significance.
†Hypothesis rejected at the 5-percent level of significance.
‡Hypothesis rejected at the 1-percent level of significance.

significantly *positive* abnormal returns to the rival firms. The CAAR for this sample is 3.5 percent over the -10 through 5 period surrounding the final outcome announcement (Z-value of 2.0, 70 percent positive). For the other event periods there is no evidence of significant abnormal performance by the rivals. This, of course, contrasts with the significant losses to the merging firms associated with these events that are reported in table 9.2. Essentially, the data imply that gains to the rival firms associated with the merger proposal do not depend on the merger's survival.

This implication is inconsistent with the collusion hypothesis and consistent with the information hypothesis listed in table 9.1. An efficient merger can convey new information that benefits other firms in the same industry as the merging firms. As discussed earlier, news of a technological innovation that can be adopted by the rivals (perhaps through mergers of their own), or news of a significant increase in the value of certain specialized resources generally owned throughout the industry, can cause a positive revaluation of the rival firms. This information is valuable to the rivals regardless of the outcome of the merger attempt. Thus, while we reject the market-power hypothesis, we cannot reject the proposition that the mergers in our sample, whether challenged before or after the implementation of the HSR Act, would have been efficient. The proposition that the HSR Act has led to a more precise identification of truly anticompetitive mergers for the purpose of Section 7 prosecution is not substantiated by our evidence.

Results Using Agency-based Rival Firms

Our test of the market-power hypothesis assumes that the rivals in our sample are sufficiently close to the merging firms, in terms of product market competition, to be significantly affected by any new production/investment strategy to be implemented by the merged firms. The positive abnormal returns to the five-digit SIC rivals, shown in table 9.3, support this assumption. The question remains, however, whether a more elaborate procedure for selecting rival firms will produce substantially different results. For example, it is possible that while the five-digit SIC rivals are sufficiently close to the merging firms to benefit from an information effect, they are too distant to be significantly affected by any effect the mergers might have on product prices. If so, our tests are biased against the market-power hypothesis and in favor of the efficiency hypothesis.

The DOJ and the FTC routinely research the product markets of merging firms to diagnose potential anticompetitive effects of the merger. As a result, they record the identity of the firms they consider to be major competitors of the merging firms. By comparing the case-related performance of these agency-based rivals to the performance of the corresponding five-digit SIC rivals we can gauge the sensitivity of our results to the choice of rival firms.

The results in table 9.4 are based on the thirty-six cases in our sample for which we were able to assemble two sets of rival firms. Using a t-test that accounts for any contemporaneous cross-correlation of returns, we fail to reject the hypothesis that the abnormal performance is identical across the two sets of rivals for any of the event periods in the table.[15] Both sets of rivals earn statistically significant positive abnormal returns relative to the proposal announcement and neither set shows subsequent price behavior consistent with the market-power hypothesis. The return patterns of the agency-based rivals reinforce our rejection of this hypothesis.[16]

Conclusion

In 1978 Congress undertook to strengthen the hand of the agencies charged with enforcing Section 7 of the Clayton Act. New enforcement powers granted under the Hart-Scott-Rodino Antitrust Improvements Act were intended to enhance the agencies' ability to select truly anticompetitive mergers for prosecution. The HSR Act imposes automatic delays on proposed mergers, so that the agencies have time to consider the mergers' competitive effects before they are completed. It also provides the agencies with the legal right to obtain merger-related information during precomplaint investigations.

Studies by Eckbo and Stillman show that the HSR Act addressed a genuine

15. The t-statistic for this test was computed as

$$t_{s-a,i} \equiv \frac{\hat{\gamma}_{si} - \hat{\gamma}_{ai}}{SE(\gamma_{si} - \hat{\gamma}_{ai})},$$

where

$$SE(\hat{\gamma}_{si} - \hat{\gamma}_{ai}) \equiv [(X_i'X_i)_{33}^{-1}(\sigma_{si}^2 + \sigma_{ai}^2 - \sigma_{sai})]^{1/2},$$

and where subscripts a and s denote the agency-based and five-digit SIC rivals of merger i; σ_{si}^2 and σ_{ai}^2 are the variances of the error term resulting from regressing equation (1) on each of the two sets of portfolios of rivals; σ_{sai} is the contemporaneous covariance of the error terms across the two regressions; $X_i \equiv [\mathbf{1}_T \hat{r}_m \mathbf{d}]$ is a $T \times 3$ matrix; $\mathbf{1}_T$ is a $T \times 1$ vector of ones; and $(X_i'X_i)_{33}^{-1}$ is the (3, 3) element of the 3×3 matrix $(X_i'X_i)^{-1}$. In a sample of N mergers, and under the hypothesis that $\hat{\gamma}_s - \hat{\gamma}_a = 0$, the sample average of $t_{s-a,i}$ multiplied by N is distributed approximately standard normal for large N.

16. A virtually identical picture emerges when we apply our CAAR methodology to the agency-based rivals of the eleven cases compiled by Stillman (1983). Stillman, who studies the same rival portfolios individually and only on days where the bidder or target firms earn statistically significant abnormal returns, fails to reject the hypothesis of zero proposal-induced abnormal performance for ten of the eleven rival portfolios. Our evidence of significantly positive average abnormal returns to Stillman's rival portfolios does not necessarily contradict his results since (i) our CAAR methodology pools the information in the sample (with a resulting efficiency gain) and (ii) the cumulative effect of several days of gradual information leakage can be statistically significant even when the abnormal return on any given day in the cumulation period is not.

Table 9.4 A Comparison of the Percentage Cumulative Average Abnormal Returns (CAAR) to Five-Digit SIC Rivals and Agency-based Rivals Relative to the *Wall Street Journal* Announcement of the Merger Proposal, the Antitrust Complaint, and the Final Case Outcome (Z-value; Percentage Positive)

Number of Cases (DOJ, FTC)	SIC Rivals/ Agency Rivals	Days Relative to the *Wall Street Journal* Announcement (Day 0)				
		−20 through 10	−10 through 5	−3 through 3	−1 through 1	0
Merger proposal announcement:						
36 (21, 15)	SIC Rivals	3.0‡ (2.3, 72)	1.9* (1.9, 61)	1.4* (1.9, 58)	.3 (.2, 47)	.1 (.2, 58)
	Agency Rivals	3.3† (2.9, 61)	2.2‡ (3.4, 67)	1.2‡ (2.5, 58)	.6* (1.8, 56)	−.1 (−.1, 47)
Antitrust complaint announcement:						
32 (21, 11)	SIC Rivals	1.3 (.9, 50)	1.2 (1.2, 50)	.5 (.7, 56)	.9‡ (2.4, 56)	.2 (.4, 60)
	Agency Rivals	1.1 (.4, 47)	.4 (.2, 59)	0 (−.2, 50)	.6 (1.5, 53)	.1 (.2, 56)
Case outcome announcement (cancellation or divestiture):						
24 (15, 9)	SIC Rivals	−.2 (−.4, 46)	−.5 (−.6, 46)	.1 (−.1, 46)	.2 (1.1, 67)	−.2 (−.5, 50)
	Agency Rivals	−.1 (.1, 46)	−.6 (.8, 63)	−.2 (−.5, 38)	.7* (1.6, 58)	.2 (1.2, 46)
Case outcome announcement (dismissal or no divestiture):						
7 (5, 2)	SIC Rivals	−3.2 (−.7, 29)	−1.1 (−.2, 43)	−3.1 (−1.4, 29)	−1.3 (−.7, 14)	−1.4† (−2.0, 29)
	Agency Rivals	−3.3 (−1.1, 29)	.1 (.2, 43)	−.5 (−.2, 57)	.4 (.8, 57)	.1 (.6, 43)

Note: Four of the thirty-six cases were challenged after September 1978. The sample relative to the complaint announcement excludes four cases in which the complaint and outcome were announced simultaneously. The sample relative to the final outcome announcement excludes two cases which were pending as of December 1983, and three cases which were lost due to delisting of rival firms.

*Hypothesis of zero abnormal returns (CAAR = 0 percent) is rejected at the 10-percent level of significance.

†Hypothesis is rejected at the 5-percent level of significance.

‡Hypothesis is rejected at the 1-percent level of significance.

problem. Both authors conclude that the challenged horizontal mergers in their samples, which cover the 1963–1978 period, were not anticompetitive. The central purpose of our research is to test the proposition that the HSR Act has produced a significant improvement in the agencies' case-selection record. We reject this proposition. The cases in our sample that were filed after 1978 were mounted against mergers that apparently would not have harmed competition—in fact, our evidence suggests that these mergers were economically efficient.

Since changes in the enforcement process apparently have not resulted in improved performance by the agencies, one must look to the agency case-selection criteria in order to explain their failure to identify anticompetitive mergers. According to the Merger Guidelines of 1968 and 1982, very modest increases in industry concentration can trigger Section 7 challenges.[17] As noted by Stigler, the economics profession has supplied "precious little" in the way of tested knowledge to support this selection policy.[18]

It is also possible that, far from providing a social benefit, the HSR Act entails a somewhat subtle social cost by reducing firms' incentives to merge. If a merger proposal conveys to the market some of the valuable inside information held by the bidder firm, the delay in the execution of the merger transaction required by the premerger notification rules can reduce the bidder's expected return from the investment. The evidence indicates that rival firms benefit from the news of a merger proposal, and a delay in execution gives these rival firms additional time to exploit the news, perhaps by competing for the target firm. This potential public-good problem lowers the *ex ante* expected returns to the firm initiating the merger negotiations, whether the merger will have anticompetitive effects or not.

Tollison (1983) has argued that all but the "most overwhelmingly large" mergers should be allowed to go forward. We find his argument appealing. A more permissive merger policy would shift Section 7 investigations to *ex post* analyses of anticompetitive effects based on the larger set of data available after the consummation of a merger. It would accommodate the mounting evidence, including the results reported in this paper, that the market-power hypothesis rests on an extremely weak empirical foundation.

17. Tollison (1983, 214) cites evidence that "over 20 percent of the mergers challenged under the 1968 guidelines fell *below* the guidelines." Eckbo (1985) finds that stock-price–based tests similar to the kind used in this paper reject the market-power hypothesis even for values of market shares and industry concentration that exceed the critical values in the Merger Guidelines.

18. Stigler (1982b). See also Brozen (1982).

CHAPTER TEN

The Employment Consequences of the Sherman and Clayton Acts

WILLIAM F. SHUGHART II and ROBERT D. TOLLISON

Introduction

The alternative approaches to the problem of monopoly—laissez faire, regulation, public ownership, and antitrust—are discussed in virtually every economics textbook. The laissez-faire alternative is usually dismissed as not politically feasible. In addition, modern empirical research has shown that in many cases the effects of regulation and public ownership diverge from the benign textbook analysis in which corrective government intervention brings competitive outcomes. The theory of economic regulation, for example, is based on the idea that regulation transfers wealth among certain interest groups rather than that it protects consumers against the abuses of market power or market failure (Stigler 1971, Peltzman 1976).

How has antitrust fared under this intellectual revisionism regarding public policy toward monopoly? Clearly, antitrust has engaged criticism, but the majority of the antitrust debate has been carried out in terms of principle. On those occasions when antitrust policy fails to move the economy toward the competitive ideal (as it does quite often by many accounts), such failures are attributed to correctable errors. Better people, for example, with better training in economics could apply the laws to better effect. The antitrust debate embodies a presumption that the antitrust laws provide a framework wherein economic welfare can be improved. There are, of course, caveats to this argument. Some scholars would abolish the Federal Trade Commission (FTC) and others would support marginal changes in the law, but most see the antitrust statutes, especially Sections 1 and 2 of the Sherman Act, as a corpus of sound doctrine whose application is beneficial to the economy.

What is missing from the antitrust debate is the type of empirical scrutiny that has been applied to alternative public policies toward monopoly such as regulation and public ownership. Antitrust and regulation, for example, are assumed to be different in their economic effects. While regulation may work in practice to impose more costs than benefits, antitrust is rarely seen in the same light. This is not to say that antitrust decisions and doctrine are not

This essay was previously published in the *Journal of Institutional and Theoretical Economics* 147 (March 1991): 38–52.

hotly debated; they are. But, by and large, no one has stepped back and asked a simpler question: What has been the impact of the law enforcement activities of the Justice Department's Antitrust Division on the economy? A record exists, and it can be evaluated. Taking a first step in this direction is the purpose of this paper.

To do so, we place economic welfare on its most basic footing by asking whether the historical activities of the Antitrust Division have had an impact on employment in the economy. In other words, what is the effect of antitrust on jobs? Our approach is empirical. Using data covering the period 1947–1981 (and earlier), and measuring antitrust intervention in terms of cases instituted per thousand dollars of real budgetary expenditures, we find a positive and statistically significant *ceteris paribus* relationship between unanticipated increases in Antitrust Division enforcement activities and the civilian labor force unemployment rate. Our results therefore suggest the existence of an antitrust analog to the short-run Phillips relation, and imply that enforcement of the antitrust laws by the Justice Department tends to reduce overall economic efficiency.

We do not pretend that this is a complete test of the impact of antitrust laws on the U.S. economy. It is, however, a step toward estimating the effects of this legislation on economic welfare, a step that is sorely needed if we are to know whether or not antitrust and regulation are really all that different in their practical consequences.

The essay is organized as follows. In the next section, we outline the alternative hypotheses relating antitrust enforcement and economic efficiency. The third section contains a discussion of the data and presents the empirical results. Concluding remarks follow in the final section.

Antitrust and Unemployment

The basic framework of American antitrust policy is embodied in three statutes enacted around the turn of the century. In brief, the Sherman Act (1890) prohibits "every contract, combination in the form of trust or otherwise, or conspiracy, in restraint of trade or commerce among the several States . . ." (Section 1), and declares guilty of a misdemeanor "every person who shall monopolize, or attempt to monopolize . . ." (Section 2). The Clayton Act (1914) prohibits price discrimination, exclusive dealing and tying contracts, acquisitions of competing companies, and interlocking directorates when the effect of the practice "may be to substantially lessen competition or tend to create a monopoly." The substantive Section 5 of the FTC Act (1914) bans "unfair methods of competition in commerce and unfair or deceptive acts or practices in commerce." Subsequent amendments have strengthened several provisions of the statutes. The most noteworthy of these are the modification of the Clayton Act's price discrimination section by the Robinson-Patman

Act (1936), and the closing of a loophole in antimerger law by the Celler-Kefauver Act (1950).

The Clayton Act is enforced jointly by the Department of Justice and the FTC, while the Antitrust Division has sole responsibility for bringing Sherman Act cases. The Commission enforces the provisions of its own enabling legislation and, beginning in 1947, the FTC was also able to condemn conduct that offends the Sherman Act under Section 5 of the FTC Act.

Despite the fact that the Sherman Act has been hailed as a " 'charter of freedom,' a constitution governing the economy of the United States," the historical enforcement record of the Antitrust Division has been the subject of substantial criticism. A large segment of the critical literature examines the economic merits of individual cases, and it is fair to say that many more "bad" than "good" decisions have been identified by these analyses. In recent memory, only the outcome of the *Sylvania* case has received general approval.[1] The more usual case study finds that the evidence presented was "weak and at times bordered on fiction," and that "neither the government nor the Courts seemed able to distinguish competition from monopolizing" (Peterman 1975a, 143). Other critics suggest alternative (procompetitive) explanations for the behavior of the defendants (see Cummings and Ruther 1979), contend that the economic theory of the case was "erroneous" (Flath 1980, 193), or focus on the deficiencies of the remedy imposed (Zelenitz 1980). There are a variety of examples along these lines (Elzinga 1970; McGee 1958; Fisher, McGowan, and Greenwood 1983).

The literature also includes empirical studies that analyze the Justice Department's record in prosecuting certain types of antitrust law violations. For example, Hay and Kelley considered horizontal price-fixing complaints brought successfully by the Antitrust Division from January 1963 to December 1972, and found that "industries colluding at one point in time often can be found to be colluding at later points in time, in spite of antitrust action in the interim" (Hay and Kelley 1974). Similarly, one interpretation of the evidence adduced by Asch and Seneca is that the antitrust authorities more often prosecute unsuccessful cartels (Asch and Seneca 1976). Palmer found that firms having below-average growth rates were represented disproportionately in antitrust suits charging horizontal restraint of trade (Palmer 1972), and by Elzinga's reckoning, the remedial measures adopted in enforcing antimerger law were less than "sufficient" in 35 out of 39 cases (Elzinga 1969).

In terms of its implications for the economy, the literature critical of antitrust suggests that enforcement of the laws may not enhance economic efficiency. Indeed, because the antitrust authorities may bring cases against the

1. See Continental T.V. Inc. v. GTE Sylvania Inc., 433 U.S. 36 (1977). A representative approving view is given by Bork (1978). For a contrary opinion, see Stuart Altschuler, Sylvania, Vertical Restraints, and Dual Distribution, 25 Antitrust Bull. 1 (1980).

wrong firms or impose relief measures that are ineffective in some instances and have unintended consequences in others, vigorous enforcement efforts may in fact lead to an economy characterized by lower rates of growth in real output, higher prices, and lower employment levels than otherwise.

Even though antitrust intervention might plausibly reduce output and employment in those firms subject to complaints, is it reasonable to expect that the economy would fail to adjust to such conditions? For example, one might expect labor markets to continue to clear in the face of antitrust activity because wages would fall in some sectors of the economy (i.e., those industries exempt from the law) as workers shifted out of the sectors targeted by antitrust complaints. But, although it is indeed reasonable to expect the economy to adjust, such adjustments are likely to take place only to the extent that antitrust enforcement is *predictable*.

What we are suggesting is an antitrust analog to the Phillips relation. In the long run (when the actual level of antitrust enforcement is equal to the amount individuals expect), observed unemployment in the economy will be invariant to case output. That is, the overall level of employment will adjust to antitrust activity through wage and other price movements brought about by a reallocation of resources between targeted and untargeted sectors of the economy. In the short run, however, unanticipated increases in law enforcement activity may cause unemployment to rise as firms are forced unexpectedly to adopt inefficient production technologies. Thus, the mechanism linking unemployment to antitrust works much like the standard Phillips relationship between unemployment and unanticipated inflation. Antitrust activity is variable, and even if aggregate case output were always perfectly anticipated, it is doubtful that the allocation of enforcement resources among the various violation types (horizontal price fixing, matters involving the legality of vertical restraints, merger cases, and so forth) could always be predicted correctly.

To see how the antitrust Phillips relationship might operate, assume that the economy is in long-run equilibrium with a given level and mix of antitrust enforcement activity. Now suppose that the Antitrust Division steps up its enforcement efforts under Section 7 of the Clayton Act and begins issuing an unexpectedly large number of complaints against mergers in some industry, say, grain milling. The agency moves to enjoin proposed mergers and, since the antitrust law has no statute of limitations, complaints may also be brought against mergers consummated in the past. Mergers prevented and divestitures ordered by the agency serve to reduce the optimal scale of grain-milling companies, causing the affected firms to lower their current and planned production rates and to lay off some of their employees. During the adjustment period, unemployment in the industry will be higher than otherwise. Moreover, if the unexpectedly large number of cases against grain-milling firms is taken as a signal of more antimerger enforcement generally, other industries, perhaps exhibiting concentration-profit data comparable to the targeted firms, may alter their behavior in a similar fashion.

As a further illustration, suppose that equilibrium is displaced by an unanticipated increase in antitrust complaints charging that the use of resale price maintenance (RPM) by a group of manufacturers facilitates a horizontal conspiracy to fix retail prices. If the allegations are correct, then a successful prosecution of the cases by the Antitrust Division will lead to increased competition in the industry, resulting in expanded output and employment. In contrast, if RPM had in fact produced more efficient exchange by, for example, providing incentives for retailers to supply ancillary services to their customers, then prohibition of the practice will cause lower sales at retail, a consequence matched upstream by reduced output and employment. By forcing firms to adopt inefficient selling techniques, unexpected increases in efforts to enforce the law against price fixing may result in higher unemployment rates in the short run.

Our hypothesis, then, is that an unexpected increase in antitrust activity can lead to an increase in the general level of unemployment. Although we have not laid out a theory of bureaucratic behavior, we see the systematic part of enforcement activity as arising from planning by agency staff members. Given its annual budgetary appropriations, the agency sets an enforcement agenda and prosecutes, *presumably,* those matters expected to have the greatest net benefit to society. Actual case loads can diverge from the level planned, however, if, for example, there is an unexpectedly large number of complaints by consumers or competitors, or if some budgeted cases turn out to be more complicated than envisaged, consuming enforcement resources that were originally intended for other matters.

Obviously, this is only one explanation of how antitrust could cost jobs, and it rests on the idea that antitrust attacks generally efficient arrangements in the economy. A second link between antitrust and unemployment, although one that seems weak in view of the economy's ability to adjust in the long run to intervention, can be derived from the so-called market-concentration doctrine. In particular, if the majority of respondents to Justice Department complaints have achieved profitability through monopoly power, then we should observe expanded output and employment in the wake of increased enforcement activity. On the other hand, if these same firms have achieved high profits by virtue of lower costs, then antitrust penalties will result in the adoption of inefficient production technologies. That is, we would expect that if antitrust is applied predominantly to firms whose profits are based on efficiency, increased enforcement efforts will lead to reductions in output and employment.

The market-concentration interpretation requires that antitrust have a substantial deterrent effect. Although only a relatively small number of firms are ever the subject of antitrust complaints in a given year, "if it becomes evident that, for example, large firms with profit margins over 10 percent have a greater probability of being prosecuted than those with profit margins under 10 percent, a large firm with a profit margin of, say, 11 percent will have an incentive to reduce its margin and thereby reduce probability of prosecution'' (Peltzman 1984). In other words, antitrust may raise unemployment by making the economy as a whole less efficient.

Empirical Results

The historical record of the two public enforcement agencies has been compiled by Posner (1970) and by Gallo, Craycraft, and Bush (1985). The FTC data are of little use for our purposes, however. The broad language of Section 5 encompasses both traditional antitrust violations and consumer protection matters such as those involving false and deceptive advertising, misrepresentation of goods, product liability, and so forth. In order to focus on the former, we limited our sample to cases brought by the Antitrust Division under the Sherman and Clayton Acts. This restriction allows us to examine the welfare effects of the two statutes regarded by most as the heart of American antitrust law.

Our basic data set consists of cases instituted annually by the Antitrust Division for the period 1890 to 1981. (We would be happy to supply these data upon request.) Although the data on enforcement date from 1890, we further restricted our sample to two subperiods, 1932–1981 and 1947–1981. The 1932 starting point marks the date when the Antitrust Division became a separate line item in the Justice Department budget, allowing us to control for changes in the real value of resources devoted to enforcement, and 1947 is the first year for which a complete set of observations on important labor market variables is available.[2]

Although many of the complaints issued by the Antitrust Division over the 1932–1981 period charged the respondent(s) with offending more than one provision of the law, it is fair to say that the majority of the cases in our sample involve allegations of price fixing, monopolizing, and violating antimerger law. For example, allegations of horizontal conspiracy—a category including but not limited to price fixing agreements—accounted for 34 percent of the violations charged in the cases instituted between 1930 and 1969 (Posner 1970, 398), and 42 percent of the illegal behaviors alleged in the complaints issued from 1963 to 1982 (Gallo, Craycraft, and Bush 1985). Next in importance were violations of Sherman Act Section 2 (15 percent of the 1930–1969 charges and 6 percent of the 1963–1982 violations), followed by Clayton Act Section 7 violations (8 percent and 18 percent, respectively).

Our hypothesis is that an unanticipated increase in antitrust enforcement

2. All macroeconomic data were obtained from the Council of Economic Advisers, Economic Report of the President (1982).

leads to an increase in the general level of unemployment. But there is also reason to believe that antitrust activity and unemployment are determined jointly (see Amacher, Higgins, Shughart, and Tollison 1985). For example, if one views the supply of antitrust violations as being a monotone transformation of the number of market transactions taking place in the economy, then increases in the level of real output should be associated with higher levels of enforcement. On the other hand, if antitrust is not all that different from traditional price-entry regulation, then increased enforcement activity may be observed during economic downturns as more firms complain of price-cutting and other "cutthroat" competition by rivals. In either case one would expect some relationship between antitrust activity and real GNP.

The above considerations raise questions about the direction of causality between unemployment and antitrust. On the one hand, the level of enforcement activity may be influenced by changes in the level of real output (employment); on the other hand, unexpected changes in antitrust are hypothesized to cause changes in the level of employment (real output). To investigate these relationships, we used the procedure suggested by McMillin and Fackler, which utilizes the definition of causality developed by Granger.

In brief, a variable X is said to Granger-cause Y if the current value of Y is better predicted from past values of X and Y than by past values of Y alone. In implementing the test, the variables are first made stationary. Law-enforcement activity was measured as cases instituted annually per thousand dollars of real budgetary expenditures. The residuals from a regression of the natural logarithm of this ratio on the natural logarithm of real GNP became our proxy for the unexpected component of antitrust intervention.[3] This series, UCPBD, required no further transformation to achieve stationarity. The unemployment series was stationary in the first differences of its natural logarithm, D1LNU.

After converting both variables to stationary series, each dependent variable was regressed on up to 7 lags of itself, and the optimal lag length was determined by selecting the lag that minimized the model's final prediction error (FPE). Two bivariate models were then formed. In one of these bivariate

3. In each of the subperiods analyzed, antitrust activity was counter-cyclical, suggesting that the Justice Department's enforcement efforts operate much like ordinary price-entry regulation. For example, the ordinary least squares estimates for the 1932–1981 period were

$$\text{LNCPBD} = 2.3668 - 0.4423\text{LNRGNP}, R^2 = 0.211,$$

where LNCPBD is the natural logarithm of cases per (thousand) real budgetary dollars, and LNRGNP is the natural logarithm of real GNP. The coefficient on the independent variable is significantly different from zero at the 1-percent level on a two-tailed test ($t = -3.75$), and the Durbin-Watson statistic allows one to accept the null hypothesis of no first-order autocorrelation ($d = 1.57$). The residuals from this and similar regressions were used as proxies for unanticipated antitrust enforcement in the various data subperiods.

models, D1LNU was regressed on the optimum lags of itself determined in the previous step plus up to 7 lags of UCPBD. The optimum lag length of UCPBD was again determined by the minimum-FPE criterion. The process was then reversed, treating UCPBD as the dependent variable. In each case, if the minimum FPE of the bivariate model was less than the FPE of the univariate model, then the added variable became a candidate for inclusion in the final model.

The results of this exercise are presented in table 10.1. In the first row, the model that best predicts unemployment contains 2 lags of itself and 6 lags of unanticipated antitrust activity. The provisional conclusion therefore is that unexpected enforcement efforts cause unemployment in the sense of Granger. (Moreover, the signs of the coefficients on the lagged values of UCPBD suggest that the causal relationship is positive: unexpected increases in antitrust intervention lead to higher unemployment rates.) Similarly, the results displayed in the second row indicate that unemployment is a candidate for Granger-causing antitrust; this causal mechanism is also positive in sign.

The final step is to treat these two equations as a system and reestimate them using Zellner's technique. The results from pooling the equations shown in table 10.2 generally confirm the ones obtained using the FPE criterion. In particular, taken as a group the 6 coefficients on lagged values of UCPBD are significantly different from zero at the 10-percent level on the basis of the calculated F-statistic. The causal relationship running from unemployment to antitrust also holds up under the relevant t-test. We thus have fairly strong evidence of bidirectional causality. Unanticipated increases in antitrust enforcement Granger-cause increases in the general level of unemployment, but there is also a feedback effect in which increases in unemployment Granger-cause increases in antitrust activity.

The causality tests suggest that a portion of the variation in the unemploy-

Table 10.1   Final Single-Equation Models

Dependent Variable*	Independent Variables†	Initial Minimum FPE‡	Final Minimum FPE
D1LNU	D1LNU (2) UCPBD (6)	0.0807754	0.0766302
UCPBD	UCPBD (1) D1LNU (1)	0.1540584	0.1469735

*D1LNU and UCPBD are, respectively, the first difference of the natural logarithm of the unemployment rate, and the residuals from the regression of the natural logarithm of the ratio of Justice Department antitrust cases to real budgetary appropriations on the natural logarithm of real GNP.
†Maximum lag length in parentheses.
‡Lagged dependent variable only.

Table 10.2   Systems Regressions: Tests of Sets of Coefficients Against Zero*

Dependent Variable	Independent Variables	F-Statistic	Degrees of Freedom
D1LNU	D1LNU (2)	1.68	2,76
	UCPBD (6)	1.86†	6,76
UCPBD	UCPBD (1)	—‡	
	D1LNU (1)	—§	

*See table 10.1 for variable definitions.
†Significant at a 10-percent level.
‡Coefficient not different from zero on a two-sided t-test ($t = 1.09$).
§Coefficient different from zero at a 5-percent level on a two-sided t-test ($t = 2.05$).

ment rate is explained by variations in antitrust activity. In order to assess the effects that antitrust enforcement may have on unemployment when other factors are held constant, we constructed an estimable equation of the following form:

$$LNU_t = a_0 + a_1 UGNP_t + a_2 PHAT_t + a_3 LNFLFPR_t + a_4 LN(B/W)_t + v_t,$$

where LNU_t = the natural logarithm of the unemployment rate in year t,
$UGNP_t$ = the residuals from a regression of the natural logarithm of real GNP on a linear time trend,
$PHAT_t$ = the inflation rate,
$LNFLFPR_t$ = the natural logarithm of the female labor force participation rate,
$LN(B/W)_t$ = the natural logarithm of the ratio of the average weekly unemployment insurance benefit to the average weekly wage in the nonagricultural sector, and
v_t = the regression error term.

This is a standard set of explanatory variables of the unemployment rate.[4] The level of aggregate demand for goods and services is one of the prime determinants of the derived demand for labor. More important for firms' employment decisions, however, is the effect of unanticipated changes in the demand for output. Unexpectedly high levels of aggregate demand, for example, will draw down accumulated inventories of finished goods and induce firms to step up their current production rates. In the short run this can be accomplished by offering overtime to existing employees, but if the demand shift is viewed as being permanent, previously laid off workers will be recalled and new employees hired. Similarly, unexpectedly low levels of

4. On the use of unanticipated demand changes and the unemployment insurance benefit-to-wage ratio as independent variables in an equation explaining the unemployment rate, see Daniel K. Benjamin and L. A. Kochin, Searching for an Explanation of Unemployment in Interwar Britain, 87 J. Pol. Econ. 441 (1979).

aggregate demand will lead to a contraction in output and employment. To capture these effects we used the residuals from a regression of the natural logarithm of real GNP on a linear time trend as a proxy for unanticipated demand changes.[5] In accordance with the above discussion, positive deviations should be associated with lower levels of unemployment, and vice-versa.

The variable PHAT allows for the existence of a short-run Phillips relation. If individuals form their expectations about future inflation rates adaptively, then an increase in the inflation rate will in the short run cause some workers to accept job offers that subsequently (when expectations have been revised upwards) pay a real wage that is too "low". The unemployment rate will fall temporarily. On the other hand, inflation rates that are unexpectedly low will cause unemployment to rise in the short run as some workers quit jobs and others refuse to accept employment offers that will later turn out to pay an acceptable real wage.

LNFLFPR measures the labor force status of women. There is substantial empirical evidence that for a variety of reasons females experience higher unemployment rates than their male counterparts. One would therefore expect that overall unemployment will rise as a larger percentage of females enter the labor force, all else equal.

If being unemployed is considered to be the occupation of searching for employment, then the variable B/W measures the average relative wage earned by job seekers. Specifically, B/W is the ratio of the average weekly benefit check paid by state unemployment insurance funds in real terms to the average real weekly wage earned by workers in the nonagricultural sector. As benefits rise relative to wages, we expect the unemployment rate to increase, *ceteris paribus*.

Finally, we augmented the unemployment rate equation with our measure of unanticipated antitrust activity, UCPBD. The results from estimating the equation by ordinary least squares (OLS) are displayed in table 10.3. The data suggest that unexpected antitrust enforcement tends to increase unemployment, *ceteris paribus*. In particular, for the 1947–1981 subperiod, an unanticipated increase of 1 percent in Antitrust Division cases per thousand dollars of budgetary appropriations leads to about a 0.17 percent increase in the economy-wide unemployment rate.

---

5. After correcting for the presence of serial correlation in the residuals, the results of this estimation for 1932–1981 were:

$$LNRGNP = 5.4974 + 0.0382TREND, R^2 = 0.848.$$

The coefficient on the linear time trend was significantly different from zero at the 1-percent level ($t = 16.17$), and the estimated first-order autocorrelation coefficient was 0.8343 ($t = 10.70$).

Table 10.3   OLS Regression Results

	Dependent Variable: Log of Unemployment Rate	
	1932–1981	*1947–1981*
Intercept	1.9355	−1.7031
UGNP	−2.8543	−4.7197
	(−3.48)*	(−3.09)*
UCPBD	0.1465	0.1728
	(1.88)‡	(2.59)†
PHAT	−0.8965	−3.2430
	(−0.72)	(−1.87)‡
Log of:		
FLFPR		1.2124
		(2.48)†
B/W		1.1125
		(0.88)
$\hat{\rho}$	0.8505	0.3964
R^2	0.254	0.606

Notes: t-statistics in parentheses; $\hat{\rho}$ is the estimated first-order autocorrelation coefficient. An asterisk denotes significance at the 1-percent (*), a dagger at the 5-percent (†), and a double-dagger at the 10-percent (‡) levels.

The remaining coefficient estimates support the predictions of economic theory. Unexpected increases in aggregate demand reduce the unemployment rate sharply, and there is evidence of the existence of a negatively-sloped short-run Phillips curve. Moreover, increased female labor-force participation raises the unemployment rate significantly, and the coefficient on the unemployment insurance benefit-to-wage ratio is of the expected sign, although it is not different from zero at standard significance levels. Overall, the regression specifications in table 10.3 explain between 25 percent and 61 percent of the variation in the unemployment rate over time.[6]

Because of earlier evidence of bidirectional causality between antitrust and unemployment, we specified a second equation in which unanticipated enforcement, UCPBD, was the dependent variable and the natural logarithm of the unemployment rate, LNU, was the independent variable. We then treated the two equations as a system and reestimated them using Zellner's

6. To check the sensitivity of the results to changes in the time periods analyzed, we reestimated both equations after dropping the last 10 observations in each sample (i.e., adopting subperiods of 1932–1971 and 1947–1971). We obtained results quite similar to those reported in table 10.3. In particular, the coefficients on UCPBD were positive and significantly different from zero at the 5-percent level in both cases.

Table 10.4 Seemingly Unrelated Regression Results

Dependent Variable: Log of Unemployment Rate

	1932–1981	1947–1981
Intercept	1.9762	−1.5670
UGNP	−2.8854	−5.5095
	(−1.63)	(−3.78)*
UCPBD	0.3654	0.2809
	(1.87)‡	(3.78)*
PHAT	−4.8911	−3.3994
	(−1.92)‡	(−1.88)‡
Log of:		
FLFPR		1.1712
		(2.62)†
B/W		1.0899
		(0.98)
R^2	0.114	0.550

Notes: See table 10.3. R^2 is the weighted coefficient of multiple determination for the two-equation system.

technique. The results for the unemployment rate regression are shown in table 10.4.[7] By and large these estimates confirm the results obtained using OLS. The coefficient on unexpected Antitrust Division enforcement is positive and significantly different from zero in both cases. Moreover, with the exception of unanticipated changes in aggregate demand in the 1932–1981 subperiod, the estimated coefficients on all other variables retain their previous signs and significance levels.[8]

In sum, our most conservative estimate (see table 10.3) suggests that an unexpected increase of 1 percent in Sherman and Clayton Act cases per thousand dollars of real Antitrust Division budgetary expenditures led to a

7. The results from estimating the second equation generally showed a positive relationship between unanticipated antitrust enforcement and unemployment. For the 1932–1981 period, for example, we obtained

$$UCPBD = -0.2870 + 0.1660LNU,$$

where the coefficient on the natural logarithm of the unemployment rate just missed significance at the 10-percent level ($t = 1.62$).

8. We also estimated our two-equation system for the 1932–1971 and 1947–1971 subperiods. In the former case the coefficient on antitrust activity was positive but not different from zero at standard significance levels. For 1947–1971, however, the results were quantitatively similar to those reported in table 10.4; the coefficient on UCPBD was positive and significant at the 1-percent level.

0.15 percent rise in the unemployment rate, all else equal. This implies that the mean unemployment rate increased by 0.0078 (from 5.2171 to 5.2249 percent), adding about 5,400 individuals to the average annual stock of unemployed labor force participants over the 1932–1981 period.

Concluding Remarks

In this paper we have presented evidence suggesting that antitrust enforcement reduces economic welfare. Specifically, using data on Sherman and Clayton Act cases brought over the period 1932–1981, we found that on balance antitrust has raised the level of unemployment in the economy. We do not claim that antitrust is responsible for all (or even most) of observed unemployment, nor do we suggest that every antitrust action throws people out of work. Rather, our most conservative results imply that on average an unexpected increase of 1 percent in antitrust case activity leads to about a 0.15 percent increase in the overall unemployment rate.

We stress in conclusion that ours is a positive and not a normative analysis. Surely, the Federal Reserve is just a special and powerful case of how unexpected government intervention impacts on the economy. It should come as no surprise that other parts of the government affect the economy in a similar way. And with respect to antitrust we should keep in mind that these laws have been around for a long time. They sound good, and their potential is often remarked. But their usefulness in the end has to be a function of how they are applied and how they work out in the economy at large. Our essay reports a small contribution to the latter problem.

CHAPTER ELEVEN
Antitrust Enforcement and
Foreign Competition

WILLIAM F. SHUGHART II, JON D. SILVERMAN,
AND ROBERT D. TOLLISON

Record trade deficits and increasing concern with the competitiveness of American business in the global economy have led recently to a number of proposals for relaxing domestic antitrust enforcement. For example, late in his second term President Reagan floated a plan to amend the Clayton Act that would, among other things, have exempted import-injured industries from the antimerger law for up to five years.[1] Similarly, President Bush publicly supported measures aimed at easing the antitrust treatment of corporate research joint ventures to spur the development of the new technologies necessary for meeting the challenge of foreign competition.[2]

These proposals for reform are based on the presumption that import competition serves as a counterweight to domestic antitrust concerns. In other words, during a time when foreign producers are seen to have made significant inroads into domestic markets, less vigilance by the antitrust authorities is thought to be required. International competition, and not intervention by the Federal Trade Commission (FTC) or the Justice Department's Antitrust Division, should provide the necessary incentives for firms to keep their prices in line with costs. Indeed, some critics have argued that vigorous domestic antitrust enforcement activities place American firms at a competitive disadvantage relative to their foreign rivals who typically operate under less stringent antitrust proscriptions.

The idea that domestic antitrust enforcement and foreign competition are *substitutes* for helping maintain a freely functioning economy may in fact play a role in explaining the origins of antitrust policy in the United States. DiLorenzo (1985) has argued that the Sherman Act was passed in 1890 partly as a means of pacifying opponents of protective tariffs. In particular, he suggests that antitrust was the price paid by interest groups representing "big business" in return for the protectionist trade legislation (known popularly as the "Campaign Contributors' Tariff Bill") introduced just three months

1. See Nadine Cohodas, Reagan Seeks Relaxation of Antitrust Laws, 44 Cong. Quarterly Weekly Report 187 (1986) and Shughart (1987).

2. Administration Said to Propose Easing Antitrust Laws on HDTV, McGraw-Hill News Service (1989).

after the Sherman Act was signed into law. The business sector's puzzling lack of opposition to the Sherman Act, a law which on the surface was antithetical to its interests, is thus seen as part of a political bargain in which domestic firms accepted the imposition of an antitrust policy in exchange for protection from foreign competitors.

The Public-Choice Perspective

The foregoing interpretation rests on the assumption that antitrust serves the "public interest" by promoting freely functioning competitive markets. If so, it is reasonable to conclude that antitrust enforcement and foreign competition are substitutes for mitigating the welfare losses associated with domestic monopoly. In this case, we would expect to observe more vigorous antitrust law enforcement activity during periods of increased trade protectionism as the agencies charged with the responsibility of protecting the interests of consumers moved to offset the competition-reducing effects of tariffs and quotas. On the other hand, antitrust enforcement would be expected to decline when trade barriers are low, on the theory that during such periods foreign competition provides an effective margin of market discipline for domestic monopolists. Indeed, the notion that import competition and antitrust are substitutes for one another is recognized explicitly in the Justice Department's merger guidelines, which call for considering actual and potential entry by foreign producers as part of the criteria for defining relevant antitrust markets.

Suppose, however, that antitrust is not intendedly procompetitive, but instead serves as means by which some firms—especially small, inefficient firms—can obtain protection from the forces of effective competition (Shughart and Tollison 1985; Shughart 1990a). If antitrust can be usefully characterized as an interest-group bargain, as an emerging body of literature suggests,[3] then trade protectionism and enforcement of the Sherman, Clayton, and FTC Acts may represent *complementary* policies for transferring wealth to groups having a comparative advantage in rent-seeking activities.

Of critical importance to this alternative hypothesis about the link between antitrust and trade protectionism is empirical evidence suggesting that import competition tends to come at the expense of small domestic firms.[4] That is, smaller enterprises disproportionately lose market share and profits in the face of increased competition from foreign producers. As such, domestic concentration ratios are positively related to the level of import penetration, not because the entry of foreign producers is triggered by the existence of

3. In addition to the papers collected in this volume, see Mackay, Miller, and Yandle (1987).
4. Richard E. Caves, Trade Exposure and the Changing Structure of U.S. Manufacturing Industries, in International Competitiveness (A. Michael Spence and Heather A. Hazard, eds. 1988) and William F. Chappell and Bruce Yandle, The Competitive Role of Import Penetration, 37 Antitrust Bull. 957 (1992) report such evidence.

monopoly rents in concentrated domestic industries,[5] but rather because imports tend to displace the sales of smaller firms which, in turn, causes the market shares of larger domestic firms to rise.

An important implication of the economic theory of regulation (Stigler 1971; Peltzman 1976) is that no one group gets all that it wants from government intervention. (One commentator characterizes this prediction as "share the gain, share the pain.")[6] For the case at hand, government might respond to the losses sustained by small firms on account of increased import penetration by raising barriers to international trade. Such a response would tend to benefit all domestic firms (both large and small) at the expense of U.S. consumers and foreign producers.

Alternatively, more active antitrust enforcement might be brought to bear on larger domestic firms in order to shift some of the costs associated with import competition away from their smaller rivals. Complaints of unlawful predatory pricing might be issued against large firms that attempt to hold on to their market shares by cutting price; attempts by large firms to consolidate their assets and become more efficient through merger might be challenged; and so on. This second option, which also tends to transfer wealth away from domestic consumers, has the advantage of focusing more of the benefits of protectionism on the small firms that have more at stake and therefore more to gain from lobbying for intervention that offsets the distributional effects of foreign competition. The use of antitrust policy also avoids imposing some of the costs of protectionism on foreign producers that might invite retaliation by their governments to the detriment of domestic export industries. Which of these options is chosen in any particular circumstance is simply a matter of selecting the protectionist policy that offers the highest political payoff to rational, self-interest-seeking policy makers.

This essay investigates the explanatory power of these two alternative hypotheses about antitrust and foreign competition by examining the relationship between the budgets of the public antitrust law enforcement agencies and the extent of import penetration. Using data for the years 1932 through 1981, we find evidence that increased competition from foreign producers leads to a statistically significant increase in funding for both the Antitrust Division and the FTC, holding constant such factors as the general level of economic activity and agency caseloads. This finding suggests that in the political marketplace, antitrust and foreign competition are not treated as substitutes for maintaining a competitive economy. Instead, the antitrust agencies' funding levels are increased during periods when foreign producers make greater inroads into the domestic economy, a result that can be rationalized under the view that antitrust enforcement operates in part to protect

---

5. Howard P. Marvel, Foreign Trade and Domestic Competition, 18 Econ. Inquiry 103 (1980).

6. Jack Hirshleifer, Comment, 19 J. Law & Econ. 241 (1976).

small domestic firms against their foreign rivals at the expense of larger domestic firms and consumers.

Empirical Evidence

Two hypotheses concerning the relationship between domestic antitrust enforcement and foreign competition were outlined above. One hypothesis suggests that antitrust and imports are substitutes for maintaining a competitive economy; the other implies that antitrust complements trade protectionism in insulating small domestic firms from the rigors of foreign competition.

The Model

We specified the following regression equation to test whether antitrust enforcement is a substitute for or a complement to import competition:

RBUDGET = f(CASES, DKT, RGNP, MDNPCT, HSRDUM, LDUM, PDUM, DEP, ϵ),

where

RBUDGET = real annual budget of either the FTC (RFTCB), the Antitrust Division (RDOJB), or the two agencies combined;

CASES = the number of antitrust cases instituted by the relevant enforcement agency or the two agencies combined;

DKT = a three-year running total of antitrust cases instituted by the relevant enforcement agency or the two agencies combined (years $t-1$ through $t-3$);

RGNP = real Gross National Product;

MDNPCT = the value of durable and nondurable imports as a percent of GNP;

HSRDUM = a binary variable set equal to zero for the years 1976– 1981, and set equal to zero otherwise;

LDUM = a binary variable set equal to zero for the years 1948– 1981, and set equal to zero otherwise;

PDUM = a binary variable set equal to zero for the years of Republican presidents, and set equal to zero otherwise;

DEP = a binary variable set equal to zero for the years 1932– 1933, and set equal to zero otherwise; and

ϵ = the regression error term.

The observations were obtained from standard government sources.[7] Dollar

7. FTC cases and appropriations were obtained from the Office of the Secretary of the Federal Trade Commission. The case data were updated and reconciled with those reported by Posner (1970) for the period 1890–1969, and by Gallo, Craycraft, and Bush (1985) for the period 1963–1984. Antitrust Division cases were taken from Posner (1970) and Gallo, Craycraft, and Bush (1985). Appropriations for the Antitrust Division were obtained from the Budget of the

values were converted to constant 1982 dollars using the implicit GNP price deflator.

Case-load statistics represent one way of measuring the quantity of output produced by the public antitrust law enforcement agencies. To the extent that Congress and, more specifically, the congressional committees having budgetary and oversight responsibilities with respect to the FTC and the Antitrust Division, use cases instituted as an indicator of bureaucratic performance, we expect a positive relationship between this variable and the size of antitrust budgets.[8] CASES is entered with a one-year lag to reflect institutional features of the budgetary process whereby the appropriations committee can observe only the previous year's output when establishing current funding levels. Moreover, Posner (1970, 377–79) has estimated that the elapsed time from the initiation of an antitrust case to its resolution is three years, on average. DKT controls for the number of cases in the production pipeline and is likewise expected to be positively related to agency budgets to the extent that a greater number of ongoing antitrust matters is viewed sympathetically by the appropriations committee.[9]

Real GNP is expected to be positively related to antitrust law enforcement budgets for at least two reasons. On the one hand, such a relationship is consistent with the operation of some version of Wagner's Law which holds that government is a normal good. On the other hand, GNP measures the total number of transactions taking place in the economy and therefore could be thought of as a proxy for the potential supply of antitrust violations. In this case, we would expect antitrust appropriations to increase with increases in GNP if the resources available to the law enforcement agencies are to keep pace with greater numbers of illegal business practices. Because of the timing of the congressional budgetary process, we also enter RGNP with a one-year lag.

MDNPCT is the principal variable of interest in our analysis. Its sign will be negative if Congress views foreign competition as an alternative to domestic antitrust law enforcement as means of limiting monopoly welfare losses in the economy. That is, if increased import penetration is seen as having salutary effects on domestic markets, raising consumer surplus by expanding output and reducing prices, then public-interest-maximizing political repre-

---

U.S. Government (various years). Real GNP and the value of durable and nondurable imports are from U.S. Department of Commerce, Bureau of Economic Analysis, National Income and Product Accounts of the U.S., 1929–1982 (1986).

8. For theory and evidence that congressional overseers rely on "visible" output measures to evaluate bureaucratic performance, see Cotton M. Lindsay, A Theory of Government Enterprise, 84 J. Pol. Econ. 1061 (1976). In addition, Katzmann (1980, 146) reports that one "yardstick that the [Appropriations] subcommittee uses in judging how well the commission is performing has to do with case-load statistics."

9. Yandle (1988) provides evidence that the backlog of antitrust cases is positively related to the Antitrust Division's budget.

sentatives would be expected to shift scarce budgetary resources away from the antitrust agencies toward alternative programs and policies through which the expected marginal benefits of public spending are greater. By contrast, the extent of import penetration will be positively related to antitrust budgets if, as we have argued previously, antitrust law enforcement activities are designed in part to protect certain domestic business interests against the rigors of international competition. Like CASES and RGNP, MDNPCT is entered with a one-year lag.[10]

HSRDUM controls for the Hart-Scott-Rodino Act of 1976, which expanded the antitrust agencies' authority in the area of antimerger law enforcement.[11] Yandle (1988) presents evidence that premerger notification requirements had a positive and significant impact on the Antitrust Division's budget and we here include HSRDUM in that spirit. Similarly, the 1948 liaison agreement between the FTC and the Antitrust Division (LDUM), which followed the Supreme Court's decision in *Cement Institute*,[12] established an interagency case-allocation mechanism that has also been shown to have raised public antitrust law enforcement budgets significantly (Higgins, Shughart, and Tollison 1987).

Presidential party label (PDUM) is included to test the conventional wisdom that Republican administrations are less activist on the antitrust front. Finally, DEP controls for the two most severe years of the Great Depression in our sample. Evidence exists suggesting that regulatory intervention tends to increase during economic downturns either to protect small business or to shore up private cartels.[13] Antitrust budgets are predicted to have been higher than normal during the Depression if similar reasoning applies.

Empirical Results

The regression model specified above was estimated for the years 1932 through 1981.[14] Separate regressions were run for the FTC, the Antitrust Division, and the two agencies combined because of evidence reported in this volume and elsewhere that the FTC is more responsive to political pres-

10. Coefficient signs and significance levels are not affected by entering the contemporaneous value of MDNPCT, however.

11. See chapter 9 of this volume for a discussion of the impact of premerger notification on the selection of merger cases by the antitrust authorities.

12. FTC v. Cement Institute, 333 U.S. 683 (1948).

13. See, for example, Amacher, Higgins, Shughart, and Tollison (1985). Evidence that trade protectionism tends to be countercyclical is reported in William F. Shughart II and Robert D. Tollison, The Cyclical Character of Regulatory Activity, 45 Pub. Choice 303 (1985).

14. The starting date of our data set was dictated by the fact that the Antitrust Division did not become a separate line item in the budget of the Department of Justice until 1932. Missing observations on antitrust cases instituted prevented us from estimating the model for years beyond 1981.

Table 11.1   Descriptive Statistics

Variable	Mean	Standard Deviation	Minimum	Maximum
RFTCB*	32,165.08	22,916.44	10,770.49	86,011.08
RDOJB*	17,623.66	12,115.24	1,262.29	50,809.80
FTC CASES	204.48	122.60	18.00	560.00
FTC DKT	624.14	305.22	169.00	1,251.00
DOJ CASES	41.24	25.23	4.00	116.00
DOJ DKT	113.58	63.23	15.00	273.00
RGNP†	1,702.09	816.86	498.50	3,248.80
MDNPCT	3.76	1.91	1.70	9.06

*Thousands of 1982 dollars.
†Billions of 1982 dollars.

sure than its counterpart bureau in the Justice Department. All variables are entered in their levels. Preliminary empirical analysis indicated that the FTC and combined antitrust budget time series follow a first-order moving average process; such a term is therefore included on the right-hand side of these two specifications.[15]

Descriptive statistics for the continuous variables are reported in table 11.1. Table 11.2 displays the ordinary least squares regression estimates.[16] The results suggest that increased import penetration leads to significantly higher law enforcement budgets for the FTC, the Antitrust Division, and the two agencies combined. Moreover, the coefficient estimates imply that the FTC's budget is much more responsive to the competitive inroads of foreign producers than that of its counterpart antitrust agency. At the variable means, a 1-percent *ceteris paribus* increase in import penetration leads to a .54-percent increase in the commission's appropriations, but to only a .26-percent increase in the antitrust budget of the Department of Justice.[17] This finding is consistent with evidence that the FTC tends to be more responsive to political pressure than the Antitrust Division. It also tends to support the conventional wisdom that small business is one of the commission's key constituencies.

15. Clive W. J. Granger and Paul Newbold, Forecasting Economic Time Series (1977) argue at 203 that "if some simple specific model is to be assumed on a priori grounds, we feel that the first-order integrated moving average process is a serious candidate for economic time series in general, and would certainly expect it typically to provide a better representation than the first-order autoregressive process. . . ."

16. Because the Durbin-Watson d-statistic falls within the inconclusive region, the Box-Pierce Q, computed for the first 20 lags of the regression residuals, is also reported. The Box-Pierce $Q(n)$, which follows a chi-square distribution, tests the null hypothesis that the first n autocorrelation coefficients are jointly not significantly different from zero against the alternative hypothesis that at least one of them is. The null hypothesis cannot be rejected in any of the three cases.

17. The responsiveness of the antitrust budgets of the two agencies combined to the competitive inroads of foreign producers is likewise inelastic. At the variable means, a 1-percent increase in import penetration leads to a .49-percent increase in total antitrust appropriations.

Table 11.2   Regression Results

	Dependent Variables		
	RFTCB	RDOJB	Combined Budgets
C	−19,178.42	−4,612.41	−24,138.89
CASES(−1)	2.17	42.11	−2.51
	(0.24)	(1.53)	(−0.22)
DKT	7.99	20.60	9.47
	(2.14)†	(1.58)	(2.10)†
RGNP(−1)	18.69	7.78	27.09
	(11.13)*	(7.47)*	(12.71)*
MDNPCT(−1)	4,589.75	1,214.09	6,451.80
	(5.75)*	(2.50)*	(6.47)*
HSRDUM	7,460.62	6,949.40	13,606.27
	(2.14)†	(3.34)*	(3.15)*
LDUM	−3,200.38	1,531.11	−1,332.53
	(−1.74)	(1.42)	(−.58)
PDUM	−2,164.74	−2,479.75	−4,745.09
	(−1.56)	(−3.05)*	(−2.73)*
DEP	9,476.64	−386.24	7,475.63
	(3.09)*	(−.21)	(1.95)
MA(1)	.73		.53
	(6.50)*		(3.78)*
R^2	.97	.97	.98
D-W	1.37	1.47	1.72
Q(20)	18.87	23.92	16.51
F	198.94	168.80	292.67
N	50	50	50

Notes: t-statistics in parentheses; an asterisk (*) denotes significance at the 1-percent level and a dagger (†) at the 5-percent level. MA(1) is the estimated first-order moving average term. Q(20) is the Box-Pierce Q-statistic computed for the first 20 lags of the regression residuals.

Appropriations likewise tend to increase as real GNP increases and as there are greater numbers of antitrust cases in the production pipeline. (The latter variable, however, is not different from zero at customary levels of statistical significance in the Antitrust Division regression.) Nevertheless, the previous year's case output, by itself, does not have a statistically significant impact on funding, which may suggest that the relevant appropriations and oversight committees take a longer-run view when evaluating bureaucratic performance.

In addition, the empirical results indicate that antitrust budgets are significantly lower during Republican administrations; that the FTC received substantial additional law enforcement resources during the Great Depression, perhaps to prevent prices from falling as much as they otherwise would have; and that both agencies benefited financially from the Hart-Scott-Rodino Act.

Overall, the regressions explain up to 98 percent of the variation in antitrust budgets over a 50-year period.

Concluding Remarks

Economic regulation of price and entry has come to be understood as part of a political process that works to transfer wealth among competing interest groups. Antitrust, as the papers collected in this volume suggest, can be analyzed fruitfully in similar terms. This chapter supplies additional evidence of the power of approaching antitrust law enforcement as the outcome of an interest-group bargain, in this case involving small firms versus large firms in an open macroeconomy.

In particular, the evidence presented herein suggests that antitrust intervention and trade protectionism are complementary policies that serve to insulate small domestic firms from the forces of global competition. Other things being the same, antitrust budgets are significantly higher following periods of increased import penetration. Rather than shifting scarce budgetary resources away from the FTC and the Justice Department's Antitrust Division when foreign producers compete more effectively with domestic firms and consumer welfare losses are arguably lower than otherwise, Congress appropriates additional funding to support more vigorous antitrust intervention in the economy.

The observed congressional response to import penetration cannot be explained by the public-interest model which asserts that antitrust is driven by the goal of protecting the interests of domestic consumers. Antitrust and import competition would be substitutes if this were the case. The empirical results are, however, entirely consistent with a private-interest theory in which the public antitrust agencies place the protection of selected domestic competitors ahead of the goal of promoting competition.

PART THREE
The Public-Choice Model of Antitrust Enforcement

LOUIS DE ALESSI

In his presidential address to the American Economic Association, George Stigler chided his colleagues for continuing to tinker with the design of marginal-cost pricing and other "optimal" regulatory arrangements to be implemented by omniscient government employees pursuing some universally accepted notion of the public interest.[1] His advice to find out how government regulation works in practice directed the attention of scholars to a new field of research.

Earlier work had prepared the ground for rigorous research. Theoretical contributions by Armen Alchian on the property rights (constraints) associated with alternative institutional arrangements and by Ronald Coase on transaction costs had shown that neoclassical economic theory could be extended to analyze the behavior of firms regulated or managed by government employees;[2] preliminary empirical findings had demonstrated that this approach was fruitful.[3] Concurrently, James Buchanan and Gordon Tullock had extended economic theory to the analysis of public choices,[4] including rent-seeking behavior (Tullock 1967). Combined with the property rights approach,[5] this

The author gratefully acknowledges helpful comments by Michael L. De Alessi and Svetozar Pejovich as well as the financial support and stimulating intellectual environment provided by the International Centre for Economic Research in Turin, Italy, during the summer of 1992.

1. George J. Stigler, The Economist and the State, 55 Amer. Econ. Rev. 1 (1965).

2. Armen A. Alchian, Private Property and the Relative Cost of Tenure, in The Public Stake in Union Power, P. Bradley, ed. (1959); Armen A. Alchian, Some Economics of Property Rights, 30 Il Politico 816 (1965); and Ronald H. Coase, The Problem of Social Cost, 3 J. Law & Econ. 1 (1960).

3. See, for example, Armen A. Alchian and R. A. Kessel, Competition, Monopoly, and the Pursuit of Money, in Aspects of Labor Economics (1962); George J. Stigler, Public Regulation of the Securities Market, 37 J. Bus. 117 (1964); and George J. Stigler and Claire Friedland, What Can Regulators Regulate? The Case of Electricity, 5 J. Law & Econ. 1 (1962). The literature is summarized in Eric Furubotn and Svetozar J. Pejovich, Property Rights and Economic Theory: A Survey of Recent Literature, 10 J. Econ. Lit. 1137 (1972), and in Louis De Alessi, An Economic Analysis of Government Ownership and Regulation: Theory and the Evidence from the Electric Power Industry, 19 Pub. Choice 1 (1974).

4. James M. Buchanan and Gordon Tullock, The Calculus of Consent: Logical Foundations of Constitutional Democracy (1962).

5. Louis De Alessi, Implications of Property Rights for Government Investment Choices, 59 Amer. Econ. Rev. 13 (1969).

190 LOUIS DE ALESSI

development opened the decisions of legislators and other bureaucrats to formal inquiry and broadened the foundations for analyzing government regulation of business.[6]

Research concerning the behavior of those being regulated and of those doing the regulating shows that the public interest paradigm lacks a theoretical basis and does not work empirically. Government employees do not pursue the public interest. In practice, the expression "public interest" simply supplies rhetoric to mask private interests.

What did work was not always clear. In studies of public utility commissions and the like, researchers could reasonably identify the gainers and losers from government regulation. They found that the self-interest hypothesis explained the behavior of both the regulators and the regulated.[7] But in studies of antitrust activities, the nature of the cost-reward structure driving the regulators remained murky until the appearance of the articles reprinted in this section. In the first paper, Roger Faith, Donald Leavens, and Robert Tollison show that U.S. antitrust agencies are strongly influenced by the legislators who control their budgets. Next, Malcolm Coate, Richard Higgins, and Fred McChesney demonstrate that the FTC's merger challenges are shaped by institutional guidelines, by congressional pressure, and by the conflicting incentives of the lawyers and economists it employs. Finally, Charlie Weir presents evidence that the decisions of the British Monopolies and Mergers Commission are determined by variables—such as whether a merger is contested—that reflect private interests.

The present discussion places antitrust activity in its public choice setting. First, it looks at how the market works and at the possible scope of antitrust; then it applies the public choice perspective to antitrust activities; next, it outlines the contribution of the papers included in this section; and finally, it provides a few concluding comments.

The Scope of Antitrust

Resources are scarce and individuals must compete for access to those that are available. Any society, therefore, must adopt a set of rules—the institutional environment—for controlling competition and resolving conflict. These rules can be formal, such as the U.S. Constitution, or informal, such as custom. Together they specify the rights that individuals may hold to the use of resources, to the income these resources yield, and to the transferability of these resources to others. The resulting system of property rights sets the range of contracts that individuals can legally form with one another. Thus,

6. James M. Buchanan and Robert D. Tollison, eds., Theory of Public Choice: Political Applications of Economics (1972).
7. For example, see Ross D. Eckert, On the Incentives of Regulators: The Case of Taxicabs, 14 Pub. Choice 83 (1973).

it determines how the economic consequences of a decision are allocated between the individual making the choice and other members of society. Because different systems of property rights present individuals with different structures of costs and rewards, they establish different opportunities for gain and affect choices systematically.

Elementary neoclassical theory dominated economics until the 1960s and continues to provide the backbone of antitrust rhetoric. This theoretical framework applies to a world of certainty in which all rights to the use of resources are fully defined, fully allocated to private owners, and freely transferable at zero transaction and information costs; all contracts are fully specified and enforced. Under these conditions, *all* future value consequences of a decision are fully capitalized into current transfer prices; the individual making a choice bears, and has the incentive to consider, *all* the ensuing harms and benefits. External effects and shirking or opportunistic behavior are ruled out. Firms do not exist (every owner of the right to the use of resources is an independent contractor) and all sellers and buyers behave like competitors.[8] It follows that cost is equal to price at every margin and all opportunities for gain are fully exploited.

The characteristics of this solution deserve emphasis. In an open market, price measures the value of the output that resources produce in their present use; cost measures the value of the output that the same resources could have produced in their next best use. If price is equal to marginal cost, then all resources are allocated to their highest-valued use. The output of one commodity cannot be increased without decreasing the output of another commodity, and one individual cannot be made better off without making someone else worse off. This solution is the competitive solution and means that, at least on allocative [Pareto] criteria, there is no scope for antitrust.[9]

Economists typically use neoclassical equilibrium conditions as a benchmark for judging the relative efficiency of actual market solutions. They view significant deviations from the competitive ideal as evidence of market "failure" and justification for government action, including antitrust. But the institutional environment and the nature of transaction costs affect every aspect of economic activity. An obvious example is the choice of the particular form of business organization, such as corporation, partnership, or sole proprietorship. Another example is the choice of production technique, which may facilitate or hinder monitoring, favor large or small teams, and entail large or small firm-specific investments. A broader example is the choice to make or buy, which affects the degree of vertical and horizontal integration

8. George J. Stigler, The Law and Economics of Public Policy: A Plea to the Scholars, 1 J. Legal Stud. 1 (1972).

9. Perfect price discrimination and perfect competition yield the same allocation of resources but drastically different distributions of gains. If one is concerned with the distribution of the gains, then techniques other than antitrust (e.g., lump-sum taxes) are available.

as well as the nature of the formal and informal contracts that bind together owners of specific capital, lenders, employees, suppliers, distributors, and customers. Moreover, these contracts may include self-enforcing provisions, such as cancellation at will, and mechanisms to monitor performance and assure compliance, such as internal operating rules and the use of hostages (e.g., trademarks).

Few, if any, of these arrangements would exist in a competitive environment under naive neoclassical conditions. As a result, arrangements that have evolved to facilitate specialization and exchange in a world of uncertainty, attenuated private rights, and positive information, transaction, and enforcement costs have been misinterpreted as anticompetitive and made the object of antitrust activity. The logical fallacy in this thinking is obvious but persistent.

An open-market system controls collusive and anticompetitive behavior, but does not eliminate it.[10] To establish whether any remaining problem offers scope for antitrust activity, the competitive outcome must be compared to the outcome that would exist under antitrust.[11] Before addressing this task, it is useful to consider the normative criteria on which antitrust is based.

Normative Bases of Antitrust

A monopolist is a firm (or a coalition of firms) with some market power in the sense that it faces a negatively sloped demand curve; thus, it can affect the price of its product. Antitrust is supposed to redress two alleged problems of "too much" market power: the "inefficient" allocation of resources and the "unfair" distribution of the gains from exchange. The answers to both problems ultimately rest on purely normative criteria.

How the gains from trade ought to be shared is a normative issue. Fundamentally, it concerns the boundaries imposed on private property rights: what are the rights of the owner of a copyright, a patent, a part or the whole stock of a resource, a firm, one's own person? Economic theory can show the consequences of alternative institutional environments, including the distribution of gains and losses and the effect on long-term economic growth. It does *not* provide value-free criteria for making the interpersonal utility comparisons necessary to aggregate the gains and losses of different outcomes and choose the "best" system.

Less obviously, the "efficient" allocation of resources also entails value

10. Supposed barriers to entry in open markets, such as economies of scale, large capital investments, and advertising, ultimately rest on the existence of positive transaction costs (Demsetz 1982b). Even in the case of "natural" monopolies, there is always the possibility of competing for the market as a whole (Demsetz 1968b).

11. Harold Demsetz, Information and Efficiency: Another Viewpoint, 12 J. Law & Econ. 1 (1969).

judgments. To predict choices, which is the role of positive economics, efficiency may be defined as constrained optimization. "Efficiency" describes the properties of an equilibrium solution that arises from the conjunction of the premises of economic theory and the (antecedent) conditions; the latter include the cost of transacting and the property relations that characterize the state of the world under consideration.[12] A change in circumstances may imply a movement to a new, efficient solution. The judgment that one equilibrium solution is more efficient than another, however, requires reference to a benchmark, and the choice of a benchmark cannot be value-free.[13]

Even Pareto criteria do not yield an unambiguous answer. A solution is Pareto-inefficient if price is greater than marginal cost; this condition implies that not all mutually beneficial gains from trade have been exploited. A perfectly discriminating monopolist, however, at the margin charges a price equal to cost and yields a Pareto-efficient solution. Thus, a sufficient but not necessary condition for Pareto inefficiency is that transaction costs are high enough to inhibit some trade. Describing a solution in a world in which transasctions are free as more efficient than a solution in a world in which they are costly is not very helpful. A more useful approach is simply to compare the outcomes associated with alternative institutional arrangements. The assessment of the outcomes, of course, is not value-free either.

Finally, the question of what is "too much" market power is not easily answered. In practice, most firms and individuals enjoy some monopoly power because they have different characteristics (e.g., quality, warranties, location) that distinguish their products or services from those offered by others. Under open-market conditions, the negative slope of a firm's demand curve reflects the ability to offer a commodity tailored to the wants of particular groups of consumers. This is a welfare-increasing activity. It does not imply either the existence of monopoly profits or, as Demsetz has shown,[14] a misallocation of resources (defined as price greater than marginal cost). From this viewpoint, possible targets of antitrust would be collusive, closed-market arrangements with "substantial" actual or potential market power.

The Limits of Antitrust

Aside from the unanswerable normative questions surrounding antitrust, what are the potential gains and losses from having an antitrust policy? The magnitude of the economic consequences of monopoly obviously matters in decid-

12. Louis De Alessi, Property Rights, Transaction Costs, and X-Efficiency: An Essay in Economic Theory, 73 Amer. Econ. Rev. 64 (1983).

13. James M. Buchanan, Social Choice, Democracy, and Free Markets, 62 J. Polit. Econ. 114 (1954) and Louis De Alessi, Efficiency Criteria for Optimal Laws: Objective Standards or Value Judgments?, 3 Const. Polit. Econ. 321 (1992).

14. Harold Demsetz, The Nature of Equilibrium in Monopolistic Competition, 67 J. Polit. Econ. 1 (1959).

ing the potential usefulness of antitrust. Estimates for the United States during the period immediately after World War I suggest that the aggregate welfare losses from monopoly are small, perhaps as little as one-tenth of one percent of gross national product (Harberger 1954; Schwartzman 1960).[15] These estimates should be adjusted upward to include the resources used in rent-seeking activities (Tullock 1967) and the higher production costs incurred by the managers of nonproprietary firms.[16] They should then be adjusted downward to allow for the effects of patents, copyrights, trademarks, and other private property rights granted to stimulate inventive and informational activities or to guarantee individual liberty. On net balance, the welfare losses from monopoly seem small.

Several other considerations support this view. First, monopoly frequently arises from product differentiation under open-market conditions. In these circumstances, the seeming discrepancy between price and marginal cost is due to the analyst's failure to allow for changes in product quality and for the satisfaction that consumers obtain from product variety.[17] Second, long-standing focus on the purely competitive model has distracted attention from the deterrent effects of potential entrants (e.g., Baumol 1982) and the broad range of contractual arrangements designed to encourage specialization and exchange by reducing transaction costs (e.g., Haddock 1982). Third, the complexity of many exchanges (e.g., quality of a product, conditions of delivery and payment) allows some price discrimination that reduces the residual opportunities for mutually satisfactory trade. Finally, collusive arrangements are typically short-lived without state support. Political rhetoric aside, the scope for antitrust seems limited.

Even if, in principle, antitrust could do some good, it does not follow that antitrust is desirable. *That* judgment depends on the alternatives available and the value criteria used. The alternatives are the economy as it would function in practice without antitrust and the *same* economy as it would function in practice with antitrust. Those responsible for antitrust are constrained by political and bureaucratic considerations as well as by a frequently naive and incomplete understanding of how the economy works. Both theory and evidence suggest that antitrust suits deter business practices, mergers, and other voluntary contractual arrangements that evolve to ease specialization and exchange and that encourage competition. Indeed, some scholars have argued that antitrust deters instead of promoting competition and is used to establish and maintain monopoly (e.g., Armentano 1982). Moreover, the

15. Even absent other considerations, the inability to measure subjective values and make interpersonal utility comparisons leaves unclear the meaning of these measures of welfare losses.

16. Alchian and Kessel, *supra* note 3.

17. Demsetz, *supra* note 14.

random component of antitrust activity generates uncertainty, which increases the cost of doing business and reduces competition and consumers' welfare (see, for example, chapters 9, 16, and 17 of this volume).

Government antitrust suits are frequently instigated by various interests (e.g., managers, owners, labor unions, local governments) who might be harmed by a takeover or by competitors who offer better products and/or lower prices. Antitrust enforcement agencies have used allegations of predatory pricing, a concept that has weak theoretical foundations and even weaker empirical support (McGee 1958), to discourage price competition. A phenomenon of at least equal importance, however, is the private use of antitrust.

In principle, private antitrust suits are supposed to complement the public enforcement of antitrust, filling gaps and serving interests that might otherwise escape the attention of dedicated public servants. In practice, the willingness of judges to give plaintiffs their day in court and the relative capriciousness of the verdicts have combined to foster a process filled with uncertainty and the opportunity for hold-up. Private suits have benefited managers seeking to obtain more generous compensation in a takeover bid or protection from competitors. Because these suits can be very expensive, a firm may well choose to pursue less aggressive competitive practices or settle out of court rather than incur the costs of a formal trial whose outcome may be random and could establish an unwanted precedent.

In the 1960s and 1970s, the number of private suits dwarfed those brought by the government. More recently, the frequency of private suits has subsided somewhat as the courts have enforced slightly more rigorous standards, but private actions still vastly outnumber those brought by the public law enforcement agencies. The threat and actual filing of many private suits continue to discourage competition, with a perverse effect on consumer welfare (Shughart 1990c).

Finally, the effects of antitrust clearly extend beyond the cases filed. Suits signal the nature of the activities that the antitrust authorities are currently seeking to forbid, and the threat constrains the choices of all firms. The usefulness of antitrust in deterring anticompetitive behavior depends on the ability of the antitrust agencies to prosecute the "right" cases. The evidence suggests that the suits brought are inappropriate and yield perverse consequences (e.g., Shughart and Tollison 1985). The possibility of having to fight an antitrust suit, even if the probability of losing is small, inhibits firms from pursuing competitive behavior that the antitrust authorities may choose to proscribe. Modern economic systems are extremely complex and their structural relationships, including the full consequences of antitrust activities, are poorly understood. The capricious and frequently perverse nature of antitrust suggests that the harm from unintended and undesired side effects is substantial.

Public Choices and Antitrust

The *stated* purpose of antitrust is to promote competition (efficiency) and
increase the welfare of consumers by attacking price fixing, market sharing,
and various collusive and monopolistic arrangements. Until recently, contractual arrangements that did not fit the Procrustean bed of pure competition
under neoclassical conditions were perceived as anticompetitive and suitable
targets of antitrust. A better understanding of market processes is developing
among economists and filtering through to the antitrust agencies. Still, current
research shows that antitrust activity in the United States continues to be
ineffective or counterproductive. The public-choice approach demonstrates
that there is no reason to expect regulators to change their behavior without
a change in their cost-reward structure.

The behavior of public utilities and regulatory commissions provided the
first insights into the nature and consequences of government regulation.
Because the owners of regulated firms cannot extract the full gains from more
profitable operation, they have less incentive to monitor management, reduce
shirking, and introduce cost-reducing or income-increasing innovations; the
principal-agent problem is exacerbated. Might countervailing forces offset
these tendencies? For example, firms in some industries (e.g., railroads,
airlines, telephony) sought or coopted their own regulation in an effort to
exclude entry and enforce collusion among themselves.[18] Transferring the
resolution of conflict from the market to the political arena, however, allows
other parties to participate in the rent-seeking process. As a result, those
subject to regulations are typically unable to capture the full gains permitted
by their protected position; owners' property rights are attenuated and managers' discretionary authority increases. Nevertheless, regulated firms are still
subject to the discipline of the market. Regulation may provide an easier
life,[19] but it does not guarantee profits or even survival.

Managers of government regulatory bureaus, whose output is not traded
in the marketplace, are less constrained by market considerations and have
greater opportunity to pursue their own self-interest within their political
constraints. Because their reward structures are not tied to measures of the
"public" interest, such as Pareto efficiency, they have little incentive to
pursue it. Government managers whose salary and tenure are set by statute,
such as commissioners of independent regulatory agencies, have incentive to
engage in less regulatory activity than government managers whose salary
and tenure are tied more closely to performance, such as bureau chiefs.
Not surprisingly, the evidence shows that commissioners are more likely to

18. See, for example, Louis De Alessi, The Economics of Property Rights: A Review of the
Evidence, 2 Res. Law & Econ. 1 (1980).

19. Ibid. For instance, government regulation of electric utilities results in higher prices,
lower output, higher owners' wealth, and greater job discrimination.

encourage anticompetitive arrangements that ease their workload, including single monopolies, market sharing, and simple pricing.[20]

Similarly, those who are responsible for antitrust activities respond to the cost-reward structures built into the system. Existing incentives within the legislative and enforcement branches of government discourage an antitrust regime that benefits consumers.

The public-choice approach denies the assumption that government employees act in single-minded pursuit of the public interest, defined as allocative [Pareto] optimality. That belief lacks any theoretical or empirical basis. Oddly enough, many who support a shift in regulation from market to government processes because the market fails to provide the "right" incentives simultaneously disregard the possibility that government institutions also fail to provide the "right" incentives. Although some government failures may be due to lack of information or mistakes, a more fundamental problem is the lack of incentive to acquire the "right" information and to make the "right" choices.

Both theory and evidence indicate that the behavior of individuals working for the government, like the behavior of individuals engaged in any other economic activity, is best explained by the self-interest hypothesis. Government employees pursue their own goals, including their personal conceptions of the public interest, within the limits imposed by institutional constraints, the state of nature, and the arts. This coherent approach to private and public choices permits a fresh look at antitrust.

At the legislative level, politicians have incentive to favor constituents who are either numerous or well-organized, and special-interest groups who contribute to their campaigns. In practice, regulation of business has meant establishing agencies that either require or allow collusive arrangements.[21] Similarly, the legislation enabling antitrust sought political objectives rather than consumer welfare (e.g., DiLorenzo 1985). Moreover, members of Congress control the budgets of the antitrust agencies and have both incentive and opportunity to favor their constituents and contributors (e.g., Posner 1969a).

At the enforcement level, employees of the U.S. Department of Justice and the Federal Trade Commission (FTC) are not rewarded according to the effects of their actions on measures of the public interest, such as reducing welfare losses from monopoly. As a result, other variables dominate. Higher-level decision-makers in these agencies are more responsive to political and bureaucratic considerations that affect their individual welfare, either directly

20. Eckert, *supra* note 7.

21. For example, see De Alessi, *supra* note 18. The intent to enforce collusion may be explicit, as in the case of the Interstate Commerce Commission, or implicit, as in the case of the Federal Aviation Administration, the Federal Communications Commission, and the various state utility commissions.

or through the health of their agencies, than to global issues of economic efficiency and consumers' welfare. They have incentive to pursue cases that appeal to them, are supported by key legislators, or are highly visible, thereby increasing the apparent output of the agency. Conversely, they have incentive to dismiss or delay cases that are opposed by key legislators or that have low visibility. At a lower decision level, much of the legal staff of the antitrust agencies consists of fresh law school graduates who are investing in human capital. These young lawyers spend a few years with an antitrust agency, acquiring courtroom experience and inside knowledge, before going to work for a private law firm specializing in antitrust. Economists do not follow this career pattern. As a result, lawyers have a greater incentive to litigate than do economists employed by the same agency. Moreover, different bureaucrats have different perceptions of the public interest and of the way to advance it through antitrust.

Given the cost-reward structures influencing legislative and bureaucratic behavior, economic theory implies that variables attempting to measure welfare losses from monopoly, monopoly profits, and related phenomena have little power to explain government antitrust activity. Several chapters in Part One of this book provide empirical support for this conclusion. Indeed, the evidence presented in Part Two shows that antitrust may actually increase industrial concentration, penalize competition-enhancing business practices, and reduce overall economic performance. The evidence suggests that antitrust may do more harm than good.

The Public Choice Model of Antitrust Enforcement: The Evidence

Regardless of their ideological orientation, few economists today would defend the historical record of antitrust (McChesney 1986, 381–82). Economists are less likely to agree, however, on why antitrust has failed. Most would fault unfortunate errors or unintended consequences, all avoidable next time.

The papers in this section demonstrate that the public-choice approach provides a rigorous—and ultimately convincing—alternative to such ad hoc theorizing and wishful thinking. Using the standard tools of economic theory, antitrust activity is analyzed as the outcome of decisions made by rational, self-seeking politicians, bureaucrats, and judges. The resulting implications are then tested at a remarkable level of empirical sophistication against real-world evidence. Earlier work relied on data aggregated at the industry level and on those cases that were actually litigated. All the chapters in this section look at disaggregated data and two of them compare cases that were brought with those that were not.

As the public-choice model predicts, calculating political behavior dominates antitrust. Roger Faith, Donald Leavens, and Robert Tollison test the hypothesis that FTC adjudications are influenced, directly or indirectly, by politicians acting at the behest of special-interest groups in their districts. The geographically based system for electing members of Congress implies that individual legislators have incentives to trade votes with other legislators to generate benefits for constituents and contributors at the expense of taxpayer-consumers in general. Voting to increase Pareto efficiency or other possible measures of the public interest has a very low payoff. A more rewarding strategy is to concentrate benefits on identifiable blocs of constituents and financial supporters while spreading the costs throughout the economy. This hypothesis implies that members of key congressional committees and subcommittees with budgetary and oversight powers over the FTC routinely pressure the agency to dismiss suits against firms in their districts and to sue competitors in other districts.

Faith, Leavens, and Tollison tested the hypothesis using data from two periods: 1961 to 1969 and 1970 to 1979. The first period covers episodes that Posner (1969a) presumably had in mind when he derived the pork-barrel hypothesis. The second period encompasses a series of reforms that, supposedly, had greatly improved the FTC's record in promoting the public interest. The findings for both periods strongly support the legislative-influence hypothesis. The FTC's adjudications systematically favor firms located in the jurisdictions of members of congressional committees responsible for overseeing the FTC or controlling its budget.

Next, Malcolm Coate, Richard Higgins, and Fred McChesney apply the political self-interest hypothesis to examine the FTC's enforcement policy toward horizontal mergers. They derive and test three implications. First, that the policy is based on the variables specified in the merger guidelines issued by the Department of Justice rather than on variables more closely identified with the public interest. Second, that the policy is influenced by members of Congress who oppose mergers that would drain resources and votes from their districts. Third, that lawyers and economists within the FTC have conflicting interests, with lawyers exhibiting a greater willingness to initiate suits. The tests use nonpublic information from the FTC's internal files. As expected, the results show that the FTC relies on the criteria contained in the Department of Justice merger guidelines, as applied by the FTC's lawyers and economists, and not on identifiable measures of the public interest; that lawyers have more influence than economists, resulting in greater litigation; and that the FTC responds to politicians' interest in keeping resources and votes from exiting their districts.

The vacuity of the public-interest hypothesis is further exposed by evidence from the United Kingdom. Although not working explicitly within the public-choice model, Charlie Weir investigates how the British Monopolies and Mergers Commission dealt with merger bids referred to it from 1974 to 1990. To Weir's surprise, various indicators of the public interest relating to competition (e.g., reduced prices, increased efficiency) carried little, if any, weight in the Commission's decision whether to challenge a merger. The most significant variables were the Commission's overall attitude to the arguments presented and whether the merger bid was contested by the target firm. As Weir notes, "None of these have anything positive to say about mergers and their impact."

But whether a merger bid is contested or not has a lot to say about its political impact. In that sense, Weir's article on merger policy in the United Kingdom relates closely to the work of Coate et al. for the United States. Contested merger bids mean that management and labor opposed to a takeover have an incentive to seek political help in blocking the transaction. Weir's finding that a contested merger is more likely to elicit a government antitrust challenge is perfectly predictable within the public-choice framework.

Conclusion

The problem of defining the role of antitrust is the problem of defining and allocating property rights. The structure of property rights determines the nature and scope of competition. It determines whether a firm has the right to compete with another firm by charging a lower price, manufacturing a better product, providing more information to consumers, building a plant of more appropriate size, or setting fire to competing factories. All these activities may have exactly the same effect on the competitors' wealth, yet only some may be sanctioned.

The structure of property rights also limits the coalitions that owners of resources can form. It establishes the range of contractual agreements that individuals can develop and adopt to create business organizations and regulate relations among themselves in order to reduce transaction costs and ease specialization and exchange. Owners of resources may be allowed to form certain kinds of coalitions, such as corporations or partnerships, but not others, such as horizontal mergers in markets with few competitors. Firms may be allowed to contract for the delivery of certain goods in exchange for some specified compensation, but may not be allowed to contract for setting prices or sharing markets.

The cost-reward structure faced by government employees responsible for antitrust is unrelated to any relevant measure of that elusive concept, the public interest. Accordingly, it is not surprising that antitrust activity is typically counterproductive. A growing number of scholars have concluded that antitrust does more harm than good. Recommendations have varied from outright repeal of the Sherman Act, the Clayton Act, the Federal Trade Commission Act, and ancillary legislation, to drastic reforms of the process. Given the present form of constitutional democracy and our rudimentary understanding of public choices, it is difficult to see how the incentive structure of those responsible for developing and managing antitrust activity in the United States could be harnessed to the appropriate criteria, could such criteria be found and agreed upon.

CHAPTER TWELVE

Antitrust Pork Barrel

Roger L. Faith, Donald R. Leavens,
and Robert D. Tollison

Introduction

Richard Posner, writing in 1969, asserted that the Federal Trade Commission
(FTC) was significantly impaired in its task of promoting the public interest
by the commission's dependence on Congress (Posner 1969a). To make this
point Posner employed a model of antitrust pork barrel. He emphasized that
each member of Congress is obligated to protect and further the provincial
interests of the citizens of the jurisdiction that he or she represents. Specifically (p. 83), "the welfare of his constituents may depend disproportionately
on a few key industries. The promotion of the industries becomes one of his
most important duties as a representative of the district." Moreover, because
the power to control the FTC is so unevenly distributed among members of
Congress, the potential exists for each member of powerful subcommittees
to exercise "a great deal of power to advance the interests of businesses
located in his district however unimportant the interests may be from a national standpoint." Posner concluded that FTC investigations are seldom in
the public interest and are initiated "at the behest of corporations, trade
associations, and trade unions whose motivation is at best to shift the costs
of their private litigation to the taxpayer and at worse to harass competitors."[1]

This model of FTC behavior builds on a fairly standard characterization

This essay was previously published in the *Journal of Law and Economics* 25 (October 1982):
329–42. © 1982 by The University of Chicago. All rights reserved.

1. Posner (1969a, 87). Posner is not the only observer to offer a pork-barrel hypothesis
about FTC behavior. Consider the following observations by other students of the commission:
"According to Joseph W. Shea, Secretary of the FTC, any letter the Commission gets from a
congressman's office is specially marked with an expedite sticker. The sticker gives the letter
high priority, assuring the congressman of an answer within five days. No distinction is made
between letters—whether from complaining constituents, which congressmen routinely 'buck'
over to the FTC, or those from the Congressmen themselves." Edward F. Cox, Robert C. Sells,
and John E. Schulz, The Nader Report on the Federal Trade Commission and Antitrust Policy
(1969), at 194. "In September, 1969, despite vigorous dissents from his colleagues, Commis-
sioner Elman supported Baum's analysis. He told a Senate group that congressional pressure
'corrupts the atmosphere' in which his agency works. He charged that congressmen make private,
unrecorded calls on behalf of companies seeking FTC approval of million-dollar mergers."
Susan Wagner, The Federal Trade Commission 211 (1971).

of how geographically based representative democracy works in practice. In effect, a geographically based system confronts the legislator with a high payoff from representing local interests in the national legislature by trading votes with other legislators to finance numerous local benefits at the expense of taxpayer-consumers in general and with a correspondingly low payoff from voting in terms of cost-benefit analysis, economic efficiency, or the "national interest." This asymmetry of payoffs to the legislator is partly based on the greater information that voters have about localized benefits as compared with general benefits and partly based on the rational calculation of the average taxpayer-consumer that it is not worth his while to try to do anything to stop such transfers of wealth. What is surprising about this model, however, is that it has generated so few efforts at empirical confirmation. The small amount of literature investigating the linkage between representation and local influence, the key proposition of the pork-barrel-and-geography model, shows a mixed bag of results, some supportive of this proposition and some not.

Our purpose in this essay is to contribute to this literature by presenting some empirical evidence on antitrust pork barrel. Basically, we examine the case-bringing activity of the FTC in order to see if there is any bias in the results of this process in favor of firms that operate in the jurisdictions of members of congressional committees that have important budgetary and oversight powers with respect to the FTC. The hypothesis that we expect to be unable to reject is that favorable FTC decisions (dismissals) are nonrandomly concentrated on firms in the jurisdictions of members of key FTC committees.

The data base for this hypothesis-testing exercise covers the case-bringing activity of the FTC from 1961–1979. For the purpose of empirical testing we will split this data into two periods. The first period, 1961–1969, allows us to test Posner's argument on the period of FTC activity that he presumably had in mind when he developed the pork-barrel hypothesis. The second period, 1970–1979, allows us to see if the argument holds up over a period in which it has been claimed that the FTC was subjected to a series of reform measures that greatly improved the commission's record for the promotion of the public interest. This latter view of FTC behavior in the 1970s has been offered in a recent book by Robert Katzmann, who explicitly rejects models of budget maximization and congressional influence as explaining very much of recent FTC behavior.[2] Without offering an alternative explanation of outcomes, he chooses to stress instead the role of internal bureaucratic processes, such as the turnover of legal personnel, in explaining the cases that the FTC selects. Although we are interested in FTC case outcomes rather than case selection, it will prove interesting to compare the explanatory power of the

2. Katzmann (1980), esp. at 181–87.

private- and public-interest theories with respect to FTC behavior in the 1970s.[3]

Empirical Procedure

The initial period of study extends from 1961 to 1969. The selection of 1961 as a starting point coincides with the beginning of a congressional session and was dictated by local Virginia Polytechnic Institute (VPI) data availability. The selection of 1969 as a breakpoint derives from the fact that two highly critical reports on the FTC were published in 1969, and reorganization and reform of the FTC were begun in 1970.[4]

According to institutional sources, congressional jurisdiction over the FTC is shared by two Senate committees, one Senate subcommittee, and five House subcommittees: the Senate Committee on Interior and Insular Affairs; the Senate Committee on Commerce, Science, and Transportation; the Senate Subcommittee on Antitrust and Monopoly of the Senate Judiciary Committee; the House Subcommittees on Independent Offices and the Department of Housing and Urban Development, on Agriculture and Related Agencies, and on State, Justice, Commerce, and the Judiciary and Related Agencies (these are all subcommittees of the House Committee on Appropriations); the Subcommittee on Oversight and Investigations of the House Committee on Interstate and Foreign Commerce; and the Subcommittee on Monopolies and Commercial Law of the House Judiciary Committee.[5] The exact jurisdictional relationship of these committees to the FTC is never made clear in institutional sources. Indeed, congressional power over the FTC seems to shift over time, especially among the five House subcommittees. We thus collected data on all of these committees and subcommittees so as to be able to work from a broad definition of congressional influence over the FTC to more narrowly based definitions. The membership of these committees and sub-

3. Clarkson and Muris (1981), in a recently published study, incisively critique the performance of the FTC in the 1970s. Their critique is based upon a broad economic analysis of the behavior of the agency and the impact of its policies on consumer welfare. Their resounding negative findings are in accord with the type of empirical results that we uncover in this paper. Also, evidence in support of the congressional-influence model with respect to the general policies of the FTC can be found in Weingast and Moran (1983). These authors focus on the entire Senate and the Consumer Affairs Subcommittee of the Senate Commerce Committee to see if the selection of cases is biased in favor of the preferences of these two Senate groups. By way of contrast, we look at all committees and subcommittees relevant to the FTC and test to see if the disposition of cases is biased in favor of firms located in these committee members' districts.

4. See Cox, Sells, and Schultz, *supra* note 1; and Bureau of Nat'l Aff., Report of the American Bar Association Commission to Study the Federal Trade Commission, Antitrust and Trade Regulation Report no. 427, Special Suppl. (September 1969).

5. Our primary source is Katzmann (1980), esp. at 141, 143, & 147–50. Also, see Wagner, *supra* note 1.

committees was traced back to 1961 using the *Congressional Quarterly Almanac*.[6] Subsequently, the districts and states represented by the membership were plotted on a map of the United States. It was necessary to use a new map for each session of Congress since membership changed over the period studied. Moreover, in 1963 and 1973, as a result of the 1960 and 1970 censuses, congressional districts' boundaries were changed nationwide. Consequently, three sets of congressional district maps had to be employed, one for the period 1961–1962, one for 1963–1972, and one for 1973–1979.[7]

FTC action against businesses can take place on several levels. While the FTC is empowered to initiate investigations on its own, by far the majority (80–90 percent) of investigations are begun at the request of the public.[8] The public is permitted to file applications for complaints with the FTC, in which case the staff reviews the application to determine whether sufficient evidence of a violation exists to warrant further investigation. At this point either the case is closed for lack of evidence or a formal complaint is drawn up.[9] If the case remains open, the business charged is notified by the commission that a formal complaint is about to be served. In effect, the business is given the opportunity to agree to stop whatever action is specified in the complaint. If the business agrees, a consent order to cease and desist is prepared, and, if approved by the commission, the consent order prevents the issuance of a formal complaint. However, if the respondent does not file an answer with the FTC in response to the advance notice or seeks to contest the complaint, a formal complaint is issued. Subsequently, the case is heard by an administrative law judge (ALJ), and only two outcomes are possible—either the case is dismissed for insufficient evidence of a violation or a cease and desist order is issued. A case to which a respondent has consented can never be dismissed later. Moreover, any business that is issued a cease and desist order has the right to appeal to the commission (if the order is issued by an ALJ) and (if the commission supports the order) to the Circuit Court of Appeals in the circuit where the firm is located or in the Washington, D.C., circuit.

The outcomes of all contested cases and consent cases are summarized each year in *Federal Trade Commission Decisions*, which reports the nature of the case (consent, cease and desist, or dismissal), the name of the respondent(s), and the respondent(s)'s headquarters address(es).[10] When more than

6. 17–25 Congressional Quarterly Almanac (1961–69).

7. The congressional maps were taken from 87th Cong., 1st Sess., Official Congressional Directory (1961); 88th Cong., 1st Sess., Official Congressional Directory (1963); and 93d Cong., 1st Sess., Official Congressional Directory (1973).

8. See Alan Stone, Economic Regulation and the Public Interest (1977), at 64–65.

9. We are precluded from gaining insight into this initial aspect of FTC case selection because data on the preliminary FTC action are confidential and not available to the public.

10. Federal Trade Commission, 58–76 Federal Trade Commission Decisions (Gov't Printing Office, 1963–71).

one respondent was named and these respondents were associated with separate businesses, the headquarters address of each separate business was recorded as if separate cases had been involved.[11]

One point should be stressed about this procedure. Assigning firms to congressional districts on the basis of the respondent's headquarters address could be misleading if a division or plant under FTC scrutiny was located in a different district from the firm's headquarters. However, it is consistent with the pork-barrel hypothesis that a representative will seek to wield his influence when the profits of one of his constituents (the firm) are in jeopardy because of an FTC action against a division or plant of the firm not located in the district. Indeed, if all pork-barrel activity occurs in the district of the plant, such misassignment of firms to districts serves only to bias our statistical tests against the pork-barrel hypothesis.

After recording all of the relevant FTC data, the respondent addresses were plotted against the maps showing the congressional districts and Senate states of the eight committees' and subcommittees' members.[12] The totals for consents, cease and desist orders, and dismissals were tallied individually for the two Senate committees, the Senate subcommittee, each of the five House subcommittees, and the five House subcommittees taken together.

Precisely the same procedure was followed in gathering the data for the 1970–1979 sample period.[13] The data for both periods are summarized in the discussion of our empirical results to follow.

A final caveat about our empirical procedure is in order. Consider the source of cases brought against firms located within a given congressional district. Some of these cases will be initiated by individuals (persons, firms, or organizations) residing outside the district, and some will be initiated by district constituents. In the first case, a dismissal is clearly beneficial to the local firm and the local politician. The pork-barrel hypothesis is straightforward in this case—proportionately more dismissals relative to cases will occur in districts where representatives sit on FTC-relevant committees.[14] In

---

11. Two additional points are relevant here. First, interlocutory or modified orders were also issued over this period, though infrequently. Since these latter orders cite respondents from earlier complaints or from complaints to follow, they were not included in the study in order to avoid double counting. Second, if a committee member's district was located in a multidistrict metropolitan area, then companies investigated by the FTC located in adjacent districts were treated as if they were actually located within the member's district. In this respect we follow Plott, who suggested that representatives of large metropolitan districts share interests in adjacent districts. See Charles R. Plott, Some Organizational Influences on Urban Renewal Decisions, 58 Amer. Econ. Rev. 306 (1968).

12. Our source map was Rand McNally Road Atlas (1980).

13. See 26–35 Congressional Quarterly Almanac (1970–79); and Federal Trade Commission, 77–93 Federal Trade Commission Decisions (Gov't Printing Office, 1970–1979).

14. Likewise, consider the case in which the complainant is a firm in an FTC-relevant district. Assuming the complainant makes known his complaint to his representative, the pork-barrel

the second case, a dismissal favors the local respondent but harms the local complainant. The representative must choose to aid one firm or the other, presumably on the basis of greater net gain to himself or herself. Under these conditions there is no reason to believe that there is any systematic bias by the representative in favor of dismissal and therefore that there is any systematic bias across districts in the proportion of dismissals to cases brought. The latter point preserves the basis for testing our formulation of the pork-barrel hypothesis, given that some complaints will be brought by district constituents against district constituents.[15]

Empirical Results: 1961–1969

We test the pork-barrel hypothesis on two sets of data. In table 12.1 the base is cases brought, which includes all case-bringing activity of the FTC (dismissals, cease and desist orders, and consent decrees). In table 12.2 the base is complaints, which includes only formal actions against firms by the commission (dismissals and cease and desist orders). Consent decrees are thus removed from the latter data, and we look for congressional influence on the pattern of formal FTC decision making.

Our category of cases brought is the broadest measure of FTC activity for which data are available. It may also be the most suitable for our tests even if systematic data on the source of complaint applications were available. First, information on what firms are being scrutinized by the FTC is not readily known either to the firm or to its representative until a complaint is brought. Second, even if the representative knew that one of his or her constituents was the source of a complaint, if the firm did not know, the gain to the representative from halting any further investigation would be minimal since the benefit to the firm of such activity would be unobservable.

In tables 12.1 and 12.2 the ratios of dismissals to cases brought and dismissals to complaints are given for the jurisdictions represented by the given committee's membership in column 1 and for the remaining congressional jurisdictions in column 2.[16] According to the null hypothesis, the difference between the proportion of dismissals within and without the relevant congres-

---

effect will result in a higher probability of *nondismissal* of the complaint, thereby reinforcing the lower ratio of dismissals to cases brought in nonrelevant FTC districts.

15. To the best of our knowledge there are no systematic data on the source of FTC complaints that are available to the public. While it is true that the source of some complaints will become known in the process of discovery, such data are not collected and published by the FTC. Indeed, if the pork-barrel hypothesis is correct (that is, the public-interest hypothesis is wrong), the FTC has an obvious institutional incentive not to make such data generally available.

16. The totals for all five House subcommittees taken together are less than the sums over the five subcommittees since some congressmen sit on more than one FTC-related subcommittee. This point carries special force in our data, particularly given our handling of multidistrict metropolitan areas as discussed in note 11 *supra*.

Table 12.1   Empirical Results for Cases Brought: 1961–1969

Congressional (Sub)Committee	Ratios of Dismissals to Cases Brought			
	Within Congressional Areas (1)	Outside Congressional Areas (2)	z-Statistic (3)	Probability (4)
Senate Committee on Interior and	17/285	148/2,190		
Insular Affairs	.0596	.0678	.52	.400
Senate Committee on Commerce,	32/570	133/1,905		
Science, and Transportation	.0561	.0698	1.14	.748
Senate Subcommittee on Antitrust	60/638	105/1,837		
and Monopoly of the	.0940	.0572	3.22	.999
Senate Judiciary Committee				
House Subcommittee on Independent	14/87	151/2,388		
Offices and the Department of	.1609	.0632	3.59	.999
Housing and Urban Development of				
the House Appropriations Committee				
House Subcommittee on Agriculture	38/461	127/2,014		
and Related Agencies of the House	.0824	.0630	1.50	.866
Appropriations Committee				
House Subcommittee on State,	60/906	105/1,569		
Justice, Commerce, the Judiciary	.0662	.0669	.06	.048
and Related Agencies of the House				
Appropriations Committee				
House Subcommittee on Oversight and	4/61	161/2,414		
Investigations of the House Committee	.0656	.0667	. . .	. . .
on Interstate and Foreign Commerce				
House Subcommittee on Monopolies	62/873	103/1,602		
and Commercial Law of the House	.0602	.0643	.65	.478
Judiciary Committee				
All five House subcommittees	84/1,104	81/1,371		
	.0761	.0591	1.69	.909

Note: Where the z-statistic is not computed, at least one of the sample populations was not large enough to meet the criteria set by Paul G. Hoel, Introduction to Mathematical Statistics (1971), at 135, for using the normal approximation to a binomial distribution.

sional jurisdictions should not be significantly different from zero. Column 3 reports the z-statistic testing for a difference in two proportions drawn from binomial distributions of different populations. Column 4 gives the probability of correctly rejecting the null hypothesis.

Institutional sources stress that the Senate committees are relatively passive overseers of the FTC. This conjecture tends to hold for the Committee on Interior and Insular Affairs. However, membership on the Commerce Committee would appear to be related to unfavorable FTC rulings in table 12.2, while membership on the Subcommittee on Antitrust and Monopoly is significantly related to favorable rulings in both tables 12.1 and 12.2. This latter result is meaningful since this subcommittee had a membership in the 1960s

Table 12.2　Empirical Results for Complaints: 1961–1969

Congressional (Sub)Committee	Ratios of Dismissals to Complaints			
	Within Congressional Areas (1)	Outside Congressional Areas (2)	z-Statistic (3)	Probability (4)
Senate Committee on Interior and	17/64	148/515		
Insular Affairs	.2656	.2874	.36	.281
Senate Committee on Commerce,	32/140	133/439		
Science, and Transportation	.2286	.3030	1.70	.910
Senate Subcommittee on Antitrust	60/163	105/416		
and Monopoly of the	.3681	.2524	2.77	.999
Senate Judiciary Committee				
House Subcommittee on Independent	14/26	151/553		
Offices and the Department of	.5385	.2730	2.93	.997
Housing and Urban Development of				
the House Appropriations Committee				
House Subcommittee on Agriculture	38/110	128/469		
and Related Agencies of the House	.3454	.2708	1.56	.881
Appropriations Committee				
House Subcommittee on State,	60/198	105/381		
Justice, Commerce, the Judiciary	.3030	.2756	.69	.510
and Related Agencies of the House				
Appropriations Committee				
House Subcommittee on Oversight and	4/20	161/559		
Investigations of the House Committee	.2000	.2880	. . .	. . .
on Interstate and Foreign Commerce				
House Subcommittee on Monopolies	62/176	103/403		
and Commercial Law of the House	.3523	.2556	2.37	.982
Judiciary Committee				
All five House subcommittees	84/234	81/345		
	.3590	.2348	3.25	.999

Note: See note to table 12.1.

that, on average, encompassed only eight states, and we find a highly significant pattern of decisions over this period favoring firms in these states.

For purposes of testing the pork-barrel hypothesis on House data, we present results for individual subcommittees and for all five subcommittees taken together. The pattern of results on individual subcommittees suggests that the Independent Offices Subcommittee wielded substantial power with respect to FTC decision making in the 1960s, both in the broad and narrow definitions of influence. The results also suggest that the Subcommittee on Agriculture and Related Agencies and the Subcommittee on Monopolies and Commercial Law were influential in FTC decision making over this period with respect to favorable rulings for within-district cases. The Subcommittee on State, Justice, Commerce, and the Judiciary and Related Agencies and the Subcommittee on Oversight and Investigations appear to bear no relation to FTC behavior.

The results for all five House subcommittees taken together are reported at the bottom of tables 12.1 and 12.2. When the broad definition of FTC activity is used, we can reject the null hypothesis at approximately the 10-percent level of confidence. On the more narrowly based definition, when a complaint has been issued, the pork-barrel hypothesis can be accepted at better than the 1-percent level of confidence. The House subcommittees, taken as an observational unit, appear to have been a ripe arena for antitrust pork barrels in the 1960s.

The idea that congressional committee members who have important oversight and budgetary powers with respect to the FTC can deflect commission decisions in favor of firms in their jurisdictions would appear to have useful explanatory power in the 1960s, supporting the suspicions of Posner and other observers. The question remains for our inquiry of whether the much touted reforms of the commission in the 1970s did anything to mitigate congressional influence in antitrust matters.

Empirical Results: 1970–1979[17]

As stressed earlier, Katzmann argues that the efforts to reform the FTC to operate more consistently in the public interest have by and large been successful.[18] By this, Katzmann does not mean that there are not biases in commission activities, only that these biases derive from such factors as personnel selection and turnover, not from such forces as congressional influence or FTC aspirations to acquire a larger budget by currying congressional favor. Our results for commission activity in the 1970s, the period of reform, do not bode well for Katzmann's assessment. These results, using the same format as employed for tables 12.1 and 12.2, are given in tables 12.3 and 12.4.

The institutional observation that the Senate committees are passive overseers of FTC activities tends to be borne out in the results for the 1970s. We can observe no statistically reliable relationship over this period between membership on the relevant Senate committees and FTC decision making. This contrasts with the results for the 1960s when the Subcommittee on Antitrust and Monopoly in particular appeared to have a significant impact on commission decisions. On the other hand, the Commerce Committee, which in the 1960s exhibited a dismissal pattern opposed to the pork-barrel hypothesis, reversed itself in the 1970s, particularly with respect to complaints. Still, in the case of the Senate, Katzmann's public-interest argument

---

17. The exact cutoff date is June 1979.

18. Katzmann (1980). Again, this view should be contrasted to that recently offered by Clarkson and Muris (1981).

Table 12.3   Empirical Results for Cases Brought: 1970–1979

| | Ratios of Dismissals to Cases Brought | | | |
| | Within Congressional Areas | Outside Congressional Areas | z-Statistic | Probability |
Congressional (Sub)Committee	(1)	(2)	(3)	(4)
Senate Committee on Interior and	8/278	56/1,562		
Insular Affairs	.0288	.0358	.59	.440
Senate Committee on Commerce,	24/558	40/1,282		
Science, and Transportation	.0430	.0312	1.54	.876
Senate Subcommittee on Antitrust	7/305	57/1,535		
and Monopoly of the	.0230	.0358	1.11	.733
Senate Judiciary Committee				
House Subcommittee on Independent	6/72	58/1,768		
Offices and the Department of	.0833	.0329	2.29	.978
Housing and Urban Development of				
the House Appropriations Committee				
House Subcommittee on Agriculture	0/3	64/1,837		
and Related Agencies of the House	.0000	.0348	. . .	. . .
Appropriations Committee				
House Subcommittee on State,	19/417	45/1,423		
Justice, Commerce, the Judiciary	.0436	.0316	1.18	.762
and Related Agencies of the House				
Appropriations Committee				
House Subcommittee on Oversight and	6/157	58/1,683		
Investigations of the House Committee	.0382	.0345	.24	.189
on Interstate and Foreign Commerce				
House Subcommittee on Monopolies	18/282	46/1,558		
and Commercial Law of the House	.0682	.0295	3.26	.999
Judiciary Committee				
All five House subcommittees	29/589	35/1,251		
	.0492	.0280	2.32	.980

Note: See note to table 12.1.

can perhaps be said to hold. An alternative explanation is that a given firm is an insignificant member of a senator's constituency (the entire state), and the net return from FTC pork barrel is negligible in the Senate.

The House, however, is another matter. The results for all five subcommittees taken as a unit tend to bear out the pork-barrel hypothesis for both definitions of FTC activity. This is probably the strongest counterevidence to the claim that the reforms of the FTC altered the basic underlying relationship of the agency with Congress. If anything, the pork-barrel process became more pronounced and apparent in the data.

Among the individual House subcommittees, the Subcommittee on Independent Offices and the Subcommittee on Monopolies and Commercial Law continued to have an important impact on FTC actions in the 1970s, with the latter subcommittee now showing a significantly favorable impact on

Table 12.4   Empirical Results for Complaints: 1970–1979

Congressional (Sub)Committee	Ratios of Dismissals to Complaints			
	Within Congressional Areas (1)	Outside Congressional Areas (2)	z-Statistic (3)	Probability (4)
Senate Committee on Interior and	8/23	56/173		
Insular Affairs	.3478	.3237	.23	.182
Senate Committee on Commerce,	25/64	39/132		
Science, and Transportation	.3906	.2954	1.33	.816
Senate Subcommittee on Antitrust	7/24	57/172		
and Monopoly of the	.2917	.3314	.39	.303
Senate Judiciary Committee				
House Subcommittee on Independent	6/6	58/190		
Offices and the Department of	1.000	.3052	. . .	. . .
Housing and Urban Development of				
the House Appropriations Committee				
House Subcommittee on Agriculture	0/0	64/196		
and Related Agencies of the House	.0000	.3776	. . .	. . .
Appropriations Committee				
House Subcommittee on State,	19/38	45/158		
Justice, Commerce, and Judiciary	.5000	.2848	2.54	.989
and Related Agencies of the House				
Appropriations Committee				
House Subcommittee on Oversight and	6/11	58/185		
Investigations of the House Committee	.5454	.3135	1.59	.881
on Interstate and Foreign Commerce				
House Subcommittee on Monopolies	18/25	46/171		
and Commercial Law of the House	.7200	.2690	4.49	.999
Judiciary Committee				
All five House subcommittees	29/55	35/141		
	.5273	.2651	3.74	.999

Note: See note to table 12.1.

both cases brought and complaints. Unlike the results for the 1960s, the Subcommittee on the Judiciary and Related Agencies had a strong impact on formal FTC actions, particularly with respect to complaints (table 12.4). In an apparent jurisdictional shift, the Subcommittee on Agriculture essentially drops out of the data in the 1970s. Finally, the Subcommittee on Oversight and Investigations continues to be unimportant in explaining FTC decisions with respect to complaints.

Overall, the individual subcommittee results suggest that most of the basic results from the 1960s carried over to the 1970s. There were some jurisdictional shifts, to be sure, but most of the important underlying patterns in the data persisted and were strengthened in a statistical sense. The hypothesis of reform in the 1970s simply does not hold up for the House.

One general comparative aspect of the data should be noted. Total cases brought fell from 2,475 in the 1960s to 1,840 in the 1970s. More important, the number of formal actions by the FTC fell from 579 in the 1960s to 196 in the 1970s. It would appear that consents became more important in the 1970s, and, moreover, the leverage of four of the House subcommittees over the diminished number of formal commission actions became quite pronounced in the 1970s. Perhaps the reduction in formal actions is the true result of the FTC reforms.

Conclusion

Our results lend support to a private-interest theory of FTC behavior over the entire period that we investigated. If anything, the pork-barrel relationship between Congress and the commission became statistically stronger during the reform period of the 1970s. We would claim that those observers who see the FTC as acting more in congruence with the public interest (whatever this may mean) over this period have been misled in their analyses. In contrast to Katzmann, in particular, we would not be so hasty in discarding budget-maximizing or congressional-influence hypotheses about regulatory bureau behavior.[19] The tendencies that we describe are hard to explain with other models.

Also, though our results mask a complicated underlying pattern of pork-barrel activity, representation on certain committees is apparently valuable in antitrust proceedings. In terms of the representation and influence problem, then, we come out on the side of the argument that suggests that representation matters in determining policy outcomes.

Finally, we should be clear that we do not claim to have a completely specified model of the relationship between Congress and the FTC or of the behavior of the FTC over time. Much work remains to be done on such problems. For example, what are the characteristics of firms (large employers? large campaign contributors?) which benefit from FTC decision making? What is the amount of wealth at stake in a typical FTC case? Does seniority matter among the overseers of the FTC? Our results, however, along with the work of Posner and others, suggest the value of approaching such questions about antitrust decision making with a healthy dose of cynicism about representative democracy, which works in this area much as it does in others.

19. Katzmann (1980). Perhaps Katzmann was led astray by excessive reliance on interviews as a research methodology. Asking people what they do is a notoriously bad way to find out what they are actually doing.

CHAPTER THIRTEEN

Bureaucracy and Politics in FTC Merger Challenges

Malcolm B. Coate, Richard S. Higgins, and Fred S. McChesney

Introduction

Since the publication of Stigler's (1971) article on the economic theory of regulation, public-interest views of regulation have yielded increasingly to self-interest explanations. That is, well-organized private groups purchase regulatory favors in the political marketplace, benefiting both themselves and politician-sellers at the expense of less well-organized groups. However, one form of government regulation, antitrust, has largely escaped characterization as a political, interest-group bargain. "Antitrust is one of the few remaining areas in which it is commonly assumed that government operates in the public interest" (Shughart and Tollison 1985, 53). Stigler himself believes antitrust to be a rare instance of benevolent regulation.[1] Some have tested this claim by examining the

This essay was previously published in the *Journal of Law and Economics* 33 (October 1990): 463–82. © 1990 by The University of Chicago. All rights reserved.

Our analysis and conclusions are our own and do not necessarily reflect the views of our respective institutions. We have reluctantly agreed to recite the following, written by the FTC's Office of General Counsel:

> This paper was prepared using nonpublic information from Federal Trade Commission internal files. Access to this information was available to Messrs. Higgins and Coate because they were employees of the Commission, and it was made available to Mr. McChesney because he was a consultant to the FTC Bureau of Economics. The Commission's Bureau of Economics has major disagreements with the methodology, analysis, inferences, and conclusions contained in this paper, and neither the Commission nor any of its members has authorized or endorsed its creation or publication. The FTC General Counsel determined that precluding publication would not be in the public interest and authorized its publication under secs. 5.12 and 5.21 of the FTC Rules of Practice, 16 C.F.R. secs. 5.12 and 5.21.

1. Stigler calls the Sherman Act "a public interest law . . . in the same sense in which I think having private property, enforcement of contract, and suppression of crime are public-interest phenomena . . . I like the Sherman Act" (Hazlett 1984, 46). See also Stigler (1966). For similarly benign views of the intent (though not effect) of antitrust law, see Bork (1978, 50–71). For further discussion of the tenacity of the public-interest view of antitrust, see Robert E. McCormick, The Strategic Use of Regulation: A Review of the Literature, in The Political Economy of Regulation: Private Interests in the Regulatory Process 26 (Robert A. Rogowsky and Bruce Yandle, eds., 1984).

cases brought by antitrust authorities but found little evidence that public-interest (social-welfare) considerations drive antitrust enforcement. However, the alternative hypothesis, that antitrust is a politically driven, private-interest sort of regulation, has also been tested and found to be largely unsupported.

This essay joins the debate by examining decisions of the Federal Trade Commission (FTC) to challenge horizontal mergers, using non-public data from that agency's files. The FTC does not purport to base its enforcement of merger law on the public-interest variables identified by previous authors; rather, the commission's merger enforcement policy focuses on variables specified in the Department of Justice's merger guidelines. All other things equal, the guidelines predictably would play a role in agency determinations to challenge a merger, a hypothesis tested here using the internal FTC data.

Our data also elucidate the separate roles played by FTC lawyers and economists in influencing FTC decisions to challenge mergers. Several studies of the FTC have advanced—but never tested—hypotheses about these two groups within the agency. Lawyers supposedly have greater incentives to initiate cases than do economists, but both lawyers and economists are said to affect agency decisions whether to file a complaint. Those and related hypotheses are also tested here.

Finally, we model antitrust enforcement by the FTC as also influenced, *ceteris paribus,* by pressure from Congress. This pressure reflects demands from management and labor of companies at risk from reorganization through mergers and takeovers. Although mergers and takeovers are socially beneficial overall, the configuration of winners and losers confronts a politician with asymmetric benefits and costs. Individual shareholders who gain are weakly organized and scattered throughout the country; institutional shareholders are too numerous and well-diversified to have strong incentives to organize. Management and labor that may lose their jobs or be transferred are better organized and more concentrated in a particular politician's district. An antitrust regime can be useful to a politician in the same way that anti-takeover legislation is, avoiding the risk that resources and votes will exit a politician's jurisdiction following completion of a merger.

The chapter begins with a brief review of previous attempts to explain antitrust, followed by presentation of an alternative model of bureaucratically and politically directed antitrust enforcement. The FTC is modeled as responsive to (a) the merger guidelines, (b) internal agreement or disagreement between its own lawyers and economists, and (c) pressure from politicians seeking to block mergers. The model is next tested by examining FTC decisions whether to challenge mergers proposed between 1982 and 1986. The model is shown to explain considerably more of antitrust enforcement than has been possible heretofore. High values for the variables identified in the merger guidelines almost guarantee a merger challenge. In addition, congressional pressure on the FTC to block mergers is found to increase significantly the likelihood that the commission will do so.

Determinants of Antitrust Enforcement

Previous Inquiries

Statistical examination of antitrust enforcement began with Posner (1970). Building on Posner's data, Long, Schramm, and Tollison (L-S-T) (1973) developed a cross-industry model of welfare loss potentially caused by antitrust infractions, and examined whether the Justice Department brought more cases in industries in which amounts of potential welfare loss were greater. They found that welfare loss "played a minor role in explaining antitrust activity. . . . Much of the explanation of antitrust activity clearly lies outside our model" (pp. 361–62).

Subsequent work to explain antitrust enforcement in social-welfare (public-interest) terms has aimed at improving the L-S-T model. Siegfried (1975), for example, ran the L-S-T tests using more disaggregated data and a larger sample. However, his results were not qualitatively different from the L-S-T results, and they generally explained even less of the Antitrust Division's enforcement activities. When Siegfried altered various L-S-T assumptions, his model's explanatory power fell even further, leading him to conclude that "economic variables have little influence on the Antitrust Division."[2] Asch (1975) noted difficulties in using industry data of any sort, since antitrust cases are filed against firms, not entire industries. Other than the need to focus more on micro (firm) levels of enforcement, however, Asch advanced no particular hypothesis about antitrust. Indeed, he concluded (p. 579) that the "appropriate interpretation" of his empirical results was "not entirely clear," even "puzzling."

Thus, in attempts to predict antitrust enforcement *ex ante,* the "public interest hypothesis has not been supported by empirical work."[3] As an alternative, antitrust has been modeled as an interest-group process akin to other economic regulation, whereby antitrust is used to benefit well-organized private interests. A priori, the hypothesis is appealing: as attested by current judicial regulation of the telephone industry, antitrust often results in de facto regulatory regimes administered by government agencies and the

2. Siegfried (1975, 573). Overall, Siegfried concluded that "government is more interested in questions concerning the division of the economic pie than in increasing its total size. . . . [T]here is apparently *no* consideration of economic benefits in the decision process for allocating antitrust cases." Ibid., at 563, 567 (emphasis in original).

3. Yandle (1988, 263). Studies of particular areas of enforcement likewise find that antitrust does not increase, and often reduces, economic welfare. Government price-fixing cases apparently target ineffective cartels, rather than successful ones that cause significant economic damage (Marvel, Netter, and Robinson, 1988). Firms successfully charged by the government with price-fixing have had lower rates of profitability than a random sample of firms (Asch and Seneca 1976). Likewise, mergers challenged by the government are generally not anticompetitive (Eckbo and Wier 1985). Noteworthy also is the considerable evidence that the remedies awarded the government in successful antitrust cases seem not to have achieved stated welfare goals. For example, Hay and Kelley (1974), Elzinga (1969), Rogowsky (1987).

courts.[4] Thus, some studies attempted to locate the private beneficiaries of antitrust, whose influence (via the political process) could explain the origin and enforcement of the antitrust statutes. Such attempts, notably those of Stigler (1985) and of Baxter (1980), have also failed empirically.[5]

A Bureaucratic-Political Model of Antitrust Enforcement

BUREAUCRATIC FACTORS

There are several likely reasons for the prior models' inability to explain antitrust enforcement. First, prior inquiries have ignored the criteria that the antitrust agencies themselves specify as determining their case selection. With mergers, for example, the Department of Justice and the FTC have officially adhered to written merger guidelines for the past twenty years.[6] The more recent guidelines (issued on 14 June 1982, and revised in 1984) define various factors that will increase the likelihood of an antitrust challenge to a merger, including the degree of and change in market concentration (measured by the Herfindahl-Hirschman Index [HHI]), the existence of significant barriers to entry, the likelihood of successful collusion for reasons other than barriers to entry, and the possibility that one firm may be failing. Prior models have not included the merger guidelines criteria as determining antitrust enforcement, perhaps because antitrust enforcers' measures of these variables have not generally been available.[7] Our access to internal FTC case files permits us, however, to determine whether these factors increase the chances of FTC enforcement action.

A second reason for the weak explanatory power of previous models, especially the private-interest models, has been their failure to model the

4. For example, Easterbrook (1984, 35, n. 72) says: "Many antitrust suits are regulatory. The Department of Justice used antitrust suits to establish district courts as regulatory agencies over industries in which the Antitrust Division was persuaded that competition was 'unworkable,' but in which the political process had not acted. Approximately 53 antitrust decrees entered through 1979 are regulatory in character. This substantially exceeds the number of industries regulated by statute." See also Sullivan (1986).

5. Stigler (1985, 8) tested the hypotheses that agrarian and small-business interests account for the origins of federal antitrust law but reported a "failure to find strong evidence for any explanation for the passage of the Sherman Act." Baxter (1980) hypothesized that two groups in particular, private antitrust lawyers and smaller firms, stand to gain from greater antitrust enforcement. Discriminating tests of his hypotheses were difficult to identify, and the data Baxter did present were inconclusive.

6. U.S. Dep't of Justice Merger Guidelines, 30 May 1968. The guidelines were amended in 1982 and 1984. For the text of the 1968, 1982, and 1984 guidelines, plus the FTC's statement that it would give "considerable weight" to Justice's 1982 guidelines, see Section of Antitrust Law, Am. Bar Ass'n, Horizontal Mergers: Law and Policy 264–336 (1986).

7. But see Rogowsky (1984). Rogowsky examined the extent to which the Antitrust Division has followed its merger guidelines, finding that from 1968 to 1981 over 20 percent of the merger cases filed by the government fell below the defined threshold of concentration. Rogowsky did not, however, specify or test a model of enforcement action.

agency decision in terms of the incentives of particular agency personnel. Lawyers and economists face different incentives to bring cases. Attorneys are said to favor more litigation than do economists because court challenges increase lawyers' human capital as litigators and thus raise their subsequent returns in private practice.[8] Even in the shorter run, heading a major investigation is required for FTC lawyers to advance to higher government employment grades (which also increases salaries); no such requirement applies to economists. The influence of economists at the FTC has grown considerably, particularly as economists have been named as commissioners and (once) even as chairman of the commission.[9] Economists tend to stay longer at the agency, instead of using federal experience to build capital for subsequent private employment.

Conflicting incentives will lead to disagreement between lawyers and economists about whether to bring cases, and disagreements will reduce the likelihood of merger challenges. One would hypothesize that the FTC brings more cases when both lawyers and economists agree that the magnitudes of the various factors set out in the merger guidelines have reached worrisome levels. Disagreement among agency personnel as to the desirability of a particular merger challenge, in contrast, probably will reduce the likelihood that a case will be brought.

POLITICAL FACTORS

There is another reason for the largely unsuccessful attempts at explaining antitrust enforcement from an interest-group perspective. Those efforts have generally considered only private industries possibly served by antitrust. The likely private beneficiaries from antitrust may, however, cut across particular industries. Examination of the private winners and losers from mergers, plus the interests of politicians themselves, suggests that merger enforcement would be politically driven by the same groups favoring restriction on corporate takeovers generally.

In a merger, the wealth of shareholders in both firms increases.[10] Even the threat of a merger will benefit shareholders of potential target firms if management seeks to operate more efficiently to avoid a takeover. Small shareholders who gain are not ordinarily organized and are geographically

8. "The principal attraction of Commission service to lawyers who wish to use it as a steppingstone to private practice lies in the opportunities it affords to gain trial experience. . . . It is the experience of trying cases, the more the better, not the social payoff from the litigation, that improves the professional skills and earning prospects of FTC lawyers" (Posner 1969a, 86). Every other study of the FTC agrees. For example, Clarkson and Muris (1981, 300). The same incentives are said to motivate antitrust lawyers at the Justice Department. For example, Weaver (1977, 38–41).

9. For example, Katzmann (1980, 52–53).

10. See generally Michael Jensen and Richard Ruback, The Market for Corporate Control: The Scientific Evidence, 11 J. Fin. Econ. 5, 9–16 (1983), which recites the empirical evidence.

dispersed; their small individual holdings give them little incentive to be politically active. Likewise, larger institutional shareholders are too numerous, dispersed, and well-diversified to have strong incentives to organize. But with gains to shareholders often come losses to two more concentrated groups—firms' current management and labor. Jobs may be eliminated and offices may be closed or moved, as a result either of the merger or of reorganization to fend off takeover threats. This means that the merger (or threat of merger) of a firm in politicians' home districts or states confronts them (and their management and labor constituents) with concentrated expected costs, while the expected benefits are spread among shareholders nationwide. Imperiled home-district management and labor will value political help to stop the merger; failure to stop it will mean not only that the district loses wealth, but that politicians may lose votes as jobs are transferred.

Of course, the districts where jobs and offices are ultimately located will benefit, so other politicians may have an incentive to favor a merger. But the particular districts that benefit are more difficult to perceive (more uncertain) *ex ante,* so potential labor and management beneficiaries have less incentive to press for the merger. Thus, the value of the probable loss to the current district is typically greater than the value of the possible gain to another. The expected costs to losing politicians outweigh the gains to winning politicians, *ceteris paribus.* To politicians who stand to lose, an antitrust challenge can be beneficial in defeating the attempted merger altogether; at a minimum it will slow down completion of the merger, increasing the likelihood that the parties themselves will call off the proposed arrangement.

In effect, the antitrust system works like private and public antitakeover devices, although the similarities have not been fully appreciated. Privately, target managements can file antitrust actions to repel hostile bidders; they can acquire assets preemptively to increase concentration levels and so elicit a governmental antitrust challenge to the proposed takeover.[11] Under either strategy, antitrust is a close substitute for other private devices (for example, poison pills) to fend off bids.

The public system of antitrust enforcement also works like antitakeover statutes, which have been shown to decrease the number of successful takeovers.[12] The Hart-Scott-Rodino (H-S-R) procedure of premerger notification requires that merger partners notify federal antitrust authorities of their proposed merger, then wait for government clearance before completing any deal. In essence, therefore, the H-S-R system works like the Williams Act, the principal federal statute regulating takeovers, which requires notification

11. For example, Panter v. Marshall Field & Co., 646 F.2d 271 (7th Cir.), cert. denied, 454 U.S. 1092 (1981). See Jarrell (1985).

12. Gregg A. Jarrell and Michael Bradley, The Economic Effects of Federal and State Regulations of Cash Tender Offers, 23 J. Law & Econ. 371 (1980).

of the Securities and Exchange Commission (SEC) and a mandatory waiting period before tender offers can be completed.[13]

Political considerations alone will not determine agency decisions. Antitrust enforcers purport to follow the government's merger guidelines in deciding what mergers to challenge, and these should also affect bureaucratic choices. At the margin, however, political demands for enforcement will increase the bureaucratic supply of mergers challenged. There is considerable anecdotal evidence that the FTC commissioners do at times bring pressure for more cases.[14] The principal implication of the model presented here is that in bringing such pressure, the FTC commissioners respond to politicians' demand for more antitrust cases. This model of antitrust has implications for a more general debate. Many social scientists, including some economists, view administrative agencies as operating with few effective constraints imposed by legislators: this view characterizes many prior studies of the Federal Trade Commission.[15] Others argue along the lines of the present hypothesis: that the benefits to politicians of controlling bureaucratic agencies are worth the costs.[16] In the end, the issue is an empirical one.

Empirical Evidence

To test the bureaucratic-political model of merger enforcement, we reviewed the internal records associated with all H-S-R "second requests" concerning

13. Just as legislators have proposed extending the Williams Act waiting period, they have also sought to extend H-S-R waiting periods before mergers can be completed. See, for example, H.R. 586, 100th Cong. 1st Sess. (8 Jan. 1987). That bill would require an "economic impact statement" for mergers. It would require (i) notice whether the proposed merger would result in the sale or closing of any facility or termination of its operations, (ii) an estimate of the number of jobs that would be lost, and (iii) an estimate of revenue that would be lost "by each governmental entity in the geographical jurisdiction." H.R. 586, 100th Cong., 1st Sess. sec. 4(b)(2) (1987).

14. In May 1987, the FTC commissioners met to "decide the fate" of the Bureau of Competition director, who was accused of bringing too few cases. "Here Comes the Pendulum," FTC Watch, 29 May 1987, at 1. "The meeting was scheduled far enough in advance that [BC Director] Zuckerman had time to visit all the Commissioners . . . and promise to get the bureau up to speed. According to knowledgeable agency officials, Zuckerman's promises to the Commissioners will require the Competition Bureau to bring on the order of thirty (30) cases in the next six months, an output which would be prodigious by recent standards." Ibid., 2. It was subsequently reported that the budget for merger surveillance and thus the number of investigations had increased considerably. "A little direct intervention by the Commissioners," it was concluded, "goes a long way." "Mergers," FTC Watch, 26 June 1987, at 5.

15. For example, Katzmann (1980); Clarkson and Muris (1981).

16. For general discussions and empirical tests, see Weingast and Moran (1983), Shughart, Tollison, and Goff (1986), Faith, Leavens, and Tollison (1982). See also Kovacic (1987, 65), concluding that the FTC's antitrust enforcement has been "consistent with, and responsive to, congressional policy preferences"; Posner (1969a, 82–85) discusses ways politicians can use the FTC to benefit their constituents.

horizontal mergers issued by the Federal Trade Commission between 14 June 1982 (the date of the new merger guidelines), and 1 January 1987. Second requests obtain the data necessary to evaluate potentially anticompetitive transactions.[17] The sample includes seventy commission decisions.[18] In forty-three cases, the merger was allowed to proceed without interference; in the other twenty-seven cases (including those in which the merger was allowed to proceed only following some agreement with the FTC, such as a negotiated divestiture) the commission issued a complaint. Of the twenty-seven complaints issued, the FTC has not lost a case.[19]

Explanatory Variables

MERGER GUIDELINES VARIABLES

The five FTC commissioners vote whether to challenge a merger on the basis of information in formal staff memoranda, which are usually submitted separately by the lawyers of the Bureau of Competition (BC) and the economists of the Bureau of Economics (BE). The files for the seventy proposed mergers prepared for the commission's decisions reveal what each staff believes to characterize the relevant legal and economic considerations about each proposed merger. To distinguish the relative influence of lawyers' and economists' views on the decision to challenge, we identified the separate views of BC and BE as to the principal criteria included in the merger guidelines.[20]

17. For a description of the Hart-Scott-Rodino procedures, including issuance of "second requests," see, for example, Heublein, Inc. v. FTC, 539 F.Supp. 123, 124–25 (D.D.C. 1982). Following a second request, the FTC staff can dispose of a matter in several ways. The investigation may be closed, based on the staff's concurrence in a recommendation to close, which is subject to reversal by the commission. Alternatively, there may be a recommendation to the commission that a complaint be issued. In this case, the commission votes either to issue a complaint or to close the investigation.

18. The seventy cases were drawn from the total of 109 H-S-R second requests issued between 14 June 1982, and 1 January 1987. Investigations were dropped from the sample if the merger was vertical (ten cases); the attempted merger was abandoned when the second request was issued, so the FTC's case file lacked information on the relevant variables (eight cases); the transaction was a joint venture, rather than a merger (four cases); the merger received early approval, presumably because the merger raised no serious competitive issues, so the FTC's case file contained insufficient information to be included in the sample (nine cases); the cases had been closed before sufficient information had been included in the files (three cases); or the HHI fell below the lower bound (1000) stated in the guidelines for a challenge (five cases).

19. Of the twenty-seven complaints issued, twenty-six cases were completed at the time of this writing; in the last one, an administrative ruling in favor of the FTC was still on appeal. As noted, the twenty-seven complaints include cases in which the merger was allowed to proceed only subject to some agreement with the commission (such as a divestiture), since complaints must be filed in such cases.

20. In cases when the director of the Bureau of Competition disagreed with his staff and sided with the Bureau of Economics, the staff position was used here as BC's position on the merger.

For each merger, we first noted lawyers' and economists' calculations of the HHI in the relevant industry and the change in the index from the proposed merger. The calculations were translated into two binary variables. The first, for BC, equals one for those mergers in which the lawyers argued that the industry HHI exceeded 1800 (making the industry "highly concentrated" under the guidelines) and that the merger would cause at least a fifty-point HHI increase (and so would be deemed "a matter of significant competitive concern" under the guidelines). The second variable, for BE, equals one for cases in which the economists argued that the HHI was below 1800 or the increase would be less than fifty points. (For mergers involving diversified firms, and so different HHI's for different markets, the highest HHI was used.) Thus, a particular case could have both variables equal to one only if the two bureaus disagreed. Disagreements occur, often when the economists and lawyers define the relevant market differently.[21] (As would be predicted, this usually happened because lawyers argued for narrower markets than did economists.)

For other variables identified as relevant in the merger guidelines, a similar procedure was followed. For barriers to entry, binary variables for the BC and BE determinations were included. The BC barrier-to-entry variable was coded one when the lawyers claimed significant entry could not occur for at least two years, the period specified in the merger guidelines. The BE barrier variable was assigned the value one when BE found that entry would easily occur within two years. Positive values for both variables again signal disagreement. Ease of collusion was handled the same way, with a dichotomous variable for each bureau. A value of one for the BC variable indicated that the lawyers thought collusion relatively easy, while a one for BE meant the economists thought the opposite. (Zeros for the barrier-to-entry or collusion variables in some cases indicate that the bureau simply did not address the issue.) Finally, when the failing-firm doctrine was cited by BC as applicable, a failing-firm variable was coded one. Ordinarily, the commission views application of the doctrine as a purely legal issue.

POLITICAL VARIABLES

To measure the effect of politics on each proposed merger, we used two variables. The first provides a proxy for political effect by measuring the amount of news coverage given the merger. Bigger mergers generate greater news coverage. The larger the merger, the more likely it is to result in job losses, plant closings or relocations, and revenue losses to local jurisdictions, and thus the likelier it will be to encounter political resistance. Our measure of news coverage, as an indirect measure of the political pressure stemming from a proposed merger, is the count of the number of articles that mentioned

---

21. For the seventy cases in the sample, the two bureaus disagreed about the definition of the relevant market sixteen times.

the merger in the *Wall Street Journal* prior to the FTC's decision. Predictably, the commission will respond to pressure brought by better-organized labor and management groups, meaning it will challenge mergers generating more publicity.

Restricting the citations variable to articles that appeared before the FTC's merger decision reduces concerns over any problem of simultaneity between the number of articles and the decision whether to challenge the merger; the decision would increase the number of citations afterward. To be sure simultaneity was avoided, the equation was also estimated with the natural logarithm of the total merger bid price substituted for the citation count. Bid price would perform as do citations, capturing the potential loss of wealth and jobs in the districts affected and so the expected cost to politicians of letting the merger proceed. Higher bid prices therefore would increase the probability of the FTC's voting to challenge the merger. However, because the FTC vote would not affect the bid price, there is no simultaneity problem.

Political pressure is included more directly in the model by a twelve-month moving average, centered on the FTC's second request date, of the number of times commissioners or senior (politically appointed) FTC staff were called before congressional committees to testify on their antitrust enforcement records. Calling commissioners and staff to defend their antitrust records is a technique that politicians use frequently to increase amounts of antitrust enforcement. The FTC commissioners and staff prepare "case counts" to show that they are active in investigating cases and filing an acceptable number of complaints. Politicians berate commission witnesses when they deem the number of cases brought too low.[22] Individual representatives and senators even advocate particular enforcement actions.[23] The debate in 1984 over amending the Export Administration Act to ban oil company mergers for five years shows the link between merger enforcement and political interest in local industries. The debate principally concerned job losses in the jurisdictions affected.[24] The budget process also reflects congressional desires for

22. See, for example, Katzmann (1980, 146), discussing FTC testimony before its appropriations subcommittee: "[One] yardstick that the subcommittee uses in judging how well the commission is performing has to do with case-load statistics."

23. Ibid., at 147–60.

24. Yandle (1988, 272) summarizes congressional concerns:

The plan for the amendment had been triggered by the 1984 merger attempt of Texaco and Getty Oil Company, which would have been the largest merger in the nation's history. In the unfolding discussion, the senators first expressed grave concern about the inevitable monopoly power . . . [and then about] specific details associated with the FTC's antitrust review of the Texaco-Getty merger and the effects of the merger on plant operations in their states. For example, Senator Lautenberg raised as an issue Texaco's Eagle Point refinery in [West Deptford], New Jersey, indicating that 500 jobs and $1.8 million in local tax revenues were at risk. Senator Dole commented on the potential closing of a refinery in [El] Dorado, Kansas, where 1,000 jobs were at stake. He then indicated that he would "be meeting with officials of Texaco and others who may be able to shed more light on this."

Table 13.1   Summary and Predicted Signs of Regression Model Independent Variables

Name	Definition	Mean	Standard Deviation	Predicted Sign
BCHERFHI	One if BC claims HHI > 1800 and change > 50, zero otherwise.	.714	.455	+
BEHERFLO	One if BE claims that HHI < 1800 or change < 50, zero otherwise.	.429	.498	−
BCBARHI	One if BC claims barriers to entry high, zero otherwise.	.814	.392	+
BEBARLO	One if BE claims barriers to entry low, zero otherwise.	.343	.478	−
BCCOLHI	One if BC claims industry conducive to collusion, zero otherwise.	.443	.500	+
BECOLLO	One if BE claims industry not conducive to collusion, zero otherwise.	.343	.478	−
FAILFIRM	One if BC claims failing-firm doctrine applicable, zero otherwise.	.057	.234	−
CITES	Number of articles mentioning merger in *Wall Street Journal* before FTC decision.	2.57	4.84	+
HEARINGS	Twelve-month moving average of FTC or political staff testimony before Congress.	5.83	3.61	+

more antitrust cases. Antitrust agency budgets are allocated according to the enforcement zeal shown; passage of the Hart-Scott-Rodino Act in 1976 in particular caused a significant increase in antitrust budgets.[25]

The Regression Model

We defined a binary dependent variable, VOTE, equal to one when the commission voted a complaint in a case (including cases of divestiture or other negotiated changes in the merging parties' original agreement) and zero when it allowed the merger to proceed as the parties originally agreed. Given the binary dependent variable, we used the probit model,

$$\text{PROB}[\text{VOTE} = 1] = F[aX],$$

where F is the normal distribution function and aX is a linear combination of the explanatory variables. Table 13.1 lists the independent variables, their means and standard deviations, and their predicted signs in the regression model.[26]

25. Ibid., at 271 (table 3).

26. The variable for congressional appearances, the effect of which is tested here, includes only hearings in which antitrust (rather than the FTC's consumer protection functions) was the subject. The means and standard deviations of BEBARLO and BECOLLO are identical, but this is coincidence. BECOLLO measures BE's assessment of the ease of collusion for reasons

The parameter estimates for each explanatory variable are presented in table 13.2. All variables have the predicted signs. The coefficients of all but the failing-firm variable are significant at the 10-percent level; most are significant at the 5-percent level. Overall, the model easily passes the chi-square likelihood ratio test, indicating that the explanatory variables significantly influence the probability of a complaint. We note in particular that the pseudo-R^2 computed from the likelihood statistic suggests that the model explains about half the variance in the dependent variable,[27] much more than previous studies of antitrust enforcement have been able to explain.

POLITICAL INFLUENCES

The coefficient estimates for the two variables measuring political pressure, CITES and HEARINGS, lead us to conclude that the commission does respond to political considerations, *ceteris paribus*. A chi-square test shows that the two variables are jointly significant at the 1-percent level. Using the point estimates of the regression coefficients and evaluating the derivative of the normal distribution function at the mean values of the independent variables, we can calculate the marginal effects of the political variables on the probability that the commission will vote to seek a complaint. The marginal *Wall Street Journal* story raises the probability of a challenge 4.7 percentage points, and one additional congressional hearing raises the probability of a merger challenge by 4.2 percentage points. Thus, commission decisions are significantly influenced by political concerns. Reestimating the equation with the log of the total merger bid price substituted for CITES yields results qualitatively the same as those in table 13.2; all coefficients retain the same

---

other than barriers to entry; the evaluation of entry barriers is captured by BEBARLO. The Pearson coefficient of correlation between the two variables (.11) is insignificant. Indeed, the correlations between the different merger guidelines variables for each bureau are generally insignificant. For the Bureau of Competition, the correlation coefficients are:

	BCHERFHI	BCBARHI
BCHERFHI		
BCBARHI	.02	
BCCOLHI	.18	.28

The coefficients for the Bureau of Economics are:

	BEHERFLO	BEBARLO
BEHERFLO		
BEBARLO	.04	
BECOLLO	−.02	.11

Thus, the data indicate that the individual variables identified by the merger guidelines are evaluated on their own separate merits.

27. R. Carter Hill, George G. Judge, William E. Griffith, Helmut Lutkepohl, and Tsoung-Chao Lee, The Theory and Practice of Econometrics 767 (1985).

Table 13.2   Probit Regression Parameters

Variable	Coefficient
BCHERFHI	1.11†
	(1.53)
BEHERFLO	−.962†
	(−1.65)
BCBARHI	1.84*
	(1.85)
BEBARLO	−.880†
	(−1.58)
BCCOLHI	1.65*
	(3.16)
BECOLLO	−.880*
	(−1.83)
FAILFIRM	−4.33
	(−.01)
CITES	.169*
	(1.82)
HEARINGS	.151*
	(1.71)
Constant	−4.01*
	(−2.47)
Likelihood ratio test	46.3*
Pseudo-R^2	.497

Note: t-statistics are in parentheses.
*Significant at the .05 level.
†Significant at the .10 level.

signs, and all that are statistically significant remain so except the HHI variables, whose significance falls to just below 10 percent.[28]

The political variables may understate the FTC's overall susceptibility to political considerations. The sample does not include attempts to merge that would have occurred but for parties' perception that merging would be unacceptable politically. Data availability and measurement difficulties also pre-

28. The estimated equation (with the absolute value of t-statistics in parentheses) was the following:

$$VOTE = -3.96 + .832\,(BCHERFHI) - .717\,(BEHERFLO) + 1.39\,(BCBARHI)$$
$$(2.44)\,(1.21) \qquad\qquad (1.27) \qquad\qquad (1.65)$$

$$-.957\,(BEBARLO) + 1.42\,(BCCOLHI) - .916\,(BECOLLO)$$
$$(1.71) \qquad\qquad (2.85) \qquad\qquad (1.92)$$

$$-4.47\,(FAILFIRM) + .234\,(PRICE) + .130\,(HEARINGS) + u.$$
$$(.01) \qquad\qquad (1.51) \qquad\qquad (1.57)$$

with PRICE (in millions of dollars) representing the logarithm of the merger bid price. (PRICE has a mean of 4.98 and standard deviation of 1.69.)

clude inclusion of a full set of political variables, so some of the unexplained variation in the dependent variable may have a political basis. Moreover, if Congress influences the bureaucratic decision to challenge mergers after development of the merger guidelines, it would also influence the bureaucratic decisions reflected in the guidelines themselves. If antitrust enforcers were to announce enforcement criteria promising fewer cases than Congress found acceptable, enforcers would be made to alter the guidelines. Mindful of this possibility, officials would adjust the criteria: for example, congressional influence would cause concentration ratios triggering second requests to be set lower than would otherwise be the case. The tests here cannot capture any political influence that affected the guidelines themselves.

Finally, BC staff's legal analysis may itself include responses to political pressure. That is, factual findings presented to the commission may already reflect political choices made at the subcommission level. To test this hypothesis, we modeled the BC staff recommendation as a function of the two political variables and of BE's reading of the economic variables. The political variables were individually and jointly insignificant, however.[29] Thus, commission responsiveness to political influences appears to reside at the level of the commissioners themselves, not at the staff level.

BUREAUCRATIC INFLUENCE

Merger guidelines variables. The evidence on bureaucratically interpreted guidelines factors also supports our hypotheses. A claim by BC that the HHI, difficulty of entry, or ease of collusion is worrisome would increase the likelihood of commission action, *ceteris paribus*. Likewise, BE claims that the HHI, ease of entry, or difficulty of collusion do not justify challenging a merger would reduce the likelihood that the commission would vote to challenge. A chi-square test indicates that the three economic variables as interpreted by BC are jointly significant at the 1-percent level, as are the same variables as interpreted by BE.

---

29. The estimated equation (with the absolute value of t-statistics in parentheses) was the following:

$$\text{BCCHOICE} = .627 - 1.04 \,(\text{BEHERFLO}) - .831 \,(\text{BEBARLO}) - .113 \,(\text{BECOLLO})$$
$$\quad\quad (1.56) \quad\quad (2.72) \quad\quad\quad\quad (2.26) \quad\quad\quad\quad (.32)$$
$$\quad - 5.75 \,(\text{FAILFIRM}) + .0321 \,(\text{CITES}) + .0426 \,(\text{HEARINGS}) + u.$$
$$\quad\quad (.01) \quad\quad\quad\quad (.81) \quad\quad\quad\quad (.78)$$

where BCCHOICE is the choice of the Bureau of Competition to favor the FTC's challenging the merger (BCCHOICE = 1) or allowing the merger to proceed (BCCHOICE = 0). While the political variables have no significant influence on BC's choice, BE's evaluation of the concentration index (BEHERFLO) and of the possible existence of barriers of entry (BEBARLO) are highly significant predictors of BC's decision.

With the political variables held constant at their means, the equation as estimated in table 13.2 can be used to estimate more precisely the relative importance of the merger guidelines criteria. When BC and BE agree that the HHI, entry barriers, and likelihood of collusion are all high, there is a 97-percent probability that the FTC will challenge a merger.[30] If both bureaus agree that entry barriers and likelihood of collusion are high, but that the HHI is not high, the probability of a challenge falls to 43 percent. The HHI is apparently the least important of the three guidelines factors, however. If the bureaus agree that entry barriers are low while the two other factors are high, the probability of a challenge falls to 21 percent. If the likelihood of collusion is agreed to be low even when the other two factors are thought to be high, the probability of a challenge is only 27 percent. The role of concentration ratios in FTC thinking, at least during the period studied, appears smaller than other considerations.[31]

Table 13.2 also shows, however, that within the two bureaus the three merger guidelines variables may be of equal importance. Although there is no reason a priori to believe that all factors would count equally, little empirical difference appears in the size of the coefficients for the HHI, entry barriers, and ease of collusion as the FTC economists reckon them. Only the coefficient for BC evaluation of the HHI is appreciably less (1.11) than those for entry barriers (1.84) and ease of collusion (1.65), and this result is not statistically significant.

A chi-square test indicates that one cannot reject the null hypothesis that within each bureau all guidelines factors are weighted equally. The same test shows, however, that the factors are weighted differently between the two bureaus.[32] It will prove useful below to reestimate the equation shown in table 13.2 on the assumption that each bureau weights the three guidelines factors the same. Two composite variables, BC and BE, were constructed to measure the sum of each bureau's dummies for the three merger guidelines factors. The reestimated model (with absolute t-values in parentheses) is

30. The probability is computed by first finding the value of the linear expression estimated in table 13.2 at the mean values of the political variables and then incorporating the different assumptions about the BC and BE evaluations of the merger guideline factors (HHI, entry barriers, and likelihood of collusion). The failing-firm variable, insignificant in table 13.2, is assumed to be zero. Next, based on a standardized-normal distribution table, the probability corresponding to the particular value of the linear expression is recorded. The same procedure is used to derive other probabilities discussed here based on table 13.2. The reader can calculate probabilities of a merger challenge for merger guideline assumptions not discussed by using the data in table 13.2 and a standardized-normal table.

31. The differences are suggestive but not statistically significant; the confidence intervals surrounding the point estimates contain the other point estimates.

32. To test this hypothesis, the equation was estimated with only one composite variable. The computed chi-square test statistic was 3.06.

$$\text{VOTE} = -4.17 + 1.56\,(\text{BC}) - .85\,(\text{BE}) - 4.52\,(\text{FAILFIRM})$$
$$(3.21)\quad(3.65)\qquad(2.93)\qquad\quad(.01)$$

$$+ .158\,(\text{CITES}) + .164\,(\text{HEARINGS}) + u,$$
$$(2.19)\qquad\qquad(2.00)$$

with the likelihood ratio test equal to 45.6 and the pseudo-R^2 equalling .489. Qualitatively, the results are identical to those in table 13.2.

Lawyers versus economists. While lawyers and economists are both influential in the decision whether to challenge a merger, lawyers' influence appears to dominate. As shown in table 13.2, the absolute sizes of the BC coefficients for the HHI, entry barriers, and ease of collusion are greater than the BE coefficients for those variables. The reestimated model above shows that the composite BC variable is greater in absolute value than the composite BE variable. Based on the coefficients from the reestimated model, table 13.3 shows more precisely the different effects of BE and BC evaluations of factors identified in the merger guidelines as anticompetitive. The table shows the probabilities that a merger will be challenged under alternative BC and BE evaluations of the number of troublesome guidelines factors. For example, if the two bureaus agree that only one factor is a problem, the probability of a challenge is only .002; if they agree that two of the three factors are problematic, the likelihood of a challenge rises to .295; if both bureaus agree that all three factors present potential problems, the probability of a challenge is .969.

Table 13.3   Probability of FTC Merger Challenge as a Function of BC and BE Merger Guidelines Evaluations

Number of Factors Alleged Potentially Anticompetitive by:					
		Bureau of Competition			
		0	1	2	3
Bureau of Economics	0	*	*	.013	.249
	1	*	.002	.083	.568
	2	*	.018	.295	.847
	3	003	.106	.623	.969

*Less than .001.

Table 13.3 is particularly interesting in measuring the effects of bureau disagreement. When the two groups disagree, BC apparently has a greater effect on a particular decision than BE.[33] If BC alleges that three guidelines

33. The data here do not capture any influence that BE has on the BC factual analysis. (Casual empiricism suggests that BC has little effect on the BE analysis.) During an investigation, economists critique the BC staff analysis. Their questions may persuade BC either to close the case before or shortly after a second request (in which event the case would not be in the sample) or to adjust their opinion in the final memorandum (changing disagreement to agreement on a

factors are problematic when BE claims only two are worrisome, the likelihood of a challenge is .847; in the reverse situation, however, when BE claims that three factors are problematic while BC alleges that only two factors are worrisome, the likelihood of suit is only .623. If BC claims that all factors are at worrisome levels when BE says that none are, the probability of a challenge is .249. If BE claims that all factors are problematic when BC says that none are, the probability of a challenge is only .003. In short, lawyers' evaluation of the variables identified in the merger guidelines has a greater effect than does the evaluation by economists.

Conclusion

In deciding whether to challenge or allow a merger, the Federal Trade Commission relies on a number of criteria, including the various criteria specified in the Department of Justice merger guidelines. With data from the commission's own files, we show that the evaluations of agency lawyers and economists concerning the Herfindahl-Hirschman Index, ease of entry, and likelihood of collusion all perform as one would predict, and all significantly influence commission decisions.

Moreover, access to the internal data permits examination of the respective roles of attorneys and economists. A disagreement between economists and lawyers about whether to challenge a merger is not a "fair fight." Lawyers have greater influence with the commission over the decision.

Finally, we hypothesize that the process is also driven by the desires of politicians to stop mergers. Merger challenges, like antitakeover legislation, prevent the exit of resources and votes from a politician's jurisdiction and, thus, allow the politician to respond to organized labor and management interests that seek to prevent the changes caused by mergers. As we show in statistical tests, greater political pressure does cause the FTC to challenge more mergers.[34]

In the end, therefore, a constellation of identifiable interests benefits from the FTC's stopping mergers. Politicians, their organized constituents opposed to mergers, and agency attorneys are apparently among the principal benefi-

---

key guidelines factor). Thus, our results may underestimate the net effect of economists at the FTC. The results reported in note 29, *supra*, indicate that BE's evaluations of guidelines factors are significant predictors of BC's decision whether to advocate challenging a merger.

34. Inferences justified by the results here are of course limited to the period under study, 1982–86. We note, however, that antitrust in the Reagan administration has supposedly been driven more by truly economic concerns, a position apparently justified by the data. See Warren P. Preston and John M. Connor, Federal Antitrust Activity under the Reagan Administration: New Evidence (unpublished manuscript, Univ. South Carolina 1987). If, as shown here, politics plays an important role in antitrust enforcement even when economic welfare is a more dominant concern, the influence of politics must have been even greater prior to the 1982 merger guidelines.

ciaries. Overall, the merger guidelines are applied with an upward bias, resulting in a greater propensity to challenge mergers in the marginal case. Greater appreciation of the ways that antitrust works and, in particular, of the role of politics in the process should begin to dispel the notion that antitrust can be viewed as driven solely by congressional and bureaucratic concerns for competition.

CHAPTER FOURTEEN

Monopolies and Mergers Commission, Merger Reports and the Public Interest: A Probit Analysis

CHARLIE WEIR

Introduction

The Monopolies and Mergers Commission (the Commission) investigates merger bids which have been referred under the conditions laid down in the 1973 Fair Trading Act. A bid is eligible for investigation if the combined market share is at least 25 percent and/or if the value of the acquired assets exceeds, now, £30 million. In all, the Commission deals with around 3 percent of eligible bids. If a bid is expected to operate against the public interest it is not allowed to proceed; if it is not expected to operate against the public interest the bid is allowed to proceed. The latter point illustrates the policy bias in favour of mergers since a bid will be allowed if, overall, it is expected either to generate benefits or to have no effect. The way in which the Commission assesses the various elements of the public interest is the subject of this paper.

The public-interest framework incorporates five main elements which relate to competition: prices and quality; cost reductions; new entry and new techniques; industrial and employment distributions; and foreign trade. Within these categories many alternatives are possible and so it is obviously of use if firms can see that, for example, if the Commission concludes that competition is likely to increase as a result of a merger, then the bid is more likely to be allowed. Alternatively, if it is shown that exports are likely to increase, does this mean that the Commission is more likely to allow the bid? These examples illustrate the importance of consistency of treatment.

If two bids are expected to lead to increased exports and one is allowed whereas the other is not, the perception is one of inconsistency. It may be, however, that the differing conclusions reflect the complexity of the bids with other costs outweighing a particular benefit. In addition, the adoption of a case-by-case approach and hence an unwillingness to use precedence may explain the two conclusions. Finally, the results may reflect differing compositions on the investigating panel.

This essay was previously published in *Applied Economics* 24 (January 1992): 27–34.

Nevertheless, for policy to be meaningful it must not be perceived as being inconsistent and so it should be possible to show that certain components of the public interest consistently carry more weight than others. For example, competition effects might outweigh balance-of-payments effects or employment effects may not be regarded as particularly important. Such consistency will enable firms to concentrate their efforts on the most relevant issues and so to raise the quality of their arguments.

The results highlight a number of issues which appear to be consistently important; unfortunately, they stress the value of the present bias in favour of mergers. For example, bids are more likely to be allowed if they do not affect either competition or prices. Thus, the stressing of potential benefits such as greater employment or increased exports does not consistently help the bidding firm. In terms of the positive aspects, only increased competition has a significant effect on the Commission's decisions. On the negative side, harming the balance of payments significantly reduces the chances that a bid will be allowed. Overall there is no evidence that market share has a detrimental effect on bidding firms and neither does it appear that the Commission discriminates against horizontal bids.

Previous Studies

The work of the Commission has been the subject of much comment over the course of its lifetime. Most, but not all, of the attention has been critical. In addition, both the Commission's treatment of the issues and the analysis surrounding it have been qualitative in nature. Thus, for example, prior to including mergers within the Commission's remit, it was argued that efficiency improvements were one of the main advantages thought to emanate from mergers. However, although bidding firms often repeated this view (Pickering 1974, 1980) very few attempted to quantify these gains (Sutherland 1970; Utton 1975; Pickering 1980). Thus, the arguments tended to be in terms of claimed improvements in efficiency rather than estimating monetary savings.

The qualitative nature of the debate is also illustrated by the criticisms levelled at the Commission for its choice of narrow market definitions rather than broad ones (Rowley 1968; Utton 1975; Pickering 1980; Pass and Sparkes 1980). It is argued that not only is the choice of market definition arrived at arbitrarily but that the narrowness invites the risk of overstating potential market power.

The most obvious source of quantitative data is financial information and indeed the Commission publishes substantial amounts, principally balance sheets, profit and loss statements, and the sources and applications of funds. In spite of this, virtually no use is made of such performance data. This point, originally made by Sutherland (1970), still holds today. Further, despite evidence which suggests that post-merger performance suffers, it is an issue which the Commission has rarely addressed (Pickering 1974; Utton 1975).

In a market economy, mergers would be expected to result in a better use of resources and hence greater competition. This applies to horizontal mergers as well as to vertical and conglomerate ones, and yet Utton (1974) and Fairburn (1985) are among those who find that the Commission has come to conflicting conclusions about the role of market share and the degree of competitiveness within a market. Indeed, Colenutt and O'Donnell (1978) show that, surprisingly, competitive factors did not appear to be particularly important to the Commission when it reached its conclusions. This view has been overtaken by events, particularly since 1984.

The difficulties involved in the weighing of issues are stressed by Korah (1982). Given arguments couched in qualitative terms, it becomes difficult to assess the extent to which increased costs such as reduced competition outweigh greater benefits such as increased efficiency. However, an understanding of the pertinent costs and benefits of different competition effects is necessary before the weighing of arguments is possible. This is all the more important given the 1984 policy statement that competitive effects were to play a paramount role in the reference procedure.

In contrast to the previous qualitative analysis of the Commission's work, probit analysis is used to provide a quantitative assessment. The objective is to identify issues which consistently appear to influence the Commission and so to provide a sort of litmus test which may be of use to both raider and target firms.

Sample and Variables Used

The sample consists of 70 Monopolies and Mergers Commission merger reports published between 1974 and 1990. Earlier merger reports were excluded because they preceded the 1973 Fair Trading Act which substantially changed the framework within which merger policy is conducted. The reports were used to construct a database which consists of binary dependent and independent variables. The dependent variable was given a value of one if the bid was allowed and zero if it was not. The independent variables were categorized according to the comments made in the conclusions chapter of the reports. In this chapter, the Commission summarizes the public-interest issues presented to it by both parties before stating its own final opinion. Thus, the public interest can be broken down into elements which may then be represented by a binary variable. For example,

1—if efficiency was expected to improve; or
0—if efficiency was not expected to improve.

A complete list of the variables and classifications is given in the Appendix.

Since the objective is to identify elements of the public interest which appear to be important to the Commission, probit analysis provides an appropriate estimation technique. This is particularly so given that all the independent variables are qualitative in nature. Assume that the Commission's decision to allow or disallow a bid depends on an unobservable index Z_i which is itself determined by an explanatory variable X_i so that the higher the value of Z_i, the more likely the Commission would be to allow a bid. Hence

$$Z_i = B_0 + B_1 X_i$$

when X_i is the relevant public-interest issue under discussion—for example, efficiency or competition effects.

The Z_i relates to the Commission's decision in the following way. Let $Y = 1$ denote an allowed bid and $Y = 0$ a disallowed bid, then assume that there is a critical threshold Z_i^* such that if Z_i exceeds Z_i^* a bid is allowed, whereas if Z_i^* exceeds Z_i it is not.

Given that Z_i^* is assumed to be normally distributed, the probability that Z_i^* is less than or equal to Z_i can be calculated from the cumulative normal probability function

$$P_i = Pr(Z_i^* \leq Z_i) = F(Z_i)$$

$$= \frac{1}{\sqrt{2\pi}} \int_{-\infty}^{Z_i} e^{-s^2/2} dS$$

with S as a standardized normal variable. The index Z_i is estimated by taking the inverse of the cumulative normal probability function such that

$$Z_i = F^{-1}(P_i)$$
$$= B_0 + B_1 X_i$$

Thus, P_i is an estimate of the conditional probability that a bid will be allowed given, for example, the expected efficiency impact or the expected competition effect.

This method of analysis enables three general hypotheses to be tested:

H1: positive Commission conclusions help raider firms.
H2: negative Commission conclusions help target firms.
H3: neutral Commission conclusions help raider firms.

This is because of the "not against the public interest" condition which means that a merger having no expected impact must be allowed.

The "public interest," as outlined in the 1973 Fair Trading Act, was divided into 18 categories (see Appendix). Initially, two samples were constructed. The first included relative profitability since it can be hypothesized that the Commission may be more favourably disposed towards a bid if the raider was more profitable than the target. This sample covered 47 bids since in the others there was no clear profit comparison. The second sample included all the reports but with the relative profitability data excluded. Since the results for both samples are virtually identical, only those relating to the second, complete sample are quoted. Probits were run on each sample for each individual public-interest issue and then for various combinations of issues. Each set of probits covered three time periods. The first involved the whole time period 1974–1990. The second dealt with 1974–1984, and the third with 1984–1990. The subperiods were designed to assess the impact of the change in emphasis in reference policy which occurred in 1984, when it was stated that competition effects were going to be the main consideration when referring a bid to the Commission.

Results

Table 14.1 gives the results for 1974–1990 for the whole sample in which the public interest categories were run individually against the decision to allow or to disallow a bid.

In terms of the initial hypothesis H1, there seems to be little to be gained by arguing the positive side of the merger. Thus, in terms of the likelihood ratio test, the following benefits yield insignificant results—price reductions, increased efficiency, improving the balance of payments, better management, more employment, and better research and development. The fact that it is not necessary to convince the Commission that anything positive will result from a merger before a bid is allowed makes these results rather surprising. It suggests, therefore, that some offsetting costs had been identified. Increased competition, however, is significant. In addition, it generates an extremely high marginal probability with the percentage correctly classified a satisfactory 58.4 percent.

Successfully arguing your case is also significant with a marginal probability of 0.86 and 80.5 percent correctly classified. Analysis of the Commission's reports makes it clear that this is not a trite conclusion since in many instances the Commission disagreed with the arguments presented to it by both sides. It is also obvious that in weighing the evidence the Commission must reject much of it. Therefore, the careful preparation of a case is extremely important. On a number of occasions, however, the Commission disagreed with the advantages claimed by the bidding firm but, because no costs were identified, the bids were allowed to proceed.

Table 14.1   Individual Public-Interest Issues 1974–1990

Variable	Coefficient	λ^2	Marginal probability	Correct classification %
Market share > 50%	0.05			
	(0.14)	0.02	0.50	45.4
Market share > 25%	0.08			
	(0.29)	0.09	0.55	36.3
MMC accept overall case	1.72			
	(5.24)†	30.69†	0.86	80.5
Horizontal merger	0.19			
	(0.62)	0.39	0.56	44.1
Contested bid	−0.93			
	(−3.11)†	10.02†	0.36	67.5
Increase competition	5.83			
	(0.01)	12.38†	1.00	58.4
Reduced prices	0.81			
	(1.23)	1.66	0.80	50.6
Increase efficiency	0.21			
	(0.65)	0.42	0.59	5.19
Improve balance of payments	0.50			
	(1.26)	1.65	0.69	53.2
Better management	0.62			
	(0.89)	0.84	0.75	46.7
Claims quantified	0.25			
	(0.65)	0.44	0.61	50.6
Competition no effect	1.46			
	(4.58)*	22.76†	0.75	76.6
Prices no effect	1.01			
	(2.89)†	8.90†	0.63	66.2
More employment	0.18			
	(0.31)	0.10	0.59	50.6
Better research and development	0.62			
	(0.89)	0.84	0.75	48.0
Fewer jobs	−0.45			
	(−1.16)	1.37	0.39	57.1
Harm balance of payments	−1.44			
	(−2.51)†	8.00†	0.11	59.7

*95% significant.
†99% significant.
t-statistics in parentheses.
λ^2 is the likelihood ratio test.

In addition, the guidelines on merger policy issued by the Department of Trade and Industry indicate that, whenever possible, claims made by firms should be supported by quantified data. This would indicate the extent of any claimed advantages. The insignificant result on the "Claims Quantified" variable coupled with a correct classification of only 50.6 percent shows that when this was done, the firms did not advance their cases. Thus firms are not "penalized" for claiming that, say, efficiency will improve without supporting this claim with figures. However, the marginal probability figure, 0.61, is high enough to perhaps encourage firms to provide estimates of claims.

Finally, in relation to H1 (although not published here), it was found that relative profitability also produced an insignificant result. This suggests that performance indicators play no part in the Commission's assessment of the public interest. Thus, it neatly sidesteps the debates about managerial objectives and, by implication, resource allocation by simply not addressing them.

There is limited evidence to support H2—namely, that bids are more likely to be disallowed if costs are identified. It is clear that job losses are not significant, although the sign is correct. Harming the balance of payments is, however, highly significant with only an 11 percent chance of a bid being allowed with such a conclusion. In addition, it correctly classifies 62.3 percent of cases. Given the insignificant result on the improvement to the balance of payments variable it does appear that the Commission has been more impressed by the possible negative impact that mergers might have on the balance of payments.

The contested bid variable may also be regarded as falling within H2 since the target firm will be stressing the negative aspects of the bid. Contesting a bid has a significant negative impact on the Commission's decision. The marginal probability of a contested bid being allowed is only 0.36 and 67.5 percent of the cases are correctly classified. Thus, it appears that a successful lobbying campaign to get a hostile bid referred could be an extremely important defensive tactic.

Given the concern that tends to be expressed about market power (notwithstanding the fluid nature of the debate) the variables relating to market share and merger type may also be included within H2. Neither market share variable was significant and both had inconclusive marginal probabilities as well as poor correct classification statistics. Thus, the Commission does not appear to regard medium to large combined market shares as inherently undesirable and so does not accept the straightforward link between market share and monopoly profits. This is further supported by the insignificant result on the horizontal merger variable which showed that horizontal mergers are not more likely to be disallowed simply because they are horizontal.

The neutral hypothesis, H3, is illustrated by the "no effect" variables for competition and price. Both yield significant positive results, high marginal probabilities—0.75 and 0.63 respectively—and good correct classifications—76.6 percent and 66.2 percent. Thus a "no effect" conclusion will improve the chances of a bid being allowed by the Commission which confirms the inbuilt bias in favour of mergers.

A variety of combinations of public-interest issues, all of which made a priori sense, were tested to see if they added to the results generated by the

Table 14.2   Combinations of Public-Interest Issues, 1974–1990, Which
Have the Largest Effect on the Marginal Probabilities

Variables		λ^2	Marginal probability
(a)	Contested bids		
	Better management	10.94†	0.61
			(0.36)
(b)	Competition—no effect		
	Merger type	32.76†	0.92
			(0.75)
	Competition—no effect		
	Efficiency improvement	27.47†	0.92
			(0.75)
(c)	Prices—no effect		
	Better R & D	9.87†	0.85
			(0.63)
(d)	Harm balance of payments		
	Fewer jobs	9.23*	0.05
			(0.11)

*95% significant.
†99% significant.
λ^2 is the likelihood ratio test.
Individual marginal probability of first-named variable from each group
in parentheses (from table 14.1).

individual issues. The purpose was to show, particularly through the impact
on the marginal probabilities, just how important additional variables were
to the Commission. The results given in table 14.2 exclude any combinations
involving two of the variables. The marginal probability of the Commission's
overall acceptance of the arguments was not improved by the addition of
further variables. The same was also true for the increased-competition
variable.

The results in table 14.2 tend to fall between the original hypotheses. For
example, if a bid is contested, a convincing argument about the improved
quality of management raises the marginal probability of the bid being allowed from 0.36 to 0.61. Another interesting result is the combination of
horizontal bids and the no-effect-on-competition variables. The improvement
to the marginal probability from 0.75 to 0.92 is understandable since the
combination implies a lack of market power and hence no monopoly actions
in terms of price or output. On the other hand, the chances of a bid being
allowed are dramatically reduced if fewer jobs are added to a "harm the
balance of payments" conclusion. Here the marginal probability falls from
0.11 to 0.05.

Table 14.3 enables us to assess the extent to which the subperiods have
been open to different influences. Both subperiods reinforce the importance

Table 14.3 Significant Public-Interest Issues During Subperiods 1974–1984 and 1984–1990

Variable	Coefficient	λ^2	Marginal probability	Correct classification (%)
(a) *1974–84*				
MMC accept overall case	−1.61			
	(−3.89)*	16.72*	0.66	79
Contested bid	−1.45			
	(−3.38)*	12.64*	0.29	73
Improve balance of payments	1.38			
	(2.29)*	6.30*	0.88	60
Competition—no effect	2.09			
	(3.82)*	20.30*	0.75	74
Increase competition	5.93			
	(0.008)	7.77*	1.00	62
Harm balance of payments	−5.94			
	(−0.009)	10.58*	1.00	47
(b) *1984–90*				
MMC accept overall case	2.12			
	(3.50)*	15.64*	0.93	73
Competition—no effect	1.38			
	(2.65)*	7.72*	0.86	63·
Price—no effect	1.68			
	(3.04)*	10.36*	0.80	66
Increase competition	5.86			
	(0.002)	4.49*	1.00	53
Reduced price	5.74			
	(0.002)	1.04	1.00	43

*99% significant.
λ^2 is the likelihood ratio test.
t-statistics in parentheses.

of the preparation and presentation of a convincing overall case. The positive sign makes this particularly relevant to bidding firms. Both subperiods also highlight the importance of increased competition and so offer some evidence in support of H1. In addition, price reductions were found to be important in the 1984–1990 period.

In terms of H2, harming the balance of payments is significant during 1974–1984. The marginal probability of being disallowed is high although the correct classification is only 47 percent. However, it becomes insignificant during the 1984–1990 period, with the marginal probability of being allowed rising to 0.50 and a correct classification of 40 percent.

Contested bids is significant, with a low marginal probability of 0.29 and a high correct classification of 73 percent for 1974–1984, but it also becomes insignificant during the second subperiod. Its marginal probability rises to 0.55 but the percentage correct classification drops to 55. Thus, its usefulness

Table 14.4   Marginal Probabilities of Selected
Combinations of Public-Interest Issues 1984–1990

Variables		Marginal probabilities
(a)	Merger type	0.72
	Increased efficiency	(0.69)
(b)	Merger type	0.86
	Claims quantified	(0.69)
(c)	Market share > 50%	0.80
	Claims quantified	(0.50)
(d)	Increased efficiency	0.83
	Claims quantified	(0.72)
(e)	Market share > 25%	0.85
	Increased efficiency	(0.59)
(f)	Market share > 25%	0.86
	Claims quantified	(0.59)

Marginal probability of first-named variable from each
group in parentheses.

to target firms as an effective defensive tactic has been lost. The change in
attitude can be traced to the Commission's 1985 Lonrho report. Prior to that,
it had tended to be sympathetic to target firms which linked contested bids
with prospective poor post-merger management relations and all the attendant
problems which that would create for the new firms. However, in the Lonrho
report, the Commission stated that it no longer gave credence to the manage-
ment-differences defense. Consequently, the fact that a bid was contested
was no longer of relevance to the Commission.

As far as hypothesis H3 is concerned, a no-effect-on-competition conclusion is significant for both time periods. In addition, the marginal probabilities
are high, as is the percentage correctly classified. Significant during 1984–
1990 only is the no-effect-on-price variable. These results indicate the continuing influence of the policy bias in favour of mergers.

The results in table 14.3 for 1984–1990 are fairly clear-cut in terms of the
importance of individual public-interest issues. The testing of combinations
of these variables made very little difference to any of the significance tests.
A number of other combinations yielded insignificant results in terms of the
likelihood ratio test but their marginal probabilities are high enough to be of
interest. A number are given in table 14.4.

They show the usefulness of providing the Commission with quantified
data, since this raised the marginal probabilities of a number of variables.
An interesting point is that the Commission has tended to be sceptical of the
figures with which it has been presented. However, even when rejecting the

claims as over-optimistic, it is usually accepted that some benefit would be gained—for example, costs would be reduced. Thus the provision of quantities helps the qualitative analysis. The market share and merger type variables again reflect the open-mindedness of the Commission on the issue of market power, since they do not exert a negative influence on its decisions.

Conclusions

The results show that very few of the issues which make up the public interest, as outlined in the 1973 Fair Trading Act and expanded in the Guidelines to Merger Policy (1978), appear to influence the Commission. Four variables appear most frequently in the results: the Commission's overall attitude to the arguments, whether a bid is contested, whether a bid has no effect on competition, and whether it has no effect on price. None of these has anything positive to say about mergers and their impact.

Perhaps more useful, however, are the issues which do not appear to be important in themselves. There is no evidence that large market share is a problem for bidding firms and neither are horizontal mergers. This seems to reflect the growing influence of the more market-oriented theories of firm behaviour in which market share indicates entrepreneurial success rather than being the source of market-power abuse. As such it hints at the latest influence of political factors in that the Commission, according to the Director General of Fair Trading, Sir Gordon Borrie, naturally reflects the philosophy of the government of the day.

Disappointingly, the more positive aspects of the public interest have been shown to play little part in the Commission's decisions. Thus arguing, and having accepted by the Commission, that a merger will improve efficiency, help the balance of payments, create jobs, or improve research and development does not consistently appear to benefit the bidding firm and neither does superior profitability. However, increased competition does.

Since 1984, the importance of two variables—contesting a bid and helping the balance of payments—has significantly diminished. A new consideration—reduced prices—becomes significant with the overall acceptance, the no-effect-on-competition, the no-effect-on-price, and the increase-in-competition variables remaining so.

Competition impacts are clearly important, and further analysis of how the Commission deals with them is currently under investigation. However, it has been shown in this paper that competition effects have been one of the few issues which have been consistently regarded as important by the Commission and, hence, firms involved in merger bids which have been referred should be clear about the possible competitive implications of their actions.

Appendix: Probit Variables

Commission decision	1 = allow
	0 = disallow
Market share > 50%	1 = combined share greater than 50 percent
	0 = combined share less than 50 percent
Market share > 25%	1 = combined share greater than 25 percent
	0 = combined share less than 25 percent
Commission's attitude to overall case	1 = accept
	0 = reject
Merger type	1 = horizontal
	0 = non-horizontal
Bid contested	1 = yes
	0 = no
Competition effect	1 = increase
	0 = no increase
Price effect	1 = reduction
	0 = no reduction
Efficiency	1 = increase
	0 = no increase
Balance of payments	1 = improved
	0 = not improved
Better management	1 = yes
	0 = no
Claims quantified	1 = yes
	0 = no
Competition no effect	1 = yes
	0 = no
Prices no effect	1 = yes
	0 = no
More employment	1 = yes
	0 = no
Better research and development	1 = yes
	0 = no
Fewer jobs	1 = yes
	0 = no
Harm balance of payments	1 = yes
	0 = no

PART FOUR

Public Choice and the Origins
of Antitrust

WILLIAM E. KOVACIC

Once the allegation is made that a certain public policy, seemingly only misguided, actually represents purposeful political behavior, a reexamination of the original statute is naturally in order (e.g., Gilligan et al. 1989). In deciding whether a particular regulation is in the public interest, the obvious question is, what motivated the adoption of the regulation in the first place?

The existence of a perceived source of "market failure" like monopoly is perhaps a necessary condition for inferring that a statute can be justified in public-interest terms. But the enactment of a law intended to deal with a genuine market-failure problem is not a sufficient basis for a public-interest rationale, because a regulatory policy justified at the time of adoption may be turned to private ends once passed—a phenomenon now known as the "capture" theory of regulation. As many (e.g., Posner 1974, 341–43) have noted, though, the capture theory has increasingly given way to a more rational model in which regulation essentially accomplishes the private-interest objectives for which it was initially proposed, not those ends toward which it is perverted once passed.

In deciding among the public-interest, private-interest, or capture theories of regulation, the origins of the regulatory statute are obviously the chronological starting point. In the area of antitrust particularly, both lawyers and economists have long been interested in legislative histories. As I discuss below, their motivations and interests sometimes differ, but in the end the two disciplines have a good deal to say to one another. Lawyers (as well as historians) pay more attention to the written record of what legislators *say* is the reason for legislating. Economists have less confidence in that record, and are more inclined to infer motivation by identifying the winners and losers from regulation. That methodological distinction is important for understanding the debate behind the chapters presented in this section of the volume.

Finally, however approached methodologically, the history of the antitrust

Portions of this essay are adapted from Kovacic (1990b) and are reproduced here with the permission of the American Bar Association. The author is grateful to Kathryn M. Fenton and Robert H. Lande for many useful comments and discussions.

244   WILLIAM E. KOVACIC

statutes is important for more than just deciding among the different schools of thought on regulation. Perceptions of the past influence antitrust in the present. Significant developments in doctrine frequently hinge on judicial interpretations of earlier federal antitrust episodes.[1] Shifts in public law enforcement activities, such as the government's industrial deconcentration cases of the late 1960s and early 1970s, have been motivated by historical commentary identifying persistent flaws in previous antitrust policy.[2] Evaluations of past experience have catalyzed change in antitrust institutions like the Federal Trade Commission (FTC), which reconstructed its antitrust agenda in the 1970s after being accused of decades-long resistance to reform.[3] The failure of antitrust officials to consider issues in their historical context has generated unintended policy effects, such as the expansion of enforcement by state governments after the Reagan Administration retrenched the activities of the Department of Justice and the FTC.[4]

1. See, e.g., California v. American Stores Co., 495 U.S. 271, 285–95 (1990) (examining origins of Sherman Act and Clayton Act remedial provisions in determining that private parties may obtain divestiture under Section 16 of the Clayton Act); Business Elecs. Corp. v. Sharp Elecs. Corp., 485 U.S. 717, 731–33 (1988) (in justifying narrow interpretation of the agreement requirement in Sherman Act Section 1 suits involving allegations of resale price maintenance, relying in part on the view that Congress in 1890 realized that the common law meaning of the term "restraint of trade" had changed over time and intended to preserve such a "dynamic potential" when it approved the Sherman Act).

2. See Kovacic (1989, 1136–38) (describing intellectual foundation for government deconcentration initiatives of late 1960s and early 1970s). Deconcentration advocates often assailed what they saw as the historical unwillingness of public enforcement agencies to use the Sherman Act to restructure dominant firms. See, e.g., Mark Green, Beverly Moore, Jr., and Bruce Wasserstein, The Closed Enterprise System (1972), at 293–94 ("[T]he Antitrust Division remains soft on concentration. . . . The Division does sue some firms who bring you kosher hotdog rolls and chrysanthemums, but ignores opportunities to attack GM and Anaconda Copper. By focusing on the transgressions of the less powerful, the enforcement agencies aid and abet the real economic royalists").

3. In 1969, the American Bar Association Commission to Study the Federal Trade Commission cited previous blue ribbon commissions that had criticized the FTC and pointed to the seemingly minimal impact of the earlier critiques to underscore its recommendation that continued failure to implement reforms should warrant the FTC's abolition (American Bar Association 1969, pp. 3, 6). The ABA panel's depiction of an agency that had stubbornly resisted proposals for reform throughout its history shaped perceptions within Congress and the antitrust community about the appropriate path for revitalizing the Commission. See Kovacic (1982, 630–31) (discussing impact of ABA Commission's evaluation of FTC).

4. As it praised federalism and focused federal enforcement on large horizontal mergers and horizontal output restrictions, the Reagan Administration gave little apparent thought to how state attorneys general might react to relaxed federal scrutiny of mergers and distribution practices. To the displeasure of Reagan antitrust officials, the redirection of federal enforcement was offset partly by expanded state efforts to invoke antitrust theories that the Reagan Administration did not favor. Greater awareness of the history of state antitrust enforcement might have alerted Reagan officials to the likelihood of a backlash from the state attorneys general. See Kovacic (1990b, 124–25).

The Efficiency Interpretation of the
Antitrust Laws Reexamined

So important are perceptions of history that a sense of the origins and evolution of American competition policy is as necessary to antitrust literacy today as is the mastery of legal rules or price theory. Those who doubt this proposition need look no further than Robert Bork's *The Antitrust Paradox*.[5] Bork (1978, 16) observed that "[o]ne of the uses of history is to free us of a falsely imagined past" and grounded his case for change in a reexamination of antitrust's legislative origins and early cases applying the new competition statutes. His argument for a fundamental redirection of antitrust doctrine and policy drew vital force from his assessment of the congressional aims underlying passage of the Sherman, Clayton, and Federal Trade Commission Acts. Without its appeal to history, *The Antitrust Paradox* would not have played so extraordinary a role in molding doctrine and setting the agenda for policy debate in the last fifteen years (Kovacic 1990a).

Bork's Efficiency Interpretation

Bork's historically based assessment of antitrust advanced two central, influential propositions. First, Congress intended the Sherman Act to enhance consumer welfare, which Bork interpreted as proscribing only conduct that reduced allocative efficiency.[6] Second, antitrust's proper focus was horizontal price-fixing agreements and similar arrangements involving direct rivals. Bork concluded that antitrust's longstanding campaign against "naked" horizontal restraints had conferred important benefits upon society and was clearly worth sustaining.[7] Each of these views played a powerful role in changing judicial perceptions about the antitrust laws and in altering government policy in the late 1970s and throughout the 1980s (Kovacic 1990a, 1442–59).

Bork's *Antitrust Paradox* not only caught the attention of judges and enforcement officials, but also became one of the small number of scholarly

---

5. *The Antitrust Paradox* drew extensively on work that Bork had published previously. The book's discussion of the legislative intent of the antitrust laws was based upon a paper Bork had published over a decade earlier. See Bork (1966a).

6. Bork (1978, 66) concluded that "[t]he legislative histories of the antitrust statutes . . . do not support any claim that Congress intended the courts to sacrifice consumer welfare to any other goal. The Sherman Act was clearly presented and debated as a consumer welfare prescription." See also Bork's (1966a, 10) finding that there was "not a scintilla of support" in the legislative history of the Sherman Act for "broad social, political and ethical mandates." Bork (1978, 79–80) also urged a single-minded efficiency focus on the ground that any other interpretation of the Sherman Act would force federal judges to engage in unadministrable, constitutionally suspect efforts to determine how political, social, and efficiency values were to be traded off and applied in each case.

7. See Bork (1978, 263) (praising per se ban against horizontal price fixing and market divisions: "Its contributions to consumer welfare over the decades have been enormous").

works to transform the agenda for debate and research among academics.[8] It inspired a renewal of interest among economists, historians, lawyers, and political scientists in the historical roots and consequences of the American antitrust system.[9] But most observers reject Bork's conception of antitrust's origins, with challenges to his efficiency thesis coming from two different directions—from those who would expand enforcement of the antitrust statutes and from those who would abolish them.

The Expansionist Critique

One group of researchers attacks Bork for unduly narrowing antitrust's scope. Such critics argue that Congress intended the antitrust laws to accomplish non-efficiency aims, such as maintaining a decentralized political and social order. Those wanting more expansive antitrust enforcement see prosecuting horizontal restraints as beneficial, but assail Bork's proposal that antitrust ignore vertical restraints, most dominant-firm exclusionary conduct, and all mergers other than large horizontal transactions.

Criticism of Bork's efficiency thesis by the expansionists has proceeded along several lines. One of the first critiques was Robert Lande's finding that the goal of preventing unjust wealth transfers from consumers to producers was the "prevailing view" of legislators who enacted the Sherman, Clayton, and FTC Acts (Lande 1982, 68). While conceding the importance of distributional concerns, other legal commentators point to evidence of non-efficiency aims beyond wealth-distribution goals in the legislative record and in the broader social and political environment surrounding the passage of the antitrust laws. Thus, David Millon's (1988) analysis of the roots of the Sherman Act emphasizes legislative concern that the emergence of dominant firms and industry-wide cartels threatened to undermine democratic institutions. Eleanor Fox (1981) has identified a central congressional aim to preserve opportunities for firms and individuals to compete. Rudolph Peritz (1990) explains

8. A list of other comparably influential academic works in the area of antitrust would include Kaysen and Turner (1959) and Areeda and Turner (1975).

9. For an instructive survey of the modern, historically based scholarship dealing with antitrust, see James May, Historical Analysis in Antitrust Law, 35 New York Law School L. Rev. 857 (1990). Bork was not the first scholar to scrutinize the historical underpinnings and effects of antitrust in the United States. Noteworthy examples of earlier, historically oriented antitrust scholarship include Dewey (1955), Hawley (1966), Hofstadter (1965, 188–237), Letwin (1965), and Thorelli (1955). Nor was Bork's research the only contemporary source of renewed academic interest in history as a source of insight about the appropriate course for current policy. For example, Alfred D. Chandler, Jr.'s The Visible Hand: The Managerial Revolution in American Business (1977) appeared one year before The Antitrust Paradox and provoked a scholarly reassessment of the causes and effects of horizontal and vertical integration by U.S. industry in the late 1800s and early 1900s. Yet, more than any other commentator, Bork's analysis and policy precepts redirected the gaze of scholars to antitrust's past.

the emergence of antitrust institutions as the product of a tension between rival concepts of competition policy and common-law property rights.

A separate line of modern historical scholarship underscores the complexity of the economic, political, and social concerns that motivated the creation of the American antitrust laws. Some professional historians criticize legal commentators Bork, Lande, and other "single-goal" enthusiasts for slighting major ambiguities in antitrust's formative era, and for combing historical records for "an immediately usable historical past" (Ernst 1990, 885). James May finds that Congress pursued no single overriding aim through the Sherman Act, but was motivated by a "powerful, widely shared vision of a natural, rights-based political and economic order that simultaneously tended to ensure opportunity, efficiency, prosperity, justice, harmony, and freedom."[10] The notion that judges might be required to make trade-offs among these goals to decide individual cases was alien to the legislators.[11]

The multi-dimensional perspective employed by May and other contemporary historians is consistent with earlier historical works that explain the enactment of U.S. antitrust legislation as the product of efforts to achieve diverse economic, political, and social objectives. Richard Hofstadter's (1965) essay "What Happened to the Antitrust Movement?" is illustrative. Hofstadter concluded that the Sherman Act was designed to achieve the interrelated goals of increasing efficiency, protecting democratic government by blocking private accumulations of power, and preserving the competitive process as "a kind of disciplinary machinery" for the development of social and moral national character.

For the most part, the modern academic commentary described above views the antitrust system favorably and prescribes an expansive public enforcement agenda. Most scholars whose historical research questions Bork's efficiency thesis have sought to justify the pursuit of more than the Chicago school antitrust agenda which Judge Frank Easterbrook (1986, 1701) calls "little other than prosecuting plain vanilla cartels and mergers to monopoly." To these observers, abandoning an efficiency focus would help extend antitrust enforcement to reach a wider array of single-firm behavior, vertical restraints, and mergers, and to overcome judicially imposed limits on the ability of private litigants to establish standing and prove injury (Flynn 1988; Lande 1982, 1988).[12] By building a strong historical case for giving effect to

10. James May, Antitrust in the Formative Era: Political and Economic Theory in Constitutional and Antitrust Analysis, 1880–1918, 50 Ohio State L. J. 257, 391 (1989).

11. James May, The Role of the States in the First Century of the Sherman Act, 59 Antitrust L. J. 93 (1990).

12. These commentators seek to expand antitrust enforcement by going outside the efficiency model. Other pro-enforcement commentators accept the centrality of efficiency, but argue that proper treatment of efficiency dictates efforts to ban conduct (e.g., various forms of single-firm exclusionary behavior) that Chicago school teaching deems benign or procompetitive. See Baker (1989); Steven C. Salop, Exclusionary Vertical Restraints Law: Has Economics Mattered? 83

other values, the expansionists hope to loosen the grip that Bork's efficiency interpretation has exerted on many federal judges (Kovacic 1990a, 1991).

The Abolitionist Critique

The second body of historically based criticism of Bork's efficiency thesis has come from researchers, including the contributors to Part Four of this volume, who regard the federal antitrust statutes as harmful regulation. Their work challenges the conventional view that Congress designed the antitrust laws as public-interest measures. Instead, these scholars analyze the antitrust statutes as interest-group legislation, mainly the products of rent seeking by farmers and small businesses, and dispute the social value of aggressive programs to punish price fixing and similar horizontal output restrictions. Scholars in this interest-group school share the disbelief of antitrust expansionists toward Bork's efficiency thesis and, like the expansionists, they appreciate the importance of claiming the high historical ground to gain support for preferred policy outcomes. Unlike the expansionists, however, those who view antitrust from an interest-group perspective tend to think that the antitrust laws should be repealed.

Bork is thus an irritant to the abolitionists, but for a different reason. He erred by making antitrust respectable in the eyes of judges and government policymakers. If the antitrust statutes were widely seen as simply one more product of private-interest rent seeking, and if past antitrust enforcement (even including the ban against horizontal price fixing) were shown to have reduced the nation's wealth, the legitimacy of the antitrust laws would be eroded and their vulnerability to repeal increased. To abolitionists, Bork tamed a beast which, if left to rampage unimpeded through the economy, eventually would be seen as a serious menace whose destruction commentators and the public would demand.

Antitrust abolitionists descend from a scholarly tradition that seeks to unmask the private-interest origins of antitrust statutes, which usually wear the mantle of the public interest in judicial decision making and in discourse about regulatory policy.[13] The modern roots of the private-interest historical interpretation of the American antitrust laws extend back to the work of Gabriel Kolko. In *The Triumph of Conservatism,* Kolko (1963) contended that Congress created the FTC and other Progressive Era regulatory programs

Amer. Econ. Rev. 168 (1993); and Carl Shapiro, The Theory of Business Strategy, 20 Rand J. Econ. 125 (1989).

13. See United States v. Topco Assoc., Inc., 405 U.S. 596, 610 (1972) ("Antitrust laws in general, and the Sherman Act in particular, are the Magna Carta of free enterprise. They are as important to the preservation of economic freedom and our free-enterprise system as the Bill of Rights is to the protection of our personal freedoms."); Appalachian Coals, Inc. v. United States, 288 U.S. 344, 359 (1933) (describing the Sherman Act as "a charter of freedom"). For a comprehensive statement of the case for abolishing the antitrust system, see Armentano (1982).

to serve business interests under the guise of reform. Despite criticism of his analysis and evidence by many other historians, Kolko's skeptical assessment of the origins of the FTC and, later (1965), the Interstate Commerce Commission helped spur the formulation of the capture theory of regulation (see Posner 1974).

Even though Kolko based his capture theory heavily on a study of the events surrounding the formation of an important antitrust institution (the FTC), scholars initially applied the private-interest model to the creation of nearly every regulatory regime *other* than antitrust. Even among Chicago school enthusiasts, the possibility that the antitrust laws might have resulted from private-interest rent seeking has received little attention (see chapter 18 of this book).

The emergence of a new line of skeptical historical inquiry is largely attributable to three papers which appeared in the early to mid-1980s. The first was authored by William Baxter (1980, 3), who attempted "to identify the political constituency for the passage and enforcement of the antitrust laws in the United States." Baxter, soon to be named Assistant Attorney General for antitrust at the Justice Department, doubted the conventional explanation that "public-spirited legislators pass these laws and the public-spirited judiciary enforces them because they benefit all consumers" by improving resource allocation. Instead, he offered the hypothesis that the adoption and enforcement of antitrust legislation is best explained as the product of efforts by small business "to retard but not halt the continuous encroachment on its territorial enclaves by larger enterprises." However, Baxter's efforts to test the small business interest-group hypothesis with historical data on antitrust litigation patterns, stock price movements, and congressional voting on antitrust measures were generally inconclusive.

The small business interest-group thesis also motivated Stigler (1985) to explore "self-interest theories of the Sherman Act." Stigler discussed Baxter's (1980) paper in framing his own examination of whether the Sherman Act could be explained as a measure to buffer small business against the emergence of larger rivals. After reviewing patterns of state antitrust lawmaking in the 1800s and congressional voting on the Sherman Act, Stigler found only "modest support for the view that the Sherman Act came from small business interests or that opposition came from areas with potential monopolizable industries, or both."

The third formative contribution was the work of Thomas DiLorenzo (1985), a contributor to this volume. His widely cited empirical article on the interest-group origins of the Sherman Act played a major role in encouraging scholars to reconsider the public-interest hypothesis most often used to explain antitrust's formative era. Of considerable interest was DiLorenzo's documentation that most of the industries supposedly monopolized by the trusts (e.g., bituminous coal, lead, leather, linseed oil, liquor, petroleum, salt,

250 WILLIAM E. KOVACIC

sugar, and steel) actually had experienced growth in output and falling prices in the decade leading up to passage of the Sherman Act.

Subsequent research by antitrust skeptics and abolitionists has taken a variety of paths. Among the most important has been examining the origin of other turn-of-the-century regulatory schemes to explore the motivation for passage of the federal antitrust statutes. Gary Libecap (1992) describes how cattle raisers and local slaughterhouses sought enactment of meat inspection laws and antitrust legislation alike to impede expansion by large, Chicago-based meatpackers. Unlike Stigler (1985), who downplays the significance of agricultural interests in promoting passage of the Sherman Act, Libecap emphasizes the importance of such interests in galvanizing political support for the Sherman Act. Thomas Hazlett (1992) studies the Sherman Act in connection with Congress's parallel consideration of the McKinley Tariff Act of 1890. He concludes that incumbent Republicans who controlled Congress embraced the Sherman Act as political cover to make palatable their approval of "the upcoming consumer-to-industry transfers in the McKinley Tariff." Hazlett finds that a seemingly ineffectual antitrust law was an acceptable price for the "redistributional coalition" in Congress to get what it really wanted: higher tariffs.

The Papers in This Section

The paper by Donald Boudreaux, Thomas DiLorenzo, and Steven Parker takes a somewhat indirect approach to investigate the purposes that animated the creation of the federal antitrust system. The authors examine the origins of state antitrust legislation in the late 1800s. In studying the evolution of state antitrust measures, the authors join a growing body of researchers who have scrutinized state experience from the 1880s through 1920 to illuminate the sources of the federal antitrust system.[14] Boudreaux et al. focus on the development of state antitrust legislation because the same economic, social, and political impulses that generated state statutes also guided Congress in passing the Sherman Act.

The authors find that the chief political spur for enactment of Missouri's antitrust law in 1889 came from agrarian interests. As in other midwestern agricultural states, rural cattlemen and butchers pressed the Missouri legislature to pass an antitrust statute in the hope of impeding competition from centralized meat-processing facilities in Chicago. Protectionism—rather than

14. See James May, Antitrust Practice and Procedure in the Formative Era: The Constitutional and Conceptual Reach of State Antitrust Law, 135 U. Penn. L. Rev. 495 (1987); May, *supra* note 10; May, *supra* note 11; Symposium, Observing the Sherman Act Centennial: The Past and Future of Antitrust as Public Interest Law, 35 New York Law School L. Rev. 767 (1990); and Symposium, National Association of Attorneys General Antitrust Centennial Symposium, 30 Washburn L. J. 141 (1990).

fear of monopolistic output restrictions and price raising by large, integrated meatpackers—is seen to have motivated the state statutes. Boudreaux et al. also offer statistical evidence suggesting that the presence of agricultural interests strongly influenced the passage of state antitrust statutes. Like Libecap (1992), the authors underscore the importance of cattle growers and local slaughtering operations in promoting antitrust legislation.

Whereas Boudreaux et al. examine the early stages of antitrust's formative period, Robert Ekelund, Michael McDonald, and Robert Tollison use the private-interest perspective to study its concluding phase. In examining the origins of the Clayton Act, the authors also reject Bork's thesis that Congress designed this measure to serve the public interest by increasing efficiency. Like a number of other commentators who have examined business-government relationships in the late nineteenth century and early twentieth century (Gilligan et al. 1989; Libecap 1992),[15] the authors do not treat the business community as an undifferentiated mass, but instead seek to identify specific business subgroups that stood to gain or lose through the restrictions ultimately embodied in the Clayton Act.

From their review of the congressional hearings leading to passage of the statute in 1914, Ekelund et al. conclude that the principal operative provisions of the Clayton Act served to benefit large incumbent firms at the expense of new entrants and smaller firms seeking to expand. This contrasts with the view of Stigler (1985, 4–5), who found that the Clayton Act reflected a "concern with predatory competition" and displayed "opposition to big business." Ekelund et al. describe how the Clayton Act's restrictions on interlocking directorates and the formation of holding companies served to impede efforts by smaller firms to achieve scale economies enjoyed by larger rivals. They also explain how the statute's prohibition on various vertical contractual restrictions (such as exclusive dealing) denied smaller firms a valuable, lower cost alternative to physical integration for establishing vertical supply and distribution relationships. By examining congressional voting on the Clayton Act, the authors also offer statistical evidence supporting the hypothesis that the Clayton Act facilitated a transfer of wealth from smaller, growing firms to larger enterprises.

Taken together, the papers by Boudreaux et al. and Ekelund et al. do more than merely raise questions about the historical soundness of Bork's efficiency thesis. Their identification of congressional redistributionist goals seems to pose a dilemma for enforcement officials and judges who accept Bork's efficiency framework. If Congress did not (as Bork argues) intend the antitrust statutes as efficiency prescriptions and instead passed them to transfer wealth

15. See also Robert Higgs, Origins of the Corporate Liberal State, 5 Crit. Rev. 475 (1992); Morton Keller, Regulating a New Economy: Public Policy and Economic Change in America, 1900–1933 (1990); and Robert H. Weibe, Businessmen and Reform: A Study of the Progressive Movement (1962).

among various producer groups, then how should these measures be enforced and interpreted in the short term—at least until the abolitionists persuade Congress to repeal them? If the antitrust statutes were intended to redistribute wealth, are enforcement agencies obliged to bring cases that accomplish those ends, and must federal judges exercise their discretion to promote redistribution? And finally, would aggressive, unapologetic efforts to effectuate redistributionist goals impose so obvious and substantial a drag on the economy that political support to topple the antitrust system would be forthcoming?

Of all researchers whose work is responsible for modern scholarly reevaluation of antitrust's campaign against horizontal restraints, none has been more influential than the final contributor to Part Four of this volume. George Bittlingmayer's paper on the output effects of the National Industrial Recovery Act (NIRA) revisits a theme that he has pursued in early works—namely, that antitrust's assault on horizontal price setting frequently ignores important efficiency rationales for such behavior. Bittlingmayer (1982, 1983) stimulated a new round of debate about the ban on price fixing with his application of core theory to the foundational late nineteenth-century case of *United States v. Addyston Pipe & Steel Co.*

In attacking the result and analysis of *Addyston Pipe,* Bittlingmayer was challenging one of antitrust's icons. In his essay for this section, Bittlingmayer takes on another firmly held tenet of modern antitrust thinking: that the National Industrial Recovery Act was a singularly misguided exercise in economic policymaking and demonstrated the error of attempting to relax stringent antitrust prohibitions on horizontal pricing agreements. As enacted in 1933, the NIRA established the National Recovery Administration (NRA), which directed the business community, organized labor, and consumer groups to collaborate (under the loose supervision of public officials) in drafting and implementing industrywide codes of conduct. Many of the codes set output and pricing levels and, in effect, dispensed with antitrust restrictions on price-setting arrangements among direct rivals (Hawley 1966).

Most modern commentary on the NRA and its cartelizing activities has been unfavorable. Historical accounts of New Deal economic policy typically find that the NRA codes retarded recovery (Miller et al. 1984, 18–19). The repudiation of the NIRA in *Schechter Poultry Co. v. United States* in 1935 and the subsequent revival of vigorous federal efforts to prosecute horizontal price fixing during the second term of Franklin Roosevelt's presidency are often cited as favorable policy adjustments.

Bittlingmayer's paper reassesses the conventional wisdom about the NRA experience by asking whether its promotion of industrywide coordination of production and pricing actually reduced or increased output. He presents evidence showing that the passage of the NIRA and the early operation of the NRA coincided with a substantial boom in production, particularly in durable goods. Bittlingmayer notes that the cause of the boom is uncertain; nonetheless, he finds a sufficiently strong connection between the NIRA and increased production and higher stock market returns to justify further inquiry into the possible expansionary traits of this New Deal experiment, including its repudiation of antitrust's traditional ban upon various forms of horizontal collaboration.

CHAPTER FIFTEEN

Antitrust before the Sherman Act

Donald J. Boudreaux, Thomas J. DiLorenzo,
and Steven Parker

Introduction

Economists and legal scholars have studied the effects of antitrust policy for decades, but only recently have the origins of antitrust received much scholarly attention. In an early analysis, Robert Bork (1966a) claimed to have found evidence in the *Congressional Record* that the "legislative intent" of Congress in passing the Sherman Act was consumer protection. Hazlett (1992), however, disputes Bork's interpretation, as do others.

Stigler (1985, 1) was among the first economists to reexamine "the problem of why the United States introduced an affirmative competition policy." He tested an agrarian-interest hypothesis—that "the Republicans passed the Sherman Act to head off the agrarian . . . movements" for price controls and other interventions—against a self-interest hypothesis that small businesses wanted a law to protect them from their larger, more efficient rivals. Stigler found little, if any, empirical support for either hypothesis.

One of us (DiLorenzo 1985) examined the origins of the Sherman Act from a public-choice or interest-group perspective and provided evidence that industries accused of being monopolized in the late 1880s were in fact cutting prices and expanding output faster than the rest of the economy was. He suggests that the Sherman Act might have been a political smokescreen to pave the way for the McKinley tariff, which was passed just three months after the Sherman Act and was sponsored in the U.S. Senate by Senator John Sherman himself.

The public-interest interpretation of the origins of antitrust—that the law was passed as a benevolent response by Congress to a form of market failure—is still by far the predominant view among economists and legal scholars. There are, however, reasons to be skeptical of this view. This essay reexamines the genuine roots of antitrust, the state-level antitrust laws that were enacted several years before the Sherman Act. In the mid-1880s, strong

We thank the late Katherine Boudreaux, Donald Dewey, Robert Tollison, an anonymous referee, and seminar participants at George Mason University, Loyola College, Holy Cross College, the University of Georgia, and Auburn University for their comments. The usual caveats apply.

Table 15.1   State Antitrust Laws by Date of Passage

State	Year of Passage
MARYLAND	1867
TENNESSEE	1870
ARKANSAS	1876
TEXAS	1876
GEORGIA	1877
INDIANA	1889
IOWA	1889
KANSAS	1889
MAINE	1889
MICHIGAN	1889
MISSOURI	1889
MONTANA	1889
NEBRASKA	1889
NORTH CAROLINA	1889
NORTH DAKOTA	1889
SOUTH DAKOTA	1889
WASHINGTON	1889
KENTUCKY	1890
LOUISIANA	1890
MISSISSIPPI	1890
ALABAMA	1891
ILLINOIS	1891
MINNESOTA	1891
CALIFORNIA	1893

political movements emerged at the state level of government in favor of "anti-monopoly" legislation that eventually took the form of antitrust statutes. Although Stigler (1985) and Thorelli (1955) noted the existence of these state statutes, only Libecap (1992) has recognized, independently of our work, the possible relation between these state antitrust movements and congressional passage of the Sherman Act in 1890.

The Sherman Act was not enacted in a Washington, D.C., political vacuum. It emerged from the same economic and political forces that gave rise to state antitrust legislation. It is particularly relevant that in 1890 state legislatures still directly elected U.S. Senators and that the Sherman Act was introduced in the Senate rather than the House.

The second section of this essay compares the public-interest and special-interest hypotheses, and then examines these hypotheses in light of the economic and political forces at work during the emergence of state antitrust legislation in the late nineteenth century, particularly in 1889. We focus on one primarily agricultural state, Missouri, which we believe to be representative of the states that enacted antitrust legislation during this period. Most states that enacted antitrust statutes in 1889 were located in or near the Mississippi valley (see table 15.1). Agrarian interests were particularly active in pressing for antitrust legislation in Missouri. Our third section further develops the special-interest hypothesis; our fourth tests the hypothesis with cross-sectional data. Our final section contains a summary and conclusions.

Missouri Agriculture in the Late Nineteenth Century: Monopoly or Competition?

If the standard consumer-welfare-enhancing interpretation of antitrust legislation explains Missouri's experience with such laws, then the following trends should be evident in the economic data on Missouri's agricultural sector for the 1870s and '80s: (1) the real price of farm outputs should have risen (or not fallen); (2) the volume of farm outputs should have fallen (or not increased); and/or (3) the real price of farm inputs should have risen.

However, if the real prices of farm outputs and inputs fell—and if the volume of outputs rose—the protests against supposed monopolization are inconsistent with what actually happened in Missouri's agricultural economy. Indeed, if real prices fell and outputs rose, the cries against monopolization are more plausibly interpreted as rent-seeking attempts of less efficient producers to protect their markets from the increasing competition of more efficient producers.

Agricultural Price Data: Inputs and Outputs

During the 1880s, cattle was Missouri's single largest agricultural output,[1] in 1889 accounting for nearly one quarter of all agricultural output in the state. Hog production and wheat production followed, accounting for more than 20 and 13 percent, respectively, of Missouri's gross agricultural product. Cattle, hogs, and wheat together accounted for almost 60 percent of Missouri's total agricultural production in 1889.[2] Table 15.2 shows the market value of Missouri-raised cattle and hogs per head from 1879 through 1891, as well as the price of wheat in Missouri for these years.

CATTLE
Although a simple comparison of, say, the 1879 per-head value of Missouri cattle with the 1889 value shows a slight increase, a different and more significant picture emerges from the trend of cattle values from the mid-1880s to the end of the decade. Compared to its peak in 1884, the per-head value of cattle in Missouri in 1889 was 28.8 percent lower (and was to fall even further by 1890). Looked at another way, the average value of cattle per

1. Robert Klepper, The Economic Bases of Agrarian Protest Movements in the United States, 1870–1900, 320 (1978).

2. Missouri was the fourth largest cattle-producing state (behind Texas, Iowa, and Kansas); the nation's third largest hog producer (after Iowa and Illinois); and the nation's fifth largest wheat producer (following California, Illinois, Indiana, and Ohio). See U.S. Bureau of the Census, Abstract of the Eleventh Census: 1890, tables 4 and 7.

Table 15.2 Prices of Missouri's Three Leading Agricultural Products, 1879–1891

	1879	1880	1881	1882	1883	1884	1885	1886	1887	1888	1889	1890	1891
Cattle (per head)	$22.95	$25.06	$27.03	$29.01	$31.18	$32.61	$31.05	$28.60	$26.49	$25.65	$23.22	$21.86	$21.92
Hogs (per head)	4.36	5.59	6.29	7.68	7.99	6.75	5.75	5.44	5.83	6.71	6.48	5.44	5.40
Wheat (per bushel)	1.01	0.89	1.19	0.85	0.88	0.62	0.77	0.63	0.62	0.88	0.64	0.83	0.80

Source: Robert Klepper, The Economic Bases for Agrarian Protest Movements in the United States, 1870–1900 (1978).

head for the years 1887–1889 was 18.8 percent lower than the average value per head for the years 1882–1884. This decline in cattle values—which affected all the major cattle-producing states—was accomplished by a steady increase during the 1880s of the quantity of cattle entering into gross national product. Measured in pounds of live weight, cattle supply during the 1880s increased by about 50 percent for the United States as a whole, while the price per hundredweight received by American cattlemen fell from an average of $5.59 in 1880 to $3.86 in 1890—a 31 percent decrease.

Not surprisingly, this increased supply and reduced price of cattle resulted in lower prices of beef (and beef by-products) for final consumers. According to American economic historian Mary Yeager, the average price of beef tenderloins in the United States fell by nearly 38 percent between 1883 and 1889.[3]

HOGS

As with cattle, the market value of hogs in Missouri peaked in the mid-1880s. The 1889 value of a Missouri-raised hog was approximately 19 percent lower than it had been six years earlier. The average value of hogs in the state for the 1887–1889 period was more than 15 percent lower than it was in 1882–1884. The nationwide output of hogs and hog products increased during the 1880s, while the price per hundredweight of hogs fell precipitously—from $6.07 in 1880 to $3.60 in 1890—a decrease of more than 40 percent.[4]

WHEAT

The trend of prices for Missouri wheat was also downward during the 1880s, although the prices fluctuated a good deal.[5] The 1889 price of wheat in Missouri was 34.7 percent lower than it was a decade earlier. The average price of wheat in Missouri during the 1882–1884 period was 97 cents per bushel as compared to 71 cents per bushel on average for the years 1887–1889. The latter price is almost 27 percent lower than the price of wheat earlier in the 1880s.

These data do not support the notion that Missouri agriculture was becoming monopolized during the 1880s. Moreover, it is doubtful that "predatory pricing" was taking place, for prices had been falling since 1870. Predatory pricing for that length of time would have been irrational (Elzinga and Mills 1989).

3. Mary Yeager, Competition and Regulation: The Development of Oligopoly in the Meat Packing Industry 70 (1981).

4. The 1870 price per hundredweight of hogs in the U.S. was, at $6.80, even higher than it was in 1880.

5. In a ranking of fourteen states by variability from year to year in their wheat prices, Missouri is eighth. Robert A. McGuire, Economic Causes of Late-Nineteenth Century Agrarian Unrest: New Evidence, 41 J. Econ. Hist. 835 (1981).

FARM-INPUT PRICES

The farm input that first comes to mind as possibly having been monopolized in the late nineteenth century is railroad transportation. Although rail rates did fluctuate over time,[6] and varied from region to region and from shipper to shipper, there is broad agreement among economic historians that railroad rates fell dramatically during the several decades following the Civil War.[7] According to Stigler (1985, 2), "average railroad freight charges per ton mile had fallen by 1887 to 54 percent of the 1873 level, with all lines in both the eastern and western regions showing similar declines." Henry Varnum Poor found that railroad rates fell from an average charge of $2.90 per ton-mile in 1865 to $0.63 in 1885—a rate of decrease of over 78 percent.[8]

Consistent with the significant railroad rate reductions was the equally significant increase in the quantity of rail services supplied during the latter part of the nineteenth century. According to Poor, total ton-miles carried by U.S. railroads increased by 700 percent between 1865 and 1885.[9] In Missouri, there were 4,234 miles of railroad track in 1880; by 1889 this figure had increased by almost 45 percent to 6,118 miles of track.[10] We are aware of no evidence indicating that railroad rates were monopolistically high during the period leading up to the passage of antitrust legislation in Missouri.[11] All evidence points in the opposite direction.

Nor is the evidence consistent with the farmers' contention that financing costs increased during the late nineteenth century. In fact, real interest rates fell dramatically during the 1880s. In the Midwest, including Missouri, real interest rates on farm mortgages fell from an average of 11.41 percent in 1880 to 7.84 percent in 1889. This fall represents a 31 percent reduction in real interest rates during the 1880s.[12]

We were unable to find detailed data on farm-machinery prices in Missouri. However, Clevenger reports that, while input, output, and consumer goods

6. Lebergott argues that the variability of rail rates during the late nineteenth century was an effect of keen competition among the railroads. Stanley Lebergott, The Americans: An Economic Record 284–85 (1984).

7. Douglass C. North, Growth and Welfare in the American Past 139–40 (1966).

8. Quoted in George W. Hilton, The Consistency of the Interstate Commerce Act, 9 J. Law & Econ. 87, 89–90 (1966).

9. Ibid., at 89.

10. Clevenger reports that in 1879 Missouri had 27 counties without railroad service, but by 1891 only 11 counties remained unserved by the railroads. Homer Clevenger, Agrarian Politics in Missouri, 1880–1896 (unpublished Ph.D. dissertation, University of Missouri, 1940), p. 33.

11. In fact, the intensity of the competition among railroads, and the resulting continual downward trend in rail rates in the decades following the Civil War, are considered to be the reasons underlying the passage of the 1887 Act to Regulate Interstate Commerce. Sponsors of this Act hoped that the Interstate Commerce Commission would effectively cartelize the railroads. See, for example, Kolko (1963), Paul W. MacAvoy, The Economic Effects of Regulation: The Trunk-line Railroad Cartels and the Interstate Commerce Commission Before 1900 (1965), and Hilton, *supra* note 8.

12. See Jeffrey G. Williamson, Late Nineteenth-Century American Development 153 (1974).

prices fell in Missouri in the 1880s, declines in farm-output prices usually occurred before decreases in the prices of consumer goods. But, the decreases in the prices of farm outputs in Missouri were generally preceded by decreases in the prices of farm inputs. "In terms of bushels of wheat, oats, or corn, a mowing machine, binder, or cultivator could be bought for less in 1892 than in 1882" in Missouri.[13]

Clevenger's claim that the prices of farm inputs in Missouri decreased in real terms during the 1880s is consistent with the trends in farm-machinery prices.for the United States as a whole during the latter part of the nineteenth century. This trend was downward during the decades following the Civil War. Towne and Rasmussen constructed an index of U.S. farm machinery prices (in constant 1910–1914 dollars) and found that this index fell from 251 in 1870, to 124 in 1880, and to 101 by 1890.[14] This index shows that farm machinery was 2.5 times more costly in 1870 than it was in 1890.[15] There is no reason to believe that the trend of farm-machinery prices in Missouri departed significantly from the nationwide trend.

Missouri's economy was undoubtedly becoming more and more commercialized and competitive in the post-Civil War era. The state's rapid economic growth and its increasing integration with the region and the nation are reflected in the number of railroad carloads of general merchandise unloaded or loaded in St. Louis. Historian David Thelan reports that 20,542 cars were loaded or unloaded in 1870.[16] By 1880 this figure had risen more than sixfold to 125,939, and by 1890 it had more than doubled again to 323,506. These data also cast doubt on the contention that the Missouri economy was falling into the consumer-welfare-reducing grip of monopolists during this period.[17]

In sum, available data on economic conditions in Missouri's agricultural sector in the decades leading up to the enactment of the state's 1889 antitrust statute contain no clear evidence of monopolization. Indeed, every sector of Missouri's economy, especially agriculture, shows signs of having been highly competitive during the last three decades of the nineteenth century.

Political Motivations

Close study of late nineteenth-century politics in Missouri suggests that agrarians were the major special interest behind state antitrust legislation. What,

13. Clevenger, *supra* note 10, at 46.

14. Marvin E. Towne and Wayne D. Rasmussen, Farm Gross Product and Gross Investment in the 19th Century, in National Bureau of Economic Research, Trends in the American Economy (1960).

15. This index fell to 94 by 1900.

16. David Thelan, Paths of Resistance 32 (1986).

17. Thelan, a historian sympathetic with populist ideals and goals, reports that "railroads transformed the size and shape of [Missouri's] market economy, forcing businessmen and farmers to produce at unprecedented rates to survive the new competition." Ibid., at 32.

then, did the agrarians in Missouri have to gain from the passage of an antitrust statute? Agrarians and local merchants in Missouri (and elsewhere) correctly perceived that larger producers were responsible for the downward pressures on the prices of their outputs.[18] Because economies of scale caused a decrease in the optimal number of producers of any particular commodity, the economy *looked* as if it were becoming more "monopolized," if "monopoly" is defined purely in terms of market structure and not in terms of the intensity of rivalry (DiLorenzo and High 1988). As such, in their attempts to protect their local markets from the lower-priced and/or higher-quality goods being shipped to towns and countrysides on the railroads from the increasingly centralized production locations, politically organized agrarians complained of the evils of "monopoly." But the term monopoly, as used by the agrarians, referred only to the larger and more efficient firms which were driving small farmers and merchants out of their traditional lines of work and business.[19] They equated "monopoly" with bigness, even if "bigger" firms meant greater economic efficiency and lower prices for consumers.

There is evidence that farmers did indeed view large-scale enterprise as a competitive threat and sought antitrust laws to protect them from competition. The Farmers Alliance was the most powerful political coalition in Missouri in the years preceding the enactment of the 1889 antitrust law. Farmers carried so much political clout that nearly all members of the state legislature identified themselves as "farmer-lawyers," "farmer-bankers," "farmer-teachers," "farmer-druggists," and so on, to signify their identification with the farm lobby, even if they had never set foot on a farm.

The Alliance confronted candidates for the state legislature in 1888 with a card containing the following promise: "I pledge myself to work and vote for the [Farmers Alliance's] demands irrespective of party caucus or action."[20] The pledge card was widely distributed to farmers who were instructed, "If any candidate refuses to sign . . . vote against him and use your influence to elect those who sign, irrespective of party."

Of the 174 state senators and representatives, 140 signed the pledge, as did every one of the congressmen-elect headed for Washington. The winners of all three statewide races in 1888 had signed the pledge as well.

One reason Missouri's farmers wanted an antitrust law was that many of

18. Ibid.

19. Our interpretation of the antimonopoly protests of the late nineteenth century is not novel, of course. For example, Arthur Dudden argues that "in the United States by the middle of the nineteenth century, monopoly was generally deplored as hampering opportunity. . . . [T]he antimonopoly spirit of the Gilded Age took shape as a widespread but essentially middle-class protest against the centralizing tendencies in transportation, land tenure, business, and industry, which characterized the period." See Arthur P. Dudden, Men Against Monopoly: The Prelude to Trust-Busting, 18 J. Hist. Ideas 587, 588 (1957).

20. Frank M. Drew, The Present Farmers' Movement, 6 Pol. Sci. Q. 282, 303 (1891).

them were being underpriced by larger, more efficient farms. Farmers repeatedly sought legislation "to obtain higher prices for all that the farmer produces."[21] For example, at an 1889 meeting of the National Farmers Alliance in St. Louis, a declaration was issued that urged "care for the widows and . . . orphans"; and called for legislation to "suppress . . . all unhealthy rivalry."[22]

Farmers were bitter about low and falling agricultural prices, and blamed the trusts for the decline in their economic position. They complained of "our depressed condition," because of the fact that "the price of the farmers' grain is below the cost of production." As historian David March wrote: "Just as the low price of raw cotton spurred the expansion of the Southern Alliance, so low grain prices in the late 1880s caused thousands of farmers in the wheat belt . . . to join the National Farmers Alliance."[23]

To the extent that agricultural prices were falling, the notion that the Missouri antitrust law enhanced consumer welfare is suspect. Missouri farmers were an appropriate special-interest group to launch an antitrust policy on grounds of self interest, if it could be expected that an "antitrust" statute would be enforced and interpreted as an anti-*bigness* statute to protect some producers from the competition of larger and more-efficient rivals.

Cattlemen, Butchers and Other Rent Seekers

The agrarian interest group that seems to have exerted the most pressure for passage of Missouri's 1889 antitrust statute was comprised of cattlemen and local retail butchers agitated over the allegedly monopolistic practices of the "beef trust"—the centralized butchering and meat-packing firms that emerged in Chicago in the early 1880s as a result of the development of an economical refrigerated railroad car. The four largest Chicago meat packers during the 1880s were Swift, Armour, Morris, and Hammond, collectively known as "The Big Four."

Efficiency and the Chicago Meat-Packing Industry

Gustavus Swift was not the first entrepreneur to ship cattle by refrigerated railroad car, but he was the first to do so economically, shipping his first refrigerated car full of beef from Chicago to Massachusetts in the fall of 1877. The "refrigeration" of this 1877 shipment of dressed beef was little more than open doors on a railroad car being hauled in cold weather. Swift saw profits, however, in the slaughter of cattle in a central location served by several railroads (such as Chicago), permitting meat shipments across the

21. Ibid., 304.
22. Ibid., 286.
23. David D. March, History of Missouri 1169 (1971).

264   BOUDREAUX, DiLORENZO, AND PARKER

country in any season. The development of an economically viable refrigerated car allowed Swift to begin year-round shipments in 1879.[24]

In addition to integrating forward into wholesaling and retailing, Swift and his rival Chicago meat packers created markets for beef and hog by-products that had never before existed, thus extracting more profit from each cow or pig slaughtered than did local butchers. Given this more productive use of the whole cow or pig, combined with the economies of scale made possible by the centralization of butchering and shipping, it is not surprising that the price of meat to consumers fell throughout the 1880s.[25]

The average quality of beef also improved during the 1880s, even though, as Libecap (1992, 254) notes, "the use of derogatory claims about the quality of a competitor's products was a common competitive strategy . . . in the late nineteenth and early twentieth centuries." Despite these claims, the quality improvement that did occur was closely connected with the fall in the price of cattle that occurred in the mid-1880s through the early 1890s. The fall in cattle prices, in turn, was responsible for the decline of the range-cattle industry beginning in the mid 1880s.

The Beef Trust

In the wake of the decline of the range-cattle industry, there emerged for the first time, in the Midwest and the West, rumors of a "beef trust." Range-cattle producers whose product—live, grass-fed cattle shipped by rail to wholesale or retail butchers or sold directly to butchers in nearby towns—simply could not compete with much less expensive and higher-quality dressed meats shipped from Chicago. These cattlemen contended that "The Big Four" meat packers were conspiring to *depress* the price of range cattle.[26]

In May 1886, the "National Butchers' Protective Association of the United States of America" was formed in St. Louis. The organized butchers' goal "was to destroy the dressed meat industry, which was shipping meat from Chicago to eastern cities and selling it for less than the meat killed by the local butchers."[27]

The complaints of the range-cattle producers and of the local butchers prompted the first investigation of the meat-packing industry by the U.S. Congress. Responding to these complaints, the Senate in May 1888 appointed a special commission to investigate the cause of the *low* price of cattle allegedly contrived by The Big Four. Senator George Vest of Missouri was appointed to chair this committee. Five midwestern and western Senators (from Illinois, Kansas, Missouri, Nebraska, and Texas) made up the so-called Vest

24. Rudolf A. Clemens, The American Livestock and Meat Industry 235–36 (1923).
25. Yeager, *supra* note 3, at 70.
26. Ibid., at 172–73.
27. Clemens, *supra* note 24, at 243.

Committee. From the start—the committee began hearings in St. Louis in November 1888, "this place being chosen because the International Cattle Range Association and the Butchers' National Protective Association were in session there"—committee members sympathized strongly with its members' cattle-raising constituents.[28] In its May 1890 final report, the Vest Committee concluded that "the principal cause of the *depression* in the prices paid to the cattle raiser and of the remarkable fact that the cost of beef to the consumer had not decreased *in proportion,* comes from the artificial and abnormal centralization of markets, and the absolute control by a few operators thereby made possible."[29]

The Vest Committee did not deny that the price of beef to consumers had fallen, it complained only that price did not fall "in proportion" to the reduction in range-cattle prices. Consumer welfare rises, of course, when the price consumers pay falls, especially when the quality of the goods rises simultaneously. This is true, regardless whether consumer prices fall more or less than in proportion to input-price declines.

The Vest Committee found no direct evidence of collusion by the major Chicago meat packers. Instead, the Committee *inferred* the existence of collusive action among the major packers in the buying of cattle from the fact that cattle prices fell during the mid- and late 1880s. The Vest Committee reported that "Mr. P.D. Armour testifies at Washington that no such [collusive] agreement existed between himself and other packers and we do *not contradict this statement.* . . . [However], it is difficult to believe that with the most apparent motive for such action the same parties, or their subordinates with their knowledge, do not avail themselves of the opportunity presented by the centralization of markets to combine for the purpose of lowering the price of cattle."[30]

Several state legislatures also attempted to take action against the "beef trust." In 1888, Governor Lyman Humphrey of Kansas called all state governors in the Mississippi Valley to a conference that would write a uniform statute for all states represented.[31] The statutes adopted would "protect the stock-grower and farmer against the manipulations of such alleged [beef] trust."[32]

To meet this goal, the conference wrote a model antitrust statute. Neither the convention nor the proposed statute mentioned any need to protect con-

28. Ibid., at 749.
29. Senate Report no. 829, at vii (emphasis added).
30. Ibid., at 6 (emphasis added).
31. See Steven L. Piott, The Anti-Monopoly Persuasion: Popular Resistance to the Rise of Big Business in the Midwest 26 (1985).
32. Journal of the Senate of Missouri, 35th General Assembly (1889), at 165. The full text of this Missouri Senate-House resolution, calling for a conference of midwestern state legislators, as well as Missouri Governor Francis's message to the Missouri General Assembly, is available from the authors.

sumers from high prices, only a need to protect stockgrowers and farmers from lower-priced competitors. The model antitrust statute declared all "trusts" to be in violation of the state corporate charter. Significantly, the model statute included in its definition of a trust the ability of "a combination of capital, skill or acts by two or more persons, firms, corporations or association of persons . . . to limit or reduce the production, or increase or *reduce* the price of merchandise or commodities."[33]

The statute eventually enacted in Missouri was titled "An Act for the Punishment of Pools, Trusts, and Conspiracies"; it passed by a vote of 98 to 1 in the House and by 27 to 4 in the Senate.[34] Missouri's legislation prohibited "restraints of trade" in the form of pooling, forming trust companies, interlocking directorates, and so on, the effects of which were "to fix or limit the amount or quantity of any article, commodity or merchandise to be manufactured, mined, produced or sold" in Missouri. The statute also prohibited actions intended "to limit or fix the price" of outputs.[35] Although the wording of the proscription against actions intended to "limit" the price of outputs is subject to interpretation, one plausible meaning of the verb "to limit" as used in this statute is "to reduce" or "to keep from rising." This interpretation of the statute as prohibiting actions intended to reduce prices is consistent with (1) the downward trend of prices in Missouri during the 1870s and 1880s; and (2) the support given by Missouri's Governor Francis and by Missouri's farmer-dominated General Assembly to the St. Louis beef-trust conference of March 1889, which had adopted a model antitrust statute that explicitly prohibited price reductions.

In sum, we interpret the political events in Missouri during the winter and spring of 1889 as generally driven by anticompetitive forces. Missouri's agrarian-dominated General Assembly passed antitrust legislation in 1889 as part of an attempt to shield politically powerful producer groups, especially range-cattle producers and independent retail butchers, from competitive pressures exerted by the centralized, vertically integrated meat-packing firms headquartered in Chicago. No evidence exists that consumers in Missouri (or anywhere else in the United States) were being harmed economically by the so-called beef trust.

In fact, as shown above, the evidence suggests just the opposite. Centralization of meat packing generated substantial benefits to consumers in the form of lower prices and higher-quality meat, as well as expanded use of meat by-products which, until the 1880s, were discarded as waste. The growth of

33. Ibid., at 407 (emphasis added). On the prevalent nineteenth-century view that the proper and legal means for controlling the size and manufacturing activities of corporations was the state corporate charter, see Charles W. McCurdy, The Knight Sugar Decision of 1895 and the Modernization of American Corporation Law, 1869–1903, 53 Bus. Hist. Rev. 304 (1979).

34. Journal of the House of Missouri, 35th General Assembly (1889), at 952–53; and Journal of the Senate of Missouri, *supra* note 32, at 410–11.

35. Laws of Missouri, 35th General Assembly (1889), at 96–97 (emphasis added).

centralized meat packing did result in lower prices for range-cattle producers and, of course, for independent local butchers. They competed head-to-head with those performing more efficiently in Chicago's slaughtering and packing houses.

A Test of the Self-Interest Hypothesis

As shown in table 15.1 above, twenty-four states passed some form of anti-trust legislation between 1867 and 1893. Twelve of these states passed laws in 1889 and six more enacted legislation in 1890–1891. Given the speed of this process, it is reasonable to assume that these laws were passed within the same political climate, as described earlier. It was also the same political climate in which the 1890 Sherman Act was passed.

The Model

Because the vote on the Sherman Act was nearly unanimous, it is difficult, if not impossible, to test the self-interest hypothesis at the congressional level in a way that could capture the interest-group dynamics. State antitrust laws, by contrast, provide fertile ground for such testing. Following Stigler's (1985) method, we assume that states' antitrust acts are similar. We seek to predict whether a state will have an antitrust statute or not (STATEACT) on the basis of the political-interest variables identified above. The tests were also run with a dependent variable (STATEACT2) that excluded Maryland, Texas, Georgia, Tennessee, and Arkansas, which passed antitrust laws prior to 1877. These states are omitted to account for the possibility that a different political climate existed before the 1880s.

A series of logit multiple regression models was estimated. These regressions model the dependent variable (whether the state passed an antitrust statute) as a function of the (1) concentration of agricultural interests within a state, (2) concentration of businesses, and (3) rate of business failures. U.S. Census data were used.

The concentration of agriculture within a state is measured by the number of farms per capita (CAPFARM). Business concentration per state is measured by the number of businesses per capita (CAPBUS). These variables control for the general character (i.e., agricultural vs. business) of a state's economy. The rate of business failures within the state is measured by the failure rate as a percentage of the total number of businesses within the state for 1890 (P90FAIL), or, alternatively, as the average rate of business failures in the period 1885–1890 (PERFAIL). Two more specific variables for beef interests in a state are also included, one measuring the number of cows per acre (COWACRE) and the other the number of butchers per capita (BUTCH). The variables and their expected signs are summarized in table 15.3.

Together, the regressions provide a test of the special-interest hypothesis. Should CAPFARM, COWACRE, or BUTCH be positive and statistically

Table 15.3   Definition of Variables in Regression Equations

Variable	Definition	Expected Sign
Dependent Variables		
STATEACT	Binary variable = 1 if antitrust law enacted prior to 1894, 0 otherwise	
STATEACT2	Same as STATEACT, except Maryland, Texas, Georgia, Tennessee, and Arkansas excluded	
Independent Variables		
CAPFARM	Average number of farms per capita, 1885–1890	+
CAPBUS	Average number of businesses per capita, 1885–1890	–
P90FAIL	Percent of business failures in 1890	+
PERFAIL	Average rate of business failures, 1885–1890	+
COWACRE	Number of cows per acre in a state	+
BUTCH	Number of butchers per capita, 1880	+

significant, as expected, the special-interest hypothesis will be supported. A significant effect of the cattle interests would be consistent with the analysis of the previous section.

A positive and significant sign for the business-failure-rate variable (P90FAIL or PERFAIL) would also be consistent with the special-interest hypothesis. That is, a higher business-failure rate would likely lead to political pressures by smaller businesses for an antitrust law to "hamper the growth of large enterprises whose greater efficiency threatened the small business sector in many industries" (Stigler 1985, 4).

Statistical Results

The logit regression estimates are presented in table 15.4. As shown, a positive and statistically significant relationship exists between the dependent variable, STATEACT, and the number of farms per capita (CAPFARM), the number of cows (COWACRE), and the variables measuring business failures (P90FAIL and PERFAIL). These variables are significant at conventional levels. The per capita numbers of businesses (CAPBUS) and of butchers (BUTCH) are not significant. The model was also estimated with the regressors entered logarithmically, with results (not presented here) qualitatively the same as those reported in table 15.4. In the logarithmic regression, however, it is the number of farms and number of butchers (but not cows per acre) that are statistically significant.

Table 15.5, altering the model by excluding states which passed antitrust laws prior to 1877, provides further support for the special-interest hypothesis. Qualitatively, the results are similar to those for all states, but the size and significance of the coefficients are greater. (The variable measuring the number of businesses per capita also becomes significant, although its sign is the opposite of that predicted.) Apparently, the basic model works better

Table 15.4   Logit Regression: Dependent Variable = STATEACT

	#1	#2	#3	#4	#5
CONSTANT	−9.85	−8.86	−9.37	−6.97	−5.89
	(2.33)	(2.20)	(2.22)	(1.81)	(1.55)
CAPFARM	54.14	57.39	47.66	39.76	43.60
	(2.42)*	(2.51)*	(2.05)*	(2.16)*	(2.24)*
CAPBUS	88.19	82.61	90.28	59.50	49.81
	(0.91)	(0.85)	(0.95)	(0.619)	(0.51)
P90FAIL	3.77	3.37	3.71		
	(2.32)*	(2.26)*	(2.28)*		
PERFAIL				2.20	1.75
				(1.765)†	(1.53)†
COWACRE	0.1 E^{-03}		0.2 E^{-03}	0.1 E^{-03}	
	(1.56)†		(1.56)†	(1.459)†	
BUTCH		0.6 E^{-04}	−0.1 E^{-03}		0.004
		(0.487)	(0.645)		(0.32)
PERCENTAGE CORRECT	83.3	78.5	83.3	78.5	71.0

n = 40
* = significant at .05
† = significant at .10

Table 15.5   Logit Regression: Dependent Variable = STATEACT2
(Excluding States with Antitrust Laws Prior to 1877)

	#1	#2	#3
CONSTANT	−18.09	−14.58	−17.40
	(2.62)*	(2.58)*	(2.55)*
CAPFARM	92.11	87.62	83.56
	(2.59)*	(2.69)*	(2.33)*
CAPBUS	240.54	201.00	239.67
	(1.73)†	(1.62)†	(1.75)†
P90FAIL	5.80	4.53	5.72
	(2.45)*	(2.40)*	(1.85)†
COWACRE	.0003		.0003
	(1.94)†		(1.85)†
BUTCH		0.0001	−0.0001
		(0.84)	(0.60)
PERCENTAGE CORRECT	84.2	81.5	82.0

n = 35
* = significant at .05
† = significant at .10

to explain political behavior circa 1890. Most important, the relative abundance in the economy of farms (CAPFARM), and of cattle (COWACRE) in particular, is an important predictor of which states passed antitrust laws after 1877.

Conclusion

The political and economic roots of antitrust lie at the state level of government. Numerous states passed antitrust laws before the 1890 Sherman Act, which was initiated in the U.S. Senate (whose members, at that time, were directly elected by state legislatures).

The political impetus for some kind of antitrust law came primarily from the farm lobbies of midwestern agricultural states such as Missouri. Rural cattlemen and butchers were especially eager for statutes that would thwart competition from the newly centralized meat-processing facilities in Chicago. The evidence on price and output in these industries, moreover, does not support any claim that these industries suffered from a monopoly problem in the late nineteenth century, if "monopoly" is understood conventionally as an organization of industry that restricts output and raises prices. As discussed in this chapter's second section, these industries were highly competitive because of relatively free entry and rapid technological advances such as refrigeration.

It is an interesting fact that, unlike economists, historians studying the period discussed here have had little difficulty perceiving the politics behind state antitrust laws.[36] Perhaps economists have remained unpersuaded because empirical evidence of antitrust's special-interest nature has been meager. But the statistical tests reported in the previous section provide cross-sectional evidence supporting the special-interest interpretation of the origins of antitrust. The passage of state antitrust laws is found to be influenced by the presence of agricultural interests, consistent with the analysis discussed in our third section. Cattlemen who were disadvantaged by the more efficient, centralized butchering processes, developed in Chicago in the 1870s and thereafter, were significant political forces agitating for protectionist antitrust laws.

36. For further evidence in support of our interpretation of the political motivation behind antitrust legislation in the case of Missouri in particular, see Clevenger, *supra* note 10; Piott, *supra* note 31; and Thelan, *supra* note 16. Many historians interpret nineteenth-century agrarian political protests, including the agrarians' ubiquitous calls for antimonopoly legislation, as attempts to stave off the increasing commercialization of farmers' occupations and lives. For example, Dudden, *supra* note 19; Robert H. Wiebe, The Search for Order, 1877–1920 (1967); Anne Mayhew, A Reappraisal of the Causes of Farm Protest in the United States, 1870–1900, 32 J. Econ. Hist. 464 (1972); and Forrest McDonald, The Phaeton Ride: The Crises of American Success (1974).

CHAPTER SIXTEEN

Business Restraints and the Clayton Act of 1914: Public- or Private-Interest Legislation?

ROBERT B. EKELUND, JR., MICHAEL J. McDONALD, AND ROBERT D. TOLLISON

> For many members of Congress the casting of a favorable vote [on the Clayton Act] was a matter of political exigency. Administrative pressure, party discipline, the political power of organized labor, and the undoubted fact that a majority of the voters at home would interpret a Congressman's vote against an "anti-trust" statute as a vote for monopoly were the dominant factors in the situation. And so many things were lumped together in the bill that it was impossible to segregate the good from the bad. (Allyn A. Young 1915, 326)

Introduction

Seminal pieces of legislation affecting antitrust and regulation, such as the 1887 Act to Regulate Commerce, which established the Interstate Commerce Commission, and the 1890 Sherman Act, have been scrutinized from the perspective of public-choice and interest-group theory (Gilligan et al. 1989; Stigler 1985; DiLorenzo 1985, 1990). A major exception thus far has been the Clayton Act of 1914, a set of rules that marked a turning point in antitrust. Surprisingly, at least according to some observers (e.g., Bork 1978, 47–48), Congress believed that certain business practices should be prohibited in their incipiency on grounds that they might lead to monopoly. The prohibited business practices included price discrimination and the establishment of horizontal (holding companies and interlocking directorates) and vertical non-price (exclusive dealing and tying contracts) restraints.

Numerous factors combine to explain the passage of the Clayton Act in

We are grateful for comments and assistance from Audrey Davidson, Robert Hébert, David Kaserman, and Mark Thornton. We assume full responsibility for any and all errors.

1914. Actual passage followed eight months of intense, confused, and byzantine negotiations in Congress. As early as 1912, there had been demands from Democrat, Republican, and Progressive party leaders and from farm and labor groups for further antitrust regulation (Martin 1959). Belief that the Sherman Act had failed to stop the "trusts" was prevalent, but the understanding of the role of the trusts and of competition in the economy was no more "scientific" when the Clayton Act was debated and passed than it had been 25 years earlier.[1]

We argue here that, contrary to the typical public-interest interpretation of the Clayton Act (Kirtner 1964, 23; Scherer 1980, 494), the business practices proscribed by the law and the establishment of the incipiency doctrine provided the means for *ex ante* wealth transfers among competing special-interest groups. First, an analysis of the legislative hearings leading to the Clayton Act provides evidence of the existence and dominance of interest groups that subsequently gained and lost from passage of the legislation. Specifically, the evidence is consistent with the hypothesis that the restrictions established in the Clayton Act benefited large incumbent firms and firms in intrastate commerce at the expense of expanding firms. Further, we present empirical tests of the interest-group hypothesis based on a probit analysis of the final Senate vote on the Clayton Act.

The second part of this essay develops the theory of special interests and regulatory choice as expressed in written testimony before Congress. The third and fourth parts establish a framework for and present the results of an empirical test of whether passage of the Clayton Act in the U.S. Senate served the public interest or, rather, served private and political interests. The fifth and final part analyzes economic arguments concerning the inception of or change in regulation. Our investigation lends support to the view that

1. As in the case of the Sherman Act, many economists of the day were aware that market structures and the business practices associated with them were undergoing rapid changes (Breit 1991). Some, like Young (1915), at least "suspected" that sweeping condemnations of capital agglomerations and business practices might be counterproductive. But while some commentators (C. C. Arbuthnot, The Factor System as Related to Industrial Combinations, 15 J. Polit. Econ. 577 [1907], for example) understood the efficiency-promoting purposes of vertical arrangements, a number of economists (see, for instance, F. Taussig, Price Maintenance, 16 Amer. Econ. Rev. 170 [1916]) did not. One explanation, as expressed by DiLorenzo (1985) with respect to the Sherman Act, is that the "process" view of competition was at variance with the solidifying academic view of competition, circa 1914. By this time, the Marshallian conception of competition had been transformed into a mechanical exercise in achieving static equilibrium, helped by the growing application of mathematical techniques in professional economics. (For evidence that the mathematical trees did not stop businessmen from seeing the dynamically competitive forest, see Kleit 1992). As contemporary economic theory expands to include such concepts as non-price competition (in quality, service, or locational dimensions, for example), total consumption costs, and full price, per se condemnations of business practices become even less cogent from the perspective of economic efficiency. This is especially so in a populist environment of rent seeking (DeBow 1991).

regulation "appears not to follow the stylized pattern of a concentrated producer group against an undifferentiated, diffuse set of consumers" but rather that "a multiple-interest-group perspective is frequently necessary to understand the inception of regulation" (Gilligan et al. 1989, 60).

Business Practices and Interest Groups: Legislative Debate

That interest groups compete for wealth transfers within a self-interested political/institutional environment is well known (Stigler 1971; Peltzman 1976, 1989). In this setting, the economist's task is to identify particular competing groups, their regulatory interests, and the outcome of political competition as revealed in enacted legislation. As discussed in the previous chapter, state-specific agricultural interests and political legerdemain apparently inspired the Sherman Act's prohibitions of unspecified trade "restraints," though there is little evidence of welfare-reducing trust activity prior to the Act's passage (DiLorenzo 1985).

In any case, dissatisfaction with the Department of Justice's enforcement efforts under the Sherman Act was almost immediate. Only sixteen antitrust cases were instituted by federal prosecutors in the nineteenth century's final decade. There were two divergent views about how the Sherman Act's perceived deficiencies might be redressed. In the U.S. House of Representatives, the favored course of action was to enumerate specific unlawful business practices and make them criminal offenses. The Senate, by contrast, wanted to reserve the task of identifying unlawful practices for a new Federal Trade Commission (FTC), which was to be set up as an expert law-enforcement body with a broad mandate to attack unspecified "unfair methods of competition."

The Clayton Act ultimately emerged as a compromise between these two positions. It enumerated specific antitrust law violations, but did not subject violators to criminal penalties. To provide the FTC with enforcement flexibility, qualifying phrases were inserted in the bill's final version making the proscribed business practices illegal only when their effect "may be to substantially lessen competition or tend to create a monopoly." Three categories of business practices were ultimately banned by the Clayton Act—horizontal restraints (interlocking directorates and holding companies), non-price vertical restraints (exclusive dealing and tying arrangements), and price discrimination (Shughart 1990a, 56).[2]

2. Furthermore, the Clayton Act, despite considerable lobbying, failed to overturn the Supreme Court's decision in Dr. Miles Medical Co. v. John D. Park & Sons Co., 220 U.S. 373 (1911), which held resale price maintenance to be illegal per se. The Court reasoned that RPM prevented price competition and was equivalent to price fixing among distributors, with no acknowledgment of fundamental differences between intrabrand and interbrand competition. Later on, however, in U.S. v. Colgate & Co., 250 U.S. 300 (1919), the Court held that manufacturers could refuse to sell to any distributor who did not maintain desired wholesale or

Horizontal and non-price vertical restraints are all potential devices for fostering competition—that is, they are all relatively low-cost means by which firms can organize in order to expand operations beyond the local level. Oliver Williamson argues that there are gradations in governance structures between a fully integrated firm and the market.[3] Holding companies and interlocking directorates are governance structures one step removed from complete horizontal integration. Exclusive dealing contracts and tying arrangements, moreover, are vertical governance structures one step removed from a vertically integrated firm. The choice of governance structure depends on transaction costs, which are minimized through the competitive market process.

Prior to the Clayton Act's passage, firms organized horizontally and vertically, using holding companies, interlocking directorates, exclusive dealing, and tying contracts in order to minimize transaction costs. Prohibition of these devices in the Clayton Act forced either vertical or horizontal consolidation of firms. If economies of scale were associated with consolidation, the relative cost of smaller firms' integration and consolidation being higher, then the law's proscriptions transferred wealth (a) to firms engaged in intrastate commerce and/or (b) to larger firms threatened by expanding companies. Consider, in detail, these propositions and the legislative testimony pertaining to them.

Horizontal Restraints

Holding companies and interlocking directorates are the main horizontal arrangements proscribed by the Clayton Act. These horizontal arrangements allow firms to expand without having to bear the costs of full ownership integration. Further, these practices permitted firms to expand across state lines without having to pay "foreign" corporation taxes—the corporate taxes of states other than those in the initial state of incorporation.

Section 7 of the Clayton Act, the "holding company" section, forbids the purchase or acquisition of all or part of the share capital of any company when the effect is to substantially lessen competition or tend to create a monopoly. Prior to the Celler-Kefauver amendment to Section 7 in 1950, the acquisition of an ownership interest in another company was legal so long as only physical assets were acquired in the transaction. We argue that the initial exemption of asset acquisitions was in fact a "loophole" intended to

---

retail prices. However, no formal or informal agreements as to prices were allowed between producers and distributors—such agreements, in addition to "threats" or "refusals to deal" would be considered Sherman Act violations. Risks of prosecution were too great, and manufacturers backed away from RPM. Attempts to legalize RPM were, in fact, a large part of the debate surrounding the Clayton Act.

3. Oliver E. Williamson, Assessing Contract, 1 J. Law, Econ. and Org. 177 (1985).

transfer wealth among firms. The asset loophole reduced the ability of some firms to integrate their operations through the arguably less costly means of stock swaps or share purchases.

In testimony favoring the prohibition of stock purchases or trades, Samuel Untemyer saw "no objection" to the outright purchase of the physical assets of competing companies.[4] Others clearly understood Section 7's intent, however. Letters from lawyers claimed that the prohibition would keep small companies small forever. The Birmingham & Southern Railway Co. and the Buckeye Steel Casting Co. also argued that the restriction on holding companies would prevent the growth of their businesses.[5] Section 7, it was alleged, would deny these and other firms access to a relatively cheap means of expansion.

The crux of the matter is this: Acquiring an ownership interest in another firm by purchasing its physical assets can be a "lumpy" transaction. This is especially true when, as is typically the case, the assets are highly specialized to one another and the value of the target firm as a going concern consequently exceeds its break-apart value. If an asset acquisition is made in such cases, the acquiring firm must buy the target, lock, stock, and barrel. The acquired assets must then be absorbed. Combining the assets of two formerly independent firms involves reorganizing and consolidating buildings and equipment, rearranging production schedules, reassigning workers and management, and so on.

For these reasons, asset acquisitions tend to be more costly than stock acquisitions. Equities, which represent claims on future profit streams, can be bought and sold more readily and in more finely divisible units than the physical assets that underlie them. (Indeed, this observation helps explain why stock markets emerged in the first place.) Hence, the proscription on holding companies in Section 7 handicapped smaller firms, which arguably faced thereby differentially higher costs of expanding into new markets by acquiring and absorbing the assets of competitors rather than by purchasing their stock.

Another wealth transfer was created by the holding company prohibition. State incorporation laws typically levied higher taxes on "foreign" companies chartered out-of-state than on "domestic" companies holding in-state charters. Prior to the enactment of Section 7, a company could obtain charters in more than one state and avoid the foreign corporation tax through the holding company device. The Gulf Oil Company, Felt & Tarrant Manufacturing Co., and the Middle West Utility Company all testified that the holding company was a means through which they could avoid such taxes.[6] More-

4. U.S. House of Representatives, Hearings on Trust Legislation Before the House Committee on the Judiciary, 63rd Cong., 2nd Sess. (1914), at 855. Hereinafter cited as Hearings.

5. Ibid., at 1727, 1730.

6. Ibid., at 115, 1025, 1791.

over, the president of Felt & Tarrant submitted a letter noting that these taxes can "be a serious financial burden on a little concern."[7]

Along with the existence of foreign corporation taxes, the passage of Section 7 constituted a wealth transfer from expanding businesses to companies operating intrastate and to larger companies which could more readily absorb the physical assets of the firms they acquired. A related proscription—actually an extension of the restrictions placed on holding companies—was the prohibition of interlocking directorates. Section 8 of the Clayton Act makes it illegal for the same person to sit on the boards of directors of two rival companies. Interlocking directorates were[8]—and are (Kirtner 1964, 108)—seen as devices that facilitate the emergence of collusive agreements between horizontal competitors.

But the effects of the Clayton Act's restrictions on interlocking directorates were similar to those of its restrictions on holding companies. As such, as firms like the International Paper Company and the Campbell Wall Paper Company testified,[9] interlocking directorates were a means by which businesses could avoid paying state "foreign" corporation taxes. Before Section 8 of the Clayton Act became law, a subsidiary could be established in another state and an owner or partner common to the two companies would sit on both boards. As noted in a letter from the Campbell Wall Paper Company, passage of Section 8 would force either liquidation, emplacement of dummy directors, or consolidation.[10] Because consolidation was impractical due to financial constraints, the letter went on, expansion would be out of the question for many smaller firms desiring growth. As with the holding company provision, the beneficiaries of the ban on interlocking directorates were national companies threatened by rising competition and companies which operated solely intrastate.

Non-Price Vertical Restraints

Vertical restraints, such as exclusive dealing contracts and resale price maintenance, provide a lower-cost means of assuring dealer performance than does direct monitoring or full-ownership integration (Klein and Murphy 1988). Exclusive dealing contracts help assure contractual performance by creating a stream of quasi-rents for the dealer that raises the long-run gain from performance above the short-run gain from nonperformance (free riding). Nonperformance will naturally lead to the contract's termination, forcing the dealer to forego the future quasi-rent stream.

As in the case of horizontal restraints, manufacturers were able to use

7. Ibid., at 1793.
8. Ibid., at 820, 921–52.
9. Ibid., at 1791.
10. Ibid., at 1741.

exclusive dealing contracts as substitutes for ownership integration into downstream retail markets prior to the Clayton Act's passage. Prohibition of the practice in Section 3 forced manufacturers either to integrate forward into retailing by purchasing existing retail operations (or by building new outlets from scratch) or to use less efficient (higher cost) methods of distributing their products to consumers. When full ownership integration was not a viable option for expanding firms, larger concerns and intrastate businesses were consequently protected from expanding manufacturers.

Those testifying in favor of prohibiting exclusive dealing contracts argued that exclusive dealing amounted to foreclosure. Retailers or distributors who could not obtain goods from manufacturers would be "foreclosed" from retail sales. The effect, so the logic went, was to limit the competition, raise prices, and create monopolies.[11] Much of the rhetoric against exclusive dealing contracts came from small tobacco retailers, who complained that exclusive dealing in cigars and other tobacco products was driving out the independent dealers who carried a range of different brands.[12] Small, independent, rural retailers were also of concern to committee members Floyd and Peterson of Arkansas, who thought that such contracts would force country stores out of business and create retail monopolies.[13]

Opponents of declaring exclusive dealing contracts unlawful offered many of the modern, procompetitive arguments for the practice (Telser 1960; Marvel 1982; Boudreaux and Ekelund 1988).[14] The overall economic efficiency of such contracts was explained to the committee by the representatives of such firms as the Ford Motor Co. and McCall & Co.[15] These individuals explained that an exclusive dealing contract assured the retailer a profit and consequently provided incentives to supply the advertising and pre- and post-sale services needed to market the good effectively. Interbrand competition was not precluded by exclusive dealing contracts because "foreclosed" retailers were free to contract with other manufacturers.

Not only would small, rural, independent retailers gain from the prohibition of exclusive dealing, but established manufacturers benefited at the expense of new entrants. The costs of new or growing competitors would be higher with the prohibition because in many cases the costs of full ownership integration are higher than the costs associated with contracting across ownership boundaries. In fact, this point was made clear in letters to the committee.

---

11. U.S. Committee Reports, Report from the Committee on the Judiciary to Accompany H.R. 15657, House Report No. 627, 63rd Cong., 2nd Sess. (1912–1914), p. 11.

12. Hearings, *supra* note 4, at 530–40, 700–03.

13. Ibid., at 969.

14. Non-price restraints have been subject to a rule-of-reason analysis in the courts since Continental Television, Inc. v. GTE Sylvania, Inc., 433 U.S. 36 (1977), which acknowledged the procompetitive effects of non-price restrictions.

15. Hearings, *supra* note 4, at 767–69, 755–57, 966–74, and 1005.

One correspondent argued that establishing an ownership presence in retail markets—required when the contracting alternative was foreclosed—was costlier. Mr. Felt of Felt & Tarrant noted that the principal manner in which a manufacturer could attract sales agents for *new* products was by providing profits through exclusive territories, adding that "the big fellows can use, and will use, this section 3 to suppress budding competition."[16]

If the cost of forward integration is less for large manufacturers than for small manufacturers, the elimination of exclusive dealing contracts would transfer wealth to the larger firms. In addition, if there are economies of scale and other efficiencies in local and regional advertising and sales effort, the effective elimination or reduction of such efforts by "franchised" wholesale and retail dealers is economically inefficient. Passage of Section 3 of the Clayton Act served the interests of small, independent, rural retailers and large, established manufacturers. The likely effect was to slow the pace of entry into manufacturing and to reduce interbrand competition at the retail level.

Tying arrangements are another means by which manufacturers can reduce monitoring costs. Monitoring costs arise when there is a technological inter-dependence between products and the quality or performance of the final product has a direct impact on the value of the upstream firm's brand-name capital. The manufacturer can help ensure quality of the final product and protect its own brand-name capital by requiring the purchaser of the product also to purchase supplies of complementary products (Bork 1978, 379–81; Klein and Saft 1985). Famous examples of tie-in sales include Kodak cameras and Kodak film, IBM's tabulating machines and punch cards, and United Shoe Machinery Company's policies allowing its customers to lease certain kinds of shoe machinery only if they also leased other of United Shoe's equipment.

The Clayton Act's prohibition of tie-in sales benefits those manufacturers who produce the complementary or interdependent product (the "tied good") whose sale is tied to purchases of the primary product (the "tying good"). It also benefits the manufacturers who compete with the manufacturer of the tying good, whose costs of protecting the value of their brand name capital have been increased. The Boylston Manufacturing Company, one of United Shoe's rivals in the manufacture of shoe machinery, had a great deal to gain from the Clayton Act's prohibition of tying arrangements. Representatives of Boylston in fact testified that United Shoe's marketing practices had fore-closed Boylston from the shoe machinery market.[17]

We have conjectured, in the foregoing discussion, that the Clayton Act provided benefits to some firms at the expense of others. Small firms, in particular, conveyed this belief in the congressional hearings. If larger firms

16. Ibid., at 1742–44.
17. Ibid., at 1033.

have a comparative advantage in expanding into new markets by purchasing physical assets, then the prohibitions on holding companies in Section 7 and on vertical non-price restraints in Section 3 transfer wealth from large firms to small firms and from those firms engaged in interstate commerce to those operating solely intrastate.

Price Discrimination

Section 2 of the Clayton Act prohibits the practice of charging different prices for the same product to different customers with the intent of injuring a competitor. The prohibition of price discrimination tends to protect small firms against the discount pricing policies of their larger, more efficient rivals and, hence, to raise prices. Small tobacco and oil concerns came to testify in favor of declaring price discrimination illegal. They claimed that prices were currently "too low," that they were being driven out of business and that, upon their exodus, industry prices would be raised. Indeed, the intent of the Committee on the Judiciary also seemed to be to raise prices. Representative Floyd of Arkansas stated baldly that price discrimination

> is not injurious to the public. It is beneficial to the public in that the community can get the goods cheaper, but it puts the individual manufacturer out of business. This section [2] is intended to prevent a wrong to an individual [manufacturer]. If they [manufacturers] were to lower prices in that community you could never say that the people of that community, as a whole, were injured by the lowering of prices of things they bought.[18]

The prohibition of price discrimination—reiterated far more strenuously in the Robinson-Patman Act of 1936—has on the whole been the most actively enforced provision of the antitrust laws. Textual evidence in the hearings suggests that small businesses were influential in inspiring the enactment of Section 2 and that its purpose was, indeed, to *raise* prices. While all small firms, urban and rural, gained from the prohibition, it is perhaps significant that the most vocal critic of allowing so-called "discriminatory practices" to continue was a committee representative from a rural state. Strong contemporary populist sentiment, along with the demographic configuration of political power in Congress, may account for the attractiveness of the prohibition of price discrimination.[19]

The Wealth-Transfer Hypothesis: An Empirical Test

Testimony relating to the Clayton Act suggests that some firms and interest groups had much to gain from its passage. Specifically, the testimony sup-

18. Ibid., at 964.
19. The role played by small business interests in inspiring passage of the Robinson-Patman Act is detailed in Ross (1984, 1986).

ports the hypothesis that the law transferred wealth from growing firms to larger ones and to firms operating intrastate from those engaged in interstate commerce. A probit analysis of the Senate vote tests whether passage of the Clayton Act was motivated by private or public interests. The vote is specified as a function of variables which proxy state agricultural interests and growth rates in manufacturing.

Variables and Their Expected Signs

Specifically, we specify a vote function as follows:

(1) VOTE $= f$(PARTY, RPOP, AGINC, VADD, GMANUF, GMINE).

The dependent variable, VOTE, takes on a value of 1 if a senator voted aye and 0 if he voted nay. We examine only the Senate vote because observations on the variables of interest are not available for congressional districts. The actual Senate vote was 35 yes, 24 no, and 37 not voting. (The House vote was 245 yes, 52 no, and 126 not voting.) Inspection of the data suggests that the results are not biased by the exclusion of abstaining senators. The 37 non-voters came from 27 different states cutting across all regions of the country. If anything, the role of small business interests in generating political support for the bill is biased downward by the exclusion of the non-voters because many of them represented states having important small business constituencies.

Political and demographic variables are included on the right-hand side of equation (1) in order to capture the impact of private and public interests on the final Senate vote. Political support for President Wilson, who favored the legislation, is proxied by the variable PARTY. PARTY is set equal to 1 if the senator was a fellow Democrat and set equal to zero otherwise.

Agricultural and Manufacturing Interests

RPOP and AGINC are proxies for the importance of agricultural interests. The percentage of a state's population that is rural is measured by RPOP,[20] while AGINC is an estimate of state agricultural income per farm worker in 1919.[21] Because states with large rural populations and agricultural sectors are importers of manufactured goods, the *public-interest* hypothesis predicts positive signs on both RPOP and AGINC. If the Clayton Act was in fact designed to hinder the creation of monopolies, senators from these states

20. U.S. Department of Commerce, Bureau of the Census, Historical Statistics of the United States, Colonial Times to 1970 (1977), pp. 24–37.

21. Richard A. Easterlin, Estimates of Manufacturing Activity, in Everett S. Lee, Ann Ratner Miller, Carol P. Brainerd, and Richard A. Easterlin, Population Redistribution and Economic Growth in the United States, 1870–1950, vol. 1 (1957), p. 755.

would have voted for the Act in order to prevent their constituents from paying supra-competitive prices. However, the *interest-group* hypothesis predicts negative signs on these variables. Senators from rural states would tend to vote against legislation that they thought would reduce competition and raise prices on manufactured goods to their constituents.

A state's percentage of total national value added in manufacturing is represented by the independent variable VADD.[22] VADD is a measure of the extent to which manufacturing interests were concentrated in a particular state and, hence, the extent to which the state's senators would have catered to those interests. The public-interest hypothesis predicts a negative sign on VADD. Senators from those states where manufacturing was less concentrated would have voted in favor of the bill in order to reduce the prices their constituents were paying for imported manufactured goods. However, the interest-group hypothesis predicts a positive sign on VADD. Senators from states where manufacturing was more heavily concentrated would have voted for the Clayton Act in order to help protect their state's businesses from competitive market forces.

Growth Proxies

To test whether the Clayton Act transferred wealth from "growing" firms to larger, established firms, several proxies for firm growth were developed. GMANUF stands for growth in manufacturing. Growth in manufacturing by *size* of establishment was chosen as an explanatory variable because both the hypothesis presented in this paper and testimony from the congressional hearings suggests that the Clayton Act tended to handicap small but growing firms. GMANUF is decomposed into three different variables that account for the growth in manufacturing by three separate firm-size categories. The *Census of Manufactures* provides a breakdown of five size classifications of manufacturers within a state determined by value of output—more than $1 million; $100,000 to $1 million; $20,000 to $100,000; $5,000 to $20,000; and less than $5,000. According to the *Census,* these categories are based on "the selling value or price at the factory of all products manufactured during the year."[23]

MARKET SHARE MEASURE (GM)

The first proxy for growth in manufacturing is growth in the state's market share by size of business from 1904 to 1914. Market share is measured as the percentage of the national value added in manufacturing accounted for by different size classes of manufacturers within the state. (All data for

22. U.S. Department of Commerce, Bureau of the Census, Census of Manufactures, vol. 1 (1918).
23. Ibid., at 4. Unfortunately, data on sales by state of firms in the "Mom and Pop" category—$20,000 and below—do not exist for the period 1904–1914 .

constructing growth proxies for states were obtained from the 1918 *Census of Manufactures*.)

GM1M is the percentage change in manufacturing value added accounted for by the firms within the state whose products were valued at more than $1 million. GM100K is the percentage change in value added for the firms within the state whose products were valued in the $100,000 to $1 million range, and GM20K is likewise defined for firms producing products valued between $20,000 and $100,000. GM1M2, GM100K2, and GM20K2 are the squared values of these three variables.

The interest-group hypothesis predicts that senators representing states where manufacturing value added was growing relatively slowly or decreasing relative to that of other states would have voted *for* the Clayton Act. Passage would limit the expansion of out-of-state manufacturers, thereby helping protect local firms' market shares.

GROWTH IN VALUE ADDED (GVA)
A second proxy for growth in manufacturing is the growth in the value added in manufacturing from 1904 to 1914 broken down by size of manufacturer. GVA1M is the percentage change in value added for firms producing products worth more than $1 million. GVA100K and GVA20K are defined similarly for firms in the $100,000-to-$1 million and $20,000-to-$100,000 size categories. GVA1M2, GVA100K2, and GVA20K2 are these three variables squared. The interest-group hypothesis again predicts that senators from those states where manufacturing value added was growing more slowly or decreasing relative to other states would have been more likely to vote in favor of the Clayton Act, *ceteris paribus*.

PERCENTAGE CHANGE IN PRODUCT VALUE (GV)
The third proxy for the growth in manufacturing is the percentage change in the value of products produced by firms in the three previously defined size categories. GV1M is the percentage change in the value of products produced by firms in the over-$1 million size category and GV100K and GV20K are the percentage changes in product values in the $100,000-to-$1 million and $20,000-to-$100,000 firm-size categories, respectively, and GV1M2, GV100K2, and GV20K2 are the squared values of the variables. Slower or declining growth rates in manufacturing are once again predicted to increase the chances of a favorable vote on the Clayton Act.

Mining

A final independent variable, GMINE, measures the importance of state mining interests. GMINE is defined as the percentage change in the value of state mining production as a percentage of the value of national mine output from 1902 to 1909. The variable is included to account for the fact that the

Clayton Act's holding company and interlocking directorate provisions may have been expected to affect expanding mining companies adversely. If so, the interest-group hypothesis predicts a negative sign on GMINE. Senators from states where mining output was growing more slowly or decreasing relative to other states would have tended to vote for the bill to help protect the interests of local miners. Growth in the mining sector is not classified by size of operation because these data were unavailable.

Public Interest or Private Interest? Empirical Results

The results of probit analyses of the Senate's vote on the Clayton Act are reported in table 16.1. The table shows three separate model specifications based on the three different proxies for manufacturing growth described in the previous section.

The first column uses growth in market share by firm size as the proxy for growth in the manufacturing sector. In this specification, as in the other two, PARTY is positive and significant at the 5-percent level. Democratic senators clearly followed President Woodrow Wilson's wishes by voting favorably on the Clayton Act. GMINE, the variable that measures the importance of mining interests by state, has the sign predicted by the special-interest theory, but the coefficient is not significantly different from zero in any of the specifications.

The coefficients associated with two firm-size classifications are significant for the growth proxy in specification 1. GM100K2 is negative and significant at the 5-percent level with a positive (but insignificant) sign attached to GM100K. This result indicates that senators from states where manufacturing market shares for firms in the $100,000-to-$1 million size class were increasing at a decreasing rate tended to vote in favor of the Clayton Act, while senators from states where manufacturing market shares were expanding more rapidly were more likely to vote against it. (The same is true for firms in the over-$1 million size category, but the results are not statistically significant). The fact that senators from these states voted for the Clayton Act does not square with the public-interest conjecture that the law was enacted to reduce the number of monopolies or monopoly power. On the contrary, the evidence suggests that favorable votes were cast with an eye toward the law's potential for protecting in-state manufacturing interests at the expense of more rapidly growing out-of-state rivals.

Further, in specification 1, GM20K is positive and significant at the 10-percent level, and GM20K2 is positive and significant at the 5-percent level. This result indicates that senators from states where smaller firms' market shares were increasing at an increasing rate tended to vote for the Act. Importantly, the national market shares of firms in this size classification declined from 20 percent in 1904 to 12.6 percent in 1914. Furthermore, the share of

Table 16.1 Probit Analysis of Senate Vote on Clayton Act
(Dependent Variable = 1 if Yes, 0 if No)

Variable	(1)	Variable	(2)	Variable	(3)
PARTY	6.07	PARTY	3.99	PARTY	5.28
	(2.45)*		(2.50)*		(2.46)*
RPOP	−4.38	RPOP	−2.81	RPOP	−7.33
	(0.90)		(0.83)		(1.87)†
AGINC	−0.01	AGINC	−0.01	AGINC	−0.01
	(1.24)		(1.08)		(1.38)
VADD	4.17	VADD	5.54	VADD	3.30
	(0.32)		(0.47)		(0.27)
GM1M	2.33	GVA1M	0.61	GV1M	0.22
	(0.96)		(0.43)		(0.51)
GM1M2	−2.75	GVA1M2	−0.01	GV1M2	−0.01
	(1.39)		(0.43)		(0.29)
GM100K	8.94	GVA100K	7.60	GV100K	16.01
	(1.35)		(1.37)		(2.01)*
GM100K2	−16.03	GVA100K2	−2.88	GV100K2	−5.59
	(1.99)*		(1.43)		(1.75)†
GM20K	38.07	GVA20K	−15.04	GV20K	−30.41
	(1.89)†		(1.82)†		(1.73)†
GM20K2	87.14	GVA20K2	19.80	GV20K2	26.37
	(1.99)*		(1.98)*		(1.71)†
GMINE	−1.17	GMINE	−1.16	GMINE	−2.47
	(0.96)		(1.09)		(1.54)
Chi-squared	62.08		59.40		60.13
N	59		59		59
% Correct Predictions	.93		.95		.93

Note: An asterisk (*) denotes significance at the 5-percent level and a dagger (†) denotes significance at the 10-percent level.

Sources: Mark Sullivan, ed., Important Roll Calls in the United States Senate (1915); Richard A. Easterlin, Estimates of Manufacturing Activity, in Population Redistribution and Economic Growth in the United States, 1870–1950, vol. 1 (1957); U.S. Department of Commerce, Bureau of the Census, Abstract of the Twelfth Census of the United States, 1900 (1905); U.S. Department of Commerce, Bureau of the Census, Thirteenth Census of the United States: 1910 Bulletin. Mining: United States Abstract—Statistics of Mining, for Industries and States (1913); U.S. Department of Commerce, Bureau of the Census, Census of Manufactures, vol. 1 (1918); and U.S. Department of Commerce, Bureau of the Census, Historical Statistics of the United States, Colonial Times to 1970 (1977).

the market accounted for this size of firm decreased in all states, indicating their vulnerability to the competitive inroads of larger firms. The aye votes of senators from states where firms of this size still had a viable market was apparently a vote to protect them from competition. A positive vote for a bill to prevent monopolies would not have benefited these firms. Smaller firms would have been better off operating under the price umbrellas established by the leading firms in highly concentrated industries, rather than being forced to compete with these same industry leaders in markets expected to be made less concentrated by the Clayton Act's enforcement.

In specification 2, growth in manufacturing is proxied by the percentage change in value added by firm size. GVA20K is negative and significant at the 10-percent level and GVA20K2 is positive and significant at the 5-percent level. This result indicates that senators from states where the value added in manufacturing for smaller firms was shrinking rapidly (decreasing at an increasing rate) voted for the bill. Where competition caused growth in manufacturing value added to decrease for smaller firms, senators voted positively to protect them from interstate competition.

Growth in manufacturing is proxied by the percentage change in the value of products by size of firm in specification 3. Here, GV100K is positive and significant at the 5-percent level and GV100K2 is negative and significant at the 10-percent level. The result indicates that senators from states in which manufacturing growth (in the $100,000-to-$1 million size class) was increasing at a decreasing rate voted for the Clayton Act. In accordance with the inferences drawn from specification 1, senators from states where growth in manufacturing was slowing voted for the Act in order to protect this sector from further competitive pressures.

Moreover, GV20K is negative and significant, and GV20K2 is positive and significant, at the 10-percent level in specification 3. These results suggest that senators from states where growth in manufacturing for firms in this size category was decreasing relative to other states voted for the bill. As in specification 2, states in which smaller firms were being displaced by expanding out-of-state rivals voted for the Clayton Act in order to protect them from competition.

In specification 3, as in the previous two, both RPOP and AGINC carry negative signs, indicating an interest-group response from agricultural states. Further, in specification 3, RPOP is negative and significant at the 10-percent level which indicates that senators representing states with large rural populations voted against the Clayton Act. We interpret this result as further evidence that the law was intended to hinder competition. Senators from heavily agricultural states voted no in order to prevent prices from rising due to the Clayton Act's anticipated anticompetitive effects.

In the final vote tally, special interests were dominant. Ninety-three percent of the votes in specifications 1 and 3, and ninety-five percent of the votes in specification 2 are predicted correctly, as indicated at the foot of table 16.1.

Overall, the results of the analysis indicate that, along with smaller manufacturers, the interests of manufacturers with product values between $100,000 and $1 million were an important factor in securing the Clayton Act's passage. The number of firms in this size classification grew as a percentage of the total number of manufacturers from 10.3 percent in 1904 to 10.9 percent in 1914. Over the same period, the rate of growth in the number of manufacturers in the greater-than-$1 million and in the less-than-$100,000 size classifications actually declined. These observations suggest that entry was occurring in the $100,000-to-$1 million size classification and that existing manufacturers within the classification were facing increased competition.

It is not clear, a priori, how large a firm would have to be to benefit from the Clayton Act's prohibitions on vertical and horizontal restraints of trade. The empirical evidence reported here indicates that manufacturers with product values between $100,000 and $1 million were the primary beneficiaries. These were firms possibly engaged in regional competition or firms in national markets producing products of relatively low value. Holding companies, exclusive dealing contracts, and tying arrangements provided avenues along which firms formerly competing on an intrastate level could expand horizontally or vertically and compete more effectively on an interstate level. Prohibition of these practices, as established in the Clayton Act, would retard the continued entry and expansion of firms in that category and transfer wealth to their competitors.

Conclusion

Our interest-group-based examination of the Clayton Act strongly suggests that economic efficiency was not the dominant issue in 1914. Special interests take center stage in explaining the origins of the Clayton Act, as they undoubtedly did with the Sherman Act that preceded it. We have presented both textual and empirical evidence suggesting that the Clayton Act transferred wealth from growing firms to relatively large firms and to small firms engaged solely in intrastate commerce. This wealth transfer was accomplished by prohibiting certain business practices, namely horizontal restraints (holding companies and interlocking directorates) and vertical restraints (exclusive dealing and tying arrangements), that served as low-cost means by which growing firms could expand and compete interstate. Furthermore, the prohibition of price discrimination protected small manufacturers from the lower prices charged by their larger, more efficient rivals. In short, the "incipiency doctrine" enshrined in the Clayton Act was a means of transferring wealth rather than an attempt to protect or preserve competition in the public interest.

CHAPTER SEVENTEEN

Output and Stock Prices When Antitrust Is Suspended: The Effects of the NIRA

GEORGE BITTLINGMAYER

Antitrust suffered two blows during the Great Depression. In March 1933, the Supreme Court scuttled the per se rule against cartels, holding that a rule of reason governed the joint sales agency in *Appalachian Coals*. In June, Franklin Roosevelt signed the National Industrial Recovery Act (NIRA), emergency legislation limited to two years that allowed the president to suspend large portions of antitrust law for designated industries.

The NIRA was the cornerstone of the New Deal's recovery program and contained, in addition to antitrust relief, labor provisions and a public works program. The agency created under the act, the National Recovery Administration (NRA), authorized the president's appointee to negotiate and approve codes proposed by industry representatives. For several major sectors this meant restricted production or capacity, or limits on machine or plant hours. Many industries also promoted the exchange of information on prices or costs, prohibited sales below cost, specified delivery or credit terms, and otherwise regulated industry behavior.

The NIRA was controversial, both in its practical operation and constitutionally. Its legislative renewal seemed unlikely in early 1935, and the Supreme Court rendered the issue moot when it declared the NIRA unconstitutional in May 1935.

In this chapter, I use *Appalachian Coals* and the NRA's rise and brief, unstable reign to study the economic effects of antitrust, or more accurately, of vastly reduced antitrust. Did the suspension of antitrust in Roosevelt's recovery bill actually promote recovery or retard it?

At first glance, the answer seems obvious. After all, textbook cartels hurt the economy. They imply higher prices and lower output for cartel members; lower prices and lower output for firms that supply the cartels; and higher prices and lower output for firms or consumers that buy from cartelized

My sincere thanks go to the John M. Olin Foundation, which supported this work while I was a visitor at the Center for the Study of the Economy and the State, University of Chicago. I also thank Sam Peltzman and Lester Telser for useful discussions, an anonymous referee for promoting a clearer exposition, Dan Nelson for help with data sources, and Louis Chan for expert research assistance.

sectors. In general equilibrium, aggregate output should fall. Extensive cartelization would lower aggregate economic activity, just as extensive taxation
would.[1]

But there is another side to the story. The seemingly indefensible practices
fostered by the NIRA—restrictions on hours of operation, capacity, or production—have an efficiency defense stemming from the problem that fixed
costs raise. A competitive equilibrium may not exist, and arrangements remi-
niscent of classic cartels may actually promote efficiency by allowing firms
to recover fixed costs. Though the notion of an efficient cartel seems odd
today, it is supported by economic theory, by recent empirical work, and by
the common law's approach to restraints of trade, as explained further below.

The first section of this essay provides background information on the
passage and implementation of the NIRA, including the structure of NRA
codes. The second section presents economic arguments and data bearing on
the issue of the NRA's effects. The passage and early administration of the
act were marked by a strong, broad-based economic recovery. Even controlling for other factors, themselves arguably influenced by the NRA, there is
no indication that NRA-stimulated cartelization caused a decrease in output.

Antitrust and Steps to the NIRA

Background

Hawley (1966) and Himmelberg (1976) emphasize the important point that
the NIRA was merely a new twist in the long political struggle over antitrust.
Business had sought protection from the Sherman Act since Theodore Roosevelt's trust-busting days. It achieved some of its aims under Coolidge, partly
in the courts but mainly through administrative discretion. Hoover's officials
reversed the Coolidge policies in 1929, unleashing a three-year push for
antitrust reform. Hoover resisted all substantive proposals to relax antitrust
enforcement, but Franklin Roosevelt did not. In fact, the National Industrial
Recovery Act that he signed restored part of the *status quo ante* under Coolidge.

The NIRA's industry provisions centered on trade associations. Under the
so-called open-price movement of the teens and twenties, trade associations
had sought to exchange information freely on prices, output, and costs. The
movement was founded—in the wake of vigorous antitrust enforcement under
Theodore Roosevelt, Taft, and Wilson—as an answer to the problem of
"cutthroat competition." The War Industries Board temporarily satisfied
some of the movement's aims during the First World War. However, plans
for a peacetime Industries Board foundered, and trade associations suffered

---

1. The macroeconomic implications of the conventional approach to antitrust are also discussed by Shughart and Tollison in chapter 10 of this volume.

antitrust setbacks in the early 1920s at the hands of the Justice Department and Supreme Court.[2]

This trend was reversed by administrative actions of the Federal Trade Commission (FTC) and by the Supreme Court. The FTC, previously shorn of much of its power by the courts and Congress and thus arguably an agency looking for a mission, started in 1925 to accelerate sponsorship of trade-practice conferences. These conferences resulted in industry codes, regarded by the FTC and industry as officially sanctioned under the FTC's statutory mandate to prohibit unfair trade practices. Critics charged that the meetings and association activities were a cover for anticompetitive practices. The Department of Justice (DOJ) also offered advice on the legality of association activities, especially after "Colonel" William Donovan became antitrust chief. The Supreme Court began to look more favorably on information exchanges by associations. By 1929, numerous industries (including petroleum, copper, electrical equipment, wool, and rubber) had adopted codes under the FTC's auspices. Anti-merger policy also was effectively suspended by the decisions in *U.S. Steel* (1920) and *International Harvester* (1927) and by a lenient Justice Department.[3]

As Secretary of Commerce, Herbert Hoover had promoted trade associations. But as president, he pushed strict enforcement of the antitrust laws against both mergers and trade associations. The policy shift occurred behind the scenes at first, but the attorney general made it public on October 25, 1929, at the American Bar Association's annual meeting. As demonstrated in Bittlingmayer (1993c), the lax antitrust policies of the 1920s explain the merger and stock market boom; and Hoover's new approach, which was quickly backed up with stricter enforcement, explains the crash and part of the volatility that followed. At the same time, the DOJ prosecuted trade associations whose activities had been approved under Coolidge (either by the FTC or by the Justice Department itself), notably in oil; wool; and bolts, nuts, and rivets. The Department also forced the FTC to revise its trade practice conferences, and trim back industry privileges under existing codes.[4]

Calls for antitrust reform followed immediately, and as the 1930 recession turned into the Great Depression, the proposals became more radical. Gerard

2. See, e.g., American Column & Lumber Co. v. U.S., 257 U.S. 377 (1921).

3. This period is discussed in J. M. Clark, Economics and the National Recovery Administration, 24 Amer. Econ. Rev. 11 (1934); Hawley (1966); Himmelberg (1976); and chapter 1 of Charles Frederick Roos, NRA Economic Planning (1937). The *U.S. Steel* and *International Harvester* cases are discussed by Milton Handler, Legal Aspects of Industrial Mergers, in Federal Antitrust Laws: A Symposium Conducted at Columbia University (1932). The activities of the War Industries Board are covered by Bernard Baruch, American Industry in the War: A Report of the War Industries Board (1921, reprinted 1941). The Federal Trade Commission conducted a lengthy study and defense of the open-price movement in 1929; the subject is taken up in its annual reports.

4. Himmelberg (1976) discusses this development in detail.

Swope, chairman of General Electric, offered a plan in 1931 that was a forerunner of the NIRA, especially in its linkage of antitrust and labor reform. It called for compulsory membership in industry trade groups and restrictions on output and prices. The Swope Plan also included workmen's compensation, unemployment insurance, disability and old-age insurance, and employee representation. Hoover rejected the plan out of hand as fascist, but business kept up the pressure for changes in antitrust.[5]

Appalachian Coals

The agreement at issue in *Appalachian Coals, Inc. v. United States*[6] was written in December 1931 under the direction of Colonel Donovan, Coolidge's antitrust chief. Since an industrywide agreement would have run afoul of the antitrust laws, the National Coal Association called for the formation of regional sales organizations, one of which was Appalachian Coals. The agreement covered about 12 percent of U.S. output of bituminous coal east of the Mississippi.

Hoover's antitrust enforcer, John Lord O'Brian, informed the producers in January 1932 that he would challenge their plan, and the suit was filed June 29, 1932; the trial opened on August 1, 1932. The district court held the organization illegal on October 3, and the appeal was heard by the Supreme Court on January 9, 1933. The textile, glass, and lumber industries entered *amicus curiae* briefs. The Supreme Court's decision, reversing the district court, established a rule of reason standard for the sales agency. It was handed down on March 13, at the end of the banking holiday that ran from March 4 through 14.

The trade press welcomed the court's new approach, regarding it as ''the first step in scrapping previous rigid interpretations of the Sherman act and ultimate liberalization of the whole concept of antitrust statutes.''[7] As had the Court itself, the press pointed out that the decision put joint sales agencies on the same footing as mergers and permitted firms greater flexibility in choosing their preferred organizational form. A merger of 12 percent of U.S. capacity, even if geographically concentrated, would have gone unchallenged in the 1920s or early 1930s. Stocks moved up sharply when the exchanges reopened on March 15, by about 18 percent on average from March 1. The trade press credited various factors for the increase: the market's approval of the president's policies, and ''the promise of rigid economy in the Federal

---

5. The debate over antitrust is summarized in Himmelberg (1976); Ellis Hawley, Herbert Hoover and the Sherman Act, 1921–1933: An Early Phase of a Continuing Issue, 74 Iowa L. Rev. 1067 (1989); and Bittlingmayer (1993c), who also tests statistically the proposition that shifting policy and the debate over antitrust reform affected stock prices.

6. 288 U.S. 344 (1933).

7. Journal of Commerce and LaSalle Street Journal, March 14, 1933, at 1.

Administration." Alternatively, the Supreme Court's renunciation of the per se rule against cartels may have moved stock prices upwards. The gain for bituminous coal was particularly strong—27.9 percent.

The First One Hundred Days and the NIRA

Pressure for antitrust reform mounted before FDR's inauguration. On February 18, while the coal case was before the Supreme Court, business representatives took a draft of proposed legislation to brain-truster and leading "business planning" advocate Adolph Berle, who in turn took it to Roosevelt. Manufacturers also contacted other advisors on the issue.[8] According to Galambos, the coal decision encouraged reform efforts, but also complicated the situation.[9] Though the antitrust issue was "getting red hot" by the end of March, according to Berle, Roosevelt paid little attention to the revisionists, except in natural-resource industries, where he had apparently made some pre-inauguration promises.[10] The administration's early proposals and actions centered on labor, public works, emergency relief, and banking.

A key legislative development was Senator Hugo Black's labor bill, reported out favorably by the Senate Judiciary Committee on March 30. It would have limited the workweek to thirty hours as a "work-sharing" measure. Roosevelt considered it too radical and economically inflexible, but an administration effort to set the limit higher, at thirty-six hours, was defeated on April 5. The original bill passed the Senate by fifty-three to thirty on Apirl 6.

Roosevelt sought some way of channeling the political pressure for economic reform. In an interview with a leader of the trade-association movement on April 11, he rejected antitrust revision as too sensitive politically.[11] However, on the same day, he instructed his advisor Ray Moley to get in touch with advocates of "recovery plans," which typically included antitrust relief. Building on the work-sharing notion in two press conferences, held April 12 and April 14, Roosevelt floated the idea of finding a constitutional means of allowing firms to curtail production.[12] Originally, he backed labor secretary Perkins's bill, which would have fixed wages and allowed the labor secretary to limit hours of operation, but dropped it because of business

---

8. Louis Galambos, Competition and Cooperation: The Emergence of a National Trade Association 187–88 (1966); Himmelberg (1976, 184).

9. Galambos, *supra* note 8, at 191.

10. Ibid., at 194; Himmelberg (1976, 187–89).

11. According to Walker Hines, "The President [said] that the matter was so controversial that he could not see his way to deal with it in the present situation." Himmelberg (1976, 189). Hines was a National Association of Manufacturers representative and former president and chairman, as well as current counsel, of the Cotton Textile Institute, later the first industry group to get an approved code under the NRA. Galambos, *supra* note 8, at 194.

12. Galambos, *supra* note 8, at 195.

opposition.[13] Rumors of an NIRA-like plan began to circulate in the press on April 14 and 19, and Roosevelt supported Senator Robert Wagner's series of conferences in late April to draft a "start-up" plan.[14] Wagner's plan included provisions for industry codes as well as for public works. The White House also dropped hints that it would support more than wage and hour legislation in the April 30 press release of FDR's May 4 speech to the Chamber of Commerce. Senator Robinson offered encouragement to antitrust reformers in a May 1 press statement, after meeting with FDR.[15] The Dow industrials increased 39.8 percent from April 1 to May 1, and the 351 Standard industrials rose 42.5 percent, using the closest dates from Standard's weekly series of March 29 and May 3.

The first draft NIRA bill was introduced in Congress on May 17. Though the constitutional hazards were widely appreciated, the bill was reported out by the House Ways and Means Committee on May 23, and accepted by the House 325 to 76 on May 26. The Dow increased another 14.5 percent in May. This remarkable, broad-based increase in stock prices in April and May is discussed further below.

As passed, the National Industrial Recovery Act's Title I declared a national emergency and suspended the antitrust laws for two years. Industry representatives could draw up codes of conduct, approvable by the president and enforceable in court. Labor was granted collective bargaining, freedom to join unions, and the requirement that employers observe maximum hours, minimum pay and other restrictions. Sectors exempted from the NIRA included agriculture, railroads, government, domestic service, the professions, non-profit institutions, and others.[16] Section 7(a) of the NIRA, allowing collective bargaining, later formed the basis for the National Labor Relations Act. Title II concerned public works.[17] The original appropriation of $3.3 billion over two years amounted to a per annum expenditure of 2.6 percent of GNP, by no means lavish given the circumstances. The final bill also included capital-stock and excess-profits taxes in Title III to help fund the public works projects. After a close vote in the Senate (see table 17.1), Roosevelt signed the bill and appointed Hugh Johnson administrator on June 16. The market reached its peak for 1933 on July 18, two days after FDR signed the first code, that for cotton textiles, which contained provisions

13. Himmelberg (1976, 198–203). Roos, *supra* note 3, claims the Perkins bill was intended to block passage of the Black bill in the house.
14. Frank Friedel, Franklin D. Roosevelt: Launching of the New Deal 423 (1973).
15. Himmelberg (1976, 200).
16. Leverett S. Lyon, Paul T. Homan, Lewis L. Lorwin, George Terbough, Charles L. Dearing, and Leon C. Marshall, The National Recovery Administration: An Analysis and Appraisal 791 (1935). Utilities and anthracite coal never had codes, but this was "due to no lack of effort, but merely the failure to reach agreement." Ibid., at 141. Agriculture was regulated by the Agricultural Adjustment Act and the Farm Relief Act, both signed May 12, 1933. Friedel, *supra* note 14, at 337.
17. Bernard Bellush, The Failure of the NRA 12–15 (1975).

Table 17.1   Selected Dates in the Passage and Demise of the NRA

	1933
Mar. 30	Black bill reported out favorably by Senate Judiciary Committee.
Apr. 5	Administration's amendment of Black bill rejected 48 to 41. Would have set maximum hours at 36 per week instead of 30.
Apr. 6	Senate adopts original bill 53–30.
Apr. 12	First FDR press conference.
Apr. 14	Second FDR press conference.
May 7	Fireside chat on new draft bill.
May 10	Meeting convenes at White House.
May 17	NIRA emerges on floor of Congress. FDR's message to Congress.
May 23	House Ways and Means reports NIRA bill favorably.
May 26	House votes 325–76 for NIRA.
Jun. 7	Two days of Senate debate.
Jun. 9	Senate votes 57–25 for bill, 58–24 in second vote.
Jun. 10	House approves conference bill.
Jun. 13	Senate votes 46–39 to accept conference bill.
Jun. 16	FDR signs NIRA, Johnson named head of NRA.
Jun. 23	Johnson reverses himself, permits price fixing.
Jul. 15	FDR delegates broad powers to administrator.
Jul. 16	FDR signs textile code.
Jul. 19	FDR signs blanket code.
Aug. 19	Iron and Steel code signed.
Aug. 29	Lumber and Timber code signed.
Sep. 2	Petroleum code.
Sep. 5	Automobile code.
Sept. 11	Cast Iron Soil Pipe code.
Sept. 18	Bituminous code.
Oct. 13	Glass Container code.
Oct. 25	Memo on what NRA would allow.
Nov. 6	Beet Sugar code.
Nov. 17	National Emergency Council created.
Nov. 27	Paper and Pulp code.
Dec. 7	Cement code.
	1935
April	Circuit Court sustains *Schechter* conviction.
May	Senate Finance Committee limits NRA to interstate business; forbids price fixing except in mineral-resource industries.
May 14	Senate OKs resolution on NRA by voice vote.
May 27	Supreme Court *Schechter* decision—voids Title I, including Section 7(a).
Jun. 14	Remnants of Title I renewed by joint resolution until 1 April 1936.

fairly generous to industry. The Dow was 95 percent above its value on March 1, and the Standard industrials were up 124 percent.

The NRA and the Codes

The National Industrial Recovery Act contained little that restricted the form of industry codes. Johnson initially rejected industry price fixing, then re-

Table 17.2   Provisions of Selected Codes Approved in 1933

		Limits on		
No.	Name and Date	Productive Mach. Hrs.	Capacity	Plant Production
1	Cotton Textile 7/16	X	X	
3	Wool Textile 8/14	X		
9	Lumber and Timber 8/29			X
10	Petroleum 9/2		X	X
11	Iron and Steel 8/19		X	X
17	Automobile 9/5			
18	Cast Iron Soil Pipe 9/11	X		
24	Bituminous Coal 10/9			
28	Transit 10/2		X	
36	Glass Container 10/13		X	X
	Sugar Beet 11/6			
44	Boot and Shoe 10/13			
109	Crushed Stone, Sand 11/20		X	
119	Newsprint 11/27	X		
120	Paper and Pulp 11/27			
128	Cement 11/7		X	
151	Can Manufacture 12/30			

Source: Leverett S. Lyon, Paul T. Homan, Lewis L. Lorwin, George Terbough, Charles L. Dearing, and Leon C. Marshall, The National Recovery Administration: An Analysis and Appraisal (1935), at 626–28, 630–31, and 634–35; and Charles Frederick Roos, NRA Economic Planning (1937), Appendix IV.

versed himself on June 23. Proposals flowed in quickly, and after negotiations with NRA administrators, codes were signed in major industries. For selected major codes, table 17.2 gives the code name, its number (sequence) and indicates whether it contained limits on capacity, production, or hours. This table does not include the many prohibitions on selling below cost (352 out of 677 codes), permissions granted to a code authority to reject as ''unfair'' (too low) prices filed by firms under an open-price system, prohibitions of ''loss leaders,'' and declarations of emergency price fixing by the NRA itself. According to critics, early code signers received these generous powers as inducements to sign up.[18] The negotiated agreements had the force of law, though enforcement was uneven, especially later.[19] A total of 162 codes were signed by the end of December, covering 12 of the 20 million employees whose industries were eligible under the act. By May of 1934, the number of covered workers stabilized at about 18 million.[20]

The first code signed governed cotton textiles. Textile manufacturers had

18. Lyon et al., *supra* note 16, at 17, 53.
19. Ibid., at 31.
20. Ibid., at 309 (chart).

long used trade associations, and were among the first industries to seek and obtain codes. The linkage between production and labor provisions (elimination of night work and a ban on the employment of children) had been used since 1929, often with Hoover's support. The Cotton Textile Institute was an early and important supporter of antitrust reform. In fact, FDR's fireside chat of May 7, 1933, in outlining the recovery bill, used cotton textiles to illustrate how antitrust laws led to competition that in turn led to "long hours, starvation wages and overproduction."[21] The cotton textile draft code was prepared in early June, before the final votes on the bill, and President Roosevelt approved it on July 16 while sailing on the Potomac.[22]

Besides the mandatory inclusion of Section 7(a), the code's major provisions were a minimum wage and maximum hours of 40 hours per week, a two-shift limit on production, and control of entry and expansion. Similar codes soon followed in related industries under the NRA's "Textile Division."[23] A brief flirtation with "suggested price lists" by the industry's Code Authority never went very far because of NRA disapproval, but terms of sale were controlled, much as they had been under the 1920s code. At the initiative of industry, an extra 25 percent decrease in hours was approved by the NRA, over the objection of the NRA's economists.[24] In the summer of 1935, after the *Schechter* decision had declared the NRA unconstitutional, 90 percent of the cotton textile firms still adhered to the NRA standards.[25]

The code for the bituminous coal industry, which included the *Appalachian Coal* defendants, was signed in October 1933. It declared illegal "selling of coal under a fair market price," with the minimum prices for various grades and sizes established by a marketing agency acting for two-thirds of the represented coal producers. The cement code allowed the Cement Institute to allocate "available business among members," subject to a majority vote. The paper and pulp code required advance notice of price changes, quotation of prices on a delivered basis, and prices that were above cost and above the "lowest price scheduled for such product . . . by any other member and then in effect."[26]

Other large-industry codes signed in the late summer and fall of 1933 appear more innocent. For example, the automobile code stipulated minimum wages, average maximum hours for workers, data collection, and the Section 7(a) provisions. The constraints were apparently not severe, and the industry

21. Galambos, *supra* note 8, at 198.
22. Ibid., at 212–13. "A swift relay carried the news to the Potomac, to Johnson's office, to New York City. Champagne corks popped and the manufacturers and association leaders celebrated their success." Ibid., at 225.
23. Lyon et al., *supra* note 16, at 626–27, list 44 textile industries with machine- or plant-hour limitations.
24. Galambos, *supra* note 8, at 247–48.
25. Ibid., at 288.
26. Lewis Mayers, A Handbook of the NRA 468–69, 491, 708–9 (2d ed. 1934).

obtained a "clarification" of Section 7(a) to permit it to keep an open shop. Negotiated in August 1933, it seems to have been a public relations ploy intended to benefit both the auto industry and the NRA.[27] Later controversy and new codes in this industry centered more on labor issues.[28]

An important early development was the President's Reemployment Agreement, the "blanket code" for which the familiar Blue Eagle insignia was invented. It dealt only with labor issues, stipulating a maximum 35-hour week for blue-collar workers, 40 hours for white-collar, minimum wages for different labor categories (40 cents per hour for labor, $15 per week for white collar employees in cities of over 500,000 population, less for smaller cities), and collective bargaining.[29] It was a bilateral "voluntary" agreement between the president and individual firms (i.e., it did not involve industry associations), and had to be submitted by the end of August.[30] Superficially, "these [agreements] gave employers higher labor costs, but no gains excepting whatever satisfaction was obtained from participating in what many no doubt regarded as a patriotic movement."[31] However, participating firms expected special consideration when their industry codes were presented to the NRA. More important, government contracts were contingent on the Blue Eagle, and signers agreed not to deal with non-signers. About 16 million employees were soon covered.[32] The possible signal value of the blanket code also deserves emphasis. Lyons et al. contend that the cotton textile code and the blanket code jointly established precedents and revealed the sorts of provisions that the president would approve through the NRA.[33]

News stories of a blanket code first surfaced on July 6, 1933. It was controversial within the administration, with Commerce Secretary Roper and others opposing it. Details of the plan appeared on July 19, when the Industrial Recovery Board—composed of cabinet members—approved the plan.[34] Roosevelt on July 20 wrote, "If it turns out that the general agreement bears unfairly on any group of employers they can have that straightened out by presenting promptly their proposed code of fair competition."[35] The Dow declined 4.7, 7.1, and 7.8 percent on July 19, 20, and 21, for a net decline of 18.4 percent. The trade press viewed the drop as correcting the spring boom. Alternatively, if the blanket code's revelation of the president's ideal labor provisions and its coercive elements caused the decline, industries with

27. Bellush, *supra* note 17, at 94–97.
28. Roos, *supra* note 3, at 213–15.
29. Lyon et al., *supra* note 16, at 306–7; Bellush, *supra* note 17, at 48–52.
30. Charles L. Dearing, Paul T. Homan, Lewis L. Lorwin, and Leverett S. Lyon, The ABC of the NRA 63 (1934).
31. Lyon et al., *supra* note 16, at 53.
32. Ibid., at 30.
33. Ibid., at 304–8.
34. Journal of Commerce and LaSalle Street Journal, July 19, 1933, p. 1.
35. Letter to New York Times, July 21, 1993, p. 1.

a large share of labor expense should have experienced the largest declines. A test of this hypothesis appears below.

Schechter

The NIRA experienced major ups and downs over the next eighteen months.[36] NRA Administrator Hugh Johnson—energetic but arguably mentally unstable—was ultimately forced to resign. Congress and an independent commission reviewed the NRA's operations amid heated charges. Conflict between small and large firms erupted, and between those vertically integrated and those not. The labor provisions also generated friction. By early 1935, the NIRA's future was in doubt. A Brookings study released early that year was critical of the law and apparently influential in strengthening opposition to it.[37] A Senate investigation yielded at best mixed support for the NRA. In mid-May 1935, the Senate Finance Committee favored only a ten-month extension with new limits placed on the NRA, while the House seemed likely to support a two-year extension with the law's old provisions largely intact.[38] But legal developments soon made all this moot.

Schechter Poultry Corp. v. United States[39] involved charges filed against a kosher poultry supplier in Brooklyn. Defendants were charged in two counts with wage and hours violations, and in ten counts with violating trade practice provisions requiring those buying from a slaughterhouse to "accept the run of any half coop, coop, or coops, as purchased by the slaughterhouse operators." Other charges included filing false reports, violating city inspection ordinances, and otherwise violating the fair competition code for "Live Poultry in and about Metropolitan New York." Schechter Poultry lost in district court in October 1934, and again in circuit court in April 1935, though it prevailed there on the claim that the wage and hours provisions were not within the powers of Congress.

The Supreme Court heard arguments on May 2 and 3, and handed down its decision on the afternoon of May 27, declaring Title I of the NIRA (including Section 7[a]) an invalid delegation of legislative power and an unconstitutional regulation of intrastate trade.[40] The Dow industrials dropped 2.6 percent the following day and 1.6 percent the day after. Volume on May 28 was 2.3 million shares, higher than on any day in the first half of 1935. As shown below, the reaction varied greatly by sector.

Although a blow to industry, the *Schechter* case was neither completely unexpected nor fatal to the cause of "industrial self-government." As dis-

---

36. See generally Hawley (1966); Bellush, *supra* note 17.

37. Lyon et al., *supra* note 16.

38. Bellush, *supra* note 17, at 165–67.

39. 295 U.S. 495 (1935).

40. For discussions, see Hawley (1966, 128); Bellush, *supra* note 17, at 168–70.

cussed above with respect to cotton textiles, some industry codes were still observed, though no longer legally enforceable. Industry representatives also put forth new plans for a "business commonwealth" (Hawley 1966, 149–51). Moreover, the NIRA had been temporary legislation; renewal, clearly a risky bet in May 1935, would have won at most two more years. And the *Appalachian Coals* decision still stood. *Schechter* also invalidated the labor provisions of the NIRA, a result seemingly of benefit to business.[41] For business, *Schechter's* unmitigated bad news was the end of the NIRA's suspension of antitrust enforcement.

Economic Effects of the NIRA

The Competing Hypotheses

The *Appalachian Coals* holding—cartels were not per se illegal but subject to a rule of reason—had already advanced producers' ability to cartelize. But the suspension of antitrust inherent in the NRA codes moved actual practice much further. The question of interest is whether these developments increased output.

The textbook economics of cartels might seem to make the answer a foregone conclusion. Cartels lower output. In the case of the NRA, the support of the government lowers the costs of organization, but political reality imposes new constraints and costs, and redistributes some rents to labor. The straightforward monopoly view of the NRA is reflected in Hawley (1966), but is doubtless the prevailing view among economists as well.

Telser (1978, 1985, 1987) offers a different perspective on cartels and cooperative behavior using the "theory of the core." Part of the theory of cooperative games, core theory shows that a competitive equilibrium often does not exist. Take an industry composed of firms with identical U-shaped average cost curves (what Telser calls a "Viner industry"). Suppose that only a few firms supply the efficient rate of output. The supply curve, which is the horizontal sum of the marginal cost curves, is scalloped. The scallops arise because we have to add or subtract discrete lumps of capacity as we change output. Industry average cost reaches a minimum only at output rates that are integer multiples of the rate at which any given firm produces at minimum average cost. Moreover, the demand curve now typically crosses the supply curve at a point where marginal cost is either greater than average cost or less than average cost. However, a competitive equilibrium requires that marginal and average cost be the same, that is, that firms operate where average cost is at a minimum. So, for most rates of demand, there is no competitive equilibrium—the core is "empty." (The exception occurs if the

---

41. Later experience with a more pliable Supreme Court showed, however, that similar labor measures could pass constitutional muster.

demand curve happens to cross supply where average and marginal cost are equal, and average cost is at a minimum.) Economists sometimes call this the "integer problem." In a more general model, a combination of increasing returns, fixed costs and variable demand is often fatal for a competitive equilibrium.

Restrictions on competition can re-establish equilibrium, so that the theory offers a new rationale for cartels and predictions about what sorts of restrictions will emerge. More broadly, this approach derives competitive and collusive outcomes as the result of given cost and demand conditions, rather than simply assuming that competition is always possible regardless of what we assume about costs and demand. Core theory has recently, but only recently, stimulated empirical work on the classic problems of industrial organization,[42] including the famous *Addyston Pipe* antitrust case.[43]

The common law of restraints on trade prior to the Sherman Act is interesting in this respect. The common law, often viewed as more likely to promote efficiency than statutes do, did not prohibit cartels outright, holding them instead to a rule of reason. Grady (1992) recently looked at the common law cases rejected by Judge William Howard Taft in his celebrated *Addyston* opinion. He concluded that the facts, as well as the reasoning offered by the judges, comport with the view that the judges weighed the costs and benefits of horizontal restraints of trade and sought to maximize economic efficiency. Specifically, the courts did not strike down cartels in industries marked by high fixed costs or relatively elastic demand—that is, when the presumption of a core problem was great or the possible harm from cartelization small.

Clearly, the fixed-cost (or integer) problem puts a new light on the relaxation of the per se rule against cartels in *Applachian Coals,* and on the NIRA's suspension of antitrust and enforcement of industry codes. The effects of more lax antitrust during this episode may have been quite different from what the conventional theory of monopoly predicts. With high fixed costs, marginal-cost pricing may not generate enough revenue to cover the economically efficient rate of output. If the prospect of antitrust revision

---

42. See, for example, William Sjostrom, Collusion in Ocean Shipping: A Test of Monopoly and Empty Core Models, 97 J. Pol. Econ. 1160 (1989); and Steven Craig Pirrong, An Application of Core Theory to the Analysis of Ocean Shipping Markets, 35 J. Law & Econ. 89 (1992). Sjostrom and Pirrong show in independent studies that ocean shipping is marked by precisely the cost conditions that lead to problems for competitive outcomes. They also offer evidence that widespread cartelization in this industry, which goes back over one hundred years, promotes efficiency.

43. Bittlingmayer (1982, 1983) finds that the cost conditions faced by cartel members in *Addyston Pipe* were incompatible with a competitive equilibrium, and that the cartel's structure fostered the efficient recovery of fixed costs. The problems raised by fixed costs also facilitated the Great Merger Wave at the turn of the century, as explained in chapter 8 of this volume and, using a different model, in Naomi Lamoreaux, The Great Merger Movement in American Business, 1895–1904 (1985).

increased the likelihood that existing or future cooperative arrangements would in fact allow the recovery of fixed costs, firms marked by high fixed costs and variable demand would have been more likely to make investments in both tangible and intangible capital. At an aggregate level, capital expenditures should have increased. So instead of dragging output down, as the standard analysis predicts, the antitrust features of the NIRA may have boosted output. The Recovery Act of 1933 may in fact have promoted recovery.

The textbook and core-theory perspectives on cartels thus make diametrically different predictions about output under suspended antitrust. Unfortunately for empiricists, the NIRA was not pure antitrust suspension. It was emergency legislation and limited to two years. It ordered compulsion where some firms wanted freedom. Politics surely played a role also, since a presidential appointee, not a common law judge, approved the codes. For example, some of the restrictions resembled the inefficient protection often offered declining industries. The far-reaching labor provisions governing wages, hours, and collective bargaining worked at cross-purposes to antitrust relief— indeed, they were the quid pro quo for it. The NRA was also disorganized, controversial, and poorly led. Finally, its vast administrative discretion threatened the power of the courts and was, perhaps for that reason, constitutionally suspect from day one. The net effect of these other aspects of the NIRA is unclear, but they probably introduced uncertainty and extra costs, and lowered output.

Aside from its narrow economic costs and benefits, and the politics and controversy it stimulated, the NIRA may have had a major effect through the signal it gave about business policy to come. Its passage showed that a Democratic Congress and president could trim back major economic regulation, at least in return for new burdens. Antitrust was historically associated with attacks on business, and the NIRA, for all its faults, achieved some long-sought antitrust reforms that business wanted.

All that said, the NIRA remains a remarkable natural experiment. The familiar theory of cartels predicts a decline in output. The efficiency explanation predicts an increase in investment and holds out the prospect of an increase in output as a whole. From theory, let us turn to actual experience.

Aggregate Movements

Figures 17.1 through 17.5 show monthly economic data for January 1930 through December 1935, the period that covers the descent into the Great Depression and the partial and erratic revival thereafter. This period has been the focus of a spirited debate on the role of money. The broad developments reveal here, as they do at other times, that movements in money, prices, and

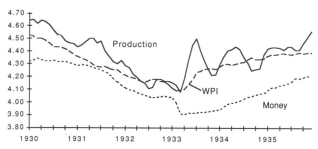

Figure 17.1   Industrial production, wholesale prices (WPI), and money, 1930–1935
Sources: Geoffrey H. Moore, Business Cycle Indicators, vol. 2 (1961); Milton Friedman and
Anna J. Schwartz, A Monetary History of the United States, 1867–1960 (1963), App. A,
table A-1; and U.S. Bureau of the Census, Historical Statistics of the United States,
1789–1945 (1949).

output are correlated, over the long-term. Monetary explanations for the
decline of both the price level and output from early 1930 through 1932
emphasize the decline in the stock of money and the failure of the Federal
Reserve to function as a lender of last resort. However, some of the short-term
movements in prices and output seem largely unrelated to monetary developments. These issues arise again in mid-1933.

Consider figure 17.1, which shows industrial production, wholesale prices,
and money. While M2 (currency plus demand and savings accounts) declined
3.1 percent through March of 1931, the decline was modest compared to that
in prices and output—15.8 and 15.7 percent. At least arithmetically, most
of the price decline was due to an increase in real balances (M2 divided by
the price level). Real balances often increase during periods of uncertainty.
Note that industrial production actually increased in the first quarter of 1931,
as did stock prices, though there were no monetary movements in the same
direction. Money, prices, and output were erratic through late 1932 and
declined markedly.

The year 1933 shows a remarkable divergence between money and the
other two aggregate measures. M2 declines by roughly 12 percent in the first
quarter of 1933, and then increases slowly over the next two years.[44] Prices
and production, in contrast, both move up sharply in the second quarter of

44. Milton Friedman and Anna J. Schwartz, A Monetary History of the United States, 1867–
1960 (1963) at 428–34, point out that part of the observed drop in money occurs because
restricted and unrestricted deposits in unlicensed banks are excluded from the money stock
measure after the March 1933 bank holiday. They construct an alternative series that *includes*
restricted deposits before and after March 1933 to obtain a consistent estimate. This measure
declines more slowly, only 7 percent from January to June 1933, but the decline extends farther
through the end of 1933. Friedman and Schwartz argue that the economically relevant measure
of money would fall somewhere in between the two series.

1933. Various causes have been advanced for the price increase, among them the declining value of the dollar abroad, forcing wholesale prices up; the Agricultural Adjustment Act, which increased farm prices; and anticipation of the NIRA. A fear of "reflationist" measures may also have influenced the price level. These varying explanations were all advanced in the mid-1930s,[45] and repeated in later commentary.[46]

What is clear is that the increase in prices cannot be explained by increases in monetary aggregates. Moreover, output growth greatly outstripped price changes: production increased by 53 percent from March to July, and prices by 14 percent. Lyon et al. attributed the surge in production to the anticipation of price hikes under the NRA, as do Friedman and Schwartz.[47] While money and prices trend upward at roughly the same 10 percent annual rate, industrial production suffers two downturns and revivals during the NRA's reign.

The evidence seems to force the following conclusion. The decline in M2 and in the price level over 1930–1933 may explain some of the fall in real output. But some unusual short-term movements in output and prices, for both 1930–1932 and 1933–1935, seem to have non-monetary origins. Clearly, the NIRA is a candidate for the surge of production; it is also not obvious from the economic data in figure 17.1 that output after the surge was lower than it otherwise would have been so as to justify the conclusion of a net *negative* effect, as the standard cartel model would predict.

The record of stock prices offers extra insight. If the NRA did force an inefficient reshuffling of production and an overall lower level during its term, broad stock indexes should have declined or at best stayed constant. The actual record shows something else. As figure 17.2 shows, stock prices largely mirror production for 1930–1935. Their first major rebound occurs in July and August of 1932, after the party conventions, when it became

45. Lyon et al., *supra* note 16, 786–89, computed a cost-of-living index that was otherwise flat, but advanced about 9 percent from June through September 1933. They play down the influence of monetary experimentation because that policy was active before the surge in prices (i.e., before April 1933), as well as after, especially with the gold- and silver-buying programs of late 1933 and early 1934. Lyon et al. conclude that the NIRA was responsible for the bulk of the mid-1933 price increase.

46. Friedman and Schwartz, *supra* note 44, at 496–98, credit anticipation of the NIRA codes and depreciation of the dollar for the 1933 spurt in prices. In fact, they attribute the price increases of the 1933–1937 period as a whole to the NIRA, the Guffey Coal Act, farm price supports, and the National Labor Relations Act. "This is the only period in the near-century we cover for which [a wage-price or price-wage spiral] . . . seems clearly justified." However, they stress the need for a rising money supply, which occurred *after* 1933. Weinstein reaches the same conclusion by using a two-equation Philips curve system and dummies for the period of the NRA. See Michael M. Weinstein, Recovery and Redistribution under the NIRA (1980), especially chap. 2.

47. "Whatever may have been the long-run effects of the NRA program, there can be no doubt that it evoked a temporary burst of industrial activity." Lyon et al., *supra* note 16, at 797. See also Friedman and Schwartz, *supra* note 44, at 493–95.

clear that Roosevelt would win the election and when *Appalachian Coals* started its fast-track progress to the Supreme Court. A goodly fraction of those gains are erased by March of 1933. However, all three Dow averages— industrials, railroads, and utilities—increase in excess of 60 percent from April through July 1933, at the time the NRA was discussed and passed. These gains are much larger than the 15-percent increase in the price level, and pose a serious obstacle to the view that the NRA merely caused an acceleration of production based on anticipated price increases.

Figures 17.3–17.5 confirm the general picture of a broad-based revival in production as the NIRA was passed and the NRA established. Figure 17.3 breaks down total industrial production into durable and non-durable goods. The data show an abrupt surge in the first half of 1933; despite fluctuations later in the year, production stayed above the level prevailing in 1931 and 1932. The single-industry components of figure 17.4—pig iron, passenger cars, and crude oil—also move up. These industries are highlighted because iron and petroleum were among the industries with the largest doses of "industrial self-government" under the NRA, while the auto industry's code was largely cosmetic, at least at first.

Figure 17.2   Natural log of Dow industrials, railroads, and utilities, 1930–1935
Source: Phyllis Pearce, The Dow-Jones Averages, 1885–1980 (1982).

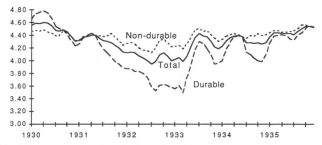

Figure 17.3   Natural log of total production, durable and nondurable, 1930–1935
Source: Federal Reserve Board, not seasonally adjusted; U.S. Bureau of the Census, *supra* Figure 17.1.

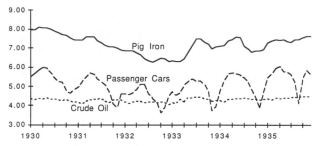

Figure 17.4   Natural log of production of pig iron, passenger cars, and crude oil
Source: Standard Statistics, various issues.

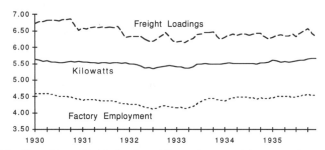

Figure 17.5   Natural log of freight loadings, kilowatt hours, and factory employment
Source: Standard Statistics, various issues.

Finally, figure 17.5 shows that three other indices of real output—freight loadings, kilowatt hours, and factory employment—show varying degrees of revival. Railroads and utilities were not codified under the NRA; their level of activity presumably reflects the general business climate. Manufacturing came under the codes for the most part, and the recorded increase in factory employment reflects the joint effects of the work-sharing provisions of the code and increased production.

Statistical Tests

Holding other things constant, was output lower *during* the NRA? Regressions presented in tables 17.3 and 17.4 explore the issue, using quarterly data from the first quarter of 1930 (1930:I) to the end of 1939 (1939:IV). The sample thus includes the recession of 1937–1938, as well as the Great Depression itself; estimates confined to 1930–1935 yield largely similar results, however.

Table 17.3 regresses the natural logs of durable and nondurable output on the natural logs of stock prices, wholesale prices, the money supply (M2) and a time trend variable. The regression model also contains a dummy

Table 17.3   Regressions of Durable and Nondurable Output on Stock Prices, Wholesale Prices, Money, and NRA Dummy: First Quarter 1930–Last Quarter 1939

	I Dependent Variable: Ln Durable Output				
Constant	.50	−19.84	−5.27	−12.49	−6.79
	(1.59)	(6.33)	(1.59)	(4.74)	(2.16)
Ln Dow	.76	—	.61	—	.38
	(11.69)		(6.01)		(2.82)
Ln WPI	—	—	—	2.52	1.41
				(5.79)	(2.53)
Ln Money	—	2.27	.61	.55	.28
		(7.51)	(1.75)	(1.49)	(.82)
NRA	.036	.328	.129	−.00	.022
	(0.58)	(3.18)	(1.61)	(0.00)	(0.25)
Trend	.011	.002	.008	.005	.007
	(5.04)	(0.70)	(3.21)	(1.88)	(2.98)
R^2	.84	.71	.86	.85	.88
D-W	1.62	.64	1.45	1.09	1.46

	II Dependent Variable: Ln Nondurable Output				
Constant	3.26	−1.91	3.15	.08	3.03
	(30.33)	(1.69)	(2.64)	(0.08)	(2.46)
Ln Dow	.22	—	.21	—	.19
	(9.69)		(5.80)		(3.72)
Ln WPI	—	—	—	.69	.11
				(3.77)	(0.52)
Ln Money	—	.59	.01	.12	−.01
		(5.50)	(.09)	(0.78)	(0.10)
NRA	−.002	.069	.000	−.020	−.008
	(0.07)	(1.90)	(0.01)	(0.51)	(0.25)
Trend	.009	.007	.009	.007	.009
	(11.9)	(5.73)	(9.53)	(7.21)	(9.21)
R^2	.89	.78	.89	.85	.89
D-W	1.20	.70	1.20	.78	1.15

Note: "NRA" is a dummy variable for 1933:III through 1935:II. Absolute value of t-statistics appear in parentheses.
Sources: Durable and nondurable output, Federal Reserve Board, averages for quarter: U.S. Bureau of the Census (1949), Appendices 7–8, p. 331. Dow, daily value from end of quarter: Phyllis Pearce, The Dow-Jones Averages, 1885–1980 (1982). Wholesale price index, BLS end of quarter values: U.S. Bureau of the Census (1949), Appendix 23, p. 344. Money (currency, demand, and time deposits): Milton Friedman and Anna J. Schwartz, A Monetary History of the United States, 1867–1960 (1963), Appendix A, table A-1, col. 8.

variable, NRA, for 1933:III through 1935:II, the period of the National Recovery Administration. The pre-NIRA surge in production during the second quarter of 1933 is thus not captured by the dummy. Since both stock prices and wholesale prices increased sharply in mid-1933, plausibly as a result of the NRA, regressions that include those two variables still attribute a good deal of the higher output levels after the middle of 1933 to other factors and not to the NRA. The regressions are stacked against finding a positive NRA effect.

The table shows, first of all, that stock prices were positively related to output, a well-established result. More surprising is the finding that the relationship between wholesale prices and output is stronger than that between money and output. Finally, the NRA's measured effects are variable, depending on whether stock prices and wholesale prices are included. Recall that the NRA began precisely when stock prices and wholesale prices shot up. Regardless of the specification, however, the estimated effect of the NRA on real output, durable or nondurable, is never significant and negative, or large and negative.

The first column of the table's results deserves special attention. If, *ceteris paribus,* the NRA increased monopoly rents and caused a decline in production, the overall surge in production in 1933–1935 was necessarily due to some other factor, and output adjusted for the historical relationship with stock prices should have been lower during the NRA's reign. However, durable-goods output was 3.6 percent higher and nondurable-goods output was 0.2 percent lower. Note that the NRA dummy has large positive values when wholesale prices are not included in the durable output regression, and an especially large value when both stock prices and the WPI index are absent. Estimated increases in durable-goods output range as high as 32.8 percent in the first three columns, that is, without wholesale prices, but zero or 2.2 percent otherwise. The results for nondurable-goods output are roughly similar: output is higher by 6.9 percent when only the money supply is used as a control, but lower by 2.0 or 0.8 percent when wholesale prices are added.

Table 17.3 indicates autocorrelation of the residuals. The estimated standard errors could be biased as a result, but not the coefficient estimates.

To correct for autocorrelation, table 17.4 uses semi-differences of the original variables. For a series X_t, the semi-differences are calculated as $DX_t = X_t - 0.5(X_{t-1})$. (I use the 0.5 weight because it falls in the middle of the autocorrelation coefficients implied by the Durbin-Watson statistics in table 17.3.) Again, durable output is higher when only money is included, or only money and stock prices—by 13.2 and 9.6 percent. If wholesale prices are included the estimated effect is small, negative, and insignificant—between -2.0 and -0.2 percent. Nondurable-goods output was no higher or lower during the NRA than its correlation with other factors would have predicted. Estimated NRA coefficients range from -3.4 to 2.2 percent. These semi-difference regressions confirm the earlier result that stock prices and wholesale prices provide most of the explanatory power.[48]

---

48. These estimates were not materially affected by the problems in measuring the money stock during 1933 reported by Friedman and Schwartz, *supra* note 44, at 428–34. Using their

Table 17.4   Semi-Difference Regressions of Durable and Nondurable Output on Stock Prices, Wholesale Prices, Money, and NRA Dummy: Second Quarter 1930–Last Quarter 1939

	I Dependent Variable: D(Ln Durable Output)				
Constant	.69	−8.07	−4.94	−6.40	−5.26
	(2.52)	(3.56)	(2.11)	(3.18)	(2.39)
D(Ln Dow)	.56	—	.38	—	.19
	(4.78)		(2.88)		(1.22)
D(Ln WPI)	—	—	—	2.46	1.89
				(3.58)	(2.29)
D(Ln Money)	—	1.91	1.15	.60	.54
		(4.42)	(2.43)	(1.15)	(1.03)
NRA	.016	.132	.096	−.020	−.002
	(0.26)	(1.83)	(1.44)	(0.26)	(0.03)
Trend	.007	.003	.003	.002	.003
	(2.90)	(1.04)	(1.32)	(0.97)	(1.12)
R^2	.57	.54	.63	.67	.68
D-W	2.07	1.28	1.89	1.80	1.99

	II Dependent Variable: D(Ln Nondurable Output)				
Constant	1.66	−0.67	.76	−.06	.67
	(19.18)	(0.81)	(0.96)	(0.08)	(0.87)
D(Ln Dow)	.20	—	.18	—	.12
	(5.43)		(3.88)		(2.27)
D(Ln WPI)	—	—	—	.90	.53
				(3.58)	(1.85)
D(Ln Money)	—	.54	.18	.05	.01
		(3.38)	(1.14)	(.29)	(.06)
NRA	−.007	0.022	.006	−.034	−.022
	(0.36)	(0.84)	(0.24)	(1.22)	(.83)
Trend	.004	.004	.004	.004	.004
	(5.96)	(3.56)	(4.46)	(3.89)	(4.36)
R^2	.74	.64	.75	.74	.78
D-W	2.02	1.26	1.83	1.31	1.65

Note: Semi-differences of the variable X_t are calculated as $D(X_t) = X_t - 0.5(X_{t-1})$. Absolute value of t-statistics appear in parentheses.

Evaluated by the aggregate data shown in figures 17.1 through 17.3, and by the regression results in tables 17.3 and 17.4, output was higher while the NIRA was in effect. The NRA dummy does have a low positive or insignificantly negative coefficient when the level of wholesale prices is viewed as exogenous, but higher prices themselves were arguably the result of the law's operation. Durable-goods production in particular seems to have increased with the passage of the NIRA. If the NIRA depressed output, as

alternative measure of M2 yields coefficient estimates for the NRA (and for the money stock) that were in all cases either nearly identical to those reported in the text or even more positive.

has been conventionally believed, that case is hard to make based on the data or results here.

Industry-by-Industry Stock Prices

An increase in broad stock indices could still be consistent with output reduction—and thus consistent with the textbook monopoly explanations of the NIRA's consequences—if monopolies were (a) not too numerous in the economy overall, but (b) over-represented among publicly traded firms. Even so, passage of the NIRA should have affected some industries more than others. In fact, some should have been clear losers if the expected effects of the NIRA were simply to force higher costs on some and bestow monopoly gains on others. Some industries were not covered by the NIRA. Railroads and utilities came under a different regulatory regime. Banks and insurance companies were not subject to antitrust in the first place. If the NRA codes were just textbook cartelizing devices, these sectors should have suffered from passage of the NIRA.

Table 17.5 shows stock returns for the Dow industrials, the Standard industrials, and 45 industry groups. These returns are shown for four periods in 1933:

—March 1–15, which covers the bank holiday, March 4–14, when exchanges were closed, and the *Appalachian Coals* decision of March 13;
—March 15–April 5, which covers the period the Black labor bill was introduced and passed;
—April 5–July 12, which begins a week before Roosevelt first floated the idea of antitrust relief linked with labor law reform, and ends with the signing of the first NIRA code; and
—July 19–26, which covers the week during which details of the blanket code were revealed and approved by Roosevelt.[49]

Table 17.5 also includes returns for one week of 1935, May 22–29, which covers the *Schechter* decision of May 27. The table's last column shows the number of weeks, out of a total of 14, that the index in question moved up from April 5 to July 12, 1933.

The broad indices—Dow industrials and the three Standard series for industrials, railroads, and utilities—show a consistent picture. The period covered by the bank holiday and *Appalachian Coals* shows a strong increase of 18 percent, the period covered by the Black bill a substantial decrease of 7 to 19 percent, the 14 weeks covered by passage of the NIRA a strong but varied increase of 68 to 141 percent, and the week covered by approval of

49. The Dow dropped sharply on July 19, 20, and 21, so that the weekly data from Standard Statistics excludes the first decline, when the Dow fell 4.7 percent.

Table 17.5 Returns by Industry Group for Dates Associated with Various Events

| Index | No. of Stocks | Returns over: | | | | | Weeks Positive |
		Appalachian Coals	Black Bill	NIRA Passage	Blanket Code	*Schechter*	
Dow industrials	30	18.2	−7.4	81.8	−8.2	−3.9	14
Industrials	351	18.3	−7.6	104.7	−8.9	−4.7	14
Railroads	33	18.0	−19.0	141.2	−11.7	−.6	14
Utilities	37	10.6	−18.8	68.3	−8.4	4.4	12
Advertising	7	17.2	−0.7	138.5	−15.8	−5.2	10
Ag. implements	4	54.4	−4.6	113.1	−13.5	−10.5	13
Airplane mfg.	9	20.4	−11.3	110.1	−15.7	−8.6	10
Air transport	4	17.1	4.6	77.3	−15.1	−4.5	11
Apparel	8	27.6	−22.1	142.2	−19.2	−7.2	11
Autos	13	27.0	−13.8	178.6	−6.7	−4.7	13
Auto parts	16	19.4	−11.7	168.4	−15.1	−4.5	13
Auto tires	7	34.4	−18.7	216.2	−9.4	−4.7	11
Building equip.	12	19.1	−1.6	183.7	−10.9	−3.7	13
Chemicals	11	20.3	−9.6	94.1	−8.4	−4.3	14
Coal, anthracite	4	16.9	−18.8	178.6	−15.8	−1.2	11
Coal, bituminous	5	27.9	4.5	127.0	−13.6	−10.5	11
Copper	8	42.3	−14.4	148.7	−9.0	−16.5	10
Cotton	10	7.5	1.1	120.1	−12.2	−4.3	12
Drugs, medicine	7	14.3	−10.1	55.8	4.7	−1.2	11
Electrical equip.	4	22.9	−12.0	123.7	−11.6	−6.4	12
Fertilizer	4	27.4	24.1	121.4	−14.6	−13.6	10
Food, no meat	22	9.6	0.9	64.7	−5.5	−3.3	14
Household prdcts.	14	18.8	−6.9	95.3	−8.4	−1.9	14
Lead and zinc	5	22.6	−6.7	112.1	−4.8	−4.3	12
Leather	4	34.1	−6.2	272.5	−15.4	−15.8	12
Machinery	10	13.6	−6.6	104.2	−10.6	−3.4	13
Meat packing	5	33.9	0.3	98.0	−11.7	−2.4	8
Mining and smelt.	10	20.6	−6.5	123.7	−7.6	−8.0	11
Misc. mfg.	10	18.9	−12.3	103.1	−9.5	−2.7	13
Misc. service	4	18.0	−12.7	122.5	−13.2	−2.5	12
Business supply	5	24.7	0.2	98.8	−13.5	−2.9	12
Paper	7	−1.3	−22.2	522.7	−15.6	−8.6	13
Petroleum	15	11.3	−5.8	92.4	−9.3	−9.6	12
Radio	10	43.5	−19.3	208.7	−13.8	−10.7	11
Railroad equip.	9	13.6	10.4	130.7	−15.2	−1.2	11
Rayon	5	1.9	−13.0	168.2	−6.1	8.6	13
Retail trade	26	19.3	−6.5	90.5	−7.1	−0.7	14
Shipping	8	−1.0	9.3	166.5	−11.9	0.3	11
Silk	6	7.0	−4.4	252.7	−12.4	−0.9	13
Steel and iron	11	30.9	−10.7	163.7	−15.1	−7.1	14
Sugar	8	29.2	10.7	77.5	−6.7	−6.7	11
Textiles	28	12.4	−5.9	155.6	−13.9	−4.4	12
Theatres	7	1.9	−18.2	242.2	−17.4	−2.2	8
Tobacco	11	12.9	−1.8	53.6	−4.3	−1.2	14
NY banks	20	8.1	−24.9	52.8	−4.9	1.7	9

Table 17.5 *continued*

Index	No. of Stocks	Returns over: Appalachian Coals	Black Bill	NIRA Passage	Blanket Code	Schechter	Weeks Positive
Fire insurance	20	10.0	21.0	87.0	−6.9	0	13
Casualty ins.	13	9.8	−14.9	83.5	−8.4	2.2	11
Commodity prices			0.3	14.1			
British pound			4.3	29.9			
							Means: $t = 2.45$
SD, 4 to 9 firms		13.8	11.9	95.6	5.1		11.2
SD, 10 or more		8.6	7.4	45.5	3.2		12.7
F(24, 21)*		2.6	2.6	4.4	2.5		

*F-test based on ratio of variances.
Source: Standard Statistics, Standard Trade and Securities, Statistical Bulletin, December 1934.
Note: Appalachian Coals and Bank Holiday: March 1–March 15, 1933
Black Labor Bill: March 15–April 5, 1933
NIRA Passage: April 5–July 12, 1933
Blanket Code (President's Re-employment Agreement): July 19–July 26, 1933
Schechter: May 22–May 29, 1935
SD = standard deviation.

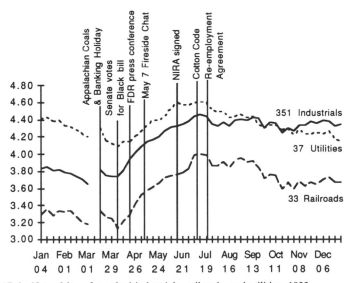

Figure 17.6   Natural log of standard industrials, railroads, and utilities, 1933
Source: Standard Statistics, Standard Trade and Securities, Statistical Bulletin, December 1934.

the blanket agreement a major decrease. Finally, *Schechter* was marked by a decline. Figure 17.6 plots the three major indices against some of the key dates for 1933.

Most noteworthy are stock returns over the period of the NIRA passage. Not only did stock prices roughly double, but the upward movement was very consistent. Each and every week for all four major indices (Dow industrials, Standard industrials, railroads, and utilities) was marked by an advance, with the exception of two weeks for the utility stocks. All stocks show increases in excess of the price level increase. (The 523-percent increase in the value of paper and paper product stocks is not an error.) U.S. commodity prices increased only 14 percent, and the British pound 30 percent. The latter figure is almost surely an overestimate of U.S. inflation. Still, using that number leaves a 70 percent increase in real terms in the 351-firm Standard industrial average.

Even more interesting, not a single industry experienced a *reduction* in stock returns during the passage of the NIRA. This includes sectors that were under a different regulatory regime, like railroads and utilities. It also includes sectors, like banks and insurance, not subject to antitrust and so unaffected by the wide suspension of antitrust enacted in the NIRA. Stock-return performance during the NIRA period was apparently not due to cartel gains by some industries at the expense of others.

Of course, some stocks did worse than average, and some stocks showed weekly increases in only 8 or 9 out of 14 weeks. However, the stock price declines were concentrated in the industry indices composed of few stocks, and they have statistical origins. With fewer stocks, an index exhibits greater variance. For all periods, as shown at the bottom of table 17.5, the standard deviations (SD) of industries with 4 to 9 stocks were larger than for those with 10 or more firms; variance ratio tests yield values of 2.5 or higher. Similarly, those indices with 4 to 9 firms had on average 11.2 weeks with positive returns out of 14 weeks, while those with ten or more had 12.7 weeks of positive returns. The difference, based on a *t*-test, is significant.

These five episodes covered abrupt changes in two types of policies: antitrust and labor. It is useful to try to isolate the effects of each policy. *Appalachian Coals* and *Schechter* both concerned antitrust. The Black bill and the blanket code concerned labor. The passage of the NIRA concerned both antitrust and labor. How well do variables that capture an individual industry's benefits or costs from these changes explain the cross-section of returns over those five periods?

Table 17.6 regresses the stock-price returns from table 17.5 on two proxies. The top panel uses payroll as a fraction of total value added (VA) to capture the importance of labor costs. Industries with relatively high labor usage should be particularly affected by the labor-related measures, the Black bill and the blanket code. The bottom panel uses a manufacturing and mining

Table 17.6 Cross-Section Regressions of Industry Returns on Industry Characteristics for Five Periods: Ordinary Least Squares (OLS) and Weighted Least Squares (WLS) by Square Root of Number of Firms in Stock Index

	Returns over:									
	Appalachian Coals		Black Labor Bill		NIRA Passage		Blanket Code		Schechter	
	OLS	WLS	OLS	WLS	OLS	WLS	OLS	WLS	OLS	WLS
Constant	.14	.09	.10	.06	.48	.23	−.05	−.02	−.04	−.03
	(1.52)	(1.08)	(1.47)	(0.98)	(0.76)	(0.40)	(1.36)	(0.66)	(1.14)	(0.80)
Payroll ÷ V A	.16	.24	−.34	−.27	2.07	2.60	−.13	−.19	−.03	−.06
	(0.84)	(1.39)	(2.49)	(2.15)	(1.61)	(2.23)	(1.88)	(3.01)	(0.37)	(0.92)
R^2/Weighted R^2	.02	.03	.17	.19	.08	.27	.11	.47	.00	.11
Constant	.12	.12	−.11	−.15	1.15	1.02	−.11	−.09	−.01	.01
	(3.54)	(5.43)	(3.66)	(7.12)	(4.85)	(6.09)	(8.02)	(9.25)	(0.48)	(0.65)
Manufacturing	.10	.08	.05	.08	.32	.44	−.00	−.02	−.05	−.06
& Mining Dummy	(2.63)	(2.72)	(1.31)	(3.07)	(1.17)	(2.11)	(0.06)	(1.29)	(3.21)	(4.37)
R^2/Weighted R^2	.14	.14	.04	.39	.03	.15	.00	.25	.19	.31

Note: The upper panel is based on 32 industries, all in manufacturing. The lower panel is based on 45 industries. Absolute value of t-statistics in parentheses. Payroll ÷ Value-added has a mean of .48 and standard deviation of .17; the manufacturing and mining dummy has a mean of .76.
Source: Payroll and value-added data at the two-digit level are 1933 values from U.S. Historical Statistics (1975, Series P61 and P65). Coverage for Fabricated Metal Products, Non-electrical Machinery, and Transportation Equipment starts in 1947, so I used the observed 1933–1947 increase of payroll per value-added of .445 to .534 for all manufacturers to adjust the 1947 data (Series P7 and P10). Three industries (Textile Mill Products, Apparel, and Instruments and Related Products) had no values for 1933, so I used those for 1929. Stock prices from Standard Statistics, Standard Trade and Securities, Statistical Bulletin, December 1934. See table 17.5.

dummy in an attempt to capture the importance of the antitrust exemption. Trade associations and their most restrictive practices—restrictions on output, capacity, price, and allocations, for example—were common in mining and manufacturing, but rare in other sectors. Moreover, as discussed earlier, railroads, utilities, banks, and insurance companies came under federal or state regulation and were rarely subject to lawsuits under federal antitrust law, at least in the 1920s and 1930s.

Some technical issues deserve attention. Since the payroll and value-added data come from manufacturing industries only, I cannot run payrolls/VA and the manufacturing and mining dummy in the same regression. Also, each pair of results is based on ordinary and weighted least squares, with the weights equal to the square root of the number of firms in the index. The weighting addresses two issues when an index is composed of few firms: the high variance of returns and the low information content of those observations. (Weighting by the number of firms yields similar results.)

The top panel shows that industries with a high ratio of payroll to value-added gained disproportionately during the NIRA's passage. An increase in that ratio from one standard deviation below the mean to one standard deviation above (from .30 to .64) implied an extra stock return of 79 to 88 percent. This is consistent with the view that the prospects of labor legislation like that of Senator Black dimmed as the NIRA's prospects brightened. It is also consistent with the view that restrictive labor legislation became less likely as the economy picked up for some other reason. However, as expected, stocks with high payroll-to-value-added dropped disproportionately over the brief two periods associated with labor initiatives. They showed little movement in response to the two court decisions, which were mainly antitrust events.

Manufacturing and mining industries, in contrast, experienced larger positive returns over the period covered by *Appalachian Coals,* and somewhat surprisingly, over the period for the Black bill, though only the weighted estimate is significant. The gains to manufacturing and mining are also greater over the period covered by the NIRA—between 32 and 44 percent—though only the weighted least squares coefficient is again statistically significant.[50] The period covered by promulgation of the blanket code, however, has no antitrust developments, and manufacturing and mining stocks were unaffected. During the week *Schechter* was announced, in contrast, manufacturing and mining stocks dropped significantly more.

Taken as a whole, the estimates in table 17.6 support the view that actual or expected developments in antitrust and labor legislation can explain some of the movements in stock prices, both for 1933 and for the 1935 *Schechter* decision. Industries in which labor accounted for a large share of value-added suffered unusually strong declines with the Black bill and the blanket code. Manufacturing and mining firms, the classic sectors for cartels and policies designed to combat them, experienced significant increases with *Appalachian Coals* and NIRA passage, and a significant decrease with *Schechter.*

Table 17.7 provides cross-section correlations of the stock-return data from table 17.5 across the five periods. Two involved Supreme Court decisions: *Appalachian Coals* scuttled the per se rule, and *Schechter* declared a particular method of suspending antitrust illegal. Two involved initiatives that implied higher labor costs, the Black bill and the blanket code. NIRA passage was a mixed bag, indicating that stringent labor legislation had lost in favor of concessions to labor paired with concessions to industry. One would pre-

50. Was the strong performance of manufacturing and mining stocks due to the lower cyclical sensitivity of other stocks? The mean coefficient from a regression of returns of the ten nonmanufacturing and nonmining industries on industrial returns—a sort of beta—is .92 (median .93), with a range from .53 (casualty insurance) to 1.44 (theaters). The value for the index of 33 railroads was 1.17, and for 37 utilities, 0.70. These results indicate that mining and manufacturing industries should have had returns greater by only 7.5 percent rather than by 32 to 44 percent as indicated in table 17.6.

Table 17.7   Correlation of Returns, Ordinary and Weighted by Square Root of Number of Firms in Stock Index

	Black Labor Bill		NIRA Passage		Blanket Code		Schechter	
	O*	W*	O*	W*	O*	W*	O*	W*
Manufacturing (n = 32)								
Appalachian	− .05	− .27	− .15	.06	− .18	− .26	− .61	− .64
Black Bill			− .41	− .49	.02	.23	.04	.25
NIRA Passage					− .41	− .57	− .28	− .41
Blanket Code							.39	.45
All industries (n = 45)								
Appalachian	.07	− .20	− .10	.11	− .15	− .26	− .66	− .52
Black Bill			− .26	− .34	− .06	.30	− .17	− .23
NIRA Passage					− .45	− .60	− .31	− .31
Blanket Code							.36	.21

*Ordinary (O) and weighted (W) estimates.
See table 17.5.

dict that the correlation between *Appalachian Coals* and *Schechter* will be negative, and between the Black bill and the blanket code positive. NIRA passage should be positively correlated with *Appalachian Coals,* negatively with *Schechter,* and negatively with the two labor initiatives.

The correlations are calculated with and without weights equal to the square root of the number of firms in the index, as before. The main result is that the returns over *Appalachian Coals* were negatively related to returns over *Schechter.* The Black bill and the blanket code are significantly positively related only using weighted observations. NIRA passage shows no correlation with *Applachian Coals,* but a strong negative correlation with *Schechter,* and a strong negative correlation with the two labor initiatives.

Overall, the pattern of correlations across events offers some additional support for the notion that antitrust and labor regulation influenced the pattern of industry returns and, arguably, of aggregate returns during this period. The evidence seems to speak especially strongly on the connection between the two antitrust decisions.

Industry-by-Industry Output

Table 17.8 shows industry-by-industry output for each quarter of 1933, relative to the average for that year. Several series were higher for the first part of the year: new bond issues, the number of business failures, the dollar value of business failures, and the average size of business failures. All other series reach their peak in the second, third, or fourth quarters—after the passage of the NIRA. Department store sales (seasonally adjusted) are higher

Table 17.8   Economic Indicators by Quarter Relative to 1933 Average

	1st Qtr.	2nd Qtr.	3rd Qtr.	4th Qtr.
New stock issues*	23	34	277	66
New bond issues*	173	172	54	1
Failures—Number*	143	108	79	70
Failures—Dollars*	154	107	73	66
Failures—Dollars/Failure*	110	101	94	96
Stocks of mfg. goods*	95	95	104	106
Stocks of raw materials*	98	88	96	118
Department store sales	88	100	108	104
Life insurance policies*	93	100	103	104
Magazine advertising*	93	107	82	118
Newspaper advertising*	93	78	105	124
Composite index	83	102	117	98
Steel ingot	52	97	148	103
Pig iron	52	79	155	114
Zinc	77	69	124	130
Lead	87	86	88	139
Tin	73	104	136	88
Railroad equipment	36	82	96	185
Electric power	94	99	105	102
Gasoline	97	100	104	99
Automobile tires	58	104	134	104
Passenger cars	83	96	148	73
Trucks	62	98	131	110
Lumber	72	93	135	100
Cotton	87	115	114	84
Wool mill	75	106	120	100
Boots and shoes	90	108	104	98
Wood pulp	79	90	120	110
Paper	83	102	116	98
Chemicals	84	92	118	106
Cigarettes	93	109	101	97
Sugar meltings	93	112	101	94
Slaughtering & meat packing	91	103	104	101
Cement	85	104	120	90
Building contracts	78	107	108	107

Note: All series are seasonally adjusted, except those marked with an asterisk (*).
Source: Standard Statistics, Standard Trade and Securities, Statistical Bulletin, December 1934.

in the third and fourth quarters than in the first and second. Stocks of raw materials, which should have increased if hoarding in advance of future price increases took place, actually declined in the second and third quarters. If hoarding took place, it was done by ultimate consumers. The number of life insurance policies sold also increases in the last half of the year, to 10 percent above the level of the first quarter. Newspaper and magazine advertising (line counts not seasonally adjusted) are influenced by seasonal factors; however, comparisons of the first and second half of the year are least likely to be tainted and show no decline for magazines and a sharp increase for newspapers. Seasonally adjusted output in the last quarter falls below the first quarter for only two industries: passenger cars and cotton.

In sum, despite cartelization, manufacturing output was up. More surprisingly, measures of activity in sectors not covered by the NRA were also up. Once again, the standard interpretation of the NRA-as-textbook-monopolizer seems inconsistent with the data.

Other Economic Programs

Clearly, the introduction, passage, and early implementation of the NIRA represents one candidate for the mid-1933 boom in stock prices and production. What other events might explain this increase? Based on painstaking research, Friedman and Schwartz conclude that the New Deal's "monetary policy was accorded little importance in affecting the course of economic affairs and the policy actually followed was hesitant and almost entirely passive."[51] But they stress the far-reaching changes in the structure of banking during the New Deal. Major actions in 1933 included the Emergency Banking Act (March), the forced sale of holdings of gold coins at face value and gold bullion to the Federal Reserve Banks (April), abrogation of the gold clause (May and June), and federal deposit insurance (June). Friedman and Schwartz argue that deposit insurance contributed greatly to the monetary stability of the United States over the long term, though denying that deposit insurance was necessarily the most preferable method of achieving stability.[52] The other policy measures of early and mid-1933 probably had little effect or retarded revival.

If stabilization of the banks fostered recovery, it was by very indirect means. A sounder banking system should have attracted funds. However, the ratio of deposits to bank reserves declined in 1933, indicating caution on the part of banks. The initial decline was autonomous; only later did the Fed increase reserve requirements. The ratio of deposits to currency held by the public increased slowly from the very low level it had reached after the February 1933 panic (4.44), but in December was still (at 5.37) below the January 1933 level (5.86) and lower, in fact, than it had been anytime since 1908.[53] A sharp jump in stock prices and output caused by re-establishment of confidence in the banking system should have seen a greater increase in deposits, yet by December deposits had increased only 6.2 percent from their low point in March. The twelve-month change in 1933 was in fact a negative 11.1 percent.

51. Friedman and Schwartz, *supra* note 44, at 420.
52. Ibid., at 441–42 and note 18.
53. Ibid., table 133.

Related evidence comes from the stock prices of banks. The twenty New York banks in the Standard index experienced the largest decrease, −24.9 percent, among forty-five industries over the period March 15–April 5, 1933, and the smallest increase, 52.8 percent, over the period April 5–July 12 (see table 17.5 above). Stabilization of the banking system did not benefit these banks. If bank reform caused the mid-1933 revival, the data offer little indication of it.

The other major New Deal program of the period March–July 1933 included the Agricultural Adjustment Act (signed May 12), which curtailed production and raised prices. It seems an unlikely candidate for the cause of the observed increase in stock prices or output.

Concluding Comments

The NIRA promoted restrictions of output and prices, and it forced firms to pay minimum wages and agree to collective bargaining. By familiar arguments, it should have lowered output overall. Cartelized, high-wage industries should have produced less, and suppliers and distributors for those industries should have produced less. Only non-cartelized, low-wage producers of substitutes should have produced more.

However, as demonstrated in this chapter, the passage of the NIRA was in fact marked by a boom, especially in durable-goods production, as shown in figures 17.1 and 17.3. Even at a more disaggregated level, the upturn was broad-based and extended beyond the cartelized sectors to retailing and financial sevices (table 17.8). Some other factor could have caused the boom, but there are few plausible candidates. The banking sector was only slowly recovering, and other New Deal policies are unlikely causes of a broad revival.

According to one conjecture, the boom was artificial, induced by the prospect of price increases. If this were true, total output over the period covered by the NIRA should have been lower, as should stock prices for the period of the NIRA's passage, at least for sectors that supplied cartels or supplied products whose prices were increased by cartels. Regressions of output on a variety of explanatory factors for 1930–1939 (tables 17.3 and 17.4) indicate that, holding plausibly and even implausibly exogenous factors constant (when stock prices and wholesale prices moved as they ordinarily do in a boom), output was not lower during the period of the NRA. Durable-goods output was perhaps greater. Since the NRA dummy in these regressions includes only the period from July 1933 to June 1935, it excludes the boom that occurred during the NIRA's passage. One should also remember that the NRA as it turned out was probably not the NRA business expected in July of 1933, nor a resurrection of Coolidge-era policies.

Stock prices offer related evidence. They increased broadly with the NIRA's passage, as shown in figure 17.2. The increases occurred in manufacturing, which would gain from cartelization. But as table 17.5 showed, increases occurred also in railroads, utilities, retailing, and other sectors where the NRA or even antitrust generally did not apply, where NRA codes were never signed, or where codes were relatively mild.

Other evidence comes from the cross-section of stock-price changes that accompanied major changes in antitrust and labor regulation (table 17.6). Industries with a high ratio of payroll-to-value-added suffered stock price declines with the Black labor bill and the blanket code, but their stock prices increased with passage of the NIRA. On the other hand, manufacturing and mining firms experienced stock-price increases when *Appalachian Coals* suspended the per se rule against cartels, and stock price declines when *Schechter* declared the NIRA illegal and so ended legal cartelization. In fact, the correlation of stock returns across industries for the weeks covering the two Supreme Court decisions is − .66 (table 17.7).

By looking at antitrust's aggregate effects, this paper may seem too ambitious. Modern macroeconomics, at least in caricature, confines itself to the effects of monetary and fiscal policy, "autonomous" spending and investment; or more recently, in the real-business-cycle literature, to autonomous technological pushes. It was not always so. Kenneth Roose's discussion of the 1930s recovery dedicates a chapter to "the political, social and economic environment."[54] He mentions—above and beyond monetary and fiscal policy—new economic legislation, Roosevelt's confrontation with the Supreme Court, and attacks on business, for example. Friedman and Schwartz summarize his discussion approvingly and expand on it.[55]

The willingness to look beyond the short list of modern macro is a tradition worth reviving, and antitrust belongs on any expanded list. Until the New Deal, antitrust and related legislation governing railroads constituted the chief instrument for federal regulation of the corporation and business in general. "Trust busting" was also volatile and politically charged. But the effects of antitrust have received little attention. Stigler's study of concentration (chapter 4 of this volume) is a notable exception. In contrast, eminent earlier economists like Wesley Clair Mitchell and Irving Fisher entertained the notion that there might be a link between antitrust and general economic and financial developments. My own work—Bittlingmayer (1992, 1993a, b, and c)—finds a connection between aggressive antitrust and the financial crashes throughout this century, including the Panic of 1907, the Crash of 1929, and the sharp decline of May–June 1962. On the other hand, lax merger policies coincided with the stock booms and merger waves at the turn of the century, in the 1920s, and in the 1980s. The claim that fluctuating antitrust may also affect output, though novel to modern ears, seems worth exploring.

54. Kenneth D. Roose, The Economics of Recession and Revival: An Interpretation of 1937–38, 59–69 (1954).
55. Friedman and Schwartz, *supra* note 44, at 495–96.

PART FIVE

Retrospect and Prospect

WILLIAM F. SHUGHART II

The intellectual exploration of antitrust has now come full circle. Although antitrust's many failures had been evident since the beginning, it was not until the late 1960s that scholars began seriously searching for systematic explanations of its effects. As seen in Part One, the search began unsuccessfully with a naive model of antitrust processes—a model based on the assumption that the law's enforcers intervene in private markets only when the social benefits of doing so exceed the costs. The repeated failure to find evidence supporting antitrust's stated public-interest goals prompted economists to start asking positive questions about what its effects have actually been (see Part Two) and, as evidence accumulated that antitrust has often been ineffective or perverse, to start looking for alternative models to explain its intent (Part Three). In the end, by helping identify the political forces at work in contemporary enforcement activities, the public-choice model has generated renewed interest in studying antitrust's political origins (Part Four).

Scholarly support for antitrust has barely wavered throughout this sequence of events, however. The majority of economists and legal commentators continue to express faith in antitrust's ideals despite persistent reminders that the evidence fails to support them. This stubborn refusal to reject the naive public-interest view of antitrust in favor of an alternative public-choice model with substantially greater explanatory power is puzzling for a number of reasons.

For one, in virtually all other policy settings, public-interest explanations of government behavior have yielded inevitably to explanations based on policymakers' narrow political self-interests. Who today takes seriously the notion that government regulation of price and entry is designed and operated for the benefit of consumers, for example? Yet, few doubt that consumer protection is antitrust's primary mission. Second, the public-interest model's continued vitality in the area of antitrust flies in the very face of the highly visible political influences on the law's enforcers.

The Papers in This Section

These are the two major themes woven throughout Part Five. In chapter 18, Fred McChesney throws the gauntlet down at the collective feet of the Chicago school. If the reluctance of scholars generally to repudiate the public-

interest model of antitrust is puzzling, then the resolute adherence to it by
the Chicago school's disciples is nothing short of astounding.

The economic theory of regulation pioneered by Chicago explicitly takes
account of the political self-interest of the regulators, instead of assuming
them to be passive maximizers of the public's interest. In the Chicago
school's approach, public regulation of price and entry serves the interests
of consumers only to whatever extent is consistent with the self-interests of
the politician-regulators nominally charged with protecting them. Moreover,
because consumers are often not well positioned to provide the regulators
with effective political support, their interests predictably get short shrift in
the regulatory process. Chicago surprisingly insists, though, that the antitrust
agencies somehow avoid yielding to political pressure, and that these agencies—uniquely among all government programs, and policies—cater not to
special interests but to the public's interest.

The illogic of this last point is underscored in the volume's final chapter
by Fred McChesney and William Shughart. The public-interest model of
antitrust persists despite widespread acknowledgment of the political forces
that shape its enforcement. Two recent examples of politically motivated
antitrust intervention, the Clinton administration's threatened use of antitrust
to prevent Northwest Airlines from entering a new market, and the Justice
Department's unprecedented follow-on investigation to the FTC's investigation of the Microsoft Corporation, illustrate these overt external influences.
Chapter 19 ends with a call for science to replace ideology. It challenges the
champions of the public-interest model of antitrust either to supply evidence
that supports its predictions or else to abandon its premises.

The plea in chapter 19 for intellectual honesty, it is important to emphasize,
is not the same thing as a plea for a major shift in the direction taken by
antitrust. After all, the near-total victory of the Chicago school approach to
analyzing public regulation of price and entry can at best be credited with
inspiring only a very modest number of actual deregulatory initiatives. Antitrust, like all government programs and policies, is shaped by ordinary politics, not by abstract ideas. Hence, it would be foolish to expect a revolution
in the way economists think about antitrust to lead to a revolution in the way
antitrust policy is actually practiced.

Economists, Lawyers, and Antitrust

A number of contributors to the literature on antitrust policy have suggested,
in fact, that the laws were enacted at the behest of the lawyers, economists,
and government employees who benefit personally from their enforcement.
It is of course easy, ex post, to identify a constituency that strongly favors
the continuation (and, indeed, expansion) of antitrust among the public officials who thereby gain promotions and larger bureaucratic empires over which

to preside, the lawyers who win large fees, and the economists who serve as highly paid experts in antitrust proceedings. But there is little reason to believe that the private interests of these groups were decisive in inspiring the enactment of the antitrust laws in the first place.[1]

The available evidence does suggest, though, that the private interests of the members of the antitrust bureaucracy may play an important role in determining the number and mix of cases brought under existing statutes. For example, based on the interviews she conducted during 1971 with staff members, private attorneys, and other observers of the Antitrust Division, Suzanne Weaver (1977, 66) sought to answer the question, "Why does the division choose to bring any particular case?" According to her, important events taking place on the antitrust front during the early 1950s, including passage of the Celler-Kefauver Act, which closed section 7's "asset loophole" (see chapter 16), and the price-fixing indictments handed down against the leading electrical equipment manufacturers, made "antitrust expertise a more valuable commodity to the business community and the law firms serving it." Because of the increased demand for such expertise, "experience in the Antitrust Division became newly valuable to a young lawyer who wanted eventually to work in private practice" (pp. 38–40). And the specific experience wanted was trial experience in the federal courts.

Weaver's study suggests that, at the margin, the objective of getting to trial carries more weight in the Antitrust Division's decision to prosecute than the potential benefits of intervention to consumers. Similar conclusions are drawn by Robert Katzmann (1980) in his study of the incentive structure faced by the attorneys employed by the Federal Trade Commission. He notes that the ultimate career goal of most members of the FTC's legal staff is a job with a prestigious law firm. Such a goal means that the FTC's senior managers will find that complicated "structural matters and industry wide cases threaten the morale of the staff because they often involve years of tedious investigation before they reach the trial stage." As a result, the commission may have a propensity to support "the opening of a number of easily prosecuted matters, which may have little value to the consumer, . . . in an effort to satisfy the staff's perceived needs" (p. 83).

Katzmann's main point, like Weaver's, is that the antitrust case selection process is dominated by the forces impinging on the antitrust bureaucracy— staff career objectives, law enforcement budgets, congressional influence, and

1. Except for the case of the Celler-Kefauver Act amendment to Clayton Act section 7, representatives of the organized bar and the public law enforcement agencies were conspicuously absent from the lists of witnesses testifying before congressional committees holding hearings on the major pieces of antitrust legislation. See Baxter (1980, 44–45), who reports that 36 (53 percent) of the witnesses who testified on the Celler-Kefauver amendment were employees of either the Antitrust Division or the Federal Trade Commission. They were unanimous in supporting the bill. DiLorenzo (1985) underscores the point that the few economists who testified on Senator Sherman's antitrust bill were generally opposed to its passage.

so forth—rather than by social welfare criteria.[2] Antitrust bureaucrats have personal stakes in the continuation of the policy they are charged with enforcing, even if that policy produces no apparent benefits for the public at large. Antitrust likewise serves the personal interests of the members of the private bar who get to defend clients, and the economists who get to read, write, and consult about it. While it is doubtful that Senator Sherman designed his bill more than a century ago solely to create jobs for today's bureaucrats, lawyers, and economists, the influence these groups bring to bear on the enforcement process must be taken into account if antitrust policy is to be understood fully.

The members of the Chicago school maintain that "better" antitrust policy will automatically follow an expanded role for economists in the law enforcement process and a greater appreciation for economics by the lawyers and judges who try antitrust cases. Yet even this superficially appealing proposition seems to be inconsistent with the facts.

Data collected by George Stigler (1982b) show the number of economists employed by the Justice Department's Antitrust Division and the FTC essentially doubling between 1971 and 1981. But this era of job growth for economists coincided with the launching of a number of clumsy structural antitrust cases based on novel, untested theories like "shared monopoly" and "brand proliferation" that ultimately collapsed of their own weight. Economists working for the antitrust bureaus also invented the idea of "raising rivals' costs" expressly to undermine the Chicago school's effective critique of predatory pricing,[3] and they were accessories both before and after the fact in further tilting merger policy toward protecting competitors rather than consumers (see chapter 9). More recently, industrial organization economists have used game-theoretic techniques almost exclusively to build increasingly exotic models of anticompetitive behavior.[4] In short, it is far from clear that better economics makes better antitrust.

The more general point, though, is that recognizing the personal benefits of antitrust policy to the members of the antitrust industry and to the industry's overseers in Congress casts further doubt on the idea that the main interest promoted by antitrust is the public's interest. This observation also suggests that substantive efforts to reform antitrust processes (or to repeal the antitrust laws) can be expected to materialize not *when* the public-choice model of antitrust displaces the public-interest model, but rather *if* the political costs of having an antitrust policy ever begin to outweigh the political benefits.

2. The papers collected in Clarkson and Muris (1981) likewise identify internal organizational conflicts, staff incentives, and external constraints imposed by Congress as key factors in the decision to prosecute. Additional evidence along these lines is presented in Coate, Higgins, and McChesney (1990). See chapter 13 of this volume.

3. See, for example, Steven C. Salop and David T. Scheffman, Raising Rivals' Costs, 73 Amer. Econ. Rev. Papers & Proceedings 267 (1983).

4. Sam Peltzman, The Handbook of Industrial Organization: A Review Article, 99 J. Polit. Econ. 201 (1991).

CHAPTER EIGHTEEN

Be True to Your School: Chicago's Contradictory Views of Antitrust and Regulation

FRED S. MCCHESNEY

> If you propose an antitrust law, the only people who should be opposed to it are those who hope to become monopolists, and that's a very small set of any society. So it's a sort of public-interest law in the same sense in which I think having private property, enforcement of contracts, and suppression of crime are public-interest phenomena.
>
> —GEORGE STIGLER[1]

Introduction

For decades, theorists known collectively as the "Chicago school" have defined the intellectual agenda of antitrust. Inspired by the ideas of Aaron Director, the Chicago school approach has been advanced by scholars like Robert Bork, Yale Brozen, Harold Demsetz, Frank Easterbrook, Richard Posner (often joined by William Landes), and George Stigler. So powerful has been their collective influence on antitrust thinking that the phrase "the Chicago revolution in antitrust" has become a platitude in the antitrust literature.

Will this intellectual dominance—salutary in so many ways—continue? In seeking to answer that question, this essay presents and develops two points about the Chicago school. First, although correct on many issues, Chicago has mistakenly concluded that it has won the antitrust war, and so has withdrawn its forces from the fray. Yet the withdrawal is premature: unopposed hostile forces remain on the battlefield.

Chicago's views of antitrust face a second, and fundamentally more difficult, challenge. Much of the normative economic analysis on which Chicago-

This essay was previously published in the *Cato Journal* 10 (Winter 1991): 775–98, and has been slightly updated here.

1. Quoted in Hazlett (1984, 46).

ans relied in proclaiming victory is manifestly inconsistent with more fundamental positive notions of economics developed by Chicagoans themselves.
In particular, Chicago's positive approach to antitrust, viewing it as public-
interest government intervention intended to correct market failure, squarely
contradicts the now-dominant economic theory of regulation that Chicago
itself popularized. The Chicago school of antitrust regulation, that is, runs
counter to the Chicago school of regulation more generally.

An underlying theme of this article is that the two basic phenomena under
discussion have produced a more complicated intellectual agenda for antitrust
in the 1990s. From 1960 until recently, the intellectual battle in antitrust
was easy to characterize: it pitted Chicago revisionism against a coalition of
anti-Chicagoans (often identified with Harvard) defending more traditional
antitrust policies. But the future debate will be multifaceted. On one side,
traditionalists will continue to challenge Chicago's conclusions that certain
practices (such as predatory pricing and vertical arrangements) are not worrisome. On the other side, public-choice theorists working within the economic
theory of regulation will increasingly challenge Chicago's public-interest
view of antitrust. Outside Chicago, antitrust is increasingly seen as another
form of regulation. If so, the debate must include recognition of the politics
of antitrust—a subject Chicagoans have persistently downplayed or ignored.[2]

Declaring Victory and Going Home: The Withdrawal
of the Chicago School

After a century of experience with antitrust, almost no one would disagree
that it has developed in thoroughly undesirable ways. Two defects stand out.

First, much of antitrust jurisprudence is economic nonsense. Everyone has
a favorite example. Some like the case in which per se liability was imposed
on a group of competitors for acts that resulted in "stabilizing prices downward";[3] others prefer the case in which per se liability was imposed for
maximum-price agreements because (according to the Court) such contracts
are no different economically from minimum-price fixing.[4] After reviewing a
number of Supreme Court opinions, one former head of the Antitrust Division
(Kauper 1986) chose as his favorite aberration the *Von's Grocery* decision.[5]

2. To avoid misunderstanding, it should be noted that those adopting a public-choice approach
generally agree with the Chicago welfare-economic analysis of particular business practices.
Chicago's contributions in this area have been enormous. The disagreement arises as to the
political economy of the antitrust statutes. In that respect, the Chicago approach has been less
helpful, as explained herein. Of course, not all Chicagoans may subscribe to all facets of what
is described here as the Chicago school of antitrust and of regulatory analysis. I believe, however,
that the views presented here are typical of the authors discussed and of the Chicago perspective
generally.
3. U.S. v. Container Corp., 393 U.S. 333 (1969).
4. Albrecht v. Herald Co., 390 U.S. 145 (1968).
5. U.S. v. Von's Grocery Co., 384 U.S. 270 (1966).

There, the government successfully blocked a merger between two grocery firms having a combined market share of 7.5 percent, in a market with 3,818 single-store and 150 chain-store competitors.[6] The rationale against the merger was stopping incipient concentration in the grocery market. As Kauper writes (pp. 2–3):

> Never has analysis been crisper, logic more refined. Confronted with a practical problem—the departure of mom and pops from the Los Angeles grocery market—the Court quickly perceived that the solution was simply to close the exit. The reaction was similar to that of Attorney General Kleindienst when, on receipt of a bomb threat, he ordered all the Justice Department doors closed and everybody kept *in*.

The second, related, defect is that the courts' blessing of economic nonsense has given private plaintiffs much ammunition for meritless (but trebly lucrative) antitrust actions. Antitrust has thereby become a weapon wielded against competition, not for it. The facts and figures on the private antitrust explosion have been presented elsewhere (e.g., Hazlett 1986). The phenomenon has caused previous partisans of antitrust (e.g., Baumol and Ordover 1985) to question its overall role in a competitive order. Many big-name "liberals" like John Kenneth Galbraith, Robert Reich, and Lester Thurow have written that it may have no role.[7]

Into this system of jumbled jurisprudence and meritless private actions, beginning in the 1950s, stepped the Chicagoans. Their contributions have been numerous, valuable, and well-discussed elsewhere. The subject of interest here is the Chicago perception of the purposes of the antitrust laws. The Sherman Act, they maintain, was intended to maximize consumer welfare (e.g., Bork 1966a; 1978, 56–66). The principal problems with antitrust, they believe, are due to courts' misunderstanding of how the competitive process actually works in maximizing consumer welfare (Bork 1978; Demsetz 1982a, 1989; Posner 1976). If courts departed from the rigid "perfect competition" model and recognized real-world problems like information and transaction costs, courts then would recognize that consumer welfare is increased by practices previously deemed undesirable under antitrust law (for example, vertical arrangements). And, in fact, courts have moved closer and closer to Chicago positions on these issues.[8]

6. "In fairness, there was a concentration trend in *Von's*—the top four went from 24.4% to 28.8%. Try that in a Herfindahl!" (Kauper 1986, 3).

7. This point is discussed by McChesney (1986, 381–82), and by Hazlett (1986, 278–79).

8. Chicagoans have proclaimed intellectual victory on the basis of courts' change of position. The reasoning has struck some as *post hoc ergo propter hoc*. Kaplow (1987), for instance, believes that the change in antitrust attitudes has been driven by politics, not economics, and thus would have happened with or without Chicago. That debate is not discussed directly here, although portions of the analysis in the third section of the paper may bear on it. See also Page (1989).

But the Chicago school's victories, evident on several fronts, have by no means been complete. Three pockets of resistance remain. First, Chicago's intellectual sorties have not been able to stem the tide of meritless private actions. Until relatively recently (Easterbrook 1984), private actions typically did not require separate analysis in Chicago. Judges who understood the consumer-welfare origins of the antitrust statutes and the true nature of competition would have all they needed to separate good from bad actions, private or public. It is apparent, however, that this just has not happened; Chicagoan suggestions for improvement in this domain (e.g., Easterbrook 1984) have been ignored.

Moreover, while commentators may agree that the reasoning of the old cases is frequently wrong, the courts have not been so quick to agree. Per se rules against agreements that limit, rather than raise, prices are still per se illegal.[9] So is the per se rule against resale price maintenance, against which Chicagoans have inveighed for a generation. Courts continue to impose liability for tying (Sims and Lande 1986, 307–8), despite Chicago's repeated demonstrations that tying is economically benign, even beneficial. Other Supreme Court decisions consistent with the Chicago approach have relied on reasoning so fragile that their durability is questioned, even in Chicago (Wood Hutchinson 1985).

Finally, antitrust partisans (e.g., Hovenkamp 1985) have been indefatigable in thinking up new, more sophisticated theories for antitrust liability. The current rage seems to be "raising rivals' costs," an old notion newly repackaged that is getting close attention from commentators (e.g., Krattenmaker and Salop 1986) and, perhaps, from the courts.[10] In addition, sophisticated models of strategic predatory pricing have replaced the older ones refuted by Chicago some time ago.

A historical perspective is helpful. The antitrust wheel of fortune has spun many times since 1890. As the wheel turns, periods of relaxed enforcement give way to renewed enforcement vigor, relying in part on new antitrust theories (Baker 1985; Sims and Lande 1986). This constant change in antitrust thinking is reflected in the waxing and waning of courts' respect for key antitrust precedents (Steuer 1985).

In other words, no one outside Hyde Park believes that with the Chicago victories of recent years the war has reached the end or even the beginning

9. Arizona v. Maricopa County Medical Society, 457 U.S. 332 (1982). For a discussion of this decision within the Chicago school paradigm, see Gerhart (1982).

10. While the Supreme Court has yet to consider a case with allegations of "raising rivals' costs," prior decisions have imposed liability on antitrust defendants for actions that in effect amounted to the same thing. See, for example, Aspen Skiing Co. v. Aspen Highlands Skiing Corp., 472 U.S. 585 (1985). As to whether the theory is actually different from more traditional notions of monopolization, see Brennan (1988). As to whether the practices even constitute monopoly, see Liebeler (1987) and Wiley (1986).

of the end. With the war still raging, however, Chicago has declared victory and gone home. The newer theories of liability remain largely unaddressed. Large numbers (arguably a majority) of commentators and courts remain to be persuaded by the Chicago approach. Yet Landes (1983, 652) declares that the economics of antitrust have been "uncontroversial for many years." With his declaration that we are all Chicagoans now ("it is no longer worth talking about different schools of academic antitrust analysis"), Posner (1979, 925) has largely abandoned the field for remoter terrain like law and literature, theories of justice, and law and feminism.[11] But even at the time, Nelson (1979, 949) commented that the economics Chicago thought it had vanquished had already been supplanted by a "newer" price theory that "is more consistent with old Harvard than the new Chicago." Nelson's point is even truer today.

The belief that by the late 1970s it was time to declare victory is evident from the Chicago antitrust writings appearing subsequently. These fall into two camps. The first reemphasizes the correctness of the Chicago approach to antitrust as a set of consumer-welfare statutes, and expresses beliefs and hopes that in the many areas where courts have not come around to appreciating Chicago's wisdom they will do so soon. Its most prominent practitioner has been Robert Bork (1978), but he has had help. Brozen (1986, 355–56), while admitting that "the antitrust laws have been used to frustrate efficiency and competition," cautions against despair; a "few halting steps" of improvement have been made, he says, and "one can only hope that there will be more to come." The same message can be said to describe Demsetz' work (1982, 1989): antitrust has proceeded from a flawed definition of competition, but if redirected to attack real (government-created) monopolies would be a useful policy.

A second camp has moved on to other areas altogether. With the important issues of substantive liability (as they perceive them) already disposed of, this second group of Chicagoans has been increasingly interested in using economics to "fine tune" antitrust procedures and damage calculations. For example, articles have appeared on optimal sanctions for antitrust violations (Landes 1983), contribution among antitrust violators (Easterbrook, Landes, and Posner 1980), standing under the antitrust laws (Landes and Posner 1979), and economic definitions of market power (Landes and Posner 1981). In these sorts of articles, Chicagoans have joined other fine-tuners (e.g., Blair 1985) who maintain in effect that the antitrust laws are fundamentally useful but could be enforced more efficiently.

Thus, the Chicagoan attitude toward antitrust today appears to be guarded

11. Posner (1979, 939–40) recognizes that the Chicago view of some practices does not dispose of opponents' claims that certain practices involving strategic behavior are anticompetitive. But as noted, there has been little attempt either to integrate those claims into the Chicago approach or, alternatively, to refute them.

optimism, based on a blend of complementary beliefs that the basic issues of antitrust liability have been resolved, that courts are slowly but surely getting it right, and that in the meantime nonliability issues can usefully be refined by welfare economics. Nowhere is Chicago's basically positive attitude toward the supposed goal and the future (if not past) performance of antitrust better manifested than in Stigler's statement, "I like the Sherman Act."[12]

A House Divided against Itself: Chicago Views of Antitrust and Regulation

Antitrust is economic regulation. Its essence is the regulation of certain kinds of economic relationships: horizontal agreements to fix prices, agreements between competitors to combine (by merger or otherwise), and so forth.[13] Antitrust thus regulates the same things that other forms of regulation have traditionally covered. Congress established the Interstate Commerce Commission and the Civil Aeronautics Board specifically to regulate competitors' prices; the Securities and Exchange Commission regulates various aspects of corporate combinations. Even the procedural aspects of antitrust and those of related forms of regulation are similar. The Hart-Scott-Rodino Act requires a waiting period to get antitrust clearance for proposed mergers from either the Antitrust Division or the Federal Trade Commission; the Williams Act, administered by the SEC, requires a waiting period before similar corporate transactions can be completed.

Given that antitrust is a form of regulation, one would think that Chicagoans would analyze it using the "economic theory of regulation." That theory was given its earliest formal statement in Stigler (1971) and further developed by other Chicagoans (Peltzman 1976; Becker 1983). Under the economic model, regulation is explained by the benefits it provides to well-organized interest groups and the politicians who represent them, rather than in terms of government officials acting altruistically to benefit the populace at large by correcting market failure.

Development of the economic theory of regulation has included significant contributions by Posner (1975), quantifying the extent of the welfare losses due to politically driven regulation; and by Landes and Posner (1975), explaining the role of a constitutionally guaranteed independent judiciary in the economic theory of regulation. Posner's thesis, elaborated through four editions of his *Economic Analysis of Law,* that the common law is generally efficient while statutory law is not, is an offshoot of the economic theory of

12. Hazlett (1984, 46).

13. Obviously, the antitrust laws cover much more than just those sorts of agreements. I mention those specifically, however, as they are generally thought to be the most problematic for competition. See Demsetz (1982, 50–53).

regulation. Intellectual recognition of the economic approach to regulation has entailed development of other ancillary theorems, as explained below.

The economic theory of regulation has resulted in an intellectual revolution among economists and lawyers. As a recent report on Chicago political economy (Tollison 1989, 295) stated, "the primary alternative to Stigler's theory of economic regulation was the Pigovian or public-interest theory of government, which was already under heavy assault from earlier contributions to public-choice theory by Buchanan, Tullock, and others. Today, virtually no one thinks in such terms. The [Chicagoan] interest-group theory of government has accumulated widespread recognition."

That antitrust is in fact regulatory is of course recognized in Chicago. Posner (1970, 389) lists 109 "regulatory decrees" in DOJ antitrust cases up until 1969, almost all of them handed down since 1945.[14] Regulatory decrees are ones that establish ongoing governmental supervision of defendants. These decrees are "disturbing," because they are anticompetitive, "tantamount to a confession that antitrust action has not succeeded in restoring competitive conditions." Moreover, Posner says, "in view of persistent and serious questions that have been raised concerning the wisdom and efficacy of formal systems of regulation in the transportation, public utility, and other industries, the creation of new schemes of regulation on an ad hoc basis is a questionable expedient."

It is interesting in itself that Posner does not refer to all of antitrust as a form of regulation, since it clearly is. Nevertheless, his admission that "regulatory" decrees have made up "a significant fraction" of all civil antitrust decrees would suggest that Posner would begin to analyze antitrust using the economic theory of regulation. Yet his major work on antitrust (Posner 1976) contains no such analysis; nor is it developed anywhere else in his writings.[15] Instead, Posner joins Bork in claiming that the Sherman Act is a government attempt to improve efficiency. "Since efficiency is an important, although not the only, social value, this conclusion establishes a prima facie case for having an antitrust policy" (Posner 1976, 4). Easterbrook (1984, 1) says simply, "The goal of antitrust is to perfect the operation of competitive markets."[16]

14. See also Easterbrook (1984, 35, n. 72), who observes that "many antitrust suits are regulatory. . . . Approximately 53 antitrust decrees entered through 1979 are regulatory in character. This substantially exceeds the number of industries regulated by statute." See also Sullivan (1986).

15. In the successive editions of *Economic Analysis of Law,* for example, Posner has never included antitrust in his discussion of regulation. See, for example, Posner's summary of antitrust (1986, 265–97). It is interesting also that in discussing Aaron Director's influence on the development of Chicago antitrust, Posner (1979, 928) states that Director's work was not motivated by "antipathy to government in the economy," but simply by a desire to correct erroneous welfare-economics views concerning firms' behavior.

16. Easterbrook's stance on antitrust is all the more curious, given his oft-stated belief that in takeovers target-firm management should be legally prohibited from resisting a hostile bidder.

Nowhere is the Chicago distinction between antitrust and regulation more evident than in Bork's discussion of "predation through governmental processes" (1978, 347–64). Recognizing that other forms of regulation are used routinely to restrict rather than enhance competition, Bork (p. 364) touts antitrust as a way to attack such behavior: "Predation through the misuse of governmental processes appears to be a common but little-noticed phenomenon. . . . In this area, antitrust cannot only perform a valuable service to consumers but, as a by-product, can also contribute to the integrity and efficiency of administrative processes." Demsetz (1989, 27) likewise expresses hope that "our antitrust laws can be marshaled to attack government sponsored protectionism."[17] Antitrust is not to be analyzed as harmful economic regulation; indeed, it should be viewed as the antidote for such regulation.

It should be noted also that Posner's belief that the Sherman Act was basically intended to increase consumer welfare is apparently inconsistent with his view that typically the common law is efficient while statutory law is not. There was, of course, a common law of trade restraints, which the Sherman Act supplanted. Chicagoans have resolved the inconsistency by claiming that the Sherman Act merely codified the common law (Bork 1978, 20), even though the Supreme Court's earliest antitrust decision specifically held that "the common law cases on restraint of trade would not be precedents in Sherman Act cases" (Grady 1990, 6). Likewise, Demsetz says, subsequent antitrust enforcement just reflects what would have happened under the common law.[18]

Such a public-interest (Pigovian) presumption in favor of antitrust regulation is the exact opposite of the economic theory of regulation. In effect, the Chicago view of the Sherman Act maintains that antitrust is the exception to the regulatory rule—it is part of the solution, not the problem. Given the

---

See, for example, Frank H. Easterbrook and Daniel R. Fischel, The Proper Role of a Target's Management in Responding to a Tender Offer, 94 Harv. L. Rev. 1161 (1981). One of the ways that management has found useful for repelling unwanted bidders has in fact been the filing of an antitrust action. See Jarrell (1985).

17. A related public-interest argument made for antitrust is that, properly implemented at the federal level, it can be used to override state-sponsored anticompetitive arrangements. See Wiley (1986b); for objections, see Spitzer (1988) and Page (1987); for a reply to the objections, see Wiley (1988).

18. According to Demsetz (1989, 26), "If the Sherman Act had not been adopted, common law procedures would have guided our policy toward competition. Would this have yielded a very different policy? Because the standard of reasonableness has played such a large role in court proceedings over the first century of the Sherman Act, the modus operandi of our antitrust policy has not differed as much as might be supposed from that which would have been used by the common law." Demsetz notes two differences between the statutory antitrust and the common law—public enforcement and the illegality of certain mergers—but believes neither of these changes has been very significant.

unique position that antitrust occupies in Chicago, it is useful to explore the reasons advanced for its favored status.

Legislative History

Bork (1978, 63) claims that the legislative history of the Sherman Act supports a public-interest interpretation, displaying "the clear and exclusive policy intention of promoting consumer welfare." Such a justification has three problems, each seemingly fatal in itself.[19] First, almost all other inquiries into the passage of the antitrust statutes have disagreed with Bork's reading of the legislative history (e.g., Lande 1982; Hazlett 1992). The supposed monopoly and cartel problems that "necessitated" the Sherman Act were apparently nonexistent (DiLorenzo 1985). There is considerable evidence that interest-group pressures explain much of the Sherman Act (Benson et al. 1987; Hazlett 1992; Libecap 1990). In its first Sherman Act opinion, the Supreme Court found that "it would be impossible to say what were the views" of the politicians voting as to the meaning of the act. As one commentator put it recently, Bork's interpretation of the legislative intent underlying the Sherman Act "is unique to Judge Bork" (Flynn 1988, 264).[20]

Second, the public-interest approach is internally inconsistent. It treats private individuals as maximizing their own welfare in attempting to cartelize or monopolize, but it treats government legislators and bureaucrats as disinterested public servants. As Shughart and Tollison (1985, 39) note, "In one setting individuals are assumed to be selfish; in another they are selfless. The analyst cannot have it both ways. A decision about how individuals behave in general must be made." A consistent approach to antitrust must begin by asking what politicians and bureaucrats maximize and how antitrust advances their goals. (This point is discussed further below.)

Perhaps most important, Bork's reliance on legislative history runs afoul of a major corollary of the economic theory of regulation. If legislation is presumptively driven by interest-group politics, it is costly for politicians to tell voters, consumers, and other victims of regulation the true motivation behind regulation. Political motivation cannot be inferred from statutory preambles, committee reports, or "speeches" never made but printed in the *Congressional Record*. Motivation is to be inferred only from the way regulation works, not what politicians say about it. As Stigler (1975, 140) put it, "The announced goals of a policy are sometimes unrelated or perversely

19. A point not considered here is the objection that it is economically meaningless to ascribe "intent" to a legislative body. Its members may vote the same way, but ordinarily do so for very different reasons. For a response to this objection, see Bork (1978, 56–57).

20. According to Flynn (1988, 267), "Everyone who has made a considered study of the legislative history of the major antitrust laws flatly rejects Judge Bork's assertion that 'consumer welfare' was the only goal Congress had in mind."

FRED S. MCCHESNEY

related to its actual effects, and the *truly intended effects should be deduced from the actual effects*." In the case of antitrust specifically, the fundamental statutes (the Sherman Act, the Clayton Act, the Federal Trade Commission Act) have been in existence for 100 years, with almost no important changes. Since Congress can always change the law if it wants, it must "intend" (accepting *arguendo* Bork's notion of institutional intent) the results that antitrust has produced for a century: bad jurisprudence and anticompetitive suits.

Lack of Economic Guidance

Chicagoans have also justified their public-interest view of antitrust by mistake theories. Allegedly, politicians and judges have wanted to do the right thing economically, but economists have failed to provide the requisite guidance (e.g., Demsetz 1982, 1989). If economists were better able to define what competition truly was and had done so, then politicians would have responded with an antitrust law that mirrored economics. According to Bork (1978, 63–64): "It is not at all clear that the congressmen who voted for the [Robinson-Patman Act] knew that they were sacrificing consumers for the benefit of small merchants. Indeed, there is evidence . . . that many congressmen thought the law would serve consumers. . . . Today we know better." Similarly, Demsetz (1989, 20) ascribes the "instability of antitrust enforcement" to a "lack of clarity as to what a crime is and as to what constitutes evidence of its perpetration." The fact that economists failed to enlighten legislators, bureaucrats, and judges (and so left the way open for the bad antitrust observed today) hardly means that antitrust was not a public-interest regulatory scheme when it was inaugurated in 1890, Chicago maintains. With greater economic understanding will come better jurisprudence, better enforcement, and fewer meritless suits. Once provided adequate economic guidance, the Chicago argument concludes, the law will conform to economics.[21]

These claims cannot be squared with the economic theory of regulation. Politicians, bureaucrats, and judges have no incentive to adopt efficient laws, and thus should not be presumed to do so. Unless it can be shown how government officials gain by seeking and using better economic information, one should not presume that they will do so. Chicago has not shown how any such incentives operate in the world of antitrust.

Moreover, the contention that the law has tried, but failed, runs afoul of another important corollary of Chicagoans' economic theory of regulation. Confronted with evidence (such as bad law and meritless suits) that regulation

21. The view that antitrust is fundamentally benevolent but flawed by economists' inability to provide the requisite guidance is well established outside Chicago. See, for example, Asch (1970, 401–2).

has not worked, public-interest partisans frequently fall back on "mistake" theories to explain why the public interest has not been served. Mistake theories fail on two counts. They cannot explain why Congress has failed to correct a century of errors, as noted above. More important, a mistake theory is an intellectual *deus ex machina;* it is offered not to explain but to obscure an inability to explain. As Stigler (1982a, 10) says, a mistake theory for real-world regulation that deviates from promised public-interest objectives is "profoundly anti-intellectual."[22] Elsewhere (1975, 140) he writes:

> Policies may of course be adopted in error, and error is an inherent trait of the behavior of men. But errors are not what men live by or on. If an economic policy has been adopted by many communities, or if it is persistently pursued by a society over a long span of time, it is fruitful to assume that the real effects were known and desired. Indeed, an explanation of a policy in terms of error or confusion is no explanation at all—anything and everything is compatible with that "explanation."

Chicago's dismissal of antitrust's dismal century as prolonged—but ameliorable—error is thus unconvincing and unacceptable.

Lack of Evidence on Effects of Antitrust

A third reason frequently offered why antitrust should be viewed as beneficial is the lack of evidence to the contrary. While many evils have admittedly arisen from antitrust, they must be offset against the good: whatever mischief antitrust has caused must be balanced against the economically undesirable things it has deterred. In the end, this third claim goes, we simply do not know whether antitrust has caused more harm than good, or vice versa. Stigler's (1966) initial study of the effects of antitrust set the tone, presenting bits of evidence very diffidently and concluding that the results were "meager" and so not much could be said one way or the other about antitrust's effects. Until more conclusive evidence is available, it is said, antitrust cannot be proven to operate like other forms of regulation.

This approach is remarkable for three reasons. First, the presumption that antitrust is a good thing runs directly contrary to the typical Chicago approach that long-term problems of cartels and monopoly are theoretically unlikely and empirically minimal (Harberger 1954). As Reder (1982, 17) notes, "Chicago concedes that monopoly is possible but contends that its presence is

22. In Stigler's view (1982, p. 10):

> Whether one accepts or rejects the high hopes that some of us now entertain for the economic theory of politics, the assumption that public policy has often been inefficient because it was based upon mistaken views has little to commend it. . . . [A] theory that says that a large set of persistent policies are [sic] mistaken is profoundly anti-intellectual unless it is joined to a theory of mistakes.

much more often alleged than confirmed, and receives reports of its appearance with considerable scepticism. . . . Normatively, Chicago economics says monopoly is bad; positively, it says it is of infrequent occurrence and limited impact.'' If so, antitrust can have few benefits. Yet Stigler (1968, 297) states confidently that ''the history of the American economy in the twentieth century testifies that a modest program of combating monopoly is enough to prevent any considerable decline in competition.'' This ''fundamental empirical truth'' is propounded without a shred of substantiation.

Second, the Chicago approach to empirical evidence presumes that antitrust regulation is benign and puts the burden on others to show that antitrust is economically malignant. Antitrust is innocent until proven guilty. If no one comes forward with sufficient evidence, antitrust goes free. That approach is contrary to the presumption ordinarily applied to regulation under the economic model. Consider Reder's (1982, 31) summary of the Chicago position:

> The state is considered an agent, and one that is exceedingly difficult to monitor or to control. Therefore the state is to be shunned as an inefficient instrument for achieving any given objective—it is better sought privately—and objectives that cannot be achieved except through the state are to be scrutinized carefully and sceptically. Either the political process will frustrate the achievement of the goals altogether, or will drastically alter them in the process of achievement and, in any case, waste resources.
>
> The argument of the preceding paragraph is sufficient basis for a generally adverse view of government intervention. Any reformer must either refute it, or minimize its importance.

Obviously, this characterization of the Chicago approach to regulation generally does not apply to antitrust specifically.

The final curiosity in the Chicago position toward empirics is the fact that there is ample statistical evidence that antitrust has *not* had any appreciable benefits. Repeated empirical investigations of the criteria on which antitrust enforcement has depended find no evidence that consumer welfare drives enforcement. For example, Long et al. (1973, 361) find that welfare loss has ''played a minor role in explaining antitrust activity.'' Siegfried concludes (1975, 573) that ''economic variables have little influence on the Antitrust Division.''

Empirical studies of certain kinds of enforcement likewise report unanimously an absence of welfare benefits. This is notably true in the two areas in which Chicagoans maintain antitrust has its most beneficial role to play: price fixing and horizontal mergers. The available evidence (Marvel et al. 1987; Asch and Seneca 1976) indicates that government antitrust actions target firms that either were not attempting to fix prices, or were doing so unsuccessfully. Likewise, actions to block horizontal mergers have concentrated on mergers that were not anti-competitive, or were even pro-competitive (Eckbo and Wier 1985). Moreover, studies of antitrust remedies

(Hay and Kelley 1974; Elzinga 1969; Rogowsky 1987) note that they systematically fail to achieve their supposed welfare goals.

Admittedly, each of these pieces of empirical work disproves only the
existence of certain kinds of benefits; the empirics cannot refute the claim—
often offered—that antitrust's benefits lie elsewhere. So, for example, it is
frequently claimed that even if enforcement is ineffective or targets firms that
were not actually violating the law, the mere presence of antitrust scrutiny
will force others in the industry to abandon any anticompetitive notions they
might harbor.[23] If so, the benefits of antitrust would be found only by investigations of the entire industry, or even the national economy. Until very
recently, such broader inquiries had not been undertaken.

Several recent papers begin to fill this gap. Shughart and Tollison (1991)
examine the macroeconomic effects of DOJ antitrust enforcement from 1932
to 1981. They report evidence from time series regressions showing a positive
and statistically significant relationship between unanticipated increases in
the number of cases instituted by the Antitrust Division and the unemployment rate of the U.S. civilian labor force. In particular, Shughart and Tollison's most conservative estimate suggests a *ceteris paribus* increase of .15
percent in the average annual unemployment rate (or about 5,400 additional
unemployed labor force participants at the data means) for every unexpected
1 percent increase in DOJ case-bringing activity. Because higher unemployment translates into lower output (and higher prices), the evidence reported
by Shughart and Tollison indicates that the DOJ's antitrust law enforcement
activities tend broadly to reduce economic welfare.

Bittlingmayer (1990) presents complementary evidence from an earlier
period, 1890–1914. Measured by different performance aggregates, the effects of antitrust enforcement during that time were consistently negative,
holding other factors constant. Antitrust cases brought during the relevant
period lowered real income, real output, stock prices, and other measures of
economic performance. The strongest negative impact was that produced by
cartel cases, an area of enforcement that is thought particularly useful under
the public-interest view of antitrust. As Bittlingmayer notes (p. 27), "the
actual—as opposed to the blackboard—effects of antitrust" run demonstrably counter to the public-interest view.

Subsequent empirical studies by Bittlingmayer reinforce this conclusion.

---

23. As two non-Chicagoans have recently stated, "The problem is, of course, that neither
the precedent nor deterrent effects of antitrust cases can be measured precisely. Among policymakers it is an article of faith that such effects are significant, and they well may be. It is
quite possible that deterrence alone produces greater social benefits than any other antitrust
results, but there is no reliable way to determine whether this is so. Lacking such knowledge,
any assertion about the quantitative economic impact of policies contains an inevitable element of uncertainty." See Peter Asch and Rosalind Seneca, Government and the Marketplace,
261 (2d ed. 1989). The papers discussed below go a long way toward removing that uncertainty.

Controlling for other factors, he (1992) finds that antitrust enforcement had a sizable impact (5–30 percent) on the variance of annual stock returns during the period 1904–1944. With each case filed, the Dow-Jones Industrial Average fell by more than 1 percent; specific antitrust episodes, like those during Teddy Roosevelt's "trust-busting" campaign, were responsible for major declines in stock prices. Bittlingmayer (1993a) has analyzed this last point in detail. He concludes that enforcement of the Sherman Act was responsible for much of the stock market's unsettledness—and, in fact, was the cause of major upheavals like the Panic of 1907—during the early days of antitrust. Indeed, swings in antitrust enforcement may explain the Great Crash: The Hoover administration's policy toward mergers and trade associations unexpectedly changed during a week in late October 1929 when stock prices fell by more than 30 percent (Bittlingmayer (1993c). In the more recent period (1945–1990), Bittlingmayer (1993b) shows, antitrust has continued to have major negative effects overall due to actions against exchange-listed firms, although the myriad price-fixing cases against nonlisted firms in the 1980s, most of which involved allegations of bid-rigging on highway contracts, seem not to have affected the markets at all.

In short, the developing statistical evidence on the effects of antitrust is considerably stronger than before. Antitrust is clearly costly—in enforcement budgets, wrongly decided cases, and private suits filed only to extort settlement offers. The earliest work tended simply to show that, in the areas investigated, antitrust had not delivered any benefits. But the many studies failing to find any antitrust benefits did not make an appreciable impact on Chicagoans, who have continued to talk—hypothetically—about antitrust's supposed ability to deter price fixing and anticompetitive mergers. That such benefits truly exist now seems very unlikely. The available evidence indicates that antitrust *reduces* output and wealth.

Antitrust's Inability to Benefit Particular Industries

A fourth reason offered by Chicagoans for their basically benevolent views of antitrust is their perception that antitrust cannot systematically benefit producers in any given industry. The focus on industry-wide producer benefits stems from the earliest (Stigler 1971) Chicago formulation of the economic theory of regulation, which models regulation as benefitting producers in a particular industry at the expense of consumers. As Stigler summarized his original model (1971, 3): "regulation is acquired by the industry and is designed and operated primarily for its benefit."

For Chicagoans, antitrust has never seemed to offer producers in most industries particular advantages, because its effects apparently are the same for all industries. Hence, it has not been seen as special-interest regulation: "The capture theory of regulation is not easily extended to antitrust since antitrust authorities do not supervise a single industry, firm or small group of these, as do most other regulatory agencies. These authorities, therefore, are not very susceptible to being manipulated by an identifiable constituency over which their power extends" (Demsetz 1989, 19). At times, Chicago school analysis has mentioned political influences on antitrust,[24] but Chicagoans' attempts to locate those influences empirically have failed.[25] Thus, given the burden of proof invoked in favor of antitrust, it continues to be characterized in public-interest terms.

There are several objections to the conclusion that a regulatory regime that cuts across industries is not likely subject to special-interest politics. First, politicians themselves clearly care for antitrust, as enforcement officials invariably learn (Baker 1985). Congressmen regularly exhort DOJ and FTC enforcers to bring ever more cases; the National Association of Attorneys General (NAAG) agitates for greater enforcement as well. Congress staunchly resisted Reagan-era initiatives to reduce enforcement at both the FTC and DOJ. Jim Miller's attempts to close FTC regional offices and to reduce his budget were successfully rebuffed on the Hill. DOJ's attempts to change the per se rule against resale price maintenance were scuttled, its horizontal merger guidelines opposed, and its vertical guidelines condemned (both by Congress and by NAAG). The FTC's ill-fated *Exxon* case to break up the eight largest oil companies was instigated in response to blatant Congressional pressure.[26] As rational maximizers of their own welfare, politicians must find something valuable about antitrust, because they spend considerable resources to obtain more of it.[27]

Moreover, one observes that, outside antitrust, regulation cutting across industries is nonetheless driven by special-interest politics. Regulatory agencies whose responsibilities cover multiple industries have nevertheless been shown to respond systematically to political pressure. The Federal Trade Commission is an oft-studied example (Mackay et al. 1987; Weingast and Moran 1983). FTC regulation of advertising benefits some industry subgroups at others' expense (Higgins and McChesney 1986). There are well-organized

24. Posner (1969a, 54) refers briefly to the "politicization of antitrust policy" in the FTC as part of the agency's "dependence on Congress" (p. 82), but does not investigate further.

25. Posner (1970, 411–13) suggested that levels of antitrust activity might depend on which political party was in power, but found no evidence to support that hypothesis. See also Stigler (1985), who examines evidence that agrarian and small-business interests were responsible for the Sherman Act, but rejects that hypothesis empirically.

26. Exxon Corp., 98 F.T.C. 453 (1981) (dismissing complaint). For a discussion, see McChesney (1986, 372–73).

27. Demsetz notes (1989, 23–24) that politicians expend resources to influence patterns of enforcement. But he apparently does not view antitrust as just another form of regulatory redistribution, because he does not believe that antitrust enforcers can be "captured" and because he sees the real problem as a lack of understanding of what competition really is. Both these points are discussed above.

pressure groups with demonstrated political power, such as unionized labor, whose affiliations span different industry groups.

Thus, the fact that antitrust is not industry-specific, and that it is administered by agencies with general jurisdictions that may not be captured by particular industries, is largely irrelevant. Neither aspect of antitrust necessarily alters the fundamental insights of the economic theory of regulation. It remains only to specify how antitrust can be used politically to benefit some groups at others' expense. Admittedly, the types of regulation imposed by antitrust are varied, meaning that each variant must be approached individually: the winners from blocked mergers and from prohibitions on resale price maintenance are most likely different groups. But this does not mean that one cannot identify the likely beneficiaries and victims, and test for antitrust's effects.

Horizontal mergers, to take one of the principal areas in which Chicagoans would admit a role for antitrust, are an example. Mergers are a phenomenon that cuts across different industries; at first glance, therefore, regulation of mergers might not seem to have the potential for rewarding politically powerful groups at the expense of politically weak ones. But one must recognize antitrust's essential similarity to the regulation of securities markets.[28] It is now well understood that well-organized groups, such as workers, will often oppose mergers, takeovers, and other changes in corporate control. While not always organized before the fact, managements of particular firms have shown that they can effectively organize *ad hoc* for political purposes, such as lobbying for passage of state and federal statutes to block takeovers that threaten their jobs. Thus, management and labor often join politically in pressing to stop takeovers.

Antitrust is a valuable political weapon in stopping mergers that are economically desirable but politically repugnant. Coate et al. (1990) show empirically that, other things equal, congressional pressure does in fact affect FTC merger enforcement. Pressure is reflected particularly in the various antitrust oversight and budget hearings at which FTC commissioners and senior political appointees for antitrust are called to testify. As that pressure intensifies, the likelihood increases that the FTC will move to block more mergers.

The trans-industry political benefits of antitrust have been identified in other contexts. While a politician's constituents may want antitrust used to stop mergers, the same groups will oppose other sorts of antitrust enforcement. Government actions opposing practices like price discrimination and vertical restraints merely reduce firm wealth. But these enforcement actions are useful to politicians, because they control the agencies that file the cases.

---

28. This similarity appears to have been recognized first by Henry Manne (1965). His seminal piece identifying "the market for corporate control," a fundamental notion in today's financial economics and securities regulation, explained why antitrust treatment of control transactions did not reflect the true economic reasons for changes in control.

The filing of an enforcement action causes the demand to rise for the services of politicians, who can wield their control over the agency to pressure bureaucrats to drop the action. As Faith, Leavens, and Tollison (1982) note, therefore, antitrust enforcement would predictably be geographically biased to favor firms operating in the jurisdictions of politicians with budgetary or oversight responsibility for antitrust. Empirically, they find that FTC cases brought against firms located in important committee members' districts are more likely to be dismissed than matters involving firms located elsewhere. The increased demands for such constituent service make antitrust valuable to politicians.

In short, the empirical evidence indicates that politicians, particularly those on committees with oversight or budgetary power over antitrust enforcement, find antitrust useful. It allows politicians to block mergers adversely affecting key interest groups in legislators' home districts; particular enforcement actions also increase the demand for politicians' services to intervene with enforcement authorities. This private-interest approach to antitrust, based on the ways that antitrust benefits legislators personally, can explain antitrust far better than public-interest models can. The special-interest model has been validated empirically, while attempts to validate the public-interest approach (Long et al. 1973; Siegfried 1975; Asch 1975) have all failed. The special-interest approach is also more consistent with the dictates of treating all actors—private and governmental—as maximizers of their own welfare.

Conclusion

The persistence of the public-interest view of antitrust is not limited to Chicago.[29] But its persistence at Chicago is remarkable, given the special-interest approach taken toward regulation more generally. The two approaches are seemingly irreconcilable. The current intellectual situation thus is not a stable equilibrium. Either the Chicago view of antitrust or the Chicago approach to regulation is wrong; both cannot be right. Strictly as a matter of internal consistency, therefore, one view or the other must yield.

In light of the empirical evidence, as well as the larger body of theory and evidence validating the economic theory of regulation, one would like to think that it is the Chicago school of antitrust that will defer to the Chicago school of regulation. That is a normative proposition, however. As a positive matter, *will* Chicagoans begin to alter their antitrust views? Lacking a model of intellectual conversion, one cannot answer the question rigorously. But one suspects that a conversion will not come quickly, for several reasons.

29. In discussing what Eastern Europe will need as it shifts to a market economy, the *Wall Street Journal* included antitrust: "Monopolies, state or private, must be broken up to allow price competition to do its vital work" (Death and Life in Germany, 1 December 1989, p. A14).

First, the public-choice approach may seem irrelevant to Chicagoans. Those who have declared victory and gone home may simply ignore the mounting challenges to Chicago orthodoxy. For others, there may be no perceived inconsistency. The more recent Chicago analysis using economics to discuss issues like antitrust standing and damages may seem unrelated to the public-choice problems presented by the wider Chicago approach to regulation. True, current discussions of standing and damages presume that antitrust is welfare-maximizing. But even if antitrust is not in the public interest (as the evidence indicates it is not), that just means that standing and damages should be considered in a second-best model. Such models are notoriously inconclusive; while not demonstrably correct in a second-best world, the existing analyses of various procedural facets of antitrust are not demonstrably wrong.

Moreover, a paradigm switch would require going outside Hyde Park. From the frequent citations made here, readers will appreciate the number of those who have disagreed with the Chicago approach. Yet for the most part, Chicagoans have simply ignored the criticisms and carried on in their public-interest analysis. Demsetz (1989, 26), for example, notes that antitrust enforcers "are never fully insulated from politics," but states as well that this fact is "of small significance." None of the empirical work showing that politics *is* a significant factor is cited or discussed.

This characteristic has drawn comment. Nelson (1979, 950) suggests that Posner "has been talking mainly to his friends" in claiming that the Chicago approach is now accepted by all. Mitchell (1989, 290–91) comments as well on how Chicago treats those working outside the Chicago paradigm as "irrelevant." So, for example, Stigler states (1982b, 52) that "it would be embarrassing" today to encounter the argument among economists that predatory pricing is used to achieve monopoly. He can be speaking only of economists in Chicago; elsewhere, economists discuss it frequently with no apparent discomfort (e.g., Salop 1981).

In sum, there is little reason at this point to expect a conversion from public interest to public choice in the Chicago approach to antitrust.

CHAPTER NINETEEN

The Unjoined Debate

FRED S. MCCHESNEY AND WILLIAM F. SHUGHART II

The prior chapter's closing pages bespeak a certain frustration. Yes, it is commonly recognized that antitrust has failed. This is not a point that divides observers along ideological lines. Even Robert Reich and John Kenneth Galbraith decry antitrust as a bust (see McChesney 1986, 381–82). "[A]ntitrust," Lester Thurow writes, "has been a failure. The costs it imposes far exceed any benefits it brings."[1]

Yet few members of the economics profession are willing to look beyond the narrow limits of the public-interest model to consider the political economy of antitrust. No systematic empirical evidence exists to support claims that antitrust has upheld either of the two prime directives most often attributed to it—protecting the interests of consumers or championing a Jeffersonian nation of yeomen farmers and shopkeepers sheltered from the harsh gales of competition. But most economists and legal scholars have failed to ask how the politics of antitrust might explain its actual performance. Hardnosed scholarship is avoided in favor of blind faith in the "modest promise of antitrust."[2]

The debate in which the public-choice school would engage the majority of economists thus remains unjoined. This inability to bring differences of opinion about antitrust to a principled debate, one that would include consideration of antitrust's politics, is frustrating for several reasons.

The Politics of Antitrust Are Everywhere

First, spotting the politics of antitrust hardly requires sophisticated mathematical modeling or complex quantitative methods. The politics are visible to the naked eye, ubiquitous, and widely reported. Consider two leading episodes from 1993.

Reno Air

Shortly after assuming power, the Clinton administration stymied Northwest Airlines' attempt to begin commercial passenger service from Reno, Nevada,

1. Lester Thurow, The Zero-Sum Society (1980), at 146.
2. Donald Dewey, Mergers and Cartels: Some Reservations About Policy, 59 Amer. Econ. Rev. 255 (1969).

to three West-Coast cities. By entering these routes, Northwest would compete head-to-head with Reno Air, a Nevada-based carrier that already flew to Seattle, Los Angeles, and San Diego. When Northwest announced its plans to fly these same routes, Reno Air complained to the U.S. Department of Transportation.

The politicians and bureaucrats responded swiftly. Since deregulation in 1978, the airlines have not legally been required to seek the Transportation Department's approval to start offering new domestic passenger service. But after Reno Air complained, Transportation Secretary Federico Peña told Northwest that he would strongly urge the Justice Department to take antitrust action against Northwest if it began flying the three routes. At a meeting called in Washington, Secretary Peña gave Northwest's president three days to reconsider the firm's plans. Congress was made aware of the affair. After pressure was applied by Richard Bryan and Harry Reid, Nevada's two Democratic senators, the Justice Department did in fact begin an investigation of Northwest's proposed entry. Northwest at last abandoned its plans to compete with Reno Air.

Why was Northwest's threatened entry objectionable? Invading markets to compete with existing firms is the essence of competition, not anticompetition. How could Northwest's entry, placing an extra carrier on the three routes affected, do anything other than enhance competition and expand consumer choice? Northwest had already announced introductory prices below Reno Air's, and even more vigorous competition between the two carriers was clearly foreseeable.

One possible objection was so-called predatory pricing. Northwest's critics charged that, despite its own financial woes (or perhaps because of them), the large, powerful carrier would under-price Reno Air and eventually drive it out of business. But mere under-pricing cannot be anticompetitive. Nor is it illegal. Only when a firm charges prices below cost and when, moreover, below-cost pricing is undertaken to bankrupt a rival, does any possible violation of the antitrust laws occur. Predatory pricing is a strong allegation—one that competitors make far more often than is justified by the facts. Indeed, the Supreme Court has said several times recently that it believes predation to be a rare event.[3] This is because predatory pricing is a rational (profitable) strategy only if the predator can plausibly recoup its losses after the prey has been bankrupted and has exited the industry. Once prices are raised with an eye toward recoupment, though, new entrants will seek to share in the predator's above-normal returns and the predatory price war must begin anew (McGee 1958).

But if Reno Air truly believed Northwest's planned actions were unlawfully

3. See, e.g., Brooke Group Ltd. v. Brown & Williamson Tobacco Corp., 113 S.Ct. 2578 (1993); Cargill, Inc. v. Monfort of Colorado, Inc., 479 U.S. 104 (1986); and Matsushita Electric Industrial Co. v. Zenith Radio Corp., 475 U.S. 574 (1986).

predatory, the place for appraising that claim was federal court. The antitrust laws allow private plaintiffs to sue for injunctive relief against anticipated injuries like those that Northwest's critics alleged would follow its entry. Instead of the courts, however, Reno Air opted for politics to stop Northwest.

The Northwest episode thus typifies the ways that antitrust is valuable politically. It offers a way for politicians to protect constituents threatened by the forces of unfettered competition. The interests of consumers get short shrift in the process. Even if Northwest's entry had ultimately driven Reno Air from the market, the effect would have been only to substitute one firm for another. And in the process, prices would be lower, consumer choice expanded, competition keener. But the winner would not be a Nevada firm—doubtless the real objection of Senators Bryan and Reid.

Microsoft

Under the terms of a 1948 liaison agreement between the Federal Trade Commission (FTC) and the Justice Department's Antitrust Division (DOJ), the two agencies divide the antitrust enforcement market between themselves (Shughart and Tollison 1985). Various industries are allocated to a particular agency—the oil industry belongs to the FTC and the steel industry to the DOJ, for example—and the other agency agrees not to compete in investigating any antitrust matter involving that industry.

Antitrust enforcement history was made in the summer of 1993, however, when the Justice Department began investigating Microsoft Corporation. The FTC had been investigating the firm for three years, and its staff was eager to initiate legal action against Microsoft for alleged monopolization. Among other things, the commission's attorneys maintained that Microsoft had unlawfully foreclosed the market opportunities of rival software companies by entering into contracts with virtually all major manufacturers of personal computers, granting substantial discounts to them in return for their agreement to include Microsoft's MS-DOS® and Windows® with all of their PCs. But the commission itself twice refused, on split votes, to issue a complaint. Following the FTC's second refusal to sue Microsoft, the Justice Department requested the FTC's files and began its own inquiry.

The FTC's investigation was in one sense unexceptional, exemplifying the now-familiar story of unsuccessful firms appealing to government for antitrust action that will handicap a highly successful rival. The investigation had centered particularly on the lack of success experienced by DR DOS®, marketed by Novell, Inc., a product that competed head-to-head with Microsoft's MS-DOS®. But the FTC's action was more interesting on another level: The commission's failure to vote out a complaint was almost surely politically driven. President Clinton had not yet named a new chairperson of the commission, and most of the commissioners voting on Microsoft were said to be seeking the nomination. But no one could discern the White House's position on the Microsoft matter. "Part of the commissioners' problem," one observer said at the time, "has been trying to divine what the administration wants to do."[4]

The commission's inaction disappointed the droves of rival firms' lobbyists and lawyers who had patrolled the corridors of the FTC building for months in hopes of getting a complaint against Microsoft. As their hopes faded, Microsoft's competitors turned to Congress. The DOJ's intervention in the Microsoft investigation occurred only after calls from Capitol Hill to Anne Bingaman, President Clinton's Assistant Attorney General for antitrust. As the *Wall Street Journal* reported,

> because Ms. Bingaman's request for the FTC documents followed prodding by two senators, her action "does appear to have taken on a bit of the political aspect," Mr. [Charles] Rule said.
> But if it's political, it's also bipartisan. Sen. Howard Metzenbaum (D., Ohio), chairman of the Senate Judiciary Committee's antitrust subcommittee, and Sen. Orrin Hatch, the ranking Republican on the full committee, both have urged Ms. Bingaman to examine the Microsoft case.[5]

The *Journal* did not report, though other publications did, that Novell's headquarters is located in Utah, the state represented by Senator Hatch. Utah is also the home of WordPerfect, Inc., whose closest competitor in word-processing software is Microsoft's Word®.

The Reno Air and Microsoft investigations are similar, in that both involve rivals, working through their political representatives, to subvert competitive market forces through antitrust processes. More important, both episodes were widely covered in the mainstream press, which included reports of the political machinations behind the administration's actions. Similarly, the press routinely reports that changes in political administrations cause changes in the enforcement objectives of the public antitrust agencies.[6]

Even to the casual observer, then, the role played by politics in shaping antitrust enforcement must be obvious. The business reporter on the beat sees and writes about it all the time. Why cannot the majority of economists see the same thing?

4. Stuart Taylor, Jr., Will FTC Break Microsoft Corp.'s Near-Monopoly?, Legal Times, 19 July 1993, p. 16.
5. Joe Davidson, U.S. Considers a Second Probe of Microsoft, Wall Street Journal, 2 August 1993, p. B8. "Rick" Rule is a former Assistant Attorney General for antitrust.
6. For example, in one of her earliest "policy" announcements, Anne Bingaman, President Clinton's Assistant Attorney General for antitrust, stated that the Justice Department would become more aggressive in bringing resale price maintenance cases. To advance that new agenda, she withdrew vertical merger guidelines adopted less than ten years earlier by the Reagan DOJ. See Catherine Young, Annie Gets Her Antitrust Gun, Business Week, 23 August 1993, p. 13.

Mistake Explanations Inevitably Fail

As noted in chapter 18 of this book, "explanations" of regulatory failures
that rely on error or ignorance explain nothing at all. No debate can be joined
on the basis of any such nonscientific "explanation." Thus, the profession's
continued belief that antitrust has a happy future, dismissing a century of
failures as mere mistakes, is frustrating.

It is disheartening as well that economists seem unable or unwilling to
apply to antitrust the lessons learned by studying other public-policy processes in which "mistake" theories eventually gave way to explanations
based on rational, self-interest-seeking political behavior. These lessons show
that the purposeful, maximizing behavior underlying supposedly "mistaken"
policies ultimately will be discerned, rendering the mistake model indefensible.

Monetary policy is a prime example. For decades, academic economists,
led by Milton Friedman, attributed the Federal Reserve System's history of
wrong-headed monetary policy to mistakes committed by well-meaning but
fallible human beings. Friedman and Anna Schwartz's *Monetary History of
the United States* is a monumental piece of scholarship, constituting one of
the most detailed empirical records ever assembled of sustained policy failure.[7] In it, they concoct perhaps the most famous mistake theory of all time,
ascribing the money supply collapse that precipitated and worsened the Great
Depression to such causes as a failure to understand the banking and liquidity
crisis, "the lack of understanding and experience" of Fed officials, the "absence of vigorous intellectual leadership" on the Federal Reserve Board, and
the fact that "contemporary economic comment" as well as the academic
literature were "hardly distinguished by the correctness or profundity of
understanding of the economic forces at work in the contraction."[8]

If the Great Depression and other monetary-policy fiascos were the result
of "mistake," it follows that the mistakes can—and should—be corrected.
The remedy for mistaken policy is simply to promote a better understanding
of the relevant economic theories and to see that better policy makers are in
place to put the theories into practice. Friedman and Schwartz's explanation
for a century of monetary-policy failures, then, was repeated mistakes—a
problem remediable with better instruction in the quantity theory of money
and with smarter bureaucrats.

Twenty years later, Friedman generously admitted that the mistake theory
would no longer work. He acknowledged criticism directed at his work by
those who advocated the superiority of "analyzing bureaucratic behavior,
not in terms of stated objectives, but in terms of the self-interest of the

7. Milton Friedman and Anna J. Schwartz, A Monetary History of the United States, 1867–
1960 (1963).
8. Ibid., at 407–19.

bureaucrats'' (i.e., from a public-choice perspective).[9] The criticism, he continued, was "largely justified":

> In the analysis of monetary policy in our book, we paid only passing attention to the self-interest of the people conducting monetary policy. More recently, we have all become familiar with the idea of applying to governmental performance the same approach that we apply to private business enterprises. The social function of business or government is one thing; the forces that control behavior may be very different.[10]

Armed with a public-choice perspective, Friedman then recounts a number of episodes directly at odds with his prior notion of mistaken (but correctable) behavior by government regulators. He identifies "mistaken" policies that, though socially baleful, turn out to be bureaucratically beneficial. Analyses pointing out errors and ways to correct them, even from the Fed's own staff, have had no impact on bureaucratic behavior; Friedman points to "a crystal clear case of a mistake made by the Fed which it has stubbornly refused to rectify under four different chairmen despite the weight of evidence, from inside and outside the system, on its adverse effects."[11] In perhaps the bitterest irony of all for mistake theorists, bureaucrats themselves are shown to embrace mistake explanations to excuse their poor performance.

Friedman is laudably gracious in conceding that repeated mistakes will not explain the policy failures he analyzed. But in his defense, public-choice theory was virtually non-existent when he and Anna Schwartz wrote their *Monetary History*; the most influential seminal work of public choice was being written at the same time.[12] Public-choice economists today improve on Friedman's work only because of more recent theoretical break-throughs.[13]

The same sequence—initial mistake theory yielding ultimately to a more convincing public-choice model—has typified the analysis of many other

9. Milton Friedman, Monetary Policy: Theory and Practice, 14 J. Money, Credit & Banking 98, 115 (1982). Friedman was referring in particular to the work of Mark Toma. See, for instance, Mark Toma, Inflationary Bias of the Federal Reserve System: A Bureaucratic Perspective, 10 J. Monetary Econ. 163 (1982). These and other important contributions to the public-choice perspective on monetary policy are collected in Eugenia F. Toma and Mark Toma (eds.), Central Bankers, Bureaucratic Incentives, and Monetary Policy (1986). Interestingly, Friedman (p. 115, n. 38) admits that while the public-choice alternative he finally accepted in 1982 had been developed "in a sophisticated and persuasive fashion" ten years earlier in non-Chicago journals like Public Choice and Kyklos, he had not been aware of these developments.

10. Friedman, *supra* note 9, at 115.

11. Ibid., at 113.

12. James M. Buchanan and Gordon Tullock, The Calculus of Consent: Logical Foundations of Constitutional Democracy (1962).

13. See, for example, Gary M. Anderson, William F. Shughart II, and Robert D. Tollison, A Public Choice Theory of the Great Contraction, 59 Pub. Choice 3 (1988) and A Public Choice Theory of the Great Contraction: Further Evidence, 67 Pub. Choice 277 (1990).

regulatory failures. Contemporaneous with Friedman's work on monetary policy, came an analysis—by another Nobel Prize winner, Ronald Coase—of broadcast spectrum regulation by the Federal Radio Commission (the forerunner of today's Federal Communications Commission).[14] Coase described the highly inefficient licensing system established by the federal government as basically a mistake, due largely to politicians' and bureaucrats' misunderstanding of the role played by private property rights in promoting the efficient allocation of broadcast frequencies. Thomas Hazlett has now shown that Coase's "error theory" is untenable.[15] "Most fundamentally, the nature of rights in the 'ether' was precisely understood; the regulatory approach adopted chose not to reject or ignore them but to maximize their rent values as dictated by [bureaucrats'] rational self-interest."[16]

To repeat, the point is not that younger economists writing today are smarter than Nobel Prize winners from the University of Chicago writing over thirty years ago. The moral is instead that theoretical advances of the past generation in the field of public choice call into question earlier conclusions that undesirable economic policy is merely mistaken. As the model of rational, self-interest-seeking behavior is applied progressively to different forms of government intervention, over and over again what at first seemed to be a mistake is later seen as logical—albeit socially undesirable—political behavior.

Among economists, antitrust is the last frontier of public-interest regulation. As Robert McCormick notes, "given the volume of research on the importance of private interests in affecting government in general and regulation in particular, it is a surprise that there remains one large research area still haunted by the ghost of Pigou. This is analysis of antitrust law."[17] But given the eventual exorcism of Pigou's ghost in other areas of public policy, partisans of antitrust must (or at least should) wonder how long the perceived public-interest explanations for antitrust can survive demonstrations of antitrust's underlying political rationale—whatever its stated economic objectives may be.

It Takes a Model to Beat a Model

The antitrust debate is unjoined because public-choice economists refuse to accept a "mistake" explanation for a policy that all sides concede has failed. As described above, the refusal to accept this mistake explanation is rooted

---

14. Ronald H. Coase, The Federal Communications Commission, 2 J. Law & Econ. 1 (1959).

15. Thomas W. Hazlett, The Rationality of U.S. Regulation of the Broadcast Spectrum, 33 J. Law & Econ. 133 (1990).

16. Ibid., at 134.

17. Robert E. McCormick, The Strategic Use of Regulation: Review of the Evidence, in The Political Economy of Regulation: Private Interests in the Regulatory Process 26 (1984).

partly in the realization that eventually such models are found wanting, forcing their proponents to recant. But impatience with mistake models also harks back to a more fundamental methodological paradigm that is supposed to govern disputes among economists.

Stigler himself has written of "the economist's insistence upon analyzing political institutions and processes with his customary apparatus of the theory of utility-maximizing behavior."[18] That apparatus includes deriving testable implications from a constrained optimization model, and testing those implications against the data.[19] Mistake theories, Stigler continues, "are not theories at all because they make no testable explanations for observable political phenomena."[20]

As the chapters in this volume (particularly those in Parts Three and Four) demonstrate, the public-choice perspective on antitrust is compelling precisely because (a) it works within a standard utility-maximization model of political behavior, and (b) it yields testable implications that have repeatedly been corroborated (i.e., not falsified) by real-world data. Of course, no claim could plausibly be advanced—not yet, at least—that the public-choice approach has answered all or even most of the important questions about the politics of antitrust. But that is beside the point, as Stigler has also discussed:

> The answer is that it takes a theory to beat a theory: if there is a theory that is right 51 percent of the time, it should be used until one comes along that is better. (Theories that are right only 50 percent of the time may be less economical than coin-flipping.)
>
> When we assume that [political actors], acting with mathematical consistency, maximize utility, therefore, it is not proper for someone to complain that men are much more complicated and diverse than that. So they are, but if this assumption yields a theory of behavior which agrees tolerably well with the facts, it should be used until a better theory comes along.[21]

The differences of opinion over antitrust will remain an unjoined debate until Stigler's point is acknowledged: It takes a model to beat a model. The chapters in Parts One and Two above show how, progressively, the public-interest model of antitrust was tested and failed. In that respect, the issue has reached the point at which there are few, if any, defenders of antitrust's record left nowadays. The only explanation of antitrust consistent with accepted economic methodology—model, implications, tests—is the public-choice explanation. Yet most lawyers, economists, and other social

18. George J. Stigler, The Theory of Price 333 (4th ed. 1987).
19. For further discussion, see Randall G. Holcombe, Economic Models and Methodology (1989), esp. chap. 3.
20. Stigler, *supra* note 18, at 333.
21. Ibid., at 7. In the original, Stigler was referring to consumers, not political actors.

scientists, while admitting the failure of the public-interest model, shun the public-choice approach.

Misunderstanding or ignorance of the public-choice model may explain the failure of some economists to open their eyes to the politics of antitrust. But, of course, it cannot serve as a general explanation for the profession's general unwillingness to join the debate. Why is there such uneasiness with the idea that the antitrust enforcement agencies are shaped by politics, as mundane as that notion is when applied to other areas of law? One possible explanation is self-interest: Plaintiffs and defendants in antitrust suits employ large numbers of attorneys and economist-experts.

Perhaps a more likely explanation is that antitrust is complex. Unlike occupational licensing requirements and many other forms of public regulation whose winners and losers are easy to identify, antitrust does not consistently promote the interests of any single, narrowly defined constituency. The politics of antitrust are often subtle, sometimes benefiting large firms, sometimes small; sometimes benefiting established enterprises, sometimes new entrants; and sometimes benefiting the law enforcers themselves. Importantly, though, neither "consumers" nor "the public" ever seem to appear on the list of demonstrated beneficiaries.

In any event, the debate over the purposes and effects of antitrust ends in frustration. "Here is our model," says the public-choice group; "here are our statistical tests. As social scientists, what is your alternative model to explain antitrust's origins, its purposes and effects? What are its implications? Where are your tests? Where is your evidence?"

Selected Bibliography

Adams, Walter, and Brock, James W. 1986. *The Bigness Complex.* New York: Pantheon Books.

Allen, Bruce T. 1972. "Vertical Foreclosure in the Cement Industry: Reply." *Journal of Law and Economics* 15: 467–71.

———. 1971. "Vertical Integration and Market Foreclosure: The Case of Cement and Concrete." *Journal of Law and Economics* 14: 251–74.

Amacher, Ryan C.; Higgins, Richard S.; Shughart, William F., II; and Tollison, Robert D. 1985. "The Behavior of Regulatory Activity over the Business Cycle: An Empirical Test." *Economic Inquiry* 23: 7–19.

American Bar Association, Commission to Study the Federal Trade Commission. 1969. *Report of the Commission to Study the Federal Trade Commission.* Chicago: American Bar Association.

Areeda, Phillip, and Turner, Donald F. 1975. "Predatory Pricing and Related Practices under Section 2 of the Sherman Act." *Harvard Law Review* 88: 697–733.

Armentano, Dominick T. 1982. *Antitrust and Monopoly: Anatomy of a Policy Failure.* New York: John Wiley & Sons.

Asch, Peter. 1975. "The Determinants and Effects of Antitrust Activity." *Journal of Law and Economics* 17: 575–81.

———. 1970. *Economic Theory and the Antitrust Dilemma.* New York: John Wiley & Sons.

Asch, Peter, and Seneca, Joseph J. 1976. "Is Collusion Profitable?" *Review of Economics and Statistics* 58: 1–12.

Bain, Joe S. 1968. *Industrial Organization.* 2d ed. New York: John Wiley & Sons.

Baker, Donald I. 1985. "Antitrust as a Political Football." Paper presented at the Nineteenth Annual New England Antitrust Conference, November.

Baker, Jonathan B. 1989. "Recent Developments in Economics That Challenge Chicago School Views." *Antitrust Law Journal* 58: 645–55.

Baumol, William J. 1982. "Contestable Markets: An Uprising in the Theory of Industry Structure." *American Economic Review* 72: 1–15.

Baumol, William J., and Ordover, Janusz A. 1985. "Use of Antitrust to Subvert Competition." *Journal of Law and Economics* 28: 247–65.

Baxter, William F. 1980. "The Political Economy of Antitrust." In *The Political Economy of Antitrust: Principal Paper by William Baxter,* edited by Robert D. Tollison. Lexington, Mass.: Lexington Books.

Becker, Gary S. 1983. "A Theory of Competition among Pressure Groups for Political Influence." *Quarterly Journal of Economics* 98: 371–400.

351

————. 1968. "Crime and Punishment: An Economic Approach." *Journal of Political Economy* 76: 169–217.

Benson, Bruce L.; Greenhut, Melvin L.; and Holcombe, Randall G. 1987. "Interest Groups and the Antitrust Paradox." *Cato Journal* 6: 801–17.

Binder, John J. 1988. "The Sherman Antitrust Act and the Railroad Cartels." *Journal of Law and Economics* 31: 443–68.

Bittlingmayer, George. 1993a. "The Stock Market and Early Antitrust Enforcement." *Journal of Law and Economics* 36: 1–32.

————. 1993b. "Government and the Stock Market: The Effects of Antitrust." Center for the Study of the Economy and the State, Working Paper No. 89.

————. 1993c. "The 1920s and the Great Crash." Center for the Study of the Economy and the State, Working Paper No. 86.

————. 1992. "Stock Returns, Real Activity, and the Trust Question." *Journal of Finance* 47: 1701–30.

————. 1990. "The Real and Monetary Consequences of Antitrust." Manuscript.

————. 1983. "Price Fixing and the Addyston Pipe Case." *Research in Law and Economics* 5: 57–130.

————. 1982. "Decreasing Average Cost and Competition: A New Look at the Addyston Pipe Case." *Journal of Law and Economics* 25: 201–30.

Blair, Roger D. 1985. "A Suggestion for Improved Antitrust Enforcement." *Antitrust Bulletin* 30: 433–56.

Block, Michael K.; Nold, Frederick C.; and Sidak, Joseph G. 1981. "The Deterrent Effect of Antitrust Enforcement." *Journal of Political Economy* 89: 429–45.

Bork, Robert H. 1978. *The Antitrust Paradox: A Policy at War with Itself*. New York: Basic Books.

————. 1966a. "Legislative Intent and the Policy of the Sherman Act." *Journal of Law and Economics* 9: 7–48.

————. 1966b. "The Rule of Reason and the Per Se Concept: Price Fixing and Market Division." *Yale Law Journal* 75: 75–105.

————. 1954. "Vertical Integration and the Sherman Act: The Legal History of an Economic Misconception." *University of Chicago Law Review* 22: 157–201.

Boudreaux, Donald J., and Ekelund, Robert B., Jr. 1988. "Inframarginal Consumers and the Per Se Legality of Vertical Restraints." *Hofstra Law Review* 17: 137–58.

Bowman, Ward S. 1967. "Restraint of Trade by the Supreme Court: The Utah Pie Case." *Yale Law Journal* 77: 70–85.

Bradley, Robert L., Jr. 1990. "On the Origins of the Sherman Antitrust Act." *Cato Journal* 9: 737–42.

Breit, William. 1991. "Resale Price Maintenance: What Do Economists Know and When Did They Know It?" *Journal of Institutional and Theoretical Economics* 147: 72–90.

Brennan, Timothy J. 1988. "Understanding 'Raising Rivals' Costs.'" *Antitrust Bulletin* 33:95–113.

Bresnahan, Timothy F. 1985. "Post-Entry Competition in the Plain Paper Copier Market." *American Economic Review* 75: 15–19.

Brozen, Yale. 1986. "The Antitrust Tradition: Entrepreneurial Restraint." *Harvard Journal of Law and Public Policy* 9: 337–56.

———. 1982. *Concentration, Mergers, and Public Policy.* New York: Macmillan.

Burns, Malcolm. 1989. "New Evidence on Predatory Price Cutting." *Managerial and Decision Economics* 10: 327–30.

———. 1986. "Predatory Pricing and the Acquisition Cost of Competitors." *Journal of Political Economy* 94: 226–96.

———. 1983. "An Empirical Analysis of Stockholder Injury under §2 of the Sherman Act." *Journal of Industrial Economics* 31: 333–62.

———. 1982. "Outside Intervention in Monopolistic Price Warfare: The Case of the 'Plug War' and the Union Tobacco Company." *Business History Review* 56: 33–53.

———. 1977. "The Competitive Effects of Trust-Busting: A Portfolio Analysis." *Journal of Political Economy* 85: 717–39.

Clarkson, Kenneth W., and Muris, Timothy J., eds. 1981. *The Federal Trade Commission since 1970: Economic Regulation and Bureaucratic Behavior.* Cambridge: Cambridge University Press.

Coate, Malcolm B.; Higgins, Richard S.; and McChesney, Fred S. 1990. "Bureaucracy and Politics in FTC Merger Challenges." *Journal of Law and Economics* 33: 463–82.

Coate, Malcolm B., and McChesney, Fred S. 1992. "Empirical Evidence on FTC Enforcement of the Merger Guidelines." *Economic Inquiry* 30: 277–93.

Colenutt, D. W., and O'Donnell, P. P. 1978. "The Consistency of Monopolies and Merger Commission." *Antitrust Bulletin* 20: 51–82.

Comanor, William S. 1985. "Vertical Price-Fixing, Vertical Market Restrictions, and the New Antitrust Policy." *Harvard Law Review* 98: 983–1002.

Comanor, William S., and Kirkwood, John B. 1985. "Resale Price Maintenance and Antitrust Policy." *Contemporary Policy Issues* 3: 9–16.

Cummings, F. J., and Ruther, W. E. 1979. "The Northern Pacific Case." *Journal of Law and Economics* 22: 329–40.

DeBow, Michael E. 1991. "The Social Costs of Populist Antitrust: A Public Choice Perspective." *Harvard Journal of Law and Public Policy* 14: 205–25.

Demsetz, Harold. 1989. "One Hundred Years of Antitrust: Should We Celebrate?" Paper presented at the Brent Upson Lecture, George Mason University Law School.

———. 1982a. *Economic, Legal, and Political Dimensions of Competition.* Amsterdam: North-Holland.

———. 1982b. "Barriers to Entry." *American Economic Review* 72: 47–57.

———. 1968a. "Do Competition and Monopolistic Competition Differ?" *Journal of Political Economy* 76: 146–48.

———. 1968b. "Why Regulate Utilities?" *Journal of Law and Economics* 11: 55–65.

Dewey, Donald. 1955. "The Common-Law Background of Antitrust Policy." *Virginia Law Review* 41: 759–86.

DiLorenzo, Thomas J. 1990. "The Origins of Antitrust: Rhetoric vs. Reality." *Regulation* 13 (Fall): 26–34.

———. 1985. "The Origins of Antitrust: An Interest-Group Perspective." *International Review of Law and Economics* 5: 73–90.

DiLorenzo, Thomas J., and High, Jack C. 1988. "Antitrust and Competition, Historically Considered." *Economic Inquiry* 26: 423–35.

Downie, J. 1958. *The Competitive Process.* London: Duckworth.

Easterbrook, Frank H. 1986. "Workable Antitrust Policy." *Michigan Law Review* 84: 1696–1713.

———. 1984. "The Limits of Antitrust." *University of Texas Law Review* 63: 1–40.

Easterbrook, Frank H.; Landes, William M.; and Posner, Richard A. 1980. "Contribution among Antitrust Defendants: A Legal and Economic Analysis." *Journal of Law and Economics* 23: 331–70.

Eckbo, B. Espen. 1985. "Mergers and the Market Concentration Doctrine: Evidence from the Capital Market." *Journal of Business* 58: 325–49.

———. 1983. "Horizontal Mergers, Collusion, and Stockholder Wealth." *Journal of Financial Economics* 11: 241–73.

Eckbo, B. Espen, and Wier, Peggy. 1985. "Antitrust Policy under the Hart-Scott-Rodino Act: A Reexamination of the Market Power Hypothesis." *Journal of Law and Economics* 28: 119–49.

Ekelund, Robert B., Jr., and Hébert, Robert F. 1990. "E. H. Chamberlain and Contemporary Industrial Organization Theory." *Journal of Economic Studies* 17: 20–31.

Ellert, James. 1976. "Mergers, Antitrust Law Enforcement and Stockholder Returns." *Journal of Finance* 31: 715–32.

Elzinga, Kenneth G. 1970. "Predatory Pricing: The Case of the Gunpowder Trust." *Journal of Law and Economics* 13: 233–40.

———. 1969. "The Antimerger Law: Pyrrhic Victories." *Journal of Law and Economics* 12: 43–78.

Elzinga, Kenneth G., and Breit, William. 1976. *The Antitrust Penalties: A Study in Law and Economics.* New Haven, Conn.: Yale University Press.

Elzinga, Kenneth G., and Mills, David E. 1989. "Testing for Predation: Is Recoupment Feasible?" *Antitrust Law Journal* 34: 869–93.

Ernst, Daniel R. 1990. "The New Antitrust History." *New York Law School Law Review* 35: 879–91.

Fairburn, J. A. 1985. "British Merger Policy." *Fiscal Studies* 6: 70–81.

Faith, Roger L.; Leavens, Donald R.; and Tollison, Robert D. 1982. "Antitrust Pork Barrel." *Journal of Law and Economics* 25: 32–42.

Fellner, William. 1949. *Competition among the Few.* New York: Knopf.

Fisher, Franklin M. 1974. "Alcoa Revisited: Comment." *Journal of Economic Theory* 9: 357–59.

Fisher, Franklin M.; McGowan, John J.; and Greenwood, Joen E. 1983. *Folded, Spindled, and Mutilated: Economic Analysis and U.S. v. IBM.* Cambridge, Mass.: MIT Press.

Flath, D. 1980. "The American Can Case." *Antitrust Bulletin* 25: 169–93.

Flynn, John J. 1988. "The Reagan Administration's Antitrust Policy: Original Intent and the Legislative History of the Sherman Act." *Antitrust Bulletin* 33: 259–307.

Fox, Eleanor M. 1981. "The Modernization of Antitrust: A New Equilibrium." *Cornell Law Review* 66: 1140–92.

Gallo, Joseph C.; Craycraft, Joseph L.; and Bush, Steven C. 1985. "Guess Who

Came to Dinner: An Empirical Study of Federal Antitrust Enforcement for the Period 1963–1984." *Review of Industrial Organization* 2: 106–30.

Gaskins, Darius W., Jr. 1974. "Alcoa Revisited: The Welfare Implications of a Secondhand Market." *Journal of Economic Theory* 7: 254–71.

Gerhart, Peter M. 1982. "The Supreme Court and Antitrust Analysis: The (Near) Triumph of the Chicago School." *Supreme Court Review 1982.* Pp. 319–47.

Gilligan, Thomas W.; Marshall, William J.; and Weingast, Barry R. 1989. "Regulation and the Theory of Legislative Choice: The Interstate Commerce Commission Act of 1887." *Journal of Law and Economics* 32: 35–62.

Gordon, Sanford D. 1963. "Attitudes towards Trusts Prior to the Sherman Act." *Southern Economic Journal* 30: 156–67.

Gould, John F., and Yamey, Basil S. 1967. "Professor Bork on Vertical Price Fixing." *Yale Law Journal* 75: 55–85.

Grady, Mark F. 1992. "Toward a Positive Economic Theory of Antitrust." *Economic Inquiry* 30: 225–41.

Haddock, David D. 1982. "Basing-Point Pricing: Competitive vs. Collusive Theories." *American Economic Review* 72: 289–306.

Harberger, Arnold C. 1954. "Monopoly and Resource Allocation." *American Economic Review* 44: 77–87.

Hawley, Ellis W. 1966. *The New Deal and the Problem of Monopoly.* Princeton, N.J.: Princeton University Press.

Hay, George A., and Kelley, Daniel. 1974. "An Empirical Survey of Price-Fixing Conspiracies." *Journal of Law and Economics* 17: 13–38.

Hazlett, Thomas W. 1992. "The Legislative History of the Sherman Act Reexamined." *Economic Inquiry* 30: 263–76.

———. 1986. "Is Antitrust Anticompetitive?" *Harvard Journal of Law and Public Policy* 9: 277–87.

———. 1984. "Interview with George Stigler." *Reason* (January): 44–48.

Higgins, Richard S., and McChesney, Fred S. 1986. "Truth and Consequences: The FTC's Ad Substantiation Program." *International Review of Law and Economics* 6: 151–68.

Higgins, Richard S.; Shughart, William F., II; and Tollison, Robert D. 1987. "Dual Enforcement of the Antitrust Laws." In *Public Choice and Regulation: A View from inside the Federal Trade Commission,* edited by Robert J. Mackay, James C. Miller III, and Bruce Yandle. Stanford, Calif.: Hoover Institution Press.

Himmelberg, Robert F. 1976. *The Origins of the National Recovery Administration: Business, Government, and the Trade Association Issue, 1921–1933.* New York: Fordham University Press.

Hofstadter, Richard. 1965. *The Paranoid Style in American Politics and Other Essays.* New York: Alfred A. Knopf.

Hovenkamp, Herbert. 1985. "Antitrust Policy after Chicago." *University of Michigan Law Review* 84: 213–84.

Howard, Marshall C. 1983. *Antitrust and Trade Regulation.* Englewood Cliffs, N.J.: Prentice-Hall.

Jarrell, Gregg A. 1985. "The Wealth Effects of Litigation by Targets: Do Interests Diverge in a Merge?" *Journal of Law and Economics* 28: 151–77.

Johnson, Ronald N., and Parkman, Allen M. 1987. "Spatial Competition and Vertical Integration; Cement and Concrete Revisited: Comment." *American Economic Review* 77: 750–53.

Kamerschen, David R. 1966. "An Estimation of the 'Welfare Losses' from Monopoly in the American Economy." *Western Economic Journal* 4: 221.

Kaplow, Louis. 1987. "Antitrust, Law & Economics, and the Courts." *Law and Contemporary Problems* 50: 181–216.

Katzmann, Robert A. 1980. *Regulatory Bureaucracy: The Federal Trade Commission and Antitrust Policy*. Cambridge, Mass.: MIT Press.

Kauper, Thomas E. 1986. "Twenty Years of Antitrust: The 'Highlights.'" Paper presented at the Twentieth Annual New England Antitrust Conference.

Kaysen, Carl, and Turner, Donald F. 1959. *Antitrust Policy: An Economic and Legal Analysis*. Cambridge: Harvard University Press.

Kirtner, Earl. 1964. *An Antitrust Primer*. New York: Macmillan.

Klein, Benjamin, and Murphy, Kevin M. 1988. "Vertical Restraints as Contract Enforcement Mechanisms." *Journal of Law and Economics* 28: 265–97.

Klein, Benjamin, and Saft, Lester F. 1985. "The Law and Economics of Franchise Tying Contracts." *Journal of Law and Economics* 26: 345–61.

Kleit, Andrew N. 1993. "Common Law, Statute Law, and the Theory of Legislative Choice: An Inquiry into the Goal of the Sherman Act." *Economic Inquiry* 31: 647–62.

———. 1992. "Efficiencies without Economists: The Early Years of Resale Price Maintenance." Bureau of Economics, Federal Trade Commission, Working Paper No. 193.

Kolko, Gabriel. 1965. *Railroads and Regulation 1877–1916*. Princeton, N.J.: Princeton University Press.

———. 1963. *The Triumph of Conservatism: A Reinterpretation of American History, 1900–1916*. New York: Free Press.

Korah, V. 1982. "Control of Mergers in the United Kingdom on Grounds of Competition Legislation, Practice and Experience." In *European Merger Control: Legal and Economic Analyses on Multinational Enterprises,* edited by K. J. Hopt. Berlin: Walter de Gruyter.

Kovacic, William E. 1993. "The Identification and Proof of Horizontal Agreements under the Antitrust Laws." *Antitrust Bulletin* 38: 5–81.

———. 1991. "Reagan's Judicial Appointees and Antitrust in the 1990s." *Fordham Law Review* 60: 49–124.

———. 1990a. "The Antitrust Paradox Revisited: Robert Bork and the Transformation of Modern Antitrust Policy." *Wayne State Law Review* 36: 1413–71.

———. 1990b. "Comments and Observations." *Antitrust Law Journal* 59: 119–30.

———. 1989. "Failed Expectations: The Troubled Past and Uncertain Future of the Sherman Act as a Tool for Deconcentration." *Iowa Law Review* 74: 1105–50.

———. 1987. "The Federal Trade Commission and Congressional Oversight of Antitrust Enforcement: A Historical Perspective." In *Public Choice and Regulation: A View from Inside the Federal Trade Commission,* edited by Robert J. Mackay, James C. Miller III, and Bruce Yandle. Stanford, Calif.: Hoover Institution Press.

―――. 1982. "The Federal Trade Commission and Congressional Oversight of Antitrust Enforcement." *Tulsa Law Journal* 17: 587–671.

Krattenmaker, Thomas G., and Salop, Steven C. 1986. "Anticompetitive Exclusion: Raising Rivals' Costs to Achieve Power over Price." *Yale Law Journal* 96: 206–93.

Krouse, Clement G. 1984. "Brand Name as a Barrier to Entry: The ReaLemon Case." *Southern Economic Journal* 51: 495–502.

Kwoka, John E., and White, Lawrence J. (eds.). 1989. *The Antitrust Revolution.* New York: Harper Collins.

Lande, Robert H. 1988. "The Risk and (Coming) Fall of Efficiency as the Ruler of Antitrust." *Antitrust Bulletin* 33: 429–65.

―――. 1982. "Wealth Transfers as the Original and Primary Concern of Antitrust: The Efficiency Interpretation Challenged." *Hastings Law Journal* 34: 65–151.

Landes, William M. 1983. "Optimal Sanctions for Antitrust Violations." *University of Chicago Law Review* 50: 652–78.

Landes, William M., and Posner, Richard A. 1981. "Market Power in Antitrust Cases." *Harvard Law Review* 94: 937–96.

―――. 1979. "Should Indirect Purchasers Have Standing to Sue under the Antitrust Laws? An Economic Analysis of the Rule of Illinois Brick." *University of Chicago Law Review* 46: 602–35.

―――. 1975. "The Independent Judiciary in an Interest-Group Perspective." *Journal of Law and Economics* 18: 875–901.

Lean, David F.; Ogur, Jonathan D.; and Rogers, Robert P. 1985. "Does Collusion Pay . . . Does Antitrust Work?" *Southern Economic Journal* 51: 828–41.

Letwin, William. 1965. *Law and Economic Policy in America: The Evolution of the Sherman Antitrust Act.* New York: Random House.

Levy, David, and Welzer, Steve. 1985. "System Error: How the IBM Antitrust Suit Raised Computer Prices." *Regulation* (September): 27–30.

Libecap, Gary D. 1992. "The Rise of the Chicago Packers and the Origins of Meat Inspection and Antitrust." *Economic Inquiry* 30: 242–62.

Liebeler, Wesley J. 1987. "What Are the Alternatives to Chicago?" *Duke Law Journal.* Pp. 879–96.

―――. 1981. "Bureau of Competition: Antitrust Enforcement Activities." In *The Federal Trade Commission since 1970: Economic Regulation and Bureaucratic Behavior,* edited by Kenneth W. Clarkson and Timothy J. Muris. Cambridge: Cambridge University Press.

Long, William F.; Schramm, Richard; and Tollison, Robert D. 1973. "The Economic Determinants of Antitrust Activity." *Journal of Law and Economics* 16: 351–64.

MacAvoy, Paul W., and Robinson, Kenneth. 1983. "Winning By Losing: The AT&T Settlement and its Impact on Telecommunications." *Yale Journal on Regulation* 1: 1–42.

Machlup, Fritz. 1952. *The Economics of Sellers' Competition.* Baltimore: Johns Hopkins University Press.

Mackay, Robert J.; Miller, James C., III; and Yandle, Bruce (eds.). 1987. *Public Choice and Regulation: A View from Inside the Federal Trade Commission.* Stanford, Calif.: Hoover Institution Press.

Manne, Henry G. 1965. "Mergers and the Market for Corporate Control." *Journal of Political Economy* 73: 110–20.

Mariger, Randall. 1978. "Predatory Price Cutting: The Standard Oil of New Jersey Case Revisited." *Explorations in Economic History* 15: 341–67.

Martin, David D. 1959. *Mergers and the Clayton Act*. Berkeley: University of California Press.

Martin, Robert E. 1982. "Monopoly Power and the Recycling of Raw Materials." *Journal of Industrial Economics* 30: 405–19.

Marvel, Howard P. 1982. "Exclusive Dealing." *Journal of Law and Economics* 25: 1–25.

Marvel, Howard P., and McCafferty, Stephen. 1984. "Resale Price Maintenance and Quality Certification." *Rand Journal of Economics* 15: 346–59.

Marvel, Howard P.; Netter, Jeffrey M.; and Robinson, Anthony M. 1988. "Price Fixing and Civil Damages: An Economic Analysis." *Stanford Law Review* 40: 561–78.

Marx, Thomas G. 1975. "Economic Theory and Judicial Process: A Case Study." *Antitrust Bulletin* 20: 775–802.

McBride, Mark E. 1987. "Spatial Competition and Vertical Integration; Cement and Concrete Revisited: Reply." *American Economic Review* 77: 754–56.

———. 1983. "Spatial Competition and Vertical Integration: Cement and Concrete Revisited." *American Economic Review* 73: 1011–22.

McCarthy, J. Thomas. 1979. "Trademarks, Antitrust and the Federal Trade Commission." *John Marshall Law Review* 13: 151–62.

McChesney, Fred S. 1993. "Antitrust." In *The Fortune Encyclopedia of Economics*, edited by D. R. Henderson. New York: Warner Books.

———. 1991. "Chicago's Contradictory Views of Antitrust and Regulation." *Cato Journal* 10: 775–98.

———. 1986. "Law's Honour Lost: The Plight of Antitrust." *Antitrust Bulletin* 31: 359–82.

McGee, John S. 1971. *In Defense of Industrial Concentration*. New York: Praeger.

———. 1958. "Predatory Price Cutting: The Standard Oil (N.J.) Case." *Journal of Law and Economics* 1: 137–69.

McWilliams, Abagail; Turk, Thomas A.; and Zardkoohi, Asghar. 1993. "Antitrust Policy and Mergers: The Wealth Effect of Supreme Court Decisions." *Economic Inquiry* 31: 517–33.

Meehan, James W. 1972. "Vertical Foreclosure in the Cement Industry: A Comment." *Journal of Law and Economics* 15: 461–65.

Miller, James C., III; Walton, Thomas W.; Kovacic, William E.; and Rabkin, Jeremy A. 1984. "Industrial Policy: Reindustrialization through Competition or Coordinated Action?" *Yale Journal on Regulation* 2: 1–37.

Millon, David. 1988. "The Sherman Act and the Balance of Power." *Southern California Law Review* 61: 1219–92.

Mitchell, William C. 1989. "Chicago Political Economy: A Public Choice Perspective." *Public Choice* 63: 283–92.

Mueller, Willard F. 1989. "The Sealy Restraints: Restrictions on Free Riding or Output?" *University of Wisconsin Law Review*. Pp. 1255–1321.

Nelson, Richard R. 1979. "Comments on a Paper by Posner." *University of Pennsylvania Law Review* 127: 949–52.

Newmark, Craig M. 1988. "Is Antitrust Enforcement Effective?" *Journal of Political Economy* 96: 1315–28.

Noll, Roger. 1987. "The Twisted Pair: Regulation and Competition in Telecommunications." *Regulation* 11: 15–22.

Office of Fair Trading (U.K.). 1978. "Mergers: A Guide to the Procedures under the Fair Trading Act 1973." London: HMSO.

Page, William H. 1989. "The Chicago School and the Evolution of Antitrust: Characterization, Antitrust Injury, and Evidentiary Sufficiency." *University of Virginia Law Review* 75: 1221–1308.

———. 1988. "Capture, Clear Articulation, and Legitimacy: A Reply to Professor Wiley." *University of Southern California Law Review* 61: 1343–55.

———. 1987. "Interest Groups, Antitrust, and State Regulation: *Parker v. Brown* in the Economic Theory of Legislation." *Duke Law Journal.* Pp. 618–68.

Palmer, John. 1972. "Some Economic Conditions Conducive to Collusion." *Journal of Economic Issues* 6: 29–39.

Parsons, Donald O., and Ray, Edward J. 1975. "The United States Steel Consolidation: The Creation of Market Control." *Journal of Law and Economics* 18: 181–220.

Pass, C. L., and Sparkes, J. R. 1980. "Control of Horizontal Mergers in Britain." *Journal of World Trade Law* 14: 135–59.

Peltzman, Sam. 1989. "The Economic Theory of Regulation After a Decade of Deregulation." *Brookings Papers on Economic Activity* 15: 1–59.

———. 1984. "Comments on FTC Line of Business Program." In *Evaluation of the Benefits of the Federal Trade Commission's Line of Business Program,* Appendix E. Washington, D.C.: Bureau of Economics, Federal Trade Commission.

———. 1976. "Toward a More General Theory of Regulation." *Journal of Law and Economics* 19: 211–40.

Peritz, Rudolph J. 1990. "A Counter-History of Antitrust Law." *Duke Law Journal.* Pp. 263–320.

Peterman, John L. 1975a. "The Brown Shoe Case." *Journal of Law and Economics* 18: 81–146.

———. 1975b. "The Federal Trade Commission v. Brown Shoe Company." *Journal of Law and Economics* 18: 361–419.

Petty, Ross. 1986. "Letter to the Editor: How IBM Raised Prices." *Regulation* 10: 4.

Pfunder, Malcolm; Plaine, Daniel; and Whittemore, Anne M. 1972. "Compliance with Divestiture Orders under Section 7 of the Clayton Act: An Analysis of the Relief Obtained." *Antitrust Bulletin* 17: 19–180.

Phillips, Almarin. 1962. *Market Structure, Organization and Performance: An Essay on Price Fixing and Combinations in Restraint of Trade.* Cambridge: Harvard University Press.

Pickering, J. F. 1980. "The Implementation of British Competition Policy on Mergers." *European Competition Law Review.* Pp. 177–78.

———. 1974. *Industrial Structure and Market Conduct.* London: Martin Robertson.

Pittman, Russell W. 1984. "Predatory Investment: *U.S. vs. IBM.*" *International Journal of Industrial Organization* 2: 341–65.

Posner, Richard A. 1981. "The Next Step in the Antitrust Treatment of Restricted Distribution: Per Se Legality." *University of Chicago Law Review* 48: 6–26.

———. 1979. "The Chicago School of Antitrust Analysis." *University of Pennsylvania Law Review* 127: 925–48.

———. 1977. "The Rule of Reason and the Economic Approach: Reflections on the Sylvania Decision." *University of Chicago Law Review* 45: 1–20.

———. 1976. *Antitrust Law: An Economic Perspective.* Chicago: University of Chicago Press.

———. 1975. "The Social Costs of Monopoly and Regulation." *Journal of Political Economy* 83: 807–27.

———. 1974. "Theories of Economic Regulation." *Bell Journal of Economics* 5: 335–58.

———. 1970. "A Statistical Study of Antitrust Enforcement." *Journal of Law and Economics* 13: 365–419.

———. 1969a. "The Federal Trade Commission." *University of Chicago Law Review* 37: 48–89.

———. 1969b. "Oligopoly and the Antitrust Laws: A Suggested Approach." *Stanford Law Review* 21: 1562–1606.

Pratt, Joseph A. 1980. "The Petroleum Industry in Transition: Antitrust and the Decline of Monopoly Control in Oil." *Journal of Economic History* 40: 815–37.

Reder, Melvin W. 1982. "Chicago Economics: Permanence and Change." *Journal of Economic Literature* 20: 1–38.

Rogowsky, Robert A. 1987. "The Pyrrhic Victories of Section 7: A Political Economy Approach." In *Public Choice and Regulation: A View from Inside the Federal Trade Commission,* edited by Robert J. Mackay, James C. Miller III, and Bruce Yandle. Stanford, Calif.: Hoover Institution Press.

———. 1986. "The Economic Effectiveness of Section 7 Relief." *Antitrust Bulletin* 31: 187–233.

———. 1984. "The Justice Department's Merger Guidelines: A Study in the Application of the Rule." *Research in Law and Economics* 6: 135–66.

Rosenbaum, David I. 1987. "Predatory Pricing and the Reconstituted Lemon Juice Industry." *Journal of Economic Issues* 21: 237–58.

Ross, Thomas W. 1986. "Store Wars: The Chain Tax Movement." *Journal of Law and Economics* 29: 125–37.

———. 1984. "Winners and Losers Under the Robinson-Patman Act." *Journal of Law and Economics* 27: 243–71.

Rowley, Charles K. 1968. "Mergers and Public Policy in Great Britain." *Journal of Law and Economics* 11: 75–132.

Rubin, Paul H. 1990. *Managing Business Transactions: Controlling the Cost of Coordinating, Communicating, and Decision Making.* New York: The Free Press.

Salop, Steven C. (ed.). 1981. *Strategy, Predation, and Antitrust Analysis.* Washington, D.C.: Federal Trade Commission.

Scherer, F. M. 1980. *Industrial Market Structure and Economic Performance.* 2d ed. Boston: Houghton Mifflin.

———. 1979. "The Welfare Economics of Product Variety: An Application to the Ready-to-Eat Cereals Industry." *Journal of Industrial Economics* 28: 113–34.

Scherer, F. M., and Ross, David. 1990. *Industrial Market Structure and Economic Performance.* 3d ed. Boston: Houghton Mifflin.

Schmalensee, Richard. 1979. "On the Use of Economic Models in Antitrust: The ReaLemon Case." *University of Pennsylvania Law Review* 27: 994–1050.

———. 1978. "Entry Deterrence in the Ready-to-Eat Breakfest Cereal Industry." *Bell Journal of Economics* 9: 305–27.

Schwartzman, D. 1960. "The Burden of Monopoly." *Journal of Political Economy* 68: 727–30.

Shepherd, William G. 1979. "Anatomy of a Monopoly." *Antitrust Law and Economics Review* 11: 103–16.

———. 1972. "The Elements of Market Structure." *Review of Economics and Statistics* 54: 25–37.

———. 1970. *Market Power and Economic Welfare*. New York: Random House.

Shughart, William F., II. 1990a. *Antitrust Policy and Interest-Group Politics*. New York: Quorum Books.

———. 1990b. *The Organization of Industry*. Homewood, Ill.: Richard D. Irwin.

———. 1990c. "Private Antitrust Enforcement: Compensation, Deterrence, or Extortion?" *Regulation* 13 (Fall): 53–61.

———. 1989. "Antitrust Policy in the Reagan Administration: Pyrrhic Victories?" In *Regulation and the Reagan Era: Politics, Bureaucracy, and the Public Interest*, edited by Roger E. Meiners and Bruce Yandle. New York: Holmes & Meier.

———. 1987. "Don't Revise the Clayton Act, Scrap It!" *Cato Journal* 6: 925–32.

Shughart, William F., II, and Tollison, Robert D. 1991. "The Employment Consequences of the Sherman and Clayton Acts." *Journal of Institutional and Theoretical Economics* 147: 38–52.

———. 1985. "The Positive Economics of Antitrust Policy: A Survey Article." *International Review of Law and Economics* 5: 39–57.

Shughart, William F., II; Tollison, Robert D.; and Goff, Brian L. 1986. "Bureaucratic Structure and Congressional Control." *Southern Economical Journal* 52: 962–72.

Siegfried, John J. 1975. "The Determinants of Antitrust Activity." *Journal of Law and Economics* 17: 559–74.

Simons, Henry C. 1948. "A Positive Program for Laissez Faire: Some Proposals for a Liberal Economic Policy." Chicago: University of Chicago Press, 1934. Reprinted in *Economic Policy for a Free Society*. Chicago: University of Chicago Press.

Sims, Joe, and Lande, Robert H. 1986. "The End of Antitrust—Or a New Beginning." *Antitrust Bulletin* 31: 301–22.

Spitzer, Matthew L. 1988. "Antitrust Federalism and Rational Choice Political Economy: A Critique of Capture Theory." *University of Southern California Law Review* 61: 1293–1326.

Sproul, Michael F. 1993. "Antitrust and Prices." *Journal of Political Economy* 101: 741–54.

Steuer, Richard M. 1985. "Monsanto and the Mothball Fleet of Antitrust." *Antitrust Bulletin* 30: 1–10.

Stigler, George J. 1985. "The Origin of the Sherman Act." *Journal of Legal Studies* 14: 1–12.

———. 1982a. "The Economist as Preacher." In *The Economist as Preacher and Other Essays*. Chicago: University of Chicago Press.

———. 1982b. "The Economists and the Problem of Monopoly." In *The Economist as Preacher and Other Essays*. Chicago: University of Chicago Press.

———. 1975. "Supplementary Note on Economic Theories of Regulation (1975)." In *The Citizen and the State*. Chicago: University of Chicago Press.

———. 1971. "The Theory of Economic Regulation." *Bell Journal of Economics and Management Science* 2: 3–21.

———. 1968. *The Organization of Industry*. Homewood, Ill.: Richard D. Irwin.

———. 1966. "The Economic Effects of the Antitrust Laws." *Journal of Law and Economics* 9: 225–58.

———. 1956. "The Statistics of Monopoly and Merger." *Journal of Political Economy* 64: 33–40.

Stillman, Robert. 1983. "Examining Anti-Trust Policy towards Horizontal Mergers." *Journal of Financial Economics* 11: 225–40.

Stocking, George W., and Mueller, Willard F. 1955. "The Cellophane Case and the New Competition." *American Economic Review* 45: 29–63.

Sullivan, E. Thomas. 1986. "The Antitrust Division as a Regulatory Agency: An Enforcement Policy in Transition." *Washington University Law Quarterly* 64: 997–1055.

Suslow, Valerie Y. 1986. "Estimating Monopoly Behavior with Competitive Recycling: An Application to Alcoa." *Rand Journal of Economics* 17: 389–403.

Sutherland, A. 1970. *The Monopolies Commission in Action*. Cambridge: Cambridge University Press.

Swan, Peter L. 1980. "Alcoa: The Influence of Recycling on Monopoly Power." *Journal of Political Economy* 88: 76–99.

Telser, Lester G. 1987. *A Theory of Efficient Cooperation and Competition*. Cambridge: Cambridge University Press.

———. 1985. "Cooperation, Competition, and Efficiency." *Journal of Law and Economics* 28: 271–95.

———. 1978. *Economic Theory and the Core*. Chicago: University of Chicago Press.

———. 1960. "Why Should Manufacturers Want Fair Trade?" *Journal of Law and Economics* 3: 12–30.

Thorelli, Hans J. 1955. *The Federal Antitrust Policy: Origination of an American Tradition*. Baltimore: Johns Hopkins University Press.

Tollison, Robert D. 1989. "Chicago Political Economy." *Public Choice* 63: 293–97.

———. 1983. "Antitrust in the Reagan Administration: A Report from the Belly of the Beast." *International Journal of Industrial Organization* 1: 211–21.

Tullock, Gordon. 1967. "The Welfare Costs of Monopolies, Tariffs, and Theft." *Western Economic Journal* 5: 224–32.

Utton, M. A. 1975. "British Merger Policy." In *Competition Policy in the UK and EEC*, edited by K. D. George and C. Joll. Cambridge: Cambridge University Press.

———. 1974. "On Measuring the Effects of Industrial Mergers." *Scottish Journal of Political Economy* 21: 12–28.

Weaver, Suzanne. 1977. *The Decision to Prosecute: Organization and Public Policy in the Antitrust Division*. Cambridge: MIT Press.

Weingast, Barry R., and Moran, Mark J. 1983. "Bureaucratic Discretion or Congressional Control? Regulatory Policymaking by the Federal Trade Commission." *Journal of Political Economy* 91: 765–800.

Weir, Charlie. 1992. "Monopolies and Mergers Commission, Merger Reports and the Public Interest: A Probit Analysis." *Applied Economics* 24: 27–34.

Wiley, John Shephard, Jr., 1988. "Capture Theory of Antitrust Federalism: Reply to Professors Page and Spitzer." *University of Southern California Law Review* 61: 1327–41.

————. 1987. "Antitrust and Core Theory." *University of Chicago Law Review* 54: 556–89.

————. 1986a. "'After Chicago:' An Exaggerated Demise?" *Duke Law Journal.* Pp. 1003–13.

————. 1986b. "A Capture Theory of Antitrust Federalism." *Harvard Law Review* 99: 713–89.

Williamson, Oliver E. 1985. *The Economic Institutions of Capitalism: Firms, Markets, Relational Contracting.* New York: Free Press.

————. 1975. *Markets and Hierarchies: Analysis and Antitrust Implications.* New York: Free Press.

————. 1968a. "Economies as an Antitrust Defense: The Welfare Tradeoffs," *American Economic Review* 58: 18–36.

————. 1968b. "Wage Rates as a Barrier to Entry: The Pennington Case in Perspective." *Quarterly Journal of Economics* 82: 85–116.

————. 1965. "A Dynamic Theory of Interfirm Behavior." *Quarterly Journal of Economics* 79: 579–607.

Wood Hutchinson, Diane. 1985. "Antitrust 1984: Five Decisions in Search of a Theory." *Supreme Court Review 1984.* Pp. 69–148.

Yandle, Bruce. 1988. "Antitrust Actions and the Budgeting Process." *Public Choice* 59: 263–75.

Young, Allyn A. 1915. "The Sherman Act and the New Anti-Trust Legislation, II." *Journal of Political Economy* 23: 305–26.

Zelenitz, A. 1980. "The Attempted Promotion of Competition in Related Goods Markets: The Ford-Autolite Divestiture Case." *Antitrust Bulletin* 25: 103–24.

Zerbe, Richard O. 1983. "The Chicago Board of Trade Case, 1918." *Research in Law and Economics* 5: 17–55.

————. 1970. "Predatory Pricing: The Case of the Gunpowder Trust." *Journal of Law and Economics* 13: 233–40.

Contributors

Peter Asch (deceased)

George Bittlingmayer
Graduate School of Management
University of California, Davis
Davis, CA 95616-8609

Donald J. Boudreaux
Department of Legal Studies
Clemson University
Clemson, SC 29634

Malcolm B. Coate
Bureau of Economics
Federal Trade Commission
Washington, DC 20580

Louis De Alessi
Department of Economics
University of Miami
P.O. Box 248126
Coral Gables, FL 33124-6550

Thomas J. DiLorenzo
Department of Economics
Loyola College in Maryland
4501 North Charles Street
Baltimore, MD 21210-2699

B. Espen Eckbo
Faculty of Commerce
University of British Columbia
Vancouver, BC V6T 1Y8
Canada

Robert B. Ekelund, Jr.
Department of Economics
Auburn University
Auburn, AL 36849

Roger L. Faith
Department of Economics
Arizona State University
Tempe, AZ 85287

Richard S. Higgins
Capital Economics
1299 Pennsylvania Avenue, N.W.
Washington, DC 20004-2402

William E. Kovacic
Law School
George Mason University
3401 North Fairfax Drive
Arlington, VA 22201

Donald R. Leavens
National Association of Realtors
777 14th Street, N.W.
Washington, DC 20005-3271

William F. Long
Bureau of the Census
Building 3
Suitland, MD 20233

Fred S. McChesney
School of Law
Emory University
Atlanta, GA 30322

Michael J. McDonald
Capital Economics
1299 Pennsylvania Avenue, N.W.
Washington, DC 20004-2402

Stephen Parker
Law School
Yale University
New Haven, CT 06520

Richard A. Posner
United States Court of Appeals
Seventh Circuit
219 South Dearborn Street
Chicago, IL 60604

Paul H. Rubin
Department of Economics
Emory University
Atlanta, GA 30322

Richard Schramm
Department of Urban Studies and
  Planning
Massachusetts Institute of
  Technology
Cambridge, MA 02139

Joseph J. Seneca
University Vice-President for
  Academic Affairs
Rutgers University
Third Floor Old Queens,
  Room 307
New Brunswick, NJ 08903

William F. Shughart II
Department of Economics and
  Finance
University of Mississippi
University, MS 38677

Jon Silverman
DRI/McGraw-Hill
1200 G Street, N.W.
10th Floor
Washington, DC 20005

George J. Stigler (deceased)

Robert D. Tollison
Center for Study of Public Choice
George Mason University
Fairfax, VA 22030

Charlie Weir
Faculty of Management
Robert Gordon University
Hilton Place
Aberdeen AB9 1FP
United Kingdom

Peggy Wier
Dean's Office
College of Arts and Sciences
University of Rochester
Rochester, NY 14627

Bruce Yandle
Department of Legal Studies
Clemson University
Clemson, SC 29634

AUTHOR INDEX

Adams, Walter, 34 n. 2
Alchian, Armen A., 7 n. 1, 189 nn. 2, 3, 194 n. 16
Allen, Bruce T., 34, 41–42
Alston, Richard M., 27 n. 11, 33 n. 1
Altschuler, Stuart, 167 n. 1
Amacher, Ryan C., 171, 184 n. 13
Anderson, Gary, M., 15 n. 8
Arbuthnot, C. C., 272 n. 1
Areeda, Phillip, 246 n. 8
Armentano, Dominick T., 34 n. 2, 194, 248 n. 13
Asch, Peter, 30, 167, 215, 332 n. 21, 334, 335 n. 23, 339

Bain, Joe S., 108
Baker, Donald I., 326, 337
Baker, Jonathan B., 247 n. 12
Baruch, Bernard, 289 n. 3
Bator, Francis M., 15 n. 9
Baumol, William J., 19, 194, 325
Baxter, William F., 216, 249, 321 n. 1
Becker, Gary S., 89, 328
Bellush, Bernard, 292 n. 17, 296 n. 27, 297 nn. 36, 38, 40
Benjamin, Daniel K., 173 n. 4
Benson, Bruce L., 331
Berle, Adolph, 26, 291
Bernholz, Peter, 25 n. 1
Binder, John J., 55–56
Bittlingmayer, George, 34, 51, 125, 135 n. 10, 252, 289, 290 n. 5, 299 n. 43, 318, 335, 336
Blair, Roger D., 327
Blalock, Herbert M., Jr., 57 n. 15
Block, Michael K., 29 n. 15, 31, 50–51
Boardman, Anthony E., 8 n. 2
Bork, Robert H., 28, 120 n. 1, 167 n. 1,

213 n. 1, 245–46, 255, 271, 278, 325, 327, 330, 331, 332
Boudreaux, Donald J., 277
Bowman, Ward S., 40–41
Bradley, Michael, 151 n. 6, 218 n. 12
Bradley, P., 189 n. 2
Breit, William, 1, 272 n. 1
Brennan, Timothy, 326 n. 10
Bresnahan, Timothy, 54–55
Brock, James W., 34 n. 2
Brozen, Yale, 129 n. 4, 163 n. 18, 327
Buchanan, James M., 9 n. 3, 19 n. 13, 22 n. 19, 189, 190 n. 6, 193 n. 13
Burns, Malcolm, 39, 46–47
Burton, John F., 86 n. 14
Bush, Steven C., 29 n. 15, 170, 182 n. 7

Caves, Richard E., 180 n. 4
Chandler, Alfred D., Jr., 136 n. 13, 246 n. 9
Chappell, William F., 126 n. 6, 180 n. 4
Chubb, John E., 12 n. 5
Clabault, James M., 29 n. 15, 86 n. 14
Clark, J. D., 138 n. 21
Clark, J. M., 289 n. 3
Clarkson, Kenneth W., 203 n. 3, 209 n. 18, 217 n. 8, 219 n. 15, 322 n. 2
Clemens, Rudolf A., 264 nn. 24, 26
Clevenger, Homer, 260–61, 270 n. 36
Coase, Ronald H., 16 n. 11, 25, 26, 189
Coate, Malcolm B., 322 n. 2, 338
Cohodas, Nadine, 179 n. 1
Colenutt, D. W., 233
Connor, John M., 229 n. 34
Cournot, Augustin, 147 n. 2
Cox, Edward F., 201 n. 1, 203 n. 4
Craycraft, Joseph L., 29 n. 15, 182 n. 7
Cummings, F. J., 167

De Alessi, Louis, 189nn.3, 5, 193nn.12, 13, 196nn.18, 19, 197n.21
Dearing, Charles L., 296n.30
DeBow, Michael E., 272n.1
Demsetz, Harold, 16n.11, 192nn.10, 11, 193, 194n.17, 325, 327, 328n.13, 330, 332, 337, 340
Dewey, Donald, 129n.4, 246n.9, 341n.2
DiLorenzo, Thomas J., 179, 197, 249, 255, 262, 271, 272n.1, 273, 321n.1, 331
Douglas, George W., 10n.4
Downie, J., 108n.3
Drew, Frank M., 262n.20
Dudden, Arthur P., 262n.19, 270n.36

Easterbrook, Frank H., 138n.19, 216n.4, 247, 326, 327, 329
Easterlin, Richard A., 280n.21, 284t
Eckbo, B. Espen, 11, 148, 157n.14, 215n.3, 334
Eckert, Ross, D., 190n.7, 197n.20
Eddy, Arthur J., 138n.20
Eichner, Alfred S., 128n.3
Eis, Carl, 140
Ekelund, Robert B., Jr., 277
Ellert, James, 148
Elzinga, Kenneth G., 1, 29, 121, 148, 167, 215n.3, 235, 259
Ernst, Daniel R., 247

Fairburn, J. A., 233
Faith, Roger L., 219n.16, 339
Fellner, William, 108
Fischel, Daniel, 329–30n.16
Fisher, Franklin M., 34, 44, 167
Flath, D., 167
Florence, P. S., 6n.7
Flynn, John J., 247, 331
Fox, Eleanor, 246
Frey, Bruno S., 27nn.11, 12, 33n.1
Friedel, Frank, 292nn.14, 16
Friedland, Claire, 26, 189n.3
Friedman, Milton, 25n.2, 131t, 301n.44, 302, 305t, 306n.48, 316nn.51–53, 318
Furubotn, Eric, 189n.3

Gaebler, Ted, 8n.2
Galambos, Louis, 291, 295nn.21, 22, 24, 25
Gallo, Joseph C., 29n.15, 170, 182n.7
Gaskins, Darius W., Jr., 34, 44

Gerhart, Peter M., 326n.9
Gilbert, Guy, 27n.11, 33n.1
Gilligan, Thomas W., 243, 251, 271, 273
Goff, Brian L., 219n.16
Grady, Mark F., 299, 330
Granger, Clive W. J., 185n.15
Green, Mark, 244n.2
Greenwood, Joen E., 167

Haddock, David D., 194
Hale, G. E., 29n.14
Hale, Rosemary, 29n.14
Handler, Milton, 289n.3
Haney, Lewis, 136n.13
Hannah, Leslie, 131t, 132n.5
Harberger, Arnold C., 95n.1, 96, 194, 333
Hawley, Ellis W., 139n.23, 246n.9, 252, 288, 289n.3, 290n.5, 297nn.36, 40, 298
Hay, George A., 29, 167, 215n.3, 335
Hazard, Heather A., 180n.4
Hazlett, Thomas, 1, 213n.1, 250, 255, 323n.1, 325, 328n.12, 331
Henderson, Gerald C., 78n.7
Higgins, Richard S., 21n.15, 121n.2, 171, 184n.13, 322n.2, 337
Higgs, Robert, 251n.15
High, Jack C., 262
Hill, R. Carter, 224n.27
Hilton, George W., 260nn.8, 9, 11
Himmelberg, Robert F., 138n.21, 140n.26, 288, 289nn.3, 4, 290n.5, 291nn.8, 10, 11, 292nn.13, 15
Hines, Walker, 291n.11
Hirshleifer, Jack, 181n.6
Hoel, Paul G., 207t
Hofstadter, Richard, 92, 246n.9, 247
Hovenkamp, Herbert, 326

Jarrell, Gregg A., 151n.6, 218nn.11, 12, 329–30n.16
Jensen, Michael C., 157n.13, 217n.10
Johnson, Ronald N., 34, 43
Jones, Eliot, 134n.8

Kamerschen, David R., 97–98
Kaplow, Louis, 325n.8
Katzmann, Robert A., 183n.8, 202, 203n.5, 209, 212, 217n.9, 219n.15, 222nn.22, 23, 321
Kauper, Thomas E., 324–25

Kaysen, Carl, 246n.8
Kearl, J. R., 27n.11, 33n.1
Keeler, Theodore E., 10n.4
Keller, Morton, 251n.15
Kelley, Daniel, 29, 167, 215n.3, 335
Kessel, R. A., 189n.3, 194n.16
Kirtner, Earl, 272, 276
Klein, Benjamin, 276, 278
Kleit, Andrew N., 272n.1
Klepper, Robert, 257n.1, 258t
Kochin, L. A., 173n.4
Kolko, Gabriel, 138nn.16, 17, 248–49, 260n.11
Korah, V., 233
Kovacic, William E., 219n.16, 243, 244nn.2–4, 245, 248
Krattenmaker, Thomas G., 326
Krouse, Clement G., 35, 50
Krueger, Anne O., 21n.14
Kwoka, John E., 29

Lamoreaux, Naomi, 299n.43
Lande, Robert, 246, 247, 326, 331
Landes, William M., 15n.8, 151n.5, 327, 328
Leamer, Edward, 25n.3
Lean, David F., 55
Leavens, Donald R., 219n.16, 339
Lebergot, Stanley, 260n.6
Letwin, William, 128n.2, 246n.9
Levy, David, 35, 54
Lewis-Beck, Michael, 141n.27
Libecap, Gary, 250, 251, 256, 264, 331
Liebler, Wesley J., 326n.10
Lindsay, Cotton M., 183n.8
Livermore, Shaw, 138n.20
Long, William, 30, 215, 334, 339
Lyon, Leverett S., 292n.16, 294t, 295, 296nn.29, 31, 32, 33, 297n.37, 302

MacAvoy, Paul W., 52, 260n.11
McBride, Mark E., 34, 42–43
McCarthy, J. Thomas, 35, 49–50
McChesney, Fred S., 14n.7, 28n.13, 198, 322n.2, 325n.7, 337, 341
McCloskey, Donald N., 25n.2
McCormick, Robert E., 21n.16, 213n.1
McCurdy, Charles W., 266n.33
McDonald, Forrest, 270n.36
McGee, John, 28, 34, 36, 37–38, 108n.3, 151n.5, 167, 195, 342

McGowan, John J., 167
McGuire, Robert A., 259n.5
Machlup, Fritz, 108
Mackay, Robert J., 180n.3, 337
McWilliams, Abagail, 31n.18, 121
Manne, Henry, 338n.28
March, David, 263
Mariger, Randall, 34, 38
Markham, Jesse W., 19n.4, 139f
Marshall, Leon C., 294t
Martin, David D., 272
Martin, Robert E., 34, 44
Marvel, Howard P., 31, 181n.5, 215n.3, 277, 334
Marx, Thomas G., 46
May, James, 246n.9, 247, 250n.14
Mayer, Thomas, 25n.2
Mayers, Lewis, 295n.26
Mayhew, Anne, 270n.36
Means, Gardiner C., 26
Meehan, James W., 34, 42–43
Miller, James C., III, 10n.4, 180n.3, 252
Millon, David, 246
Mills, David E., 259
Mitchell, William C., 340
Moe, Terry M., 12n.5
Moore, Beverly Jr., 244n.2
Moore, Geoffrey H., 301f
Moran, Mark J., 203n.3, 219n.16, 337
Mueller, Willard F., 36, 56
Muris, Timothy J., 203n.3, 209n.18, 217n.8, 219n.15, 322n.2
Murphy, Kevin M., 276

Nelson, Ralph L., 130t, 131t, 132n.5, 134t, 139f, 142t
Nelson, Richard R., 327, 340
Netter, Jeffrey M., 31, 215n.3
Newbold, Paul, 185n.15
Newmark, Craig M., 31
Noll, Roger, 53
North, Douglass C., 260n.7

O'Donnell, P. P. 233
Ogur, Jonathan D., 55
Olson, Mancur, 13n.6
Ordover, Janusz, 19, 325
Osborne, David, 8n.2

Page, William H., 325n.8, 330n.17
Palmer, John, 167

Parkman, Allen M., 34, 43
Parsons, Donald O., 45
Pass, C. L., 232
Pearce, Phyllis, 303f
Pejovich, Svetozar, 189n.3
Peltzman, Sam, 12, 165, 170, 181, 273,
    322n.4, 328
Pérez-Castrillo, J. David, 21n.15
Peritz, Rudolph, 246
Peterman, John L., 1, 44–45, 167
Petty, Ross, 35, 54
Pfunder, Malcolm, 148
Phelps, E., 25n.1
Phillips, Almarin, 108n.3, 117
Pickering, J. F., 232, 233
Pigou, A. C., 16n.10
Piott, Steven L., 265n.31, 270n.36
Pirrong, Steven C., 299n.42
Pittman, Russell W., 34, 35, 53–54
Plaine, Daniel, 148
Plott, Charles R., 205n.11
Pommerehne, Werner W., 27n.11, 33n.1
Poor, Henry Varnum, 260
Pope, Clayne L., 33n.1
Posner, Richard, 1, 12, 15n.8, 20–21,
    29–30, 35, 46, 89, 95, 101, 104n.5, 105,
    109, 138nn.18–20, 139f, 140nn.24, 26,
    142t, 151n.5, 170, 182n.7, 183, 197,
    199, 201, 215, 217n.8, 219n.16, 243,
    249, 325, 327, 328, 329, 337nn.24, 25
Pratt, Joseph, 39–40
Preston, Warren P., 229n.34

Radnitsky, Gerald, 25n.1
Rasmussen, Wayne D., 261n.14
Ray, Edward J., 45
Reder, Melvin, 333–34
Ripley, William, 136, 138
Robinson, Anthony M., 31, 215n.3
Robinson, Kenneth, 52–53
Rogers, Robert P., 55
Rogowsky, Robert A., 1, 29, 121, 213n.1,
    215n.3, 216n.7, 335
Roos, Charles F., 289n.3, 294t, 296n.
    28
Roose, Kenneth D., 318
Rosenbaum, David I., 35, 50
Ross, David, 34, 35, 47–48
Ross, Thomas W., 279n.19
Rowley, Charles K., 232
Ruback, Richard, 157n.13, 217n.10

Rubin, Paul, 28–29, 33
Ruther, W. E., 167

Saft, L., 278
Salop, Steven C., 247n.12, 322n.3, 326,
    340
Scheffman, David T., 322n.3
Scherer, Frederic, 1, 34, 35, 47–48, 97n.2,
    108–9n.3, 272
Schmalensee, Richard, 35, 47, 48–50
Schneider, Frederick, 27n.11, 33n.1
Schramm, Richard, 30, 215
Schulz, John E., 201n.1, 203n.4
Schwartz, Anna J., 131t, 301n.44, 302,
    305t, 306n.48, 316nn.51–53, 318
Schwartzman, D., 194
Schwert, G. William, 149n.4
Sells, Robert C., 201n.1, 203n.4
Seneca, Joseph J., 167, 215n.3, 334,
    335n.23
Seneca, Rosalind, 335n.23
Shapiro, Carl, 247–48n.12
Shepherd, William G., 48, 111, 112n.13
Shughart, William F., II, 1, 15n.8,
    21nn.15, 16, 121n.2, 122n.4, 171,
    179n.1, 180, 184, 195, 213, 219n.16,
    273, 331, 335, 343
Siegfried, John J., 30, 215, 334, 339
Simons, Henry, 28
Sims, Joe, 326
Sjostrom, William, 299n.42
Solow, Robert A., 121n.3
Sparkes, J. R., 232
Spence, A., Michael, 180n.4
Spitzer, Matthew L., 330n.17
Sproul, Michael F., 31, 32
Stein, Herbert, 26
Steuer, Richard M., 326
Stigler, George J., 1, 4, 10, 11, 12, 26, 27,
    28, 29, 65, 66, 147, 163, 165, 181,
    189nn.1, 3, 213, 216, 249, 250, 251,
    255, 256, 260, 267, 268, 271, 318, 322,
    323, 328, 331, 333–34, 336, 337n.25, 340
Stillman, Robert, 11, 148, 161n.16
Stocking, George W., 36
Stone, Alan, 204n.8
Sullivan, E. Thomas, 216n.4
Sullivan, Mark, 284t
Suslow, Valerie Y., 34, 44
Sutherland, A., 232
Swan, Peter L., 34, 44

Taussig, Frank, 272n.1
Telser, Lester G., 128n.2, 277, 298
Thelan, David, 261, 270n.36
Thorelli, Hans, 143n.28, 246n.9, 256
Thurow, Lester, 341
Tippets, Charles S., 138n.20
Tollison, Robert D., 1, 9n.3, 15n.8,
   19n.13, 21nn.15, 16, 22n.19, 25n.4,
   30, 122n.4, 163, 171, 180, 184, 190n.6,
   195, 213, 215, 219n.16, 329, 331, 335,
   339, 343
Towne, Marvin E., 261n.14
Tullock, Gordon, 19n.13, 21, 22, 189, 194
Turk, Thomas A., 31n.18, 121
Turner, Donald F., 246n.8

Utton, M. A., 232, 233

Vaughn, Michael B., 27n.11, 33n.1
Verdier, Thierry, 21
Vining, Aidan R., 8n.2

Wasserstein, Bruce, 244n.2
Weaver, Suzanne, 217n.8, 321
Weingast, Barry R., 203n.3, 219n.16,337

Weir, Charlie, 199–200
Welzer, Steve, 35, 54
Werden, Gregory, 151n.5
White, Lawrence J., 29
Whiting, Gordon C., 33n.1
Whittemore, Anne M., 148
Wiebe, Robert H., 251n.15, 270n.36
Wier, Peggy, 157n.14, 215n.3, 334
Wiley, John S., Jr., 326n.10, 330n.17
Williamson, Jeffrey G., 260n.12
Williamson, Oliver E., 33, 37, 41, 117,
   108n.2, 120, 152n.8, 274n.3
Wimmer, Larry T., 33n.1
Wood Hutchinson, Diane, 326

Yandle, Bruce, 126n.6, 180nn.3, 4,
   183n.9, 184, 213n.1, 215n.3, 222n.24,
   223n.25
Yeager, Mary, 259, 264nn.25, 26
Young, Allyn A., 271, 272n.1

Zardkoohi, Asghar, 31n.18, 121
Zelenitz, A., 167
Zerbe, Richard O., 51–52

SUBJECT INDEX

Addyston Pipe. See *United States v. Addyston Pipe & Steel Co.* (1899)
Albrecht v. Herald Co. (1968), 324 n. 4
Alcoa. See *United States v. Aluminum Co. of America* (1945)
American Column & Lumber Co. v. U.S. (1921), 289 n. 2
American Tobacco. See *United States v. American Tobacco Co.* (1911)
Anticompetitive actions, 191–92
Antitrust
  as benevolent regulation, 213
  Chicago school distinction between regulation and, 330, 339–40
  Chicago school influence and attitude, 323–29, 332
  effect of, 195, 200, 332, 336
  failure of, 341
  politically driven, 214
  private use of, 195
Antitrust actions
  after enactment of Robinson-Patman, 77–78
  after enactment of Sherman Act, 78–80
  consequences of cases prosecuted, 195
  cost measurement, 101–2
  counterproductive nature, 200
  intervention politically motivated, 320
  mergers following, 133–38
Antitrust cases
  aggregate welfare benefits and losses in prosecuted, 99–100
  brought by Justice Department (1890–1950), 73–81, 139
  brought since Sherman Act passage (1890), 73–81
  brought under state-level laws, 80–81
  bureaucracy's role in selection, 321–22

  against cement industry, 41–43
  civil and criminal filed since 1890, 81–86
  costs to bring, 97–103
  criminal remedies, 86–92
  criminal remedies of Department of Justice, 86–92
  decisions related to merger activity, 133–34
  Department of Justice cases by presidential term, 92–94
  effect of Chicago theories, 326–27
  government, 195
  indirect estimates of costs to bring, 101–2
  regulatory decrees from Department of Justice, 83, 85–86
  relation between cases brought and benefits, 100–101
Antitrust concept
  benefits to industry producers (Chicago), 336
  defects, 324–25
  justification for, 17, 27
  link to unemployment, 168–77
  as political weapon, 338–39
  in public-choice setting, 190
  standard view of, 19, 27–28
Antitrust enforcement
  bureaucratic-political model, 216–29
  cycles (1904–1920s), 139–40
  economic impact, 166–70
  effect of unexpected, 171–77
  evidence for, 335–36
  expansion of state-level, 244
  geographic bias, 339
  merger guidelines as criteria for, 216
  prior statistical analyses, 215–17
  private interest shaping of, x
  public-choice model evidence, 198–200

as substitute for trade protection, 179–82, 187
test of substitution hypothesis, 182–87
unanticipated increase in, 170–77
Antitrust exemptions. *See* Exemptions
Antitrust laws
  campaign against horizontal restraints (Bork), 245
  distinct from regulation (Chicago), 325–30
  as economic regulation, 328–29
  effect on collusion, 69–72
  effect on industry concentration, 66–67
  efficient collusion in violation of (Stigler), 71
  empirical studies of violations, 167
  F. D. Roosevelt's interpretation, 295
  as harmful legislation, 248–50
  influence of Bork's analysis, 245
  NIRA reforms, 300
  private-interest historical interpretation, 248
  proposed reform, 179
  public-interest interpretation, 255
  stated purpose, 196
  suspension under NIRA, 292
Antitrust laws, state-level
  cases brought under, 80–81
  in development of oil industry, 39–40
  effect of federal laws on, 63
  Missouri (1889), 250, 266
  Missouri agrarian interest, 261
  as origins of national laws, 255–57
Antitrust policy
  firm acceptance, 179–80
  late in Roosevelt administration, 139
  pressure for reform (1930s), 289–91
Appalachian Coals v. United States (1933), 133n.7, 139, 248n.13, 287, 290–91, 295, 298, 299, 303, 308–10, 313–14
Arizona v. Maricopa County Medical Society (1982), 326n.9
Aspen Skiing Co. v. Aspen Highlands Skiing Corp. (1985), 326n.10
AT&T. See *United States v. AT&T Co.* (1982)

Barriers to entry
  Brown Shoe case, 44–45, 58, 60
  Pennington case, 41, 58, 60
Benefits
  of antitrust activity, 97–103, 334–35

beneficiaries of Clayton Act, 276
  in self interest policy approach, 14–15
Bigelow v. RKO Radio Pictures, Inc. (1946), 80
In re Borden, Inc. (1978), 48–50
Borden, Inc. v. FTC (1982), 48–50
Brooke Group Ltd. v. Brown & Williamson Tobacco Corp. (1993), 342n.3
Brown Shoe. See Federal Trade Commission v. Brown Shoe (1966)
Bureaucracy
  antitrust selection process of, 321–22
  influence on mergers, 226–29
  self-interest hypothesis applied to, 197
  self-interest in antitrust actions, 197–98, 200
  self-interest in public-choice theory, 197
Business Elec. Corp. v. Sharp Elecs. Corp. (1988), 244n.1

California v. American Stores Co. (1990), 244n.1
Capture theory of regulation, 243, 249, 336–37
Cargill, Inc. v. Monfort of Colorado, Inc. (1986), 342n.3
Cartels
  under common law, 299
  core theory of cooperative games related to, 298–300
  industry agreements, 134–36
  judicial policy focus (1896–1900), 128–29
  mergers related to actions against, 144
  during World War I, 140
Celler-Kefauver Act (1950). *See* Clayton Act (1914)
Cellophane, 36–37
Cement Institute. See FTC v. Cement Institute (1948)
Chicago Board of Trade v. United States (1918), 51–52
Chicago school
  antitrust distributes unevenly, 336–39
  distinction between regulation and antitrust, 330, 339–40
  economic theory of regulation, 165, 320, 322–23, 328–33, 336
  evidence on antitrust effects, 333–36
  law conforms to economics, 332
  mistake theories justification, 332–33
  opposition to per se rule, 326
  public-interest theory of antitrust, 2, 320, 322–24, 337, 348–49
  Sherman Act protection, 325

Clayton Act (1914)
    antimerger amendment (1950), 67–69, 72
    business practices banned by, 273
    Celler-Kefauver Amendment (1950),
        147n.1, 167, 274, 321
    enforcement, 167
    factors in passage, 271–72
    incipiency doctrine, 272, 286
    origins and focus, 251
    passage, 140
    probit analysis of Senate vote, 280,
        283–86
    proposed amendment, 179
    provisions, 166
Coalitions
    actions in interest-group model, 12–13
    conditions for activation, 19
    limited by property rights structure, 200
Codes of conduct, industry
    allowing production curtailment under
        NIRA, 289, 292–93
    blanket code, 296, 308–14
    force of law under NIRA, 294–96
    Schechter case decision against, 297–98
Collusion
    Clayton Act proscription against, 274–76
    correlation with firm profitability, 111–16
    efficient (Stigler), 70–71
    hypothesis of market power, 150–51
    legal focus in definition, 109
    obstacles to study of, 107–8
    relation to firm profitability, 30–31,
        109–16
Common law
    efficiency of, 328–29
    restraint of trade, 299
Competition
    anticompetitive actions, 191–92
    determined by property rights structure,
        200
    effect of antitrust laws on, x, 194–95, 325
    history of U.S. policy, 245–50
    intrabrand in Sealy antitrust case, 56,
        59–60
    perfect competition model, 16–17
    rules of society to control, 190
    state-level antitrust laws as protection
        from, 256–67
    in states' purpose of antitrust, 196
    in U.K. Monopolies and Mergers Commis-
        sion investigations, 232, 241

for wealth transfers among interest groups,
    273
Concentration. See Antitrust laws; Market
    concentration doctrine; Mergers; Sherman
    Act (1890)
Consumer interest
    failure of antitrust to protect, x, 1
    problems of organizing, 12
    protection from monopolies, 19
    in result of price-fixing cases, 31
Consumer welfare
    with antitrust legislation, 119–20
    argument for state-level antitrust laws,
        262–63
    Chicago school interpretation of Sherman
        Act, 325, 331
    conditions for mergers improving,
        120
    lack of incentive related to, 196–97
Continental T.V., Inc. v. GTE Sylvania
    (1977), 35, 46, 167n.1, 277n.14
Contracts, 200
Coolidge administration, 288–90
Core theory of cooperative games, 298–300
Costs
    of antitrust activity, 97–103
    welfare cost of monopoly, 21
Customer assignments, 70–71

Data sources
    antitrust enforcement effect, 170
    antitrust pork barrel, 202–6
    firm profitability and collusion analysis,
        110–11
    Missouri's antitrust law, 257–61
    Monopolies and Merger Commission
        work, 233
    of U.K. Monopolies and Mergers Commis-
        sion, 232–33
Dr. Miles Medical Co., v. John D. Park &
    Sons Co. (1911), 273n.2

In re E. I. du Pont de Nemours & Co.
    (1980), 48
Efficiency, economic
    in allocation of resources, 192
    effect of antitrust enforcement on, 167–70
    as stated purpose of antitrust, 196
Efficiency hypotheses
    Bork's antitrust, 245–48, 251–52
    information hypothesis, 151

predictions of, 149–52
productivity increases, 151
Electrical equipment manufacturers' conspiracy, 55, 79
Exemptions
industry antitrust, 68–69
under NIRA antitrust law suspension, 292
proposed repeal of McCarran-Ferguson provisions, ix
Exxon Corp. v. FTC (1981), 337

Fair Trading Act (1973), United Kingdom
conditions for merger bid investigations,
231
public interest outlined in, 235, 242
Farmers Alliance, Missouri, 262
Federal Trade Commission (FTC)
actions against businesses, 204–5
actions not in public interest, 201
analysis of locations and firms in favorable
decisions, 202–12
congressional intent in creation of, 248–49
congressional jurisdiction over, 203–4,
207–12
effect of political pressure on, 219–29
legislator relation to cases brought
(1961–69, 1971–79), 206–12
Federal Trade Commission (FTC) Act
(1914), 140, 166
Federal Trade Commission v. Brown Shoe
(1966), 44–45, 57
Firm divestiture
American Tobacco, 138
American Tobacco case, 46–47, 58, 60
Standard Oil case, 39–40, 58, 60, 138
Firm profitability
correlation with collusion, 30–31, 109–16
correlation with industry concentration,
112–13
Firms
disappearance in mergers, 129–33
incentives under Hart-Scott-Rodino Act,
163
in perfect competition model, 16–17
as rent seekers, 19–23
FTC v. Cement Institute (1948), 184
FTC v. Kellogg et al., 47–48

Gains
transitional, 22
in wealth transfer activity, 12–15, 21

Government employees. *See* Bureaucracy
Government intervention
to correct sources of market failure, 8–9
in justification of antitrust, 17
market failure as justification for, 15–16
standard antitrust view, 19, 27
See also Antitrust actions, Antitrust enforcement; National Industrial Recovery
Act (NIRA); Public sector

*Hanover Shoe, Inc. v. United Shoe Machin-
ery Corp.* (1968), 80n.10
Hart-Scott-Rodino Antitrust Improvement
Act (1976), 121, 161, 163, 218–19
Hepburn bill, 140
Herfindahl-Hirschman Index (HHI), 65–66,
216, 221
Heublein, Inc. v. FTC (1982), 220n.17
Hoover administration, 228–90, 336
Horizontal arrangements, Clayton Act,
273–76

IBM. See United States v. IBM Corp.(1969)
Incipiency doctrine (Clayton Act), 272, 286
Industry concentration, 66–67, 112–13
Interest-group hypothesis
of antitrust law, 243, 249–50
prediction of Senate vote on Clayton Act,
281–86
Interest-group or capture theory
of government (Chicago), 329
wealth transfers, 12–15
Interest groups
agrarian interests in Missouri, 261–67
gains under Clayton Act, 272, 275–76,
279–83
pressures for Sherman Act, 331
*International Business Machines Corp. v.
United States* (1936), 35
International Harvester v. Kentucky (1927), 289

Joint sales agency system, 70–71
*Joint Traffic. See United States v. Joint Traf-
fic Ass'n* (1898)

*E. C. Knight. See United States v. E. C.
Knight* (1898)

Labor market. *See* Unemployment
Legislation, NIRA provisions, 139, 287,
288, 292, 295, 300

Legislation, proposed
  Hepburn price-fixing bill, 140
  Perkins bill (1933), 291
  work-sharing bill of Hugh Black (1933),
    291, 308–14
Leh v. General Petroleum Corp. (1965),
  80 n. 10
Logrolling, 14

Market concentration doctrine, 169–70
Market failure
  circumstances for, 15–16
  monopoly-induced, 18
Market-power hypothesis
  predictions, 149–51
  tests of, 158–60
  weakness of, 163
Markets
  outcomes of economic and political, 23
  for wealth transfers, 11–15
Markets, private sector
  incentives for resource allocation, 7
  in perfect competition model, 16
Matsushita Electric Industrial Co. v. Zenith
  Radio Corp. (1986), 342 n. 3
Merger bids
  antitrust action to deter, 218
  Monopolies and Mergers Commission in-
    vestigations, 231
Merger enforcement
  policy of Federal Trade Commission,
    214
  political pressure effect, 338–39
  test of bureaucratic-political model,
    219–29
Merger guidelines
  of Department of Justice, 163, 214, 216,
    229
  related to foreign producers in antitrust
    markets, 180
  role in challenge to merger, 214
Mergers
  anti-merger amendment to Clayton Act
    (Stigler), 67–69, 72
  bureaucratic influence measurement,
    226–29
  E. C. Knight decision, 128
  effect on allocative and productive effi-
    ciency, 120
  efficiency hypotheses, 151–52
  FTC basis for challenge to, 220–21, 229

increase in U.S. and Britain (1890–1905),
    128–33
  of industries with antitrust exemption,
    68–69
  industry concentration measurement with,
    65–66
  iron and steel industries, 134–35
  or firm disappearances (1890–1950), 139
  political influence measurement, 221–26,
    229
  railroads, 136–38
  relation to antitrust decisions, 133–34
  in U.S. manufacturing (1898–1902),
    127
  winners and losers, 217–18
  See also Hart-Scott-Rodino Antitrust Im-
    provement Act (1976)
Mistake theories, 125–26, 332–33, 345–
  48
Monopolies and Mergers Commission,
  United Kingdom
  hypotheses in analysis of, 234–41
  merger bid investigations, 231–32
  prior analyses of work, 232–33
  probit analysis results, 235–41
Monopoly
  Alcoa case, 43–44, 58, 60
  antimonopoly campaign (1939–42), 145
  cellophane manufacture and sale, 36–37,
    58, 60
  circumstances for, 194
  as defined by Missouri special interests,
    262
  Du Pont case, 48, 58, 60
  General Motors diesel engine case,
    45–46, 58, 60
  with perfect competition, 18–19
  Standard Oil case, 37–40, 58, 60
  in standard view of antitrust, 19
  welfare losses, 194
  welfare loss from resource misallocation,
    96–97

National Industrial Recovery Act (NIRA)
  antitrust suspension under, 139, 287
  criticism of, 252–53
  exemptions, 292
  output under, 300–308
  probable effect, 299–318
  provisions focusing on trade associations,
    288

purpose and provisions, 291–97
Schechter decision, 297–98
See also Codes of conduct, industry
Neoclassical economic theory, 191–92
Northern Securities v. United States (1904), 132, 138, 139, 141, 144

Oligopoly
collusive, 107–8
effect of antitrust law on formation of, 40
Oligopoly theory (Stigler), 70, 147 n. 2, 151 n. 5
Output
during Great Depression and NIRA period, 304–8
industry-by-industry (1933), 314–16
under NIRA, 300–308

Panama Canal Act (1964), 63–64
Panter v. Marshall Field (1981), 218 n. 11
Pennington v. United Mine Workers et al. (1965), 41–43, 57
Perma Life Mufflers, Inc. v. International Parts Corp. (1968), 80 n. 10
Per se rule
Chicago opposition to, 326
against price fixing, 138, 140, 145
of resale price maintenance, 337
Political activity, 337–38
Political economy, Virginia School, x
Politics
of antitrust, 341–44
effect of antitrust activity, 92–94, 214, 218–19, 320
pressure for state-level antitrust laws, 270
Predatory pricing
AT&T case, 52–53, 59–60
IBM case, 53–54, 59–60
ReaLemon case, 48–50, 59–60
Standard Oil case, 37–40, 58, 60
Price discrimination
banned in Clayton Act, 273–74, 279
circumstances for, 194
Robinson-Patman Act prohibition, 279
Utah Pie case, 40–41, 58, 60
Xerox case, 54–55
Price fixing
Addyston Pipe case, 51, 59–60, 127
bread industry case, 50–51, 59–60

Chicago Board of Trade, 51–52, 59–60
early cases under Sherman Act, 127
effect of antitrust enforcement, 30–32
electrical equipment manufacturers, 55, 59–60
Hepburn bill, 140
Joint Traffic, 127
railroad cartel cases, 55–56, 59–60
Trans-Missouri, 127
U.S. Steel case, 45, 58, 60
Private interests
of antitrust bureaucracy, 321–22
drive policy outcomes, 12
probit analysis of votes on Clayton Act, 283–86
profit or rent seeking, 19–23
Private sector
antitrust cases brought by, 78–80, 218, 326
awards in antitrust cases, 90
incentives for efficient resource allocation, 7–8
profit seeking, 20–21
rent seeking, 19–23
Product differentiation, cereal industry, 47–48, 58, 60
Property rights
in defining role of antitrust, 200
public and private sector systems of, 7–8, 191
under rules of society, 190–91
Protectionism
antitrust enforcement as substitute for trade, 179–82, 187
Missouri antitrust laws, 250–51, 257–63
Public-choice model
of antitrust enforcement, x, 198–200, 349
based on economic theory, 24
Public-choice theory
antitrust activity in, 190
application to antitrust, 8
self-interest focus and motives, 9–11, 24
self-interest of government bureaucrats, 197
Public interest
government employee conception of, 197
issues influencing Monopolies and Mergers Commission, 231–41
issues in Monopolies and Mergers Commission reports, 233–34
paradigm, 190

probit analysis of votes on Clayton Act,
283–86
served by antitrust policy, 119–20,
179–80
Public-interest hypothesis
elements related to competition, 231–32
internal inconsistency in interpretation,
331–32
in prediction of antitrust enforcement, 215
prediction of Senate vote on Clayton Act,
280–81
Sherman Act interpretation (Bork), 331
Public-interest model of antitrust, Chicago
school, 2, 320, 322, 323–24, 337,
348–49
Public policy, business-related, 9
Public sector
antitrust enforcement, 218–19
decision making under public choice theory, 9, 24
incentives for efficient resource allocation,
7–8
interest group seeking privileges from, 22
rent seeking, 22–23
See also Antitrust enforcement; Bureaucracy

Railroad cartel cases, 55–56, 57
ReaLemon. See In re Borden, Inc. (1978);
Borden, Inc. v. FTC (1982)
Regulation
antitrust as, 328
capture theory, 243, 249
economic theory of Chicago school, 165,
320, 322–23, 328–33, 336
of industries exempt from antitrust laws,
68–69
ineffective, 196
nature and consequences of counterproductive, 196
as outcome of Department of Justice antitrust cases, 83, 85–86
wealth transfer among interest groups, 165
Rent, 19
Rent seeking
private sector, 19–23
public sector, 22
relation to profit seeking, 19–20
theory, 21
Resale price maintenance, per se rule, 326
Resource allocation

economic efficiency, 192
efficient, 7–8
monopoly misallocation, 96–97
Restraint-of-trade cases, 76–78
Rights, 190
Robinson-Patman Act (1936)
FTC cases brought since enactment,
77–78
modification of Clayton price discrimination provisions, 166–67
as price-control legislation, 76–77
price discrimination prohibition, 279
Utah Pie case, 40–41
Roosevelt (FDR) administration
implementation of NIRA, 295
industry blanket code, 296
role in NIRA legislation, 288, 291–92, 295
Roosevelt (TR) administration, 288, 336
Rules of society, 190

Schechter Poultry Co. v. United States
(1935), 252, 295, 297–98, 308–11,
313–14
Schwinn. See United States v. Arnold
Schwinn & Co. et al. (1967)
Sealy. See United States v. Sealy (1967)
Self-interest hypothesis
behavior of government employees in, 197
logit regression estimates, 268–70
in public-choice theory, 9–10
test using state antitrust laws, 267–68
Shareholder wealth, 217
Sherman Act (1890)
Chicago school perception, 325, 328,
329–31
as codification of common law (Chicago), 330
as deterrent to concentration (Stigler), 67, 72
Department of Justice civil and criminal
antitrust cases filed since, 81–86
enforcement, 167
intent (Bork), 245, 255
intent (Hofstadter), 247
origins in state-level antitrust legislation, 256
in Panama Canal Act, 63–64
as political smokescreen, 255
Posner's position, 329–30
private antitrust cases brought after enactment of, 78–80
protection as rationale for passage, 179–80
provisions, 166
thrust of, 69

Standard Oil v. United States (1909, 1911), 34, 37–40, 57, 138
Stock price performance
  comparison of merger firms and rival firms, 154–59
  of firms rivaling merging firms, 160–62
Stock prices and returns
  during Great Depression, 302–3
  legislation and court decision effect, 308–14
Stock prices and returns
  other New Deal programs effect, 316–17
  Standard Oil dissolution, 39
Sylvania. See Continental T.V., Inc. v. GTE Sylvania (1977)

Trade associations
  antitrust law enforcement against, 288–89
  Appalachian Coals decision against, 290–91, 298
Trade protection. *See* Protectionism
Trans-Missouri. See United States v. Trans-Missouri Freight Ass'n (1897)
Tying arrangements
  Clayton Act prohibition, 273, 278
  as vertical governance structures, 274

Unemployment
  link to antitrust actions, 168–77, 335
  link to increases in antitrust actions, 172–73
United States v. Addyston Pipe & Steel Co. (1899), 51, 57, 127 n. 1, 133, 141, 144, 252, 299
United States v. Aluminum Co. of America (1945), 34, 43–44, 120 n. 1
United States v. American Tobacco Co. (1911), 39, 57, 103
United States v. Arnold Schwinn & Co. et al. (1967), 35, 46
United States v. AT&T Co. (1982), 52–53
United States v. Colgate & Co. (1919), 273 n. 2
United States v. Container Corp. (1969), 324 n. 3
United States v. E. C. Knight (1989), 128, 133, 143–44
United States v. E. I. du Pont de Nemours and Co. (1956), 36–37
United States v. General Motors (N.D.), 45–46
United States v. IBM Corp. (1969), 53–54

United States v. Joint Traffic Ass'n (1898), 55–56, 127 n. 1, 136, 141, 143–44
United States v. Sealy (1967), 56, 57
United States v. Sears, Roebuck & Co. (1953), 64 n. 5
United States v. Swift & Co. (1969), 83 n. 12
United States v. Terminal Railroad Ass'n of St. Louis (1912), 83 n. 11
United States v. Topco Assoc., Inc. (1972), 248 n. 13
United States v. Trans-Missouri Freight Ass'n (1897), 55–56, 123 n. 5, 127, 133, 136, 141, 143–44
United States v. Trenton Potteries Co. (1927), 108–9 n. 3, 133 n. 7, 138, 140
United States v. United Shoe Machinery Corp. (1953), 120 n. 1
United States v. United States Steel Co. et al. (1915, 1920), 45, 133 n. 7, 289
United States v. Von's Grocery Co. (1966), 324
Utah Pie Co. v. Continental Baking Co. et al. (1967), 40–41

Vertical integration
  cement industry mergers to create, 41–43, 58, 60
  restraints banned in Clayton Act, 273–74, 276–79
  Sylvania case, 46
Vest Committee (1888), 264–65
Von's Grocery. See United States v. Von's Grocery Co. (1966)

Wealth transfers
  Clayton Act, Section 7, provisions related to, 274–77
  interest-group model interpretation, 12–15
  market for, 11–15
  related to Clayton Act incipiency doctrine, 272, 286
  test for Clayton Act effect on, 281–82
  theory of economic regulation idea of, 165
Welfare loss
  with antitrust enforcement, 177
  measurement of, 97–98
  model, 96–97
  Welfare loss triangle, 96–97
Williams Act, 218–19

In re Xerox Corp. (1975), 54–55